Critical Acclaim for
Elgen M. Long and Marie K. Long's
Amelia Earhart: The Mystery Solved

"At last, an in-depth account that finally lays the Amelia Earhart mystery to rest. Elgen and Marie Long lead us through the final flight and prove conclusively that Earhart and Noonan simply missed Howland Island, ran out of fuel, and set down in the sea. A must-read of a rock-solid verdict."   —Clive Cussler

"The most levelheaded and persuasive [book about Amelia Earhart's disappearance] of all."   —Adam Woog, *The Seattle Times*

"Numerous authors have written about the Earhart tragedy. None possess the qualification of Elgen M. Long."   —Calvin Bass, *Tulsa World*

"The quiet expertise and painstaking intelligence of this book are a tribute to all aviators and a real gift to aviation history."
                                —Reeve Lindbergh, author of *Under a Wing*

"A carefully researched narrative."
                          —Tom Steadman, *News & Record* (Greensboro, NC)

"A book that's hard to put down."
                    —Edward C. Fennell, *The Post and Courier* (Charleston, SC)

"The Longs create a tense and at times hair-raising narrative out of the simple routines and extraordinary perils of piloting the primitive aircraft of the early 20th century."   —*Publishers Weekly*

AMELIA EARHART

THE MYSTERY SOLVED

ELGEN M. LONG
AND MARIE K. LONG

SIMON & SCHUSTER PAPERBACKS
NEW YORK   LONDON   TORONTO   SYDNEY

Simon & Schuster Paperbacks
A Division of Simon & Schuster, Inc.
1230 Avenue of the Americas
New York, NY 10020

This Simon & Schuster trade paperback edition October 2009

SIMON & SCHUSTER PAPERBACKS and colophon are registered
trademarks of Simon & Schuster, Inc.

For information about special discounts for bulk purchases,
please contact Simon & Schuster Special Sales at
1-866-506-1949 or business@simonandschuster.com.

The Simon & Schuster Speakers Bureau can bring authors
to your live event. For more information or to book an event,
contact the Simon & Schuster Speakers Bureau at
1-866-248-3049 or visit our website at www.simonspeakers.com.

Designed by Karolina Harris
Maps by Jeff Ward, based on original maps by Elgen M. Long

Manufactured in the United States of America

10   9   8   7   6   5   4   3   2   1

The Library of Congress has cataloged the hardcover edition as follows:
Long, Elgen M.
    Amelia Earhart: the mystery solved/ Elgen M. Long and Marie K. Long.
       p.   cm.
    Includes bibliographical references and index.
    1. Aeronautics—Flights.   2. Flights around the world.
3. Earhart, Amelia, 1897–1937.   I. Long, Marie K.   II. Title.
TL540.E3L65   1999
629.13'092—dc21   99-35861
[B]   CIP

ISBN 978-1-4391-6466-2
ISBN 978-0-7432-0217-6 (ebook)

PHOTO INSERT: *Page 1:* Courtesy of Purdue University Library; Courtesy of Pratt & Whitney
Aircraft; Courtesy of Mrs. Harry Manning. *Page 2:* Photo by Albert L. Bresnik (top and
middle photos); Courtesy of Purdue University Library. *Page 3:* Pan Pacific Press Bureau;
Photo by Albert L. Bresnik. *Page 4:* Courtesy of Nimitz Museum, Frederick Goerner
Collection; Courtesy of F. Ralph Sias. *Page 5:* Courtesy of Norman W. King; Courtesy of James
Collopy, Dept. of Civil Aviation, Australia. *Page 6:* Courtesy of Nimitz Museum, Frederick
Goerner Collection; Courtesy of James Collopy, Dept. of Civil Aviation, Australia. *Page 7:*
Photo by Elgen M. Long; Courtesy of Lieutenant Frank Stewart, USCG ret. (middle and
bottom photos). *Page 8:* Courtesy of Lieutenant Frank Stewart, USCG ret.; U.S. Navy Photo.

CONTENTS

6 • Contents

AMELIA EARHART

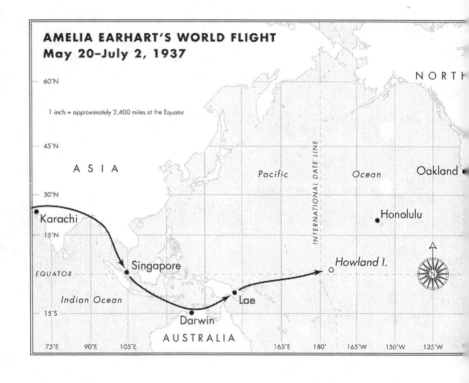

AMELIA EARHART'S WORLD FLIGHT
May 20–July 2, 1937

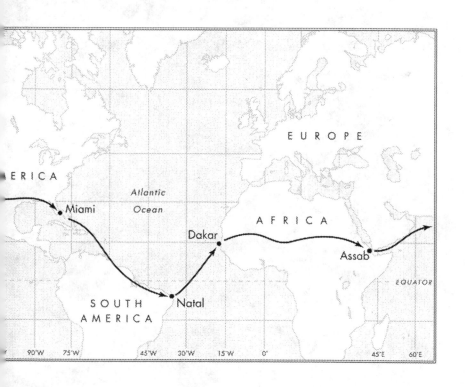

PREFACE

THE solution of the mystery surrounding Amelia Earhart's disappearance is an amazing story that has never been told.

The recent discovery of long-lost documents has finally enabled the authors to relate the events that led to solving the mystery. The story of Earhart's final flight is told in what we hope is an easy-to-read narrative style, yet the book is packed with important historic documentation.

As radio operators' transmissions were translated into plain language, any change or even shading of the original meaning was avoided. When a scene-setting or other verbal bridge was constructed to aid the flow of factual material, we took care not to inject poetic license into any matter of consequence. To ensure integrity, notes at the end of the text will guide the interested reader to the original source for complete verification.

America's foremost woman flier disappeared more than sixty years ago. Some of the language, as well as aviation and radio terms used in the 1930s, may be unfamiliar now. The terms that need explanation are defined as they appear in the book.

First, we will follow the progress of Earhart's flight from her perspective, revealing only the information that was available to her. Later, we will examine the flight from the viewpoint of those waiting for her at Howland Island. The comparison plainly reveals the tragic sequence of events that doomed her flight from the beginning.

The story begins as Amelia Earhart is leaving Lae, New Guinea, for Howland Island.

1 : TRAGEDY NEAR HOWLAND ISLAND

F RIDAY morning, July 2, 1937, Lae, New Guinea. It was not yet ten o'clock, but the tropical sun already beat down unmercifully on the twin-engine Lockheed Electra. Inside the closed cockpit, Amelia Earhart and her navigator, Fred Noonan, could feel the heat build as they taxied away from the Guinea Airways hangar.

The heavily loaded plane lumbered slowly across the grassy airfield toward the far northwest corner. Soon they would take off southeastward toward the shoreline, to take advantage of a light breeze blowing off the water. When they reached the jungle growth at the end of the field, Earhart swung the plane around to line up with the runway for departure. Only 3,000 feet long, the grass runway ended abruptly where a bluff dropped off to meet the shark-infested waters of the Huon Gulf.

Earhart was preparing to take off with the heaviest load of fuel she had ever carried. She and Noonan had flown 20,000 miles in the previous six weeks. Now only 7,000 miles of Pacific Ocean separated them from their starting point in California. The Electra, nearly 50 percent overloaded, was weighted to capacity with 1,100 gallons of fuel for the 18-hour flight to the next stop, Howland Island. Less than a mile wide,

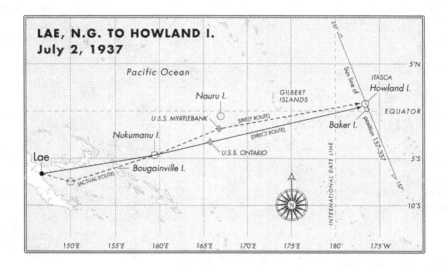

LAE, N.G. TO HOWLAND I.
July 2, 1937

two miles long, and twenty feet high, their destination was just a speck of land that lay nearly isolated in the middle of the Pacific Ocean. It was truly a pioneering flight over a route never flown before, and they would be the first to land at the tiny island's new airfield. Two more firsts for the famous thirty-nine-year-old aviator, who upon reaching California would become the first woman pilot to have flown around the world.

Fred Noonan, at age forty-four, was famous in his own right. As chief navigator for Pan American Airways he had navigated the Pan American Clippers on all their survey flights across the Pacific. Now, both he and his pilot knew that the grossly overloaded takeoff would put their lives at great risk.

Fred watched closely as Amelia ran up each engine and checked it for proper operation. She gave the instruments a final scan, and they were ready to go. The moment of truth had arrived.

Amelia advanced the engine throttles full forward and released the brakes. The roaring, straining airplane slowly accelerated as it began its ponderous takeoff roll. Her feet were busy on the rudder pedals, moving them left, right, back, and forward to keep the plane going straight down the runway. They passed the smoke bomb that marked the halfway point to the shoreline. The tail wheel was already off the ground; they were going over 60 mph. There was no stopping the heavy plane now; it was fly or die, and the bluff at the end of the runway was coming up fast. Amelia applied back pressure on the control wheel to lift off the ground. The force required was lighter than she expected, and the plane over-rotated slightly as the wheels left the runway. She relaxed some of the pressure, allowing the nose-high attitude to decrease slightly.

They were off the ground, but their airspeed was too slow for optimum climb. When they were beyond the edge of the bluff, Amelia let the plane sink slowly until it was only five or six feet above the water. She signaled Fred to retract the landing gear, and the electric motor began cranking the wheels up into the nacelles to reduce drag. The seven seconds required to retract the landing gear seemed more like seven minutes as the engines struggled at full power to increase the airspeed.

After several seconds, Amelia could tell that she needed less back pressure on the control wheel to hold the craft level. This signaled that the battle between the engines and the drag of the airplane was slowly being won by the engines. The airspeed was increasing; they were going to make it. When the indicated airspeed increased to optimum climb speed, Amelia let the plane rise from its dangerous position just over the water. After they were safely a couple hundred feet in the air, she gently turned the plane to a compass heading of 073 degrees, direct for Howland Island. She reduced the engines to climb power and quickly scanned the engine gauges to check that everything was normal. They breathed easier as the plane slowly rose to the recommended initial cruising altitude of 4,000 feet.

Fred wrote down their takeoff time from Lae as 0000 Greenwich civil time (GCT), July 2, 1937. Having calculated that the flight to Howland Island would take 18 hours, they had to time their arrival to occur at daylight the following morning. Fred would need the stars to be visible for celestial navigation until just before they reached the island.

Amelia had arranged for a message to be sent from Lae to notify the Coast Guard cutter *Itasca* at Howland Island of her departure. The 250-foot Lake class cutter was waiting just off the island to provide communications, radio direction-finding, weather observations, and ground servicing for her flight. The captain of the *Itasca* was to notify all other stations, including the U.S. Navy auxiliary tug *Ontario*. The *Ontario* was positioned approximately halfway between Lae and Howland Island, in order to provide weather reports and transmit radio homing signals for Earhart.

Harry Balfour, the Guinea Airways radio operator at Lae, was receiving new wind forecasts for Earhart's flight just as she was taking off. The messages indicated that the headwinds to Howland Island would be much stronger than reported earlier, when they had expected only a 15 mph headwind. Fred had subtracted this headwind from the 157 mph optimum true airspeed to calculate a 142 mph ground speed. At 142 mph it would take them 18 hours to fly the 2,556 statute miles to Howland Island.

Earhart's radio schedule with Lae called for her to transmit her messages at 18 minutes past each hour, and to listen for Lae to transmit its messages at 20 minutes after the hour. Balfour attempted to report the stronger headwinds to Earhart by radio at 10:20, 11:20, and 12:20 local time, but she never acknowledged having heard him. In addition, for more than 4 hours after she departed from Lae, local interference prevented signals sent by the plane from being intelligible until 0418 GCT.

At 0418 GCT (2:18 P.M. local time), Balfour finally received a radio transmission from Earhart using the daytime frequency of 6210 kilocycles. She reported: "HEIGHT 7,000 FEET SPEED 140 KNOTS" and some remark concerning "LAE" then "EVERYTHING OKAY."

At four hours and eighteen minutes into the flight they were already experiencing stronger headwinds than anticipated. The increased winds had made them recalculate their optimum speed. Amelia reported the change to 140 knots (161 mph) in her message.

Maintaining the correct airspeed was important, but Earhart also had to fly at the correct altitude for optimum fuel efficiency. As the engines burned fuel, the plane's weight would decrease and the optimum altitude would increase. At any given aircraft weight there is a specific altitude for best fuel economy. The higher temperatures common in the tropics reduce the density of the air. Above the optimum altitude the temperature's effect on air density is equivalent to approximately a 2,000-foot increase in altitude and a corresponding increase in fuel consumption. The Electra would lose fuel efficiency below the optimum altitude but not nearly as rapidly as when flying above it. For maximum efficiency in the tropics, the Electra had to be flown approximately 2,000 feet below the recommended pressure altitude.

Balfour heard the next report from Earhart in Lae one hour and one minute later, at 0519 GCT. She reported: "HEIGHT 10,000 FEET—POSITION 150.7 EAST, 7.3 SOUTH—CUMULUS CLOUDS—EVERYTHING OKAY."

Perhaps the cumulus clouds or the 9,000-foot mountains of Bougainville Island had forced them to the very uneconomical altitude of 10,000 feet. The worst had happened; they were flying at a density altitude close to 12,000 feet. The gross weight of the plane at this point would require them to burn an unconscionable amount of extra fuel to reach and cruise at that altitude. The resulting inefficiency could cost them a significant portion of their fuel reserve.

The position indicated by the reported geographical coordinates, longitude 150.7 east and latitude 7.3 south, is less than 220 statute miles from Lae and well over 450 miles from where the Electra would have been at 0519 GCT. Since it was standard practice for ships at sea to give their position at noon every day, it's possible that this was their position at twelve noon local time. It definitely was not their position at 0519, when Earhart transmitted the message.

Lae heard nothing from Earhart during her 0618 GCT transmitting schedule, but at 0718 GCT Balfour heard her report clearly on 6210 kilocycles: "POSITION 4.33 SOUTH, 159.7 EAST—HEIGHT 8,000 FEET OVER CUMULUS CLOUDS—WIND 23 KNOTS."

This position, approximately 850 statute miles from Lae, was right on their planned course to Howland Island. Significantly, the position was just to the west and in sight of Nukumanu Island. Noonan had navigated perfectly so far; they were exactly on course with a positive visual fix. A true airspeed of 161 mph reduced by a 26.5 mph (23-knot) wind would give them a ground speed of 134.5 mph. Again, the geographical position reported is not where they were at the time when the report was received by Harry Balfour in Lae; Earhart would have been at the reported position near Nukumanu Island approximately one hour earlier. Perhaps the activity resulting from sighting Nukumanu explains why Balfour in Lae did not hear from Earhart during her 0618 GCT transmitting schedule. Her signals on 6210 kilocycles were strong before and after 0618, and if she had transmitted, he should have heard her. (The reason why the radio position reports made by Earhart to Lae were not correlated to the time she transmitted them is unknown.)

At Nukumanu Island, Earhart and Noonan were approximately one-third of the way to Howland Island. They had been flying about six and a half hours and had a positive visual fix of their position. They knew their ground speed and the heavy plane's hourly fuel consumption precisely. None of the news was good. It would be prudent for them to reevaluate the remainder of their flight.

No pilot appreciates strong headwinds that make a flight fall behind schedule, but Earhart was doubly handicapped on fuel. The 26.5 mph headwind required her to fly at 140 knots (161 mph) to obtain maximum range. That was 11 mph faster than the required zero-wind speed of 150 mph. This increased fuel consumption by about 9 percent per hour, but her progress over the ground was also increased by about 9 percent. (For every wind component there is a recommended speed for maximum range. The stronger the headwind, the faster a plane must fly. It may sound incongruous, but consider an extreme situation with a headwind of 155 mph: A plane flying at the no-wind speed of 150 mph would be driven backward. At a speed faster than 155 mph, it will run out of gas much sooner but will be farther along the way when this happens.)

Whether or not Earhart had heard the messages from Lae concerning the increased headwinds, she had already encountered the actual winds. She acknowledged their importance by reporting the 23-knot (26.5 mph) wind at 0718, and significantly she did not then, or ever again, end a message with her earlier sign-off, "Everything okay."

So far, Earhart had maintained the optimum airspeed, but if the excessive fuel consumption continued they would arrive at Howland Island with little if any fuel remaining. The situation was very serious. If they were going to return to Lae, they had to turn about before they were beyond the point of safe return.

A number of factors had to be weighed as Earhart made her decision to continue or return. The badly overloaded takeoff from Lae was punishing to the plane. The margin of safety had been so minimal that she would not want to expose them to it again unnecessarily. Even with a headwind it had required every bit of engine power that the plane could produce with 100-octane fuel, and there was no more 100-octane available at Lae. Earhart could not responsibly attempt another takeoff using only the 87-octane fuel that was available. A major delay would be caused by having to transport more 100-octane fuel to Lae.

Pilot and navigator had to weigh the hazards of continuing against the hazards in returning. It would be dark in an hour or two, and the 24-day-old waning moon would not rise until after one o'clock in the morning. There were no high peaks between Nukumanu Island and Howland Island, but there were the 9,000-foot peaks back on Bougainville Island between them and Lae. With their excess weight, if they lost an engine they might not be able to maintain altitude to clear the mountains. Lae was surrounded by mountains over 12,000 feet high on three sides, and near the airfield the terrain was over a thousand feet high. There were no landing or obstruction lights, so they could not land safely until daylight. Sunrise at Lae would be about 2020 GCT, nearly an hour and a half after they were due to arrive at Howland Island. No high terrain lay ahead, and if the weather cooperated they should be able to keep the plane operating optimally for the rest of the trip. They had now burned off enough fuel to be flying at comfortable weights.

As Earhart continued toward Howland Island, she descended to 8,000 feet to get closer to the optimum altitude. It was still too high, but as they would not have to climb back up to it later, it was a reasonable choice. With better fuel economy and a tailwind replacing a headwind, they could safely return to Lae after 10 hours. They could not land back there before 2000 GCT anyway, so she could delay her decision until 1000 GCT.

The sun had set about an hour before. It was dark as the Electra continued eastward toward Howland Island. On his map, Noonan could measure that at 0810 GCT they would be about 200 miles west of the Navy guard ship *Ontario,* which for over a week had been keeping near the midpoint position waiting for Earhart to pass.

The coal-burning Navy auxiliary tug was not equipped with the high-frequency radio equipment needed to receive Earhart's transmissions on 3105 or 6210 kilocycles. The low-frequency radios on the ship prevented it from communicating with its base in American Samoa except at night.

Earhart had requested by cablegram before takeoff that the *Ontario* send a series of Morse code "N's" at 10 minutes after each hour on 400 kilocycles. She wanted to be able to take radio bearings on the ship with her radio direction-finder as they flew by. If she listened to her Bendix radio receiver for the "N's" at 10 minutes after the hour, she heard nothing.

At 0815 GCT, Earhart was scheduled to transmit a quarter-after-the-hour report on the nighttime frequency of 3105 kilocycles to the Coast Guard cutter *Itasca,* waiting just offshore at Howland Island. Neither the *Itasca* nor Balfour back at Lae heard anything. This was not surprising, as both were over a thousand miles away, and her Western Electric transmitter was rated at only 50 watts.

At 0910 GCT she may have listened again for "N's" on 400 kilocycles, because at a ground speed of 134.5 mph she would be passing by the ship just before 0940 GCT. She must have been disappointed when she did not receive any of the scheduled signals from the *Ontario.* She had no way of knowing that her departure message from Lae had been delayed. The *Ontario* never logged sending "N's" on 400, and soon after 1500 GCT set course to return to American Samoa. The tug was running short of coal.

Earhart and Noonan were past the *Ontario* and more than halfway to Howland Island by 1000 GCT. They were approaching the point of safe return, and it was time to reevaluate their progress. They decided not to return to Lae and committed themselves to continue. There was no known airfield within a thousand miles of Howland Island. From that moment on, if Earhart was to successfully complete the flight around the world, a landing at Howland's airfield was mandatory. There was no alternative.

It was coming up on 1030 GCT when Earhart saw lights on the ocean ahead. As the lights came closer she could see that it was a ship and transmitted a report of the event. It was about 1030 GCT when she reported "A SHIP IN SIGHT AHEAD."

The ship SS *Myrtlebank,* with Capt. Cort J. Holbrook in command, was out of Auckland, New Zealand, bound for Nauru Island. The 434-foot cargo ship of the Banks Line Ltd. was under charter to the British Phosphate Company and due to arrive at Nauru Island at dawn. The *Myrtlebank*'s estimated position at 1030 GCT was 80 miles southward of Nauru. Harold J. Barnes, officer in charge of the radio station at Nauru Island, copied Earhart's message. He called her over Nauru's radio station VKT on 3105 kc. The *Itasca* heard VKT, but evidently Earhart did not.

From Lae to the *Myrtlebank*'s 1030 position was approximately 1,414 statute miles. It had taken Earhart 10½ hours to get there, at an average ground speed of about 134.5 mph. There were 1,142 statute miles still ahead to their destination. If they continued at the same speed, it would take them 8½ hours to get to Howland Island. Their new estimated arrival time would be about 1900 GCT, nearly an hour after the stars had disappeared.

The plane continued eastward, with nothing but ocean and clouds below, until about 1315 GCT. Amelia must have welcomed the waning moon when a pointed end of its crescent shape poked above the horizon right in front of them. (Even a moon in its last quarter is a help when making one's way across a sky shared with towering cumulus clouds. It is much less tiring and stressful when a pilot can see what is coming and avoid plowing unexpectedly into the rain and turbulence of a cumulus buildup.)

It was overcast as they approached the Gilbert Islands. At 1415 GCT, Earhart transmitted her quarter-after-the-hour radio message on 3105 kilocycles. When the plane passed high overhead in the cloudy sky, the local time in the British-administered Gilberts was after two in the morning.

Amelia and Fred were now only 4 hours from Howland Island. Though the headwind had not slackened, they had been able to come reasonably close to keeping their fuel consumption on target. The 26.5 mph headwind had necessitated holding their true airspeed at 160.5 mph for maximum range. The higher-than-planned airspeed automatically increased their fuel consumption, but they were still progressing the same optimum number of miles over the ground for each pound of fuel burned. They were burning 8.5 percent more fuel each hour to do it but at the same time were progressing 8.5 percent more miles toward their destination each hour.

With only four more hours to go, the specter of running out of fuel before reaching Howland Island was greatly diminished. They could rationalize that it would not be considered unusual, or even improper, for a pilot to fly a 4-hour visual flight in the United States and land with only a 45-minute fuel reserve. But of course this was not a visual domestic flight.

At 1515 GCT, Amelia turned on her transmitter and sent the following message: "ITASCA FROM EARHART—ITASCA FROM EARHART—OVERCAST—WILL LISTEN ON HOUR AND HALF HOUR ON 3105—WILL LISTEN ON HOUR AND HALF HOUR ON 3105."

They would leave the Gilbert Islands before their next quarter-after-the-hour transmission, and the sky was still overcast. A positive visual fix from the island would be possible only if the clouds cooperated. They still had over three and a half hours to go, and Fred could calculate that the sun would rise just before 1800 GCT. That would be shortly after they crossed the international date line, at 180 degrees longitude. Nautical twilight would begin 49 minutes before sunrise. It was imperative that he get a celestial fix before daylight obscured his view of the stars.

At 1615 GCT the sky was only partly cloudy and Fred could presumably see stars for a celestial fix. Standard procedure was for Amelia to take the plane off the automatic pilot and hold it as level as possible while Fred took a series of sightings with his octant. By 1622 GCT he would have had time to finish his observations, and Amelia could turn control back to the Sperry autopilot. It was already past the time for her quarter-after-the-hour transmission. Eight minutes late, at 1623 GCT, she transmitted a report in which the *Itasca* heard her say it was "PARTLY CLOUDY." As long as it remained partly cloudy, daylight would not obscure the stars for at least another hour. Fred could readily take additional celestial fixes if he needed or wanted them.

A celestial fix at 1622 GCT would have shown them to be about 354 miles from Howland Island. The wind was slowing their ground speed to 133 mph. If Earhart could get radio bearings from the *Itasca,* they could continue straight toward the island following the courses indicated by the radio bearings. If they flew straight in, their estimated time of arrival would be about 1902 GCT. If no radio bearings were received to guide them, Noonan would have to depend on something else to set an accurate final course for the island.

They were flying an easterly course, and the morning sun would rise right in front of the plane. A sun line, or single line of position from the sun, plotted on Noonan's chart would be at right angles to the sun. The sun line would lie on his chart running approximately northward and southward across their course to Howland. The sun line would accurately update their position along the course to the east and west, but it could provide little indication whether they were maintaining the intended course direct to the island or actually flying off to the north or south of it. Their arrival time at the island was not crucial, but it was imperative they not accidentally fly past the island to the north or south without seeing it.

The standard solution to this problem was for Noonan to make a judgment of the maximum distance it was reasonable for them to be accidentally off to the north or south of his intended course. (In navigation, this is called the *area of uncertainty*.) Noonan would then make a deliberate choice, north or south, to head the airplane off the distance of his uncertainty to one side. He would then know beyond a reasonable doubt that his actual position was off to the north or to the south side of the island, whichever he had chosen. When the sun line of position indicated they had progressed eastward as far as Howland Island, he would turn in the appropriate direction (northward or southward, depending on which side he had chosen) and fly directly toward the island. This was a standard procedure that Noonan had used many times.

This effectively eliminated any course errors they might have accumulated since the 1622 GCT (or any later) celestial fix. It would give them a relatively accurate fresh start on the final course line as they approached the island. Meanwhile, to ascertain that they were off to the north or south side of the island would require them to fly an extra 15 or 20 miles, delaying their arrival time 8 or 10 minutes to about 1912 GCT.

It was approximately 1715 GCT when the last fuselage tank ran empty. Amelia switched the selector valves to run the engines off the last main wing tank, which was still full with 97 gallons. The design of the fuel system required her always to run both engines off the same tank. The engines were each burning about 20 gallons per hour. At a total of 40 gph, the tank would run dry in slightly less than 2½ hours, or at approximately 1945 GCT. Amelia would select the stripper pump and carefully pump out by hand any fuel left by the engine pumps in the fuselage tank. This transferred every remaining drop into the last main wing tank and assured that all the gas left on the airplane was in that one tank. When it ran dry, they would be completely out of fuel.

The eastern sky was getting lighter, heralding the coming sunrise. The calculations from the celestial fix would have them 200 miles out of Howland at 1732 GCT and 100 miles out at 1817 GCT. They were now approaching the island, and Amelia still hadn't heard from the *Itasca*. Before the flight she had cabled the *Itasca* that she would transmit by voice on 3105 kilocycles as she approached. She had also told them she would broadcast at a quarter to the hour when she could.

The *Itasca* transcribed Earhart's 1744 GCT message and information as follows: "WANTS BEARING ON 3105 KCS/ON HOUR/WILL WHISTLE IN MIC."

She gave them a moment so they would be ready to take the radio bearing, then transmitted at 1745 GCT: "ABOUT TWO HUNDRED MILES OUT//APPX//WHISTLING//NW."

A few minutes later Amelia would need her darkest sunglasses. The sun, coming up in the front of the plane, would shine directly into her eyes through the cockpit windshield.

Amelia was expected to listen at 1800 GCT for the *Itasca* to transmit during her on-the-hour listening schedule. She would select band 4 on the Bendix receiver and set the dial to 3105 kilocycles. When receiving signals she would turn the CW (code) switch off and listen intently for a voice on 3105 kilocycles to tell her the radio bearing, as she had requested. The volume would be set high as she searched both sides of the 3105 dial, reading for any voice signal. There was nothing but noise and static, and after listening for a few minutes she could only tell Fred there was no bearing from the ship. The only thing she could do was try again during her quarter-after-the-hour transmitting schedule.

Fred had his octant in the cockpit so he could sight the sun through the windshield. They must shortly begin their descent to below the clouds. He had to take his sightings before they started down.

At 1815 GCT, it was time for Amelia to transmit on the quarter-after-the-hour schedule. If the *Itasca* hadn't heard her before, she was hopeful they would get a bearing on her now. She sent the following: "PLEASE TAKE BEARING ON US AND REPORT IN HALF HOUR/I WILL MAKE NOISE IN MICROPHONE—ABOUT 100 MILES OUT."

When Amelia was finished, Fred needed her to hold the plane steady while he took a series of sights of the sun with his octant. He would be finished by 1825 GCT. The sun was about 7 degrees above the horizon, and he would calculate its azimuth (direction) to be 067 degrees.

Fred had completed his sightings, and Amelia put the plane back on autopilot. They needed the bearing she had requested from the ship, and she listened intently at 1830 GCT. Once again, there was nothing but noise and static. She hadn't received any voice signals from the *Itasca* during either the 1800 or the 1830 GCT schedule. Either the *Itasca* wasn't transmitting to her with voice at that time, or her receiver wasn't receiving the signals. As far as she knew it was possible the *Itasca*'s 3105 transmitter wasn't working, and they were transmitting on 7500 kilocycles instead. She had no way of knowing what was wrong.

Noonan plotted the 1825 GCT sun line perpendicular to the sun's 067-degree azimuth. The plotted sun line thus ran 157–337 degrees across their course on his map. After many years of aerial navigation, he had learned that on average a sun line was accurate within 10 miles. The plot of the 1825 GCT sun line showed they had traveled about 272 miles since the 1622 GCT celestial fix. It fit well with his dead-

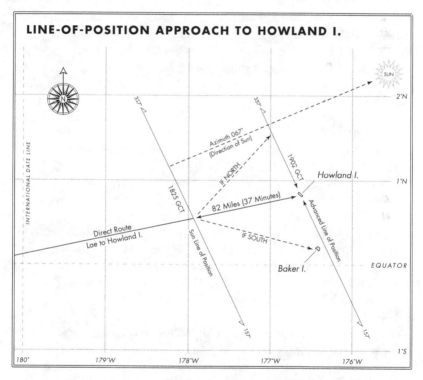

LINE-OF-POSITION APPROACH TO HOWLAND I.

If Noonan believed that he was heading north of Howland Island, he would have aimed for a point approximately 20 miles to the north so he could have turned south and flown over the island. If Noonan believed that he was heading south of the island, he would have aimed for a point roughly 20 miles south and turned north. In no case would he have aimed directly for the island itself, because if he missed it, he would not have known whether to turn to the north or the south to find it.

reckoning position and confirmed that their ground speed was about 133 mph. If he lined up their final approach course into Howland with the plotted 157–337 sun line, Noonan could be confident that his average final course to the island would be accurate within 10 miles east or west of that course. He would only have to allow for any possible dead-reckoning errors that might accumulate after 1825 GCT. (This procedure is called a *line-of-position* approach. It is a close cousin to the latitude sailing methods used by maritime navigators for centuries.)

In order to use the 1825 GCT sun line as a guiding course for coming in to Howland Island, Noonan would draw on his map a new advanced parallel line 157–337 that ran right through the island. He could then measure the distance between the 1825 GCT line and the new advanced line, along the eastward course they were flying. It was 82 miles from the original plotted 1825 GCT sun line to the new advanced line that ran through Howland. Noonan could then calculate that at a ground speed of 133 mph, it would take 37 minutes to fly the 82 miles. He would tell Earhart to turn toward the island at 1902 GCT, exactly 37 minutes after 1825. She would turn to fly a heading calculated to keep them on the new advanced course line, 157–337, until they saw the island.

Earhart started to descend at about 1833 GCT, when they were approximately 65 miles out of Howland Island. They needed to be below the cloud base before their estimated arrival time. They must not accidentally go past the island while it was hidden under clouds. They had received no radio bearings for guidance, so Noonan had to change the compass heading to make sure they were far enough off to one side of the island to cover any uncertainty when they intercepted the new advanced line, 157–337 degrees, at 1902 GCT.

Earhart could reduce the power by pulling back on the throttles as the plane gained speed in the descent. The fuel flows would drop in unison as the power was reduced. As long as the engines didn't quit or run rough, she could continue to let them run with lean fuel mixture. She would want to do everything possible to conserve fuel. If she selected the main wing fuel tank gauge, it should have read slightly over half full.

As the plane continued to descend, the relatively cool, dry air in the cockpit at the higher altitudes would have slowly given way to the warm, moist air normal on the surface at the equator. At 1,000 feet they were below the cloud base, and Noonan and Earhart could look carefully in all directions to try to spot the island. They were approaching the turning point and were busy searching every quadrant of the empty sea below. There were no whitecaps on the surface. That would indicate that the 26.5 mph headwind they had bucked since leaving Lae had finally died down. Without a smoke bomb they could not determine the wind's actual direction or velocity; they just knew that without whitecaps on the water, it was blowing less than 12 mph.

At about 1902 GCT Earhart turned toward Howland Island and flew a heading to maintain a course on the new advanced 157–337 line of position. Noonan's standard procedure would put the island about 15 or 20 miles dead ahead. They searched the water in front of them and to either side for any sign of the island or the cutter *Itasca*. The atmospheric visibility was good, and they could effectively search the ocean's surface for the island except when they looked toward the morning sun. The sun was only 17 degrees above the horizon, and it created a glare off the water. It was difficult to see anything in that direction. Also, the shiny aluminum surfaces of the wings and engine nacelles acted like mirrors. The sun's rays were reflected off the metal into their eyes, further hampering their vision toward the east.

The ten minutes Fred had estimated to get to Howland Island had elapsed, and there was still nothing in sight. At 1912 GCT Amelia made her quarter-after-the-hour transmission. While they continued to look out over the water for Howland Island, she reported on 3105 kilocycles, "KHAQQ CALLING ITASCA WE MUST BE ON YOU BUT CANNOT SEE YOU BUT GAS IS RUNNING LOW BEEN UNABLE REACH YOU BY RADIO WE ARE FLYING AT ALTITUDE 1000 FEET."

The line-of-position approach procedure required that they keep flying down the line until they reached the island, or at least until Noonan was certain they had passed it. He knew the sun line of position he had taken 47 minutes before should be accurate to within 10 miles. They had flown little more than 100 miles since then. Even if Noonan added 10 percent of the distance traveled, 10 miles, for maximum dead reckoning error, they would be no more than 20 miles off course. It had been agreed by cablegram before takeoff that the *Itasca* would make smoke in the daytime as the plane approached the island. The smoke would make it easier for them to see the low-lying coral island. If the smoke went high enough, they should spot it from 30 miles away. (Many times at sea, if the atmosphere and wind are right, a telltale column of smoke can be seen high above a ship traveling out of sight below the horizon.)

Earhart probably chose to pull the propellers back to minimum rpm, then advance the throttles just enough to keep the indicated airspeed around 85 mph for maximum endurance. They needed time to look for the island. By maintaining maximum endurance airspeed they would burn the least fuel per hour.

They continued onward for 16 more minutes and by 1928 GCT had flown along the new line 157–337 for a total of about 40 miles. When they had first started to fly along the line at 1902 GCT, they could have scanned 20 miles in the opposite direction before turning onto the line. Now they could see 20 miles farther ahead. Altogether, they had visually searched about 80 miles on the new advanced line of position. Howland Island wasn't there.

As the navigator, Fred had the knowledge and insight to judge just how accurate their position was at that moment. This was not a judgment he would make lightly, as their lives so clearly depended on it. By 1928 GCT he must have been sure they had already passed to the east or west of Howland Island. He judged the island must now be behind them, and had Amelia begin circling so they would not fly farther away. They must get a radio direction-finder bearing to resolve whether the island was to the east or west.

Amelia had already tried twice, without success, to get the *Itasca* to report a bearing to her by using voice on 3105 kilocycles. She set the receiver to band 5, set the dial on 7500 kilocycles, and turned the CW switch on. She was going to try a different strategy. Two minutes before the *Itasca*'s scheduled time to transmit on the half hour, she transmitted on 3105 kilocycles, at 1928 GCT: "KHAQQ CALLING ITASCA—WE ARE CIRCLING BUT CANNOT HEAR YOU GO AHEAD ON 7500 EITHER NOW OR ON THE SCHEDULE TIME ON HALF HOUR."

Amelia had turned on the receiver's CW (code) switch to activate the receiver's beat frequency oscillator, so she could receive the agreed-upon "A's" in Morse code on 7500 kilocycles instead of the voice transmissions she had listened for on 3105 kc. Soon there were loud Morse code *dit-dah*s of "A's" being repeated over and over. She adjusted her radio direction-finder's loop coupler to make sure it was selected to band 5, and tuned the "A's" for their loudest reception. Then she switched to take a bearing, and turned the loop to find the direction the signals were coming from.

The "A's" signal volume should have weakened and dropped off to minimum strength when the loop was turned across the direction the signal was coming from. Amelia turned the loop completely around, but there was no point where the signal "A's" signal volume would drop off. She couldn't get a minimum on the *Itasca*'s signal anywhere.

Finally the "A's" stopped, and Amelia could hear Morse code sending something for a few seconds. Then silence. She picked up the microphone and at 1930 GCT said: "KHAQQ CALLING ITASCA WE RECEIVED YOUR SIGNALS BUT UNABLE TO GET A MINIMUM PLEASE TAKE BEARING ON US AND ANSWER 3105 WITH VOICE." And then she made long dashes for them to take a bearing on.

Amelia cranked the receiver back to band 4 and set the dial to 3105 kilocycles. She turned the CW switch off and listened for the *Itasca* to answer with speech as she had requested. There was nothing but noise and static on 3105. She gave it up after a few minutes and resumed looking for the island.

If she activated the hydrostatic fuel gauge, it would now indicate less than a quarter tank of fuel remaining. Amelia was undoubtedly feeling increased tension in her muscles. They had saved an additional half hour's worth of fuel by descending and flying at endurance airspeed, but that would be the last of it. They had 35 to 40 minutes to find the island and must choose the option that would give them the best chance in the time allotted.

Noonan could be certain that his navigation had placed them within 50 miles of the island to the north or south, and within 20 miles to the east or west. They had already searched the advanced line of position to the north and south without seeing any sign of either the *Itasca* or Howland. They obviously had passed to the east or west of the island, but without a radio bearing they could not determine which. Regardless of whether they chose to move over to the east or contrarily to the west, they had only a fifty-fifty chance of being correct. It would take over 30 minutes to search the selected side, leaving not enough fuel even to get to the other side. If they'd had an hour and 15 minutes' worth, they could have covered both the east and the west sides and solved their dilemma. With a couple hours' fuel reserve, Noonan could even have started a square search pattern to look for the island in all directions. But they had only 35 or 40 minutes of fuel remaining. They had to make a decision.

Reasonable error placed the advanced 157–337 line of position within 20 miles of Howland to the east or west, but there was a good chance they were even closer. They decided to retrace their flight along the 157–337 line and visually search the ocean on both sides of the plane with renewed vigor. There was still one more chance, on the hour at 2000 GCT, for the *Itasca* to give them a radio bearing with voice on 3105 kc. It was important they remain as close to the island as possible. If they did get a radio bearing, there was little time left to follow it into the island.

The last chance for Amelia to turn on the Bendix receiver and listen for the *Itasca* to transmit on 3105 with voice came at 2000 GCT. Unfortunately there was nothing but noise and static, no voice signal from the *Itasca* to give them a radio bearing. She returned to searching for any sign of the island on the ocean. Their last hope for a bearing was gone, and she could only hope that the island might miraculously appear in the few remaining minutes. Her body would react to the anxiety, and the adrenaline would flow to prepare for the impending emergency.

The other tanks had been stripped, and the last main wing tank was now showing empty. Amelia turned on the Western Electric transmitter for a final call. She decided there was no hope for a radio bearing now. Meanwhile, two hours had passed since sunrise. Her agreement had been to use 3105 kilocycles, but this time she would repeat the message on the daytime frequency of 6210 kilocycles just in case something was wrong with 3105.

At 2013 GCT, with her voice pitched noticeably higher from the tension in her throat, Amelia spoke rapidly, transmitting the following on 3105: "WE ARE ON THE LINE OF POSITION 157–337, WILL REPEAT THIS MESSAGE, WE WILL REPEAT THIS MESSAGE ON 6210 KCS. WAIT LISTENING ON 6210 KCS. . . . WE ARE RUNNING NORTH AND SOUTH."

Amelia released the microphone button. She leaned over to crank the transmitter control from 3105 kilocycles to 6210. When the engines began to surge, she would have to drop the microphone and use both hands to reach for the control wheel and disengage the autopilot. For a few seconds, the engines cutting in and out would cause the plane to yaw back and forth. Finally, the engines would quit completely. To follow standard procedure Amelia would lower the nose to maintain a safe gliding speed, and configure the plane for ditching in the water. She would put the flaps full down and leave the landing gear retracted. With the drag of full flaps and the windmilling propellers, she would have to lower the nose considerably to maintain safe airspeed. The plane's rate of descent would increase accordingly.

The stall speed of an empty Electra with full flaps would be less than 60 mph. When the aircraft neared the water, Amelia would have to time precisely the critical raising of the plane's nose to stop the rapid descent. If she leveled off too high or too early, the plane could stall and she might lose control before it hit the water. If she was too low or too late when she leveled off, the plane could hit the water too fast. The dead-stick ditching of a plane into the ocean wasn't something you could practice; you had to get it right the first time.

As they approached the water, Fred could have rationalized his inability to find the island as plain bad luck. He had navigated other flights that had taken longer. The distance from Lae to Howland wasn't much farther than earlier pioneering flights he had made with Pan American Airways. As far as navigation was concerned, the course from Lae was neither particularly difficult nor extraordinary. Except for the absence of radio navigation and communications at Howland Island, the flight was little different from dozens he had made before. They had known from the start that it might require radio direction-finding to bring them in and had provided two systems in case one failed. Regardless, with a normal fuel reserve they could have searched the area to the east and west of Howland, or used a standard square search pattern to find the island.

Beyond all reasonable odds, the random hand of fate seemed to have conspired against them completely. Why couldn't Amelia get a minimum with her Bendix radio direction-finder? Why couldn't she hear the *Itasca* transmitting voice on 3105 kilocycles? Why hadn't they seen smoke rising from the *Itasca*? Why was Noonan's navigation so far off that they missed the island entirely? Whatever the causes, they were directly responsible for the failure of the flight.

Amelia had been apprehensive during the last 12 hours of the flight that everything was not okay. After all of the careful planning, how could everything have gone so wrong?

There was little time for reflection as the aircraft, now strangely almost silent, glided toward the sea. A couple of minutes after the engines quit, Amelia Earhart was flaring the plane above the reasonably placid waters of the Pacific Ocean, somewhere near Howland Island.

She had worked and sacrificed for years to gain recognition of women's abilities. The flight had been designed to demonstrate to a skeptical world the contributions women were capable of making. History would be charged to record her effort honestly and determine if it had been truly worthwhile. Earhart could only hope that from this moment of failure, she would be vindicated for daring to lead the way.

But what demonic trick of fate had caused this tragedy?

2: IN THE SHADOW
OF HISTORY

AMELIA Mary Earhart was born on July 24, 1897, at the home of her maternal grandparents in Atchison, Kansas.

William McKinley was president of the forty-five United States with their nearly seventy-five million inhabitants. Riverboats carried passengers and freight on the waterways, but railroads were cutting deeply into their business. Horses provided local transportation, but automobiles would soon become common. The industrial age was creating rapid and sweeping changes across the land.

Families in the heartland of America were attempting to instill in their children the nineteenth-century Victorian standards of morality and taste. Amelia Earhart and her younger sister, Muriel, were raised to live by those standards along with Episcopalian dutifulness.

Amelia's parents, Amy and Edwin Earhart, did not enjoy a tranquil marriage. Edwin's earnings as a railroad claims attorney in Kansas City were usually sufficient only for the essentials. Amy had been raised in the relative luxury and economic security provided by her father, Judge Alfred Otis. The stress of raising a family on a minimal budget resulted in hurt egos and frequent discord. The children would sometimes be sent to visit their grandparents. In Atchison, the girls enjoyed a secure upper-middle-class lifestyle under the strict but caring supervision of Judge and Mrs. Otis.

During some of their grammar school years, Amelia and Muriel lived full-time in Atchison and attended a private school. There, Amelia first displayed her aversion to explaining herself. Her teacher reported that Amelia "deduces the correct answers to complex arithmetic problems but hates to put down the steps by which she arrived at the results."

Back home Amelia and Muriel experienced a loving but sometimes chaotic existence living with their financially strapped parents. Regardless of his faults, Edwin was a doting father whose quick mind, sense of humor, and open affection contributed greatly to the education of his daughters.

Edwin constantly preached to his daughters, "Never run away!" They heard that moral so many times over the years, they reacted instinctively. Running away was not an option. But deaf to his own teachings, Edwin ran away and hid in the stupor of alcohol. The marriage and his work suffered accordingly. The family was forced to move whenever he was transferred from his job. He was finally fired, and the family resources rapidly dwindled to near zero.

In 1915, Amy and Edwin separated. Amelia attended six high schools before she finally graduated from Chicago's Hyde Park High School. During those critical years Amelia was never to enjoy the luxury of longstanding relationships with her peers. Small wonder that her sister would later write: "There was little room for nostalgia in AE's character. She believed in living each day to the utmost, without wasting time in futile regrets over severed friendships or neglected opportunities."

Amelia graduated in June of 1916, and the date marked a turning point for the whole Earhart family. Amy gained control of an inheritance from her mother. There was enough money for Amy and her daughters for the first time. Amy and Edwin reunited the family in Kansas City, and that fall Amelia could afford to go to Ogontz College in Rydal, Pennsylvania.

At Ogontz, Amelia matured and began looking toward her future. Her outlook was rare. She collected magazine and newspaper clippings about women who had established themselves in positions and occupations that were unusual or previously forbidden to her sex.

One item was about a woman doctor elected president of a county medical association; another concerned the first woman to hold the post of United States civil service commissioner; a third told of Oklahoma's only female bank president; a fourth, how India had admitted the first woman attorney to the bar. Clearly Amelia was considering a future in much broader terms than the usual roles of wife and mother.

During the 1917 Christmas holiday, instead of traveling home to Kansas City, Amelia decided to visit her sister, now in Canada. The United States had entered the World War earlier that year, but the military casualties had not yet deeply affected the fabric of life. For the first time, Amelia saw on the streets of Toronto the maimed and wounded soldiers returning from the battlefields of France. Her conscience dictated that she volunteer to care for the wounded. After receiving Red Cross training as a nurse's aide, Amelia was assigned to Spadina Military Hospital in Toronto.

Until the end of the war, Amelia worked ten hours a day with the sick and wounded. Her jobs included everything from emptying bedpans, making beds, and rubbing backs to working in the kitchen. She was deeply moved by the horror of the physical and mental mutilation that the war had heaped upon the brave young men she cared for.

Amelia became acquainted with an officer in the Royal Flying Corps who was stationed at the flying field at Armor Heights near Toronto. He invited her to come to the field and watch the training planes as their pilots made takeoffs and landings.

Amelia later wrote in her book *20 Hrs. 40 Min.*:

I remember well that when the snow blown back by the propellers stung my face I felt the first urge to fly. I tried to get permission to go up, but the rules forbade. . . . Aviation was the romantic branch of the service and inevitably attracted the romanticist. The dark side did not impress the enlisted men or me.

I have even forgotten the names of the men I knew then. But the memory of the planes remains clearly, and the sense of the inevitability of flying. It always seemed to me one of the few worth-while things that emerged from the misery of war.

After the war, Amelia returned to the United States in early 1919 with a high regard for airplane pilots and physicians. That fall, she entered the premedical program at Columbia University in New York City.

In the meantime her parents had moved from Kansas City to Los Angeles and wanted Amelia to join them. After her first year at Columbia, Amelia left in the summer of 1920 for California.

All around Los Angeles there were many new, exciting, and captivating things for the Earharts to see and do. Amelia and her father attended an air meet at Daugherty Field in Long Beach. Amelia told her father for the first time that she would like to fly. Surprised, he nevertheless made an appointment for her to take a flight the next day.

Amelia was twenty-three years old when her father paid ten dollars for her first airplane ride, a short flight from Rogers Field in west Los Angeles. She knew from that moment that she must learn to fly. Instruction cost five or six hundred dollars, but Amelia was ready to sign up at any price. She wanted to arrange to be taught by a woman flyer she had heard about.

Her father could not afford her flight training, but he did go with her to Kinner Airport in south Los Angeles to see the woman flight instructor, Neta Snook. Miss Snook agreed to take her as a student and encouraged Amelia by observing that in her experience women could learn to fly as well as men.

Amelia had a few Liberty Bonds that had been bought during the war. If Neta Snook would accept them as payment, that would be enough to get started. By then the instructor could determine whether she had any ability.

Snook agreed to accept the Liberty Bonds, and future payments in lieu of cash, for the flights. Before she went up, Amelia had to sign a liability release for the Kinner Airplane and Motor Corporation. It stated in part: "It is acknowledged that being transported through the air by so-called Flying Machines is a dangerous thing, and that the machines themselves are a dangerous instrumentality. The Kinner Airplane and Motor Corporation is not a common carrier of passengers, and accepts for trips by air only such persons as are willing to, and actually do, accept and assume the entire risk incident to aerial transportation." After signing the form, Amelia took her first flight instruction on the morning of January 3, 1921.

Amelia spent much of her time during the following months at the airfield. She wanted to learn all that she could about the aircraft and their engines. Everyone, including aircraft and engine designer Bert Kinner and Neta Snook, was favorably impressed by the young lady with the quick mind and unobtrusive manner. From almost the beginning, Earhart's training and flying experience diverged considerably from the norm. First, against the advice of her peers, she paid four times the cost of a surplus World War I trainer for a new Kinner Airster of modern design. Amelia soloed in about the conventional ten hours, but she had insisted on first receiving training in advanced maneuvers.

After soloing, she flew alone for a few hours and then returned to flying with an instructor to practice emergencies and develop advanced skills in handling them. She learned the limits of her own and her equipment's capabilities, and demonstrated an unusual sense of risk management. The result of her self-imposed training was that from the time she soloed in 1921 until she sold the Airster in 1924, she never had an incident that seriously damaged plane, passenger, or pilot.

While she owned the plane Amelia flew it whenever she could. Her job at the telephone company usually precluded flying on weekdays, but on most Saturdays and Sundays she was at the airfield. On some of the evenings after flying, Amelia and Neta would attend shows or go for drives with young men they were acquainted with. Neta noticed that Amelia did not take to the younger boys when they behaved irresponsibly. She appeared more comfortable around those who conversed and acted with maturity.

In the evenings after work, Amelia began going to lectures and concerts with a young man named Samuel Chapman. Sam, a Tufts graduate from Marblehead, Massachusetts, was at the time renting a room from the Earharts. He was quite taken with Amelia, and over time the young couple developed a deep friendship.

Before 1921 was over, Amelia was entered in the Air Rodeo at Sierra Airdrome, in Pasadena, California. The posters promised exhibitions by Miss Amelia Earhart in her Kinner Airster, and Miss Aloyfia McLintic in her Laird Swallow.

Amelia decided she would try to set a new altitude record for women. She was a member of the Aero Club of Southern California, and they agreed to seal a barograph in her plane as an official measure of the altitude. The results were published the next day in the newspapers:

> Miss Amelia Earhart, local aviatrix, established a new altitude record for women yesterday under the auspices of the Aero Club of Southern California.
>
> Flying her own Kinner Airster, containing a 60-foot power motor, she ascended more than 14,000 feet.
>
> Her sealed barograph registered little vibration until about 12,000 feet, where Miss Earhart said something went wrong with the motor. At the time she was climbing easily, at about 50 feet per minute, which would have continued perhaps for several thousand feet more if the engine difficulty had not arisen.

Amelia did not try to make any money from her flying. She considered it a sport. She did receive considerable publicity, but had no evident desire or knowledge of how to convert that publicity into financial gain. She seemed to have an aversion to explaining publicly the details of how and why she did things. It may have been only a natural ingrained midwestern desire for privacy, but it effectively prevented people from relating to her. Bert Kinner, who had no such reservations, published an advertisement with a letter from Amelia, written on May 20, 1922, extolling in detail the virtues of her Kinner Airster.

Amelia worked at various jobs trying to make enough money to fly her airplane whenever she could. She learned very early that flying was expensive. If flying was a sport, like polo it was a rich man's sport, and not a very practical one for an ordinary worker.

On May 16, 1923, Amelia was issued certificate number 6017 by the Fédération Aéronautique Internationale. It stated that the National Aeronautic Association of the United States certified that Amelia M. Earhart, born July 24, 1898 [sic], having fulfilled all of the conditions required by the Fédération Aéronautique Internationale for an Aviator Pilot, was now brevetted as such.

Apparently, in May of 1923 Amelia found it desirable to report herself as being a year younger than she really was. She would carry on this deception in publicity releases for the rest of her life. Many textbooks still list her birth year as 1898.

Amelia had already set herself apart from the millions of other young women in America. Though it appears that approximately six thousand FAI certificates had been issued to men worldwide, Amelia was among the first score of women so certified. It was not by chance. She had taken social, physical, and financial risks to make it happen. By the end of 1923 Amelia had accumulated less than 300 solo flight hours, but she and her little plane had already dared to fly higher than any woman had ever flown before.

In 1924 her parents' marriage ended, and Edwin Earhart received an uncontested divorce from Amy. After the divorce, Amelia's mother decided to leave Los Angeles for Boston, where Muriel was studying for her A.B. degree. Amelia wanted to fly her mother across the country in the Airster, but her mother would not pay the expenses for the trip. Instead Amy agreed to pay off the amount owed on the plane, but only if Amelia would quit flying for a while and settle down to more earthly pursuits. Amelia sold the plane and with the proceeds bought a yellow

Kissel roadster. The twenty-six-year-old Amelia and her mother took a circuitous route across the country to New England, arriving at Boston in July 1924.

Summer was coming to an end and the Earhart women had uprooted themselves completely. Amelia had agreed not to pursue flying for a while, and she contemplated returning to school at Columbia. Her mother offered to pay the tuition if she wanted to continue with college. After being away for four years, Amelia returned to New York City and Columbia University for the fall semester of 1924.

Though the nation was prospering, Mrs. Earhart was not. By the end of the spring semester, her finances were depleted to the point that Amelia had to return to Medford, Massachusetts, and go to work.

Amelia's leave from aviation would prove to be short-lived. She had joined the Boston chapter of the National Aeronautic Association and had somehow managed to find a few dollars to invest in Harold T. Dennison's new airport near Quincy, Massachusetts. Bert Kinner was looking for an agency in Boston to sell his airplanes. It was arranged for a Kinner plane to be kept at the Dennison Aviation hangar. Amelia was to demonstrate the Kinner plane in exchange for use of the plane when it was not busy. At least on some weekends Amelia was able to fly and keep her skills intact.

Sam Chapman had followed the Earharts from Los Angeles and found employment with the Boston Edison Company. Amelia and Sam dated frequently, but when Sam proposed marriage she declined. Sam insisted his wife must not work outside the home. He was disappointed by Amelia's rejection but never seemed to understand her. They continued their friendly relationship but were not engaged.

In September 1925 Amelia accepted a part-time job teaching foreign students in a university extension program. She continued teaching for a year, though the job barely paid enough to cover her expenses. The following year Amelia got a second job as a half-time social worker at Denison House, Boston's second-oldest settlement house. With all of that, she still had her weekends free for flying. Without any serious accident, she had accumulated nearly 500 hours of solo flying, a very respectable accomplishment.

From May 21, 1927, onward, the world would never look the same. Charles A. Lindbergh's solo nonstop flight from New York to Paris made the world a smaller place. A few months after Lindbergh's flight, Amelia was made a full-time staff member at Denison House. Not for an instant could it have crossed her mind that someday she might become a friend and associate, maybe even a rival, of America's new Lone Eagle.

As 1928 began, Amelia was a composed, educated, intelligent, energetic, unencumbered woman. She possessed a daring spirit for new ideas and adventure that was yet to be recognized or tapped. She was now thirty years old, and all options remained open. She was well prepared for whatever the future might bring.

3 : THE LEGEND BEGINS

O<small>N</small> a spring day in April 1928, much like any other day at Denison House, Amelia's work was interrupted by a telephone call from Hilton H. Railey on behalf of the New York publisher George Palmer Putnam about a flight that might involve some risk. Intrigued by the call, Amelia secured his references and agreed to meet with Railey later in the day.

Mr. Railey told her that Commander Richard E. Byrd's trimotor Fokker plane was being readied in Boston for a flight across the Atlantic. The sponsors wanted an American woman to be on the flight and asked if Amelia was interested. She was. About ten days later, Amelia was called for an interview with the flight's sponsors at the offices of G. P. Putnam's Sons Publishing Company in New York City. She knew, as she entered Mr. Putnam's office, that her participation in the Atlantic flight would be decided by the interview. What she did not know was that the future path of her entire life, both public and private, was to be completely changed.

George Palmer Putnam II was born in Rye, New York, on September 7, 1887, a grandson and namesake of the publishing house's founder.

His father was also named George, and to distinguish them their family, friends, and associates called the youngest G.P.

At age forty in May of 1928, G.P. was already an accomplished and distinguished man. Tall and lean, his six-foot-two-inch frame made him a handsome and imposing figure. He was a man of action, more than likely to take an active role in making events unfold. In 1908, at age twenty-one, knowing that his older brother would follow their father in the publishing business, G.P. had left home to make his fortune. In May of 1909 he found himself in Bend, Oregon, with $300 in his pocket. During the next five years G.P. would marry Dorothy Binney of Connecticut, and his first son, David, would be born. He would also serve Bend as mayor, having become a publisher and prosperous businessman. He moved from Bend in late 1914 when he was appointed secretary to Governor Withycombe of Oregon. More than a hundred townspeople gave the "Boy Mayor of Bend" a farewell banquet in appreciation for what he had accomplished there.

In 1916 G.P.'s father died. As expected, G.P.'s brother, Robert, took over their father's position. The United States entered the World War, and G.P. joined the Army, commissioned as an artillery officer, in December 1918. The great influenza epidemic at the end of the war took its toll of the Putnam family. Robert Putnam died, and G.P. returned with his family to New York, to assume the family's junior position at G. P. Putnam's Sons. The firm responded to his youthful outlook and energy, and over the next decade grew and prospered.

G.P. was instrumental in getting film producer Jesse Lasky to make Hollywood's first aviation movie, *Wings*. Starring Clara Bow, Buddy Rogers, and Gary Cooper, *Wings* was the first picture to receive an Academy Award. In 1928, sales of the book *We*, for which G.P. paid Charles Lindbergh a $100,000 advance, passed the half-million mark. G.P. was looking for the next best-seller when the young lady from Boston entered his office.

The interview with Amelia Earhart went very well, and everyone present was favorably impressed. They discussed what a contract would specify and asked her to return to Boston until they notified her of their decision. G.P. did something unusual: when Amelia left his office, he personally escorted her to the train station.

Amelia returned to Boston and shortly afterward was notified that she had been accepted; if still interested, she could make the Atlantic flight.

She met with Wilmer L. Stultz and Louis E. Gordon, the pilot and mechanic on the Atlantic crossing now christened the *Friendship* flight. Amelia thought she might occasionally be able to relieve them at the controls or help with the navigation. She purchased the *American Practical Navigator—An Epitome of Navigation and Nautical Astronomy,* by Nathaniel Bowditch. The copious notes and computations she made as she studied the 849-page text attest to her serious effort to learn celestial navigation.

During the weeks before the Atlantic flight, the forty-year-old Putnam, sometimes accompanied by his wife, Dorothy, could often be found in Boston. There were frequent breaks from study of the charts and books for dinners, plays, and socializing. The famous publisher was constantly on hand, and Amelia was spending time with Commander and Mrs. Byrd at their home on Brimmer Street. The intoxicating spirit of adventure was everywhere. Amelia enjoyed the excitement of the secret preparations immensely. At age thirty she was being introduced into the good life of celebrity and luxury.

The Fokker trimotor *Friendship* took off from Boston Harbor with the three fliers aboard early Sunday morning, June 3, 1928. They made it easily to Trepassey, Newfoundland, where gasoline was stored for the transoceanic flight. Then, for nearly two weeks local conditions or poor weather over the North Atlantic held them captive. Several times they attempted to take off, but the heavily laden plane could not get off the water. While awaiting each opportunity the grounded aviators whiled away the hours fishing, hiking, playing cards, and reading. Amelia read *The Story of the Titanic Disaster,* and kept a diary of the daily events.

However, at G.P.'s instigation newspapers throughout the western world were soon following the story of the woman who was to fly across the Atlantic. Amelia's tall, lean figure and all-American girl appearance started them writing of her as Lady Lindy, comparing the flight with the sensational flight Charles Lindbergh had made from New York to Paris the year before.

Finally, after all extra fuel and every piece of unnecessary equipment had been removed, at about 11:00 A.M. on Sunday morning, June 17, the *Friendship* made it into the air and headed for Europe.

Approximately 20 hours and 40 minutes later, on Monday, June 18, 1928, they landed at Burry Port, Wales. They had crossed the Atlantic to Europe. Amelia was in the record books forever, as the first woman to have flown the Atlantic. Her life would never be the same. From that moment on she would always be a celebrity.

In the next few days Amelia glimpsed how celebrities turned their fame into fortune. She arrived in Europe with little more than a comb, a toothbrush, and the clothes on her back. She would leave with three steamer trunks of fine clothes, a book contract, an airplane, first-class cabin tickets, and an invitation to dine at the captain's table.

The week in England was a whirlwind of activity for the young woman who worked at a settlement house. She met Lady Nancy Astor, purchased an Avro Avian airplane from Lady Mary Heath, and befriended department store tycoon H. Gordon Selfridge and his daughter, Violette.

Amelia tried constantly to give credit for the flight to Stultz and Gordon, but the press and public were enthralled by the first woman to have flown the Atlantic, and the stories in the papers always featured her. She protested that she had not even touched the controls and was just a sack of potatoes. The press responded that she was modest.

During this week Amelia discovered, somewhat to her bewilderment, that crowds of people responded automatically to a natural personal charisma that she did not know she possessed. She had never interacted as a celebrity with a large crowd before. When the opportunity finally occurred in England, it was like magic. Amelia was a sensation. The newspaper reporters gave her great press reviews.

Ten days later Amelia was in Southampton, England, with Stultz and Gordon, boarding the United States Lines' SS *President Roosevelt* for their return to New York. This was Amelia's first ocean voyage, and it was also the first trip in command of the *Roosevelt* for the ship's captain, Harry Manning. Amelia and the handsome thirty-one-year-old captain discovered they had much in common before they reached New York.

Harry Manning was six months older than Amelia, having been born in Hamburg, Germany, on February 3, 1897. With no money for college, at sixteen years of age he had entered the New York Merchant Marine School. When he graduated in October 1914 there were unusual opportunities for advancement because of the war in Europe. At age twenty-four he became a chief officer, and in July 1921 he joined United States Lines, eventually rising to be commodore of the line.

In January 1929 Harry Manning would become a true hero of the sea. He later received the Congressional Medal of Honor for personally rescuing the crew of a stricken freighter during a fierce Atlantic storm. Manning was also a pilot and had expressed his interest in flying. Before parting, Manning and Earhart promised to keep in touch and to make a flight together sometime.

The *President Roosevelt* arrived in New York Harbor early in the morning of July 6, 1928, and was met by Mayor Jimmy Walker's private yacht. The *Friendship* crew boarded the yacht to be greeted by dignitaries and G.P. before they were taken ashore.

Earhart, Stultz, and Gordon were heroes of the day. They were given a Broadway ticker tape parade to New York City Hall and multiple receptions that lasted till midnight, with G.P. there to guide them throughout. The publisher recognized Amelia's talent and knew the value of her newfound fame. She was a commodity now, and as with Charles Lindbergh, if her fame was to grow it must be nurtured. That was how publicists earned their money and how publishers sold their books. G.P. excelled at both.

A whirlwind tour was arranged to take the *Friendship* crew from New York to Boston and Chicago. With the tour complete, Amelia spent the last half of July and most of August at the Putnam home in Rye writing her first book, *20 Hrs. 40 Min.* With his wide range of contacts G.P. managed to keep Amelia's name in the papers. She made appearances for various public benefits, gave lectures, and had her photo taken with other celebrities. By September Amelia had finished the book and was off on another flying adventure.

This time she flew the Avro Avian she had purchased from Lady Heath on a cross-country trip to California, successfully navigating by herself. She had only maps to guide her over thousands of miles of the country she had never flown over before. It was the first solo flight ever made by a woman from the Atlantic to the Pacific and back again. She arrived in California in time to attend the 1928 National Air Races, which were being held in Los Angeles. She flew back to New York, arriving on October 16, in time for the November publication of her first article as part of the editorial staff of *Cosmopolitan* magazine.

As 1929 began, Amelia was at work writing articles for *Cosmopolitan* and traveling to give lectures, sometimes flying her Avian. On March 29, 1929, she passed her exams and flight tests and received her Transport Pilots license from the Department of Commerce. With her cross-country flight she had proven she was a competent pilot who could make record-setting flights by herself. Now she was certified by a Department of Commerce inspector as a competent transport pilot, one of only seven women in the United States to have earned the Transport Pilots license.

By midyear Transcontinental Air Transport (later to evolve into TWA) was starting its combination rail and air service from New York to Los

Angeles. Amelia was hired to help the marketing department convince women that flying was safe. It was at TAT that Amelia began a lifelong association and friendship with aviation entrepreneurs Eugene Vidal and Paul Collins. On July 7, 1929, the first passengers left New York, and Amelia was one of the ten people selected. Charles and Anne Lindbergh met the flight in Arizona, and Amelia flew with them on the final part of the trip into Los Angeles.

Amelia had given up her little open-cockpit Avro Avian for a closed-cockpit plane. Manufactured by Lockheed Aircraft, the Vega was a modern high-wing monoplane powered by a nine-cylinder air-cooled radial Pratt & Whitney Wasp engine. The single-pilot cockpit was immediately behind the engine. As there were no dual controls, the plane's design was suitable only for experienced and competent pilots.

The first all-women air race in history (later called the "Powder Puff Derby") began at Clover Field in Santa Monica, California, on August 18, 1929. The finish line was at Cleveland, Ohio, where the 1929 National Air Races were being held. In competition against eighteen of the most qualified women pilots in America, Amelia entered the race, flying her newly acquired Vega. Of the nineteen women competing in the race, fifteen crossed the finish line in Cleveland within the allotted time. Of the four who did not finish, one, Marvel Crosson, was killed in a crash. Louise Thaden won the race, Gladys O'Donnell was second, and Amelia Earhart came in third.

After the race in Cleveland there was a meeting in Amelia's hotel suite to discuss starting an organization of licensed women pilots. Invitations to become charter members were sent out to the 120 women who qualified. Eventually ninety-nine accepted the invitation. Amelia was chosen by her peers to be the first president of the Ninety-Nines.

On November 22, 1929, Amelia was back in Los Angeles, attempting to break the women's speed record in a Lockheed Vega. She flew at an average speed of 184.17 mph. She had learned the first commandment of the publicist: fame requires frequent public activity to keep your name in the news.

While Amelia was in Los Angeles, Dorothy Putnam went to Reno, Nevada, to establish the residency required for a divorce from G.P. A divorce was granted December 19, 1929.

On June 25 and July 5, 1930, at Grosse Isle Airport in Detroit, Michigan, Amelia in a Vega set three world speed records for women. At the same time she was working with Paul Collins and Eugene Vidal to create a new airline. She was to be vice president in charge of public relations, promoting the new airline's hourly shuttle service connecting New York, Philadelphia, and Washington.

New York, Philadelphia, and Washington Airways service was inaugurated on September 1, 1930, with the slogan "On the Hour Every Hour." The airline was financed by Charles and Nicholas Ludington of Philadelphia, and after a trial period was renamed the Ludington Line. Because of her appearances for TAT and Ludington and her paid lectures, Earhart was traveling almost constantly to every corner of the United States.

In 1930 G.P.'s eldest uncle died, leaving his interest in G.P. Putnam's Sons to his son Palmer C. Putnam. G.P. offered to buy his cousin Palmer's interest or to sell him his at a fair price. Palmer decided to buy out G.P. When the transaction was completed, G.P. held a promissory note from his cousin for future payments of about $100,000. After more than a decade at his grandfather's publishing house, G.P. left to become a vice president with another New York publisher, Brewer and Warren.

On February 7, 1931, Amelia and G.P. were married. Amelia moved into the Putnam home in Rye, New York. The couple made an informal agreement that neither would interfere with the other's career. They further agreed that if, after one year, either of them was unhappy, they would dissolve the marriage. After the ceremony, they were so busy there was little time to celebrate or have a honeymoon.

Shortly after she married, Amelia became interested in a new type of aircraft that did not have wings. A forerunner to the helicopter using rotating blades to provide lift, it was called an autogiro. Manufacturer Harold F. Pitcairn convinced Amelia to fly the craft to demonstrate some of its unique capabilities. With only a few minutes of instruction, she attempted an altitude record. On April 7, 1931, she successfully flew the Pitcairn autogiro to a record height of 18,415 feet. The following month, on May 29, she left Newark, New Jersey, for a flight to California with a Pitcairn craft owned by the Beech-Nut Gum Company. She arrived in Oakland, California, on June 6, 1931, becoming the first woman, and second person, to have piloted an autogiro across the continent.

On May 20, 1932, Earhart thrust herself center-stage on the international aviation scene by again flying across the Atlantic, this time not as a "sack of potatoes" but alone in her single-engine Lockheed Vega. The flight was made from Harbour Grace, Newfoundland, to near Londonderry, in Northern Ireland. Before making the flight she had to learn to pilot the Vega solely by instruments. She practiced flying blind for hours until she was confident of her ability. She had never learned to operate a radio, and there was no radio on her plane. Like Lindbergh five years before, Earhart navigated across the Atlantic solely by dead reckoning. She held compass headings and waited for Europe to come into view. Thirteen hours and 30 minutes after leaving Newfoundland she became the first woman to have flown solo across the Atlantic. She was an international sensation, and her husband joined her for a triumphant tour of Europe.

Amelia Earhart was a celebrity, received by the pope, entertained by royalty, and honored by governments across the continent. Amelia and G.P. returned to New York aboard the *Île de France* on June 20, 1932. New York City gave her a welcome the likes of which had not been seen since Lindbergh. She was now America's First Lady of the Air, an international heroine, and one of the best-known women in the world.

After they returned from Europe, G.P. left Brewer and Warren to become the head of the editorial board at the Paramount motion picture studios. He maintained an office and lived in New York but found it necessary to travel often to Hollywood. Amelia also traveled often to California and in August 1932 flew her plane to Los Angeles. It was still equipped with long-range fuel tanks, and she was determined to make a nonstop flight back to New York. She departed Los Angeles on August 24, 1932, and approximately 19 hours and 5 minutes later she landed at Newark, New Jersey. The 2,477-mile flight set an official U.S. record for distance without refueling and was the first nonstop transcontinental flight ever made by a woman.

By the end of 1932, at thirty-five years of age, Earhart was virtually on top of the world, and her proceeds from lecturing were keeping pace. For weeks on end she crisscrossed the country lecturing to packed audiences, earning the money to keep flying her plane, and keeping her name before the public. She, and everything she did, was news wherever she went. In Poughkeepsie, New York, Eleanor Roosevelt and Lady Nancy Astor both introduced Amelia at one of her lectures. A few months later she and G.P. attended Franklin Roosevelt's presidential inauguration as Eleanor's guests. Later they lunched and stayed overnight at the White House.

By early 1933 Amelia had sold the Vega in which she had soloed the Atlantic, but she kept the excellent Pratt & Whitney Wasp engine to install in a newer Vega that Lockheed was working on. The Lockheed factory was located in Burbank, California, near the Union Air Terminal.

Her earlier business venture, the Ludington Line, with its hourly flights had been a good idea whose time would eventually come, but economic hard times had forced its halt. Earhart, Paul Collins, Eugene Vidal, and a mutual friend, Sam Solomon, started another airline in New England, each putting up 25 percent of the capital. They incorporated as National Airways but called the airline Boston-Maine Airways after the railroad that was cooperating with them. At the last minute Eugene Vidal, son-in-law of U.S. Senator Thomas Gore of Oklahoma, was offered the post of director of the Bureau of Air Commerce in Washington, D.C. He accepted the appointment and had to withdraw from the airline.

Collins was named president, Earhart first vice president, and Solomon second vice president. On August 11, 1933, the first flight of Boston-Maine Airways departed Boston's Logan Airport for Portland and Bangor, Maine. Aboard the inaugural flight were Amelia Earhart and Eugene Vidal, in his new capacity as director of the Bureau of Air Commerce. Amelia worked hard to get passengers to buy tickets on the new line, and she put her stepson, David Putnam, to work as a dispatcher in Augusta, Maine. Her efforts were successful and the routes still survive. More than sixty years later, after consolidations, name changes, expansions, and mergers, the little Boston-Maine Airways is now part of the Delta Air Lines system.

President Franklin D. Roosevelt was attempting to invigorate the economy by sponsoring and funding various public works projects, including many new airports and airway facilities. The airplane designers and manufacturers had outstripped the existing suitable airports and airways.

Aviation in Europe was expanding rapidly as well. European airlines faced similar navigation and communications problems, but for political and geographical reasons they had settled on a different solution. Compared to the United States, England, France, Spain, and Italy are all relatively small countries with long coastlines. A sophisticated marine radiotelegraph communications and navigation system serving commercial shipping was already in place. (Radiotelegraph uses the dots and dashes of code exclusively, not voice.) The European maritime system was complete with radio direction-finding, radio beacon, and weather services. It had the tremendous political advantage of already having standardized on a single international language, the dots and dashes of Morse code. When flying over countries in Europe, Africa, and most of Asia, any airborne radio operator could exchange messages and navigational information with any ground station, provided that the aircraft carried radiotelegraph equipment and a radiotelegraph operator who could copy Morse code.

This contrasted sharply with the situation in the United States, where maritime radiotelegraph stations could not serve the vast interior regions. With local aeronautical radio stations located approximately every two hundred miles, U.S. aircraft could safely use less powerful and shorter-range radiotelephone transmitters that could be operated by the pilot. (Radiotelephone uses voice exclusively, no dots and dashes of code.) This was the radio system Amelia Earhart used throughout her career.

It is interesting to note that when Lindbergh and his wife, Anne Morrow, decided to make flights outside the United States, it was Anne, not Charles, who learned the Morse code and became the radio operator. She studied for months to become sufficiently practiced to qualify for a radiotelegraph operator's license.

Earhart was still receiving $250 for each lecture as 1934 began. She had a busy schedule of engagements, though it had been over two years since her solo Atlantic flight. She had made a good showing in a couple of air races and had set transcontinental speed records, but in 1933 she had had to share the Fédération Aéronautique Internationale "woman of the year" award with French aviator Maryse Hilsz. It was time for another spectacular flight to shore up her public image. Luckily, a group of Hawaiian businessmen had offered a $10,000 prize for a flight from Hawaii to the mainland.

In the fall of 1934 Earhart was staying in the North Hollywood section of Los Angeles; Paul Mantz, who was to become an important colleague, lived just a few blocks away. Mantz owned a business, United Air Services, located close to the Lockheed factory. Mantz, six years younger than Earhart, had been raised in northern California. In November 1927 he had been accepted for flight training by the Army and was sent to March Field in Riverside, California. After six months and 125 hours of instruction he was dropped from the program for not following orders, but his instructor had rated his piloting skills as excellent.

Mantz returned to the San Francisco Bay Area, where he gave flight instruction and flew charter flights until 1931. He went to Hollywood and successfully broke into the tight circle of pilots who flew for the motion picture companies. He also started an airplane maintenance business at Union Air Terminal.

Earhart had met Mantz when she had flown in to visit the Lockheed factory at Burbank. His business was multifaceted; he did more than just service airplanes and perform stunt flights for the motion picture industry. Among other things, he flew special charters for Hollywood celebrities. Mantz had a Lockheed Vega nicknamed the *Honeymoon Express,* which was kept busy carrying movie stars and wealthy people wherever they wanted to go for a dollar a mile.

Earhart hired Mantz to be her technical adviser and commissioned United Air Services to prepare her own Vega for the flight from Hawaii to California.

A new regulation required any aircraft flying over oceans to have a radio transmitter powerful enough to maintain continuous communications. Earhart, who had never learned to operate by Morse code, needed two things before her voice could be transmitted over the long distances of the Pacific. First, she needed a two-channel transmitter, with 3105 kilocycles for airway and nighttime work and 6210 kilocycles for long-range daytime radio-skip transmissions. The 3105-kilocycle frequency was monitored continuously by all Department of Commerce stations. The 6210-kilocycle channel was monitored by certain coastal or other stations that might want long-range communications. Usually, in the daytime 3105 could be heard for only a couple hundred miles, whereas 6210 could reach several times as far. Pilots would use 6210 in the daytime only to contact a station that was too far away to be reached on 3105. Almost all private flying was done in the daytime, and because all airplanes transmitted on the same frequency, it was essential that the transmitted radio signals not travel much farther than the nearest Department of Commerce station.

Because radiotelephone voice transmissions were not normally as powerful as telegraph, the second thing that Earhart needed was a very good antenna. The only way to create a good antenna on Earhart's plane was to install a long trailing wire. United Air Services installed the transmitter along with a trailing wire antenna system that could be reeled in and out below the plane like a long fishing line.

Christmas 1934 found Amelia and G.P., along with Paul Mantz and his wife, Myrtle, aboard the Matson liner *Lurline* en route to Honolulu, Hawaii. Tied down on the aft tennis deck was Amelia's Lockheed Vega, where it was watched over constantly by her mechanic, Ernest Tissot.

When they arrived in Honolulu everyone went to the Royal Hawaiian Hotel except Mantz and Ernie, who off-loaded the plane onto a barge and floated it to the Fleet Air Base, located on Ford Island in the middle of Pearl Harbor. There, they checked the plane over before Mantz could fly it from Ford Island's 3,000-foot runway to Wheeler

Field for further work. Wheeler Field was 6,000 feet long; flying a plane heavy with fuel, Earhart would need the longer runway.

A former charterer of Mantz's *Honeymoon Express,* Christian Holmes, cabled Mantz offering the group the use of his home in Waikiki. The next day they moved to the beautiful estate, where Holmes's Scottish house manager and Japanese servants attended to their every need. They stayed there while preparing the Vega for the flight to California. If everything went well, Earhart hoped to go all the way to Washington, D.C., with only one stop.

By Friday afternoon, January 11, 1935, the weather was right; Earhart took off from the wet, soggy grass of Wheeler Field into a leaden, overcast sky at 4:44 P.M. Hawaiian standard time (HST). (Hawaiian Islands time was $10^{1/2}$ hours behind Greenwich civil time, and the West Coast was 8 hours behind Greenwich, creating a $2^{1/2}$ hour time difference between Hawaii and California.)

As soon as G.P. was sure Amelia was not going to return to Wheeler, he left the field and went to the commercial radio broadcast station KGU in Honolulu, where they had prearranged for him to have a shortwave receiver to listen to Amelia's radio transmissions. G.P. would then use KGU's powerful radio transmitter to send a response to her.

After passing Makapuu Point, leaving Oahu behind, Amelia reeled out her trailing wire antenna and turned on the transmitter to broadcast her first message on the 3105-kilocycle frequency. It was 5:45 P.M. HST, and she was about 110 miles from Honolulu. She reported that the weather was overcast but everything was okay. After transmitting, Amelia listened with her receiver tuned to KGU. She was listening to music when the program was interrupted. She heard her husband's voice saying, " 'AE,' the noise of your motor interferes with your broadcast. Will you please try to speak a little louder so we can hear you." She was only a little over a hundred miles away, but her 3105 groundwave signal was already less than loud and clear.

Amelia had advised everyone before the flight that she would transmit her messages at 15 minutes and 45 minutes after the hour. She continued to transmit her radio reports, but some of the messages were only partially audible because of weak signals and atmospheric static.

It was dark when Amelia reported at 7:45 P.M. HST, "EVERYTHING IS FINE AND THE WEATHER IS FAIR." She was 3 hours out and about 400 miles from Honolulu. They were now hearing her 3105 signal bounced in by the nighttime sky wave. G.P. then requested that she shift her transmitter frequency to 6210 kilocycles. As it turned out, the 6210 frequency was not as good as 3105 kilocycles for nighttime sky-wave reception; Amelia was not heard again for 2 hours.

Then at 9:47 P.M. HST she reported: "FLYING ABOUT 8,000 FEET OVER LOW CLOUDS. ALL IS WELL." The 700-mile distance from her plane to Honolulu was now proper for bouncing in the 6210 frequency nighttime sky wave. By 12:15 A.M. HST, Amelia's signals were becoming too weak to hear in Hawaii, but she was coming in stronger to the stations on the mainland. Almost every half hour she was heard to report her altitude, the general cloud conditions, and her usual, "Everything is okay."

Radio station KFI in Los Angeles reported that her radio signals were getting weaker, while San Francisco was reporting that her signals were getting stronger. The relative strength of her signals led them to believe she was coming close to Oakland and was heading for Oakland, not Los Angeles.

Earhart was very pleased with the way the radio had worked. She could turn on her transmitter, broadcast a request, and in 15 minutes or less get an answer on her receiver. She reeled up the trailing wire antenna over the California coast as she was preparing to land.

The Vega landed at the Oakland airport at 1:31 P.M. PST, 18 hours and 17 minutes after Earhart had taken off from Wheeler Field. A tumultuous crowd of five thousand people was at the airport to greet her on arrival. Amelia Earhart was the first woman to have flown from Hawaii, and the only pilot to have flown it solo. The front page of nearly every newspaper in the country headlined the feat. The press did not know of her disappointment in not being able to continue her flight to Washington, D.C.

Amelia flew her plane down to Union Air Terminal in Burbank, and rested in North Hollywood while waiting for her husband and the Mantzes to return by ship from Honolulu. After G.P. was home they immediately started making plans for her next flight.

Earhart had been invited by the government of Mexico to fly to Mexico City. Her plane was still equipped for long-range flying, so she decided to accept the invitation. On April 19, 1935, she departed from Burbank for the 1,700-mile flight to Mexico City. Something got in her eye, and she lost her way. She had to make an unplanned stop at the little village of Nopala to get directions. When she finally arrived in Mexico City, there was a crowd estimated at ten thousand people to greet her. It rivaled anything she had ever experienced before.

There were weeks of almost continuous festivities before Earhart took off from Mexico City early in the morning of May 8, 1935. Her destination was New York City, approximately 2,100 miles away. Flying over the Gulf of Mexico, she mused about the luxury it would be to have more than one engine when flying over oceans. It occurred to her that a suitable multi-engine plane could fly safely over any ocean, maybe even on a trip around the world. She would have a talk with G.P. about this.

The Department of Commerce radio station at New Orleans, Louisiana, heard her report at 12:16 P.M. CST: "FLYING AT 10,000 FEET. EVERYTHING OKAY. SOUTHEAST OF NEW ORLEANS."

She landed at Newark airport in New Jersey 14 hours, 18 minutes, after takeoff. It was the first nonstop flight ever made from Mexico City direct to New York. The crowd of thousands at the airport were so excited by her arrival that they broke through police lines. Earhart had to be rescued by a police guard unit that had to use their nightsticks to clear a path for her. At age thirty-seven, she was now queen of the air.

Aboard her plane were fifty souvenir letters and a sheet of specially issued stamps commemorating her flight to Mexico. Now, it was up to G.P. to sell them so Amelia could have that multi-engine plane for her future ocean crossings and a possible round-the-world flight. The funds came up very short. G.P.'s cousin Palmer had declared bankruptcy, wiping out the remaining $75,000 he owed G.P.—all the money G.P. had left from his family publishing business. Luckily he had a good job with Paramount Pictures, but now he joined all the others who were living from paycheck to paycheck.

Amelia was considering entering into a partnership with Paul Mantz to operate a flight school at United Air Services in Burbank. The movie business now required G.P. to spend a lot of his time in Hollywood. He rented out the house in Rye, New York, and they bought a small house and a lot at 10042 Valley Spring Lane in the Toluca Lake area of North Hollywood. The house would need to be enlarged and remodeled before they could move in permanently.

Amelia wanted to attend the 1935 National Air Races in late August in Cleveland. She decided to enter the Bendix Air Race with her Vega. She took off from Burbank and did all of the flying in the cockpit, while Paul Mantz and Al Menasco, of Menasco Engine Company, played gin rummy in the cabin. Her elapsed time to Cleveland was 13 hours, 47 minutes, and 6 seconds, which put her in fifth place. The $500 prize money paid the expenses for the entire trip.

G.P. came to Cleveland to meet Amelia, and after the races Amelia, G.P., Mantz, and Al Menasco flew back together in the Vega.

After they returned from Cleveland, Amelia and Paul Mantz entered into an agreement to set up a flight school at United Air Services that would use a Link Trainer to teach blind-flying to pilots. G.P. would help them to publicize the business, but Mantz would maintain the controlling interest.

In November Amelia and G.P. traveled to Purdue University in West Lafayette, Indiana, where Amelia served as a part-time career counselor for women. Amelia was serious about the counseling work. She encouraged the young women students to expand their horizons and not to let past practices or conventions restrict their futures.

At a dinner party hosted by Edward C. Elliott, president of Purdue University, Amelia and G.P. explained to industrialist David Ross and the other Purdue benefactors how Amelia could use a multi-engine airplane as a flying laboratory for aviation research, maybe even for a trip around the world. Mr. Ross offered to back the project with a $50,000 donation. Later J. K. Lilly of the Eli Lilli Company, together with other donors, contributed another $30,000 to make a total of $80,000—a fortune in 1935.

For legal liability reasons, the Purdue Foundation grant would purchase the flying laboratory for Amelia in her name. She would be solely and completely responsible for its ownership and use. For the same liability reasons, in April 1936 Purdue University gave her an official leave of absence from her post as career counselor.

In preparation for delivery of the new twin-engine Lockheed Electra, Amelia needed a lot of additional money. She sold her stock in National Airways and resigned from the board as first vice president. She also withdrew from her business arrangements with United Air Services, while retaining Paul Mantz as a technical adviser.

Amelia remembered her sea captain friend, Harry Manning, and their promise to make a flight together sometime. While in New York she got in touch with Manning, who was still with United States Lines. He had been flying his own plane for several years. During his years at sea he had also become proficient at radio operating. It was decided that Captain Manning would accompany Amelia on the round-the-world flight as her navigator.

Amelia was lecturing constantly and Captain Manning had his voyages to make, but when they were in New York they planned and worked on the hundreds of details necessary for a round-the-world flight. They were determined to select the best equipment and use the latest technologies to ensure the flight's success. Getting prepared to handle every obstacle and challenge they might meet would not be easy.

A few heavier-than-air aircraft had already flown completely around the world, but none was piloted by a woman. In 1924, U.S. Army Air Service planes had completed the first circumnavigation in 175 days. Seven years later in 1931, Wiley Post and navigator Harold Gatty flew around the world in 8 days. The following year, Wolfgang von Gronau and his seaplane crew completed a world flight in approximately 110 days. In 1933, flying solo this time, Wiley Post made a second flight around the world, in 7 days. Little could be learned from the experiences of these earlier flights that would help Earhart and Manning plan theirs.

In 1936 there was little cooperation or organization among the countries of the world on matters of civil aviation. Each country decided what best suited its needs and organized its aviation communications and navigation systems accordingly.

In the United States a civil airway system of light beacons had been posted every few miles between major air centers in 1926, when airmail pilots started flying at night. The system depended on pilots' maintaining visual contact with the lights and proved useless during storms or fog. A tragic trail of crashed planes and dead pilots soon proved the system inadequate for all-weather flying. The airmail pilots were the pioneers who placed their lives on the line to discover what worked and what didn't.

In 1930 a system of low-frequency radio stations for all-weather radio navigation was set up between New York and Cleveland. By 1936, civil airways crisscrossed the nation served by the beams of the low-frequency radio ranges. The commercial airlines, and a few civilian planes equipped with radios, could use the airways within the United States to maintain year-round service in most weather conditions. Reasonably reliable and safe airline operations within the United States became feasible as new modern all-weather twin-engine planes like the Boeing 247 and Douglas DC-2 entered service. Airline operations across the oceans were just beginning, and each airline independently provided its own communications and navigation services.

By 1935, Captain Edwin Musick and Navigator Frederick Noonan of Pan American Airways were surveying the Pacific to learn whether scheduled airline service was practical. They followed earlier pathfinders Sir Kingsford-Smith, Wiley Post, Charles Ulm, and others who dared to lead the way. Eventually, all would pay the ultimate price.

This was the patchwork of incompatible systems—or their absence—that Earhart and Manning faced in finding workable solutions to problems of navigation, communications, and flight operations. First, they would have to learn how things were done in all the places they were to fly and how to conform to the local methods. Then, they would have to devise their own techniques to use where no one had ever flown before. All of this was taking place while their normal lives and the demands of work continued as usual.

4 : PREPARATIONS FOR

THE WORLD FLIGHT

B Y May of 1936, plans for the expansion of G.P. and Amelia's house on Valley Spring Lane in North Hollywood were complete. She was as excited about the house as she was about her new Electra. When not on lecture tours, she was in California happily dividing her time between watching the progress on her plane and the construction work on her home.

Mantz was to check on the plane when Earhart was out of town. Except for the absence of cabin windows and the installation of larger engines and fuel tanks, the plane was really a standard Lockheed Model 10, built to specifications similar to those of the previous fifty-four. By July, Lockheed was installing the special equipment, and her Model 10E was moved into the final assembly shop to be readied for delivery.

Earhart needed a full-time mechanic to fly with her and maintain the plane. Through Mantz, she hired Ruckins "Bo" McKneely, who had just completed six years as an overhaul mechanic of Pratt & Whitney engines. Bo was born in Patterson, Louisiana, in 1908 and was eleven years younger than Earhart.

Right on schedule the plane was ready for production tests. Earhart took her first flight in the new Electra with Lockheed's chief test pilot on July 21. Three days later, on her thirty-ninth birthday, she took delivery of the $80,000 "flying laboratory." She and Mantz both took instruction flights with the chief pilot to become proficient at flying the twin-engine plane.

To gain further experience, she decided to enter the 1936 New York–Los Angeles Bendix Air Race, with Helen Richey as her copilot. Richey had been the first woman in the United States to pilot a commercial airliner on a regularly scheduled flight. They departed New York in the Bendix Race and finished in Los Angeles fifth in a field of five. The $500 prize money didn't cover expenses, but Earhart had gained another 30 hours' experience in flying her new plane.

In October Amelia, G.P., and Bo flew the plane to the Purdue University airport in West Lafayette, Indiana. It was based there for the next few weeks while Bo worked on the fuel lines and installed equipment. Meanwhile, Earhart spent several weeks on the lecture circuit.

Flying a plane around the world entails hundreds of tasks. Each country has its rules and regulations governing aircraft licensing, landing rights, overflying rights, passports, visas, vaccinations, insurance, airports, charts and maps, weather, fuel, maintenance, communications, hotels, and last but not least, money. In those days it could take three months just to exchange letters of inquiry with a distant country. Multiply that by twenty or thirty different jurisdictions and the magnitude of the task becomes apparent. Earhart would have to use every resource at her disposal if she was to get the world flight off the ground.

Finding a practical route required weeks of studying charts and measuring distances. Previous flights around the world had bypassed the Pacific by flying the northern route through Alaska, but Earhart wanted to do something no one had ever done. She wanted to fly around the world as close to the equator as possible. The expanse of the Pacific Ocean was an obstacle. They considered a seaplane and aerial refueling, but in the end a friend held the solution.

The Department of Commerce had colonized some islands in the middle of the Pacific to establish U.S. sovereignty, believing the islands would be needed when future air routes to Australia were established. William "Bill" Miller, of the Bureau of Air Commerce (a subdivision of the department), had laid out possible airfields before turning the islands' administration over to the Department of the Interior in 1936. The bureau, under the direction of Eugene Vidal, was now planning to build an airfield on Howland Island within range of airfields in New

Guinea and Hawaii. Here was the refueling point Earhart needed to make her equatorial flight.

Gathering information and making arrangements for fuel and maintenance throughout Africa, Asia, and Australia constituted a monumental undertaking. Personal connections played a great part in this task. For instance, Amelia had remained friends since 1928 with Violette Selfridge of London, and G.P. had published Violette's book *Flying Gypsies* in 1930. Violette was now married to Viscount Jacques de Sibour, who was the London representative for Standard Oil Aviation Products and had contacts throughout the British Empire. Amelia and G.P. enlisted Viscount Sibour's aid for the flight.

Because of poor communications, getting clearances from each of the many different countries was all but impossible. Through Eleanor Roosevelt at the White House, Earhart was able to get help from the U.S. Department of State and the secretary of the Navy in making arrangements for the flight. G.P. supplied requested information, coordinated efforts, monitored progress, and kept track of the paperwork. His main job, though, was to find financial sponsors to support the world flight.

When the Electra was in Burbank it was kept in the United Air Services hangar, and Mantz watched over Bo and the plane whenever Earhart was out of town. He was still known as her technical adviser, but there was little for him to advise about after the plane was delivered.

In New York, Manning was working on plans for communications and navigation. He determined that as soon as they left U.S. territory all normal aircraft communications would require telegraphy. To contact ships or maritime coastal stations for radio direction-finding, they must be able to transmit on the international standard distress and calling frequency of 500 kilocycles. Western Electric said they could modify the transmitter for telegraphy on 500 kilocycles, but the receiver could not receive on 500. Celestial observations would be good for navigation en route, but a radio direction-finder would be required to ensure locating a small island or other destination in poor visibility. They needed a different receiver and a radio direction-finder loop.

In late November Earhart flew the plane to New York, where the transmitter modifications were discussed with Western Electric. A third channel for 500 kilocycles would be added, but tuning the transmitter to 500 kc would require a 250-foot trailing wire antenna.

G.P. had contacted Vincent Bendix as a possible sponsor for the world flight. Amelia visited Bendix in South Bend, Indiana, and came away with a promise of $5,000 and some new Bendix aircraft radio equipment. The promised Bendix radios would meet Manning's radio receiver and direction-finder requirements.

Late in December, with Jacqueline Cochran as her copilot, Earhart flew the Electra from New York back to its California base in Burbank. There were still lectures Amelia had to finish in January before she could give full time to preparing for the world flight.

Harry Manning had arranged to take three months' leave from United States Lines. He came to California to help with the final preparations; in early February 1937 he flew back with Earhart to New York. Bo was also onboard, and it gave them an opportunity to flight-check the new equipment. Manning was able to practice taking celestial observations from the plane and gain experience in navigating the much faster aircraft.

At a press conference in New York on February 12, 1937, Amelia Earhart officially announced the world flight and introduced Captain Harry Manning as her navigator.

Cyril D. Remmlein, from the Bendix Radio Research Division, met with Earhart and Manning at the airplane at Newark airport. Remmlein brought with him a prototype of the radio receiver they were going to install in the Electra. The actual airplane had to be measured because of the limited space available. As the receiver was to be remotely controlled from the cockpit, they had to select the best locations for the equipment. Earhart and Manning approved of Remmlein's final placement of the control head and receiver unit.

The Bendix receiver was so new that the first unit was still in the manufacturing process. The design engineer, O. Vernon Moore, hadn't made the coils for the first receiver yet. Earhart and Manning chose to have the receiver cover from 200 kilocycles to 10,000 kilocycles in five bands. As soon as the first production receiver and the modified direction-finder loop coupler box were completed, they would be shipped immediately to Burbank for installation.

On February 17 Amelia, along with G.P., Harry, and Bo, departed Newark in the afternoon for Cleveland and took off early the next morning to continue their journey back to Burbank.

Harry was still practicing his navigation in the back of the plane. He passed a note to Amelia in the cockpit giving a position in southern Kansas when they were actually in northern Oklahoma. Amelia realized that they were only a few miles south of the Kansas border; in reality the position wasn't all that far off. G.P. took the worst possible view and expressed concern because Manning didn't even have them in the right state.

Trying to synchronize the propellers, Earhart discovered that one propeller would not change pitch; it was frozen in position. (This is like having a car's manual transmission stuck in high gear. As long as you are driving along at normal speeds, everything is okay, but if you have to start from a stop, or go up a steep hill, you will have trouble.) With the propeller's pitch stuck in the cruise position, Earhart could not get full power out of that engine. The high-pitch blade angle normal at cruise speeds would not allow the engine to turn over fast enough to develop full power. She landed at Blackwell, Oklahoma, and Bo labored into the night to get the errant propeller working properly again. They were able to take off from Blackwell the next morning, Friday, February 19, for the approximately 8-hour flight to Burbank.

They had a good flight from Blackwell to Burbank. The propellers had worked fine, but Earhart was unable to receive any signals on the Western Electric radio receiver. She brought the plane down to a perfect three-point landing at the Union Air Terminal. Mantz was waiting at the United Air Services hangar and came toward the plane as she shut down the engines. As the others were deplaning, she told him that the radio receiver wasn't working, and she needed a radioman to look at it.

Mantz telephoned United Airlines at Burbank to ask if their radioman Joseph H. Gurr could look at Earhart's radio. It was the end of his workday and he came right over to the hangar. There were no manuals or diagrams of the radio for Gurr to study overnight, but he promised to come back the next day and take a look.

They met Gurr at the plane the next morning. After a few minutes of inspecting the plane, he found the receiver under the copilot's seat. The antenna was lying on the floor, not hooked up to the receiver, which came to life as soon as he made the connection. It was easy, but to Amelia and G.P. it seemed a miracle. From then on, Gurr was the person they called whenever they needed a radioman.

The following Monday, Remmlein notified them that the Bendix receiver was ready. He would be flying in from Washington, D.C., on Thursday, February 25, to help install both the receiver and the direction-finder. Thursday he arrived on schedule, and the next day Earhart and Manning met with him to make final installation plans. They agreed that they would put a telegraph key, a microphone, and earphones at both the navigation station and the copilot's seat to enable Manning to work the transmitter and listen to the receiver in either the aft cabin or the cockpit. Manning would have to be back in the cabin to manually switch the transmitting antenna from the trailing wire to the top V antenna or vice versa. Photographer Albert Bresnik arrived and took a series of photographs of Earhart with the direction-finder loop coupler control box and the loop antenna.

With Joe Gurr helping after work and on his days off, the Bendix RA-1 receiver was installed with its power supply on top of the fuel tanks on the right-hand side. The remote control box for the receiver was placed on the eyebrow panel, just above the left windshield in front of the pilot. The radio direction-finder loop was put on the centerline on top of the plane, a few inches in front of the cockpit overhead hatch. The loop had to be turned crosswise before the overhead hatch was opened or the loop would hit the hatch. It was easy to turn the loop by hand from the inside or the outside if it was in the way. The trailing wire antenna was installed through the cabin floor aft of the transmitter.

While Remmlein and Gurr finished installing the radios, Manning left on a commercial flight to Oakland. He met with Bill Miller, superintendent of airways for the Bureau of Air Commerce, who had recently laid out the potential airfields on the Pacific Islands. Before Eugene Vidal resigned as director of the Bureau of Air Commerce, he had sent Miller to Oakland to help Earhart in coordinating arrangements with the various government agencies.

On Tuesday, March 2, Manning and Miller conferred with officials of Pan American Airways at the airline's headquarters in Alameda, California. They made arrangements for the airline to cooperate with Earhart's flight from Oakland to Honolulu. Miller had made arrangements for temporary space in the Oakland airport administration building. At G.P.'s expense he hired Vivian C. Maatta as a secretary.

On the third Manning came back from Oakland on a commercial flight and reported to Earhart that Pan American had agreed to assist her. The next morning he went to the Federal Communications Commission office in Los Angeles to get his license to operate the Electra's transmitter as a telegraph station. He was given a test of the operating rules and a Morse code test at the required speed of fifteen words per minute. After passing the tests, Manning was issued operator's license number P-11-1695, with an endorsement authorizing him to operate aircraft radiotelegraph stations.

The installation of the new receiver and direction-finder was complete. When they turned on the Bendix equipment in the plane for the first time, Remmlein explained to Manning how to operate the equipment for best results.

The new Bendix receiver employed a high-quality, state-of-the-art eight-tube superheterodyne design, with an enhanced ability to reject unwanted signals. Off-frequency signals that had caused interference on earlier radio receivers would not even be heard on the new Bendix. The receiver had five bands and, with the exception of 1500 to 2400, any frequency between 200 and 10,000 kilocycles could be tuned. After explaining to Manning the function of the Bendix receiver's controls, Remmlein turned on the power to the radio direction-finder; its on-off switch was located on the loop coupler control box.

Remmlein took great care to explain to Manning how the radio direction-finder loop coupler worked. The correct operation of the loop coupler controls was essential for the loop to obtain a sharp minimum signal. Manning had to listen carefully, as there were no manuals to study; Remmlein was the only source of information on its correct operation. It would prove to be a significant error of omission that Earhart wasn't there to learn from Remmlein.

The loop coupler control box had been custom-made to electronically adapt the standard Navy RDF-1-B direction-finder loop to the new Bendix RA-1 receiver. Five frequency-band numbers were shown on the face of Earhart's loop coupler, but the Navy model had six bands. The actual frequency range of each band was listed on a chart concealed inside the inner bottom cover plate of the unit. The limited space on the face of Earhart's loop coupler required that the frequency bands be labeled 1, 2, 3, 4, and 5. Remmlein cautioned Manning that the radio direction-finder loop was designed to take bearings only on frequencies between 200 and 1430 kilocycles, whereas the receiver could receive signals on frequencies up to 10,000 kilocycles. If Earhart or Manning tried to take a bearing on a high-frequency signal using the Bendix receiver's upper bands, the resonance of the loop would be so far out of tune they probably could not get a minimum signal.

In addition, the five frequency bands of the Bendix receiver were not related to the five band numbers printed on the face of the loop coupler. Without an operating manual, the five direction-finder loop bands could easily be misinterpreted to be the same as the Bendix receiver's five bands. This natural, seemingly harmless mistake was to be made by both Joe Gurr and Amelia. It would frustrate every attempt Earhart made to use the Bendix direction-finder loop on her last flight.

On Friday, March 5, Clarence "Kelly" Johnson, Lockheed performance engineer, conferred with Earhart and Mantz about making performance flight-tests now that all of the equipment and antennas had been installed. The flights were to determine the best speeds, altitudes, and power settings for Earhart to obtain maximum range. The test flights were completed by Sunday evening. Kelly took several days with his slide rule to work up the optimum flight procedures and power charts for Amelia to use on the world flight.

On Monday, a meeting was held to discuss any lingering problems. G.P. brought up the incident in Oklahoma where Manning had given them a position that was not even in the right state. He asked Mantz if he had any doubts about Manning's ability to navigate a fast-moving airplane. Mantz pointed out that navigating an airplane was different from navigating a ship, and he suggested they take Manning on a flight out to sea to test his ability to get them back by celestial navigation. Joe Gurr could test the radios at the same time. They agreed it was a good idea and set up the flight for early Wednesday morning. If everything went all right, Earhart would fly the plane to Oakland that afternoon.

It was very dark Wednesday morning when Mantz, Manning, G.P., and Gurr taxied out in the Electra from the United Air Services hangar for a takeoff to the west. They were airborne at 3:35 A.M. and headed northwestward from Burbank toward San Francisco Bay. The plan was to have Manning navigate them to San Francisco; then they would swing westward out to sea well beyond sight of land. From there, Manning was to navigate back to Burbank using only celestial observations for guidance. As they flew northward, Gurr checked all of the radios and was able to maintain constant radio contact. Gurr used the nighttime frequency of 3105 kilocycles for his transmissions. Even though it was not yet daylight, the signals became so poor by the time they were 400 miles out that he had to switch to transmitting on 6210 kilocycles.

About 5:50 A.M., Manning indicated they were at San Francisco and had them turn to the west. A solid bank of low clouds stretched from the coast out over the Pacific Ocean. Behind them to the left, a faint glow was visible from the approaching morning sun. About twenty minutes later, Manning turned them southeast, back toward Burbank.

In a few minutes the sun would appear above the horizon. The sky had become so light the stars were no longer visible. Manning looked from horizon to horizon. He could see nothing but the tops of stratocumulus clouds completely covering the ocean below. He could not take a drift sight without seeing the water, and a smoke bomb would just disappear in the clouds.

The sun would soon be high enough in the sky for him to take an accurate observation. A 26-day-old moon was visible as a white crescent in the southern sky, about 45 degrees to the west of the sun. By shooting both the sun and the moon he could get a celestial fix that would be accurate to within about 15 miles. Manning took the sun and moon shots when they were about an hour out and about 150 miles from Burbank. While they were traveling the remaining 150 miles, a possible 10 percent dead-reckoning error of 15 additional miles could put Manning's position off by as much as 30 miles. Under the unwitting conditions of their test, Manning could miss the airport at Burbank by as much as 30 miles without having made any unreasonable error. That was the reality of aerial celestial navigation, and one reason why direction-finders and radio beacons were being installed at over-water destinations throughout the world.

Mantz and G.P. were both unhappy because Manning's position was off by more than 20 miles as they approached Burbank on their return. If Burbank had been a small island in the middle of an ocean they could have missed it. Manning knew he had done as well as could be expected with the navigational situation he had confronted. After nearly twenty years of experience as a navigator and seven years of flying as a pilot, Manning was confident he had performed competently under the circumstances. There was no reason for him to offer any argument or explanation; the experience simply confirmed the decision to get a radio direction-finder.

They arrived back at Union Air Terminal at 8:25 A.M. and turned the Electra over to Bo for servicing.

There was a message for G.P. to telephone Bill Miller at the Oakland office. Miller asked how the flight had gone and learned of their concern about the navigation. Miller informed G.P. that Fred Noonan, the chief navigator on the Clippers for Pan American Airways, had recently resigned and was living in Oakland. The forty-three-year-old Noonan had been with Pan Am for seven years and was considered one of the best and most experienced aerial navigators in the world. Miller said he could set up an appointment with Noonan, and G.P. told him to go ahead. They would be flying up to Oakland sometime that afternoon.

Miller also reported that the Coast Guard cutter *Shoshone* had already departed Honolulu for Howland Island with thirty-one drums of aviation gasoline and two barrels of lubricating oil for Earhart. The Navy tug *Ontario* would be leaving American Samoa as soon as it took on needed supplies and was refueled. The guard ships were on schedule.

After lunch Amelia and G.P. went to the airport to finish loading the equipment and prepare to fly the Electra north for the second time that day. Bo and Remmlein met them at the hangar. After storing all of the spare parts, supplies, and luggage, they took off for Oakland. With room for only four people in the plane, Manning, along with Mantz and Mantz's fiancée, Terry Minor, would follow by car.

As the plane made its way northward, in spite of the engine noise a very tired G.P. dozed fitfully. He would have to interview the experienced aerial navigator Fred Noonan and have Amelia make a quick decision if she wanted to hire him.

At the Oakland airport a long blast of a siren warned all planes waiting at the field that a plane was landing. The Electra appeared out of a leaden sky to the east of the airport and made one circle of the field before landing. Amelia made a sharp turn to exit the landing area and taxied to the concrete apron by the Navy hangar. The commanding officer of the U.S. Naval Reserve aviation base at Oakland airport and Bill Miller were there to meet them.

The Electra was secured in the Navy hangar. They loaded their luggage into Miller's car and drove to the hotel. As he drove along, Miller pointed as they passed a street sign that read "Amelia Earhart Road." The road had been named for Amelia after her flight from Hawaii to Oakland in 1935. Miller continued to the front entrance of the Oakland Airport Inn, where they were staying. He told them he had set up a temporary office in the airport administration building where the weather bureau, telegraph companies, and Department of Commerce offices were located.

After a night's sleep, Earhart arranged the next morning to have the plane serviced and rolled out onto the ramp for an instrument flight check. A new Department of Commerce regulation required that pilots pass a flight test for blind flying before they could fly on instruments. Earhart had never taken the test. R. D. Bedinger, Bureau of Air Commerce inspector, gave her a flight check that required her to demonstrate her ability to fly solely by instruments. For an hour she flew the Electra blind, with the cockpit windshield covered, executing various maneuvers. At the end, Bedinger had her make a complete instrument approach using the beams of the Oakland radio range for guidance to the airport.

G.P. had arranged a meeting with reporters at the Navy hangar on their return. When Bedinger alighted from the plane and the reporters asked him how Earhart did on her blind-flying check, he answered, "She can do it."

The reporters turned with their questions to Amelia, who told them everything was all set and except, perhaps, for a few minor adjustments, the plane was in perfect condition. She didn't want to put any more time than necessary on the motors before she set out. "We will just study the weather and wait to see if conditions are favorable on Monday. Then if they are, away we'll go." Asked if she was scared, she told them, "No, not scared, just thrilled."

The reporters asked G.P. if he worried about the dangerous flight facing his wife. "He told them that he wasn't worried, he would like to go along, but on a flight like this, when it comes to a question of 185 pounds of husband and 185 pounds of gasoline, the gasoline wins."

Manning and Mantz had arrived from Burbank and met with Amelia, G.P., and Bill Miller for a final review of all flight preparations. G.P. was worried over the workload Amelia was carrying. She was not sleeping well and was stressed by the multitude of tasks that she had to perform. He wanted to discuss how they might help reduce that load.

G.P. suggested that Paul Mantz might fly with Amelia on the first leg from Oakland to Honolulu, to relieve her of some of the duties. In Honolulu Paul could oversee servicing the plane for the flight to Howland Island while she rested. If any problems showed up during the first leg he would be right there to take care of them. Amelia would be busy with press conferences and writing daily articles for a syndicate formed by the *New York Herald-Tribune*. She could use more help, especially at the start. The plan was to complete the Pacific crossing in three segments in rapid succession. It was going to be too much for just Amelia and Harry Manning alone.

Mantz agreed to go as far as Honolulu if they would send Terry Minor ahead by ship to meet him there. They agreed to pay Terry's fare, and Mantz arranged to get her on a ship. They would meet with the former Pan American navigator, Fred Noonan, to see if he would agree to aid Captain Manning with the navigation as far as Howland Island. Amelia didn't want any announcements made to the press before everything was definitely arranged and agreed to.

It was after 4:00 P.M. when a postal telegraph message arrived from Lockheed confirming Kelly Johnson's optimum power and flight procedures. He had calculated that they should take off for Honolulu with a fuel load of 900 gallons. He also reminded them to check the spark plugs before departure, and to stay within 2,000 feet of the recommended altitudes if winds under 10 mph were encountered.

• •

O N a rainy Friday morning, G.P. and Manning met with Noonan. He agreed to assist in navigating as far as Howland Island. Earhart joined the group and they drove to Alameda for a final meeting with Pan American Airways and Coast Guard officials. Pan American was making a survey flight to New Zealand, with Captain Musick departing for Honolulu a little before Earhart. The Electra was faster than the Sikorsky Clipper and would overtake the "flying boat" somewhere en route. They would have to be separated by altitude to avoid colliding. If the Sikorsky flew no higher than 6,000 feet, and Amelia flew no lower than 8,000 feet, they would be safe.

Lieutenant Frank K. Johnson, communications officer for the U.S. Coast Guard's San Francisco division, met with Manning to work out the details of how to handle communications with the plane. The Coast Guard's radio station NMC, located on the coast south of San Francisco, would monitor all frequencies for the Electra's radio transmissions. It was agreed that the plane would send all of its messages and receive all radio bearings directly from the Pan American Airways stations in Alameda and Hawaii. The plane would transmit on a frequency of 3105 or 6210 kilocycles, and use either voice or Morse code. The plane would listen for Pan American to reply with Morse code telegraphy on a frequency of 2986 kilocycles. Since Pan American had no voice transmitting capability, Manning would have to turn on a switch on the Bendix receiver known as a CW or BFO switch to receive their signals. (A CW—continuous wave—or BFO—beat frequency oscillator—switch made it possible for a radio receiver to pick up Morse code signals. These abbreviations and the term "code" were used interchangeably.) If communications were normal, the plane would not make direct contact with the Coast Guard station. If it became necessary, Manning would call NMC between 31 and 36 minutes past the hour. The plane would send for the first two minutes on 3105 kilocycles, the second two minutes on 6210 kilocycles, and the third on 500 kilocycles. (Note the priority sequence of the frequencies Manning listed: first 3105, then 6210, and last 500 kilocycles.)

Manning informed Lieutenant Johnson that the plane had a direction-finder that covered 200 to 1430 kilocycles, and an all-wave receiver for receiving telegraphy. The plane could take radio bearings on the ship at Howland Island when the ship made MO's (a standard telegraphy signal used for taking bearings) on 500 or 375 kilocycles. No amateur contacts would be made, and all transmissions would be on frequencies listed. Manning requested that they send Morse code at speeds no faster than fifteen words per minute when transmitting to the plane. The arrangements for radio communications at New Guinea would be made when they were in Honolulu.

The *Shoshone* was now at sea en route from Honolulu to Howland Island. Lieutenant Johnson wanted a detailed communication plan that he could forward to the captain of the *Shoshone*. Manning would need some time to work out the details, but he agreed to prepare a plan and send it as soon as he could. With the conferences concluded, they returned to the Oakland airport.

From Miller's office at the airport they sent a message informing Kelly Johnson that they needed to climb immediately to fly 4,000 feet higher than the altitude he had recommended. They requested new power and fuel burn charts for starting their cruise at 8,000 feet.

Meteorologist E. H. Bowie in San Francisco said he expected there would be a short break in the local weather tomorrow morning. They decided to fly out over the ocean to test the compasses and radios, and this would give Fred Noonan a chance to check out the aircraft's navigation equipment. They were to meet at the Navy hangar at 10:00 A.M. Noonan didn't have his own octant and asked that Manning bring his for the flight.

Before Amelia and G.P. went back to the hotel, G.P. asked Manning to meet with the press. Earhart wanted Manning to announce that Noonan would be going with them as far as Howland Island, and to answer reporters' questions about the flight. Manning asked her if she had any special messages or radio requests she wanted included in his message to the *Shoshone*. She advised him to use his own judgment.

Manning gathered the reporters in the lobby and announced that Frederick J. Noonan, formerly of Pan American Airways, would be going along with them as far as Howland Island to assist with the navigation. Asked if he was nervous about the flight, Manning told them that he had been waiting impatiently for the flight and was eager to get started.

When asked about the radios, he summarized the situation thus: They had met with Pan American and the Coast Guard and they would send all traffic and get radio bearings from the Pan American stations. The Electra's radio call sign was KHAQQ. They would transmit on either 500, 3105, or 6210 kilocycles using both telegraphy and voice. A Pan American survey flight to New Zealand would be departing for

Honolulu within a few hours of their departure, but in no way was it a race between the two planes; their routing would diverge at Honolulu. The Clipper was going via Kingman Reef and Samoa to Auckland, New Zealand. Earhart would fly via Howland Island and Lae, New Guinea, to Darwin, Australia. Manning closed by telling the reporters about the planned flight out over the ocean in the morning for a final check of the radios and compasses.

Manning left the reporters and went back to Miller's office to prepare the communications plan for the *Shoshone* at Howland Island. It took him the better part of an hour to write the message; then he sent it to Lieutenant Johnson in San Francisco. It read as follows:

QUOTE FOR CUTTER AT HOWLAND ISLAND SIX HOURS AFTER DEPARTURE OF PLANE FROM HONOLULU CUTTER PLEASE CALL THE PLANE FROM 1 TO 6 MINUTES PAST THE HOUR AND THE FIRST 2 MINUTES ON 3105 KCS THE 2ND 2 MINUTES ON 6210 AND THE 3RD 2 MINUTES ON 500 KCS UNTIL CONTACT IS ESTABLISHED PERIOD IF NO CONTACT MADE AFTER 3 HOURS CUTTER SHOULD TRANSMIT MO LONG DASHES ON 375 KCS FOLLOWED BY CALL LETTERS FOR PLANE TO TAKE BEARINGS PERIOD THIS TRANSMISSION SHOULD BE SENT EVERY TEN MINUTES COMMENCING ON THE EVEN HOUR LASTING 4 MINUTES ATTEMPTS WILL BE MADE BY THE PLANE TO CONTACT THE NEAR SHIP AFTER THE MO TRANSMISSION IS FINISHED IN THE MANNER DESCRIBED ABOVE SHIP SHOW SEARCHLIGHT AS PLANE APPROACHES ISLAND DURING DARKNESS AND MAKE SMOKE DURING DAYLIGHT UNQUOTE

The message was relayed to the *Shoshone* at 9:05 the following morning, with a copy to the Coast Guard in Honolulu for their information. It was permanently logged into the communications files of the Coast Guard in San Francisco and Honolulu. The commander of the San Francisco division detailed in this message the procedures to be used by the Coast Guard cutter at Howland Island when it communicated with Earhart.

Meteorologist Bowie's local forecast was correct. Saturday morning, March 13, had indeed broken bright and clear at the Oakland airport. Amelia and G.P. went by Miller's office to settle on the arrangements to be made in Honolulu and at Howland Island for her flight forecasts.

At 9:35 Miller sent the following message to Richard B. Black, Earhart's representative aboard the *Shoshone:*

. . . CONTACT SAMOA NAVAL RADIO AND REQUEST WEATHER INFORMATION FROM AUSTRALIA AND NEW GUINEA STOP IF THERE IS A FINANCIAL CHARGE

FOR OBTAINING WEATHER INFORMATION THE COST WILL BE PAID BY MR PUT-
NAM STOP NO ARRANGEMENTS HAVE BEEN MADE OTHER THAN REQUESTING
GOVERNOR AMERICAN SAMOA TO OBTAIN ALL POSSIBLE WEATHER INFORMA-
TION IN THE ANTIPODES STOP ANSWERS TO INQUIRIES IN YOUR RADIO
MARCH ELEVENTH AND FINAL DATA PERTAINING TO MISS EARHARTS FLIGHT
BEING TRANSMITTED THIS DATE STOP FOLLOWING FOR CAMPBELL HOWLAND
ISLAND REQUEST HAZARDOUS AREA ON RUNWAYS BE FLAGGED OFF STOP NO
CHANGE IN FLIGHT SCHEDULE TO DATE STOP WILL ADVISE ANY CHANGE ALSO
TIME MISS EARHARTS DEPARTURE FROM OAKLAND————W T MILLER

Earhart left the office just before ten o'clock to meet as planned at
the Navy hangar with Mantz, Manning, and Noonan. They took off at
10:30 and headed out over the Golden Gate to give all of the equipment a final check, a dress rehearsal for the flight to Honolulu. Manning called the Pan American Airways station at Alameda on the radio.
They reported his signal coming in clear as a bell. The answering signal
from Pan American was so loud Manning had to lift the earphones off
his ears. Fred Noonan shot the sun with Manning's octant and found it
awkward, as he wasn't used to that particular type of instrument. When
they got back on the ground he would see if he could borrow the kind
he had used at Pan American. After landing at Oakland they put the
plane into the Navy hangar, where it would stay until they were ready
for the flight to Honolulu.

Amelia met with reporters and announced that Paul Mantz would be
coming on the flight as far as Honolulu. According to the newspaper
report,

She told them she was able to enlarge the crew because the final fuel
consumption tests had proven far more satisfactory than they dared
hope. Instead of filling the tanks with the full 1,151 gallons they
would start with only 900 gallons, a weight saving of about 1,500
pounds.

Weather permitting, she said, they would be leaving the next afternoon sometime between 2:00 and 4:30 P.M. Asked why she was making the flight, she told them it was because she "wanted to"; then,
more seriously, she added that she wanted to arouse the interest of
women in aviation, in addition to testing some of the latest scientific
aids to aerial navigation.

When she checked with Miller's office she found that Kelly Johnson
had answered their request for his recommended power settings and

fuel consumption at 8,000 feet. After comparing the hourly fuel consumption rates on the 4,000-foot and 8,000-foot recommended power charts, she could see they were going to burn an extra two gallons per hour for each of the first six hours of the flight. No wonder Kelly had advised that they stay within 2,000 feet of the recommended altitude. Going to the higher altitude would cost them extra fuel.

They left for the hotel and remained there until Sunday morning, when a quick check with the weather bureau was not encouraging. There were brisk headwinds for 1,500 miles on the route to Honolulu and crosswinds from the north the rest of the way. Amelia announced to the press that the flight would be delayed until Monday afternoon. She was anxious to be on her way, but Amelia told them, "I am too old a hand at this game to be impatient over necessary delays."

Amelia and G.P. returned to the hotel and stayed secluded for the rest of the day. She rested until the next morning, Monday, March 15.

Leaving the hotel to go to Bill Miller's office, G.P. ran into reporters and told them that all was in readiness for the 27,000-mile flight around the world. The plane was packed and ready to go, he said, adding, "All that remains to be done is to arrange some lunch and fill the thermos bottles."

Mantz and Manning were already with Miller in his office when Earhart arrived. Miller had received a message from the Coast Guard in Honolulu informing them that all three runways on Howland Island were completed. By cable, Amelia thanked Mr. Black and all the crew of the Interior Department and Coast Guard personnel who had cooperated so generously.

They conferred with Pan American Airways by telephone. The weather had not changed enough from yesterday. The regular Hawaii Clipper flight had returned to Alameda because of strong headwinds, and now two Clippers would be leaving before the Electra. Neither the Hawaii Clipper nor the Sikorsky Clipper would leave that afternoon. Amelia decided that she would wait also.

Fred Noonan called to ask if they would be leaving today and was told that Amelia had decided to wait until tomorrow. Noonan had been unable to borrow an octant. If they had time to get one from the Navy he would appreciate it. Commander Ragsdale at the Navy hangar said he would contact the North Island Naval Air Station in San Diego, California, to see if they had an octant. Miller informed Ragsdale that if the Navy had one, Manning would sign for custody of it, as he was a lieutenant commander in the Naval Reserve.

Rain showers persisted Tuesday morning the sixteenth, when Amelia and G.P. left the hotel to meet with Mantz and Manning at Miller's office.

Meteorologist Bowie and Pan American predicted that the rain showers would slacken and the weather en route to Honolulu would steadily become more favorable over the next 24 hours. Pan American was delaying the two Clippers for 24 more hours, rescheduling them to leave for Honolulu Wednesday afternoon.

Mantz inspected the runway and reported that with another day to dry out it would be okay for them to take off. They wanted to arrive in Honolulu just after dawn. The no-wind flight time at 150 mph would be about 16 hours. With the time zone difference of two and a half hours, the dawn would be that much later in Honolulu than in Oakland. If they took off at 5:00 P.M. and flew for 16 hours, it would be 9:00 A.M. in Oakland but 6:30 A.M. in Honolulu, just after sunrise, when they arrived.

Earhart held a press conference and told the reporters that she was delaying the flight for 24 hours and planned to take off for Honolulu at 5:00 P.M. the next day. The weather bureau predicted steadily improving conditions along her route to Honolulu. With another day to dry out, the runway at Oakland would, they believed, be suitable for their plane's heavy takeoff.

Bill Miller sent a message to the commander, San Francisco Division, USCG, and asked him to notify all interested parties of the delayed departure of Earhart's around-the-world flight: "Weather conditions improving and departure from Oakland March 17 looks definite." He would advise them again March 17 with further information relative to her flight from Oakland.

The Naval Reserve Aviation Base notified them that the secretary of the Navy had approved the loan of the Navy octant without any required deposit. The North Island Naval Air Station in San Diego was shipping the octant air express on United Airlines; it was due to arrive in Oakland at 2:50 P.M. The shipment was being sent collect, with charges to be paid by Miss Earhart or her representative. The instrument was to be turned over immediately on arrival and custody receipt of Lieutenant Commander Harry Manning, USNR, who was to return it to North Island Naval Air Station.

After dinner, Amelia and G.P. looked at the afternoon *Oakland Tribune* and saw a notice that Mr. Frederick Noonan was filing for divorce from his wife. G.P. remarked that it would have been better if they hadn't headlined it "Amelia's navigator seeks Mexico divorce from wife."

The following morning, one look out the hotel window was enough to make them wonder if they would get away after all. A steady light rain was falling, and there were no breaks in the heavy clouds overhead. It was Saint Patrick's Day, and Amelia was already two days behind schedule. Amelia and G.P. went to Bill Miller's office to get the latest weather reports.

The weather bureau assured them that the last part of the weather system was already moving through the San Francisco Bay Area. By late afternoon it would be clearing. Pan American Airways had scheduled the regular Hawaii Clipper to depart Alameda at 3:00 P.M. and the pioneering Sikorsky Clipper to leave before 4:00 P.M. Amelia planned her takeoff from Oakland for around 4:30 P.M.

She and Mantz went out to check on the runway they had laid out. They had just put out white paper flags to mark the special runway as it ran from the northeast to the southwest diagonally across the airport. The wind was predicted to be out of the southwest, and the Electra would start on a concrete apron, run southwesterly across the regular runways marked on the paved field, and then, if not airborne, cross onto the graveled runway that had been prepared ten years before for the 1927 Dole flights to Hawaii. Altogether the takeoff path was 4,300 feet long. Mantz thought they could be off in 3,500 feet.

The noon positions and weather reports from the ships to the U.S. Weather Bureau showed that the flight would encounter crosswinds on the first 300 miles, with a tailwind on the remainder of the route. The tailwind, expected to average about 15 miles per hour, would boost their ground speed.

Already hundreds of spectators were streaming to the airport to watch Earhart take off. A detail of seventy-five Oakland police officers directed traffic and kept the crowds away from the runway.

Amelia announced to the reporters that this time the start was definite. The weather looked fine over the Pacific and she was going to try it. She grinned happily as she made the announcement she had been waiting four days to make. She told the reporters she did not intend to use up her engines in an attempt at speed for the Hawaii crossing. With the heavy overload she would be well satisfied to make 150 miles per hour. She wanted the motors in good shape over India and would not misuse them to gain speed during the first leg of the long flight.

Back in Miller's office, Earhart and Mantz decided to take 47 gallons more fuel than Kelly Johnson had recommended, making a total of 947 gallons onboard. Mantz was to put 753 gallons of 87-octane gas in the extra tanks. He would fill the left and right 97-gallon main wing tanks with the special 100-octane gas that would allow them to use full throttle for takeoff. (Like a high-performance, high-compression engine in a car, an aircraft engine running on high-octane gas won't *ping*. *Ping*ing is the sound a car's engine makes when the engine detonates. Aircraft engines are not built as ruggedly as car engines, and when they detonate worse things than *ping*ing can happen.) The 100-octane gas would keep the Electra engines from detonating at higher than normal cylinder pressures so they could use full throttle for takeoff. Pratt & Whitney, which manufactured the Wasp S3H1 engines, approved this procedure only with 100-octane fuel.

Just after three o'clock the navy men helped Bo McKneely push the airplane out of the hanger onto the apron. Everything was loaded, and only fuel needed to be added before they were ready to go. Navy men helped with the fueling, and Mantz supervised from the cockpit.

The Hawaii Clipper took off from Alameda at 3:13 P.M., and the Sikorsky, under the command of Captain Musick, lifted off the water at 4:21 P.M.

Manning and Noonan were in the rear cabin compartment when Earhart came in the rear cabin door. She made her way over the top of the fuselage tanks to the cockpit. Mantz was already in the right-hand seat as she gingerly came off the top of the tanks into the left pilot's seat. The 4:00 P.M. weather report showed the wind out of the southwest at 14 mph, with a temperature of 48 degrees Fahrenheit. The wind was blowing directly down the makeshift runway, and the headwind would shorten their takeoff run considerably.

The fueling was complete and they were ready to start the world flight. Mantz yelled out the right-hand cockpit window that everything was set, and they started the engines. Earhart received the all-clear signal and advanced the throttles just enough to start the Electra rolling. She taxied on the concrete apron to the northeast corner of the field. Coming to the end of the marked runway, she kept the line of flags to the left as she lined up facing southwest. They checked the engines, props, controls, trim tabs, gas selector, and flaps, and set the directional gyro compasses to match the wet compass. They were ready to go.

The rain had stopped. For the first time all day the sun broke through the clouds to the west. A quick glance at the wind sock showed it blowing right down the runway. Mantz advanced the throttles evenly and Earhart released the brakes. The plane slowly began rolling across the apron, gaining speed. The roar of the motors, beating in perfect unison, reverberated for the crowd of over three thousand who had come to witness Amelia's departure.

The wheels went through a puddle on the runway. A spray of water splashed high on either side. The spray subsided as the plane, moving rapidly, crossed the main runway and headed for the old Dole runway. Another big spray of water surrounded the main wheels just as they lifted from the ground. The plane inched its way upward, slowly gathering speed, and then momentarily settled back toward the runway. Amelia caught the sink with back pressure on the elevator control and resumed a positive rate of climb.

G.P. was jubilant with the fine way Amelia had taken the plane off from a wet and muddy runway. The stopwatch registered that it had taken exactly 25 seconds from the time the wheels began to turn to when the plane left the ground. In the process it had used only 1,897 feet of the runway.

Bill Miller sent a message to the Coast Guard in San Francisco. It began:

MISS EARHART OFFICIAL TAKEOFF FROM OAKLAND AIRPORT FOR HONOLULU IS FOUR THIRTY SEVEN AND A HALF PM PACIFIC TIME————

5: THE FLIGHT TO HONOLULU

THEY had used less runway than expected for the Oakland takeoff. Mantz reduced the power for climb, while Earhart continued a shallow right turn over the bay toward San Francisco. She leveled the wings and kept the tower of the Ferry Building, at the foot of Market Street, ahead to her left. She looked down into the cockpit to check the engine instruments and make sure Mantz had set the power correctly. The plane was climbing sluggishly, but they easily cleared the towers of the west span of the San Francisco Bay Bridge. Opposite the Ferry Building, Earhart banked gently to the left to turn slowly toward the Golden Gate Bridge and the broad Pacific Ocean beyond.

This was by far the most ambitious and costly flight she had ever attempted. It had taken more than a year of work and planning, and she was finally on her way. There would be challenges in the hours, days, and weeks ahead, but the prospect of meeting and conquering them one by one was exhilarating. The flight was of truly worldwide proportions and presented the opportunity of a lifetime for high adventure.

The sun was shining and the few scattered cumulus clouds were easy to avoid. As long as they remained visually in the clear there was no danger of running into either of the Pan American Clippers. Rather than climb immediately to 8,000 feet, Earhart decided to save fuel by leveling the plane off at 3,500 feet. She would fly closer to the recommended 4,000-foot optimum altitude for the first three hours.

Mantz set the power as recommended by Kelly Johnson's telegram for the first three hours of cruise. He allowed the engines to stabilize for two or three minutes before slowly adjusting the carburetor mixture controls. Soon Mantz had to increase the engine rpm and manifold pressure slightly to hold the indicated airspeed above 140 mph. The fuel burn was now over 60 gph on the Eclipse fuel flow meters, which was to be expected as they had taken on extra gas and were heavier than Johnson had planned.

Before they were an hour out, they spotted a small speck in the sky ahead of them. As they watched, the speck grew larger until they could make out the shape of the Sikorsky Clipper, with Captain Musick, above them. Earhart kept the four-engine flying boat to her right as they passed at 5:40 P.M. PST. The faster Electra soon left the Clipper far behind.

At 6:04 P.M. PST Manning reported to Pan American in Alameda, "All's well," and received back by Morse code a weather report. Approximately 250 miles from San Francisco the winds were reported out of the northwest at 35 mph. There were squalls in the area, and the visibility was 10 miles.

The moisture in the air became evident when the right engine began coughing and running rough as ice formed in its carburetor. Mantz put both mixture controls in rich, and opened the carburetor heat valves to direct heated air into the carburetors to melt the ice and keep it from forming again. In a few minutes, after the engines had stabilized, they repeated the mixture leaning procedure. Again, the airspeed fell below 140 mph and he had to add additional engine manifold pressure.

It started to get dark, and Earhart was glad they had departed with still a couple of hours of daylight remaining. A sharp horizon line helps a pilot to keep an overloaded plane on an even keel. Some of the squalls they had flown through would have been tough to penetrate in darkness with a heavily loaded plane.

She decided to climb above the cloud layer. Mantz adjusted the mixture controls and set the engines to climb power. At 8,000 feet they were on top of the clouds. Earhart held the plane level while the indicated airspeed slowly built up to just over 130 mph. The indicators were showing only 130 mph in the less dense air at 8,000 feet, but the true airspeed (the indicated airspeed corrected for temperature and altitude) was still approximately 150 mph. The fuel flow meters showed they were burning approximately 30 gph per engine for a total fuel burn of about 60 gph. After they burned off the weight of the extra fuel, Johnson's power and fuel burn recommendations were working well.

The Sperry autopilot was doing most of the work of flying the plane, but the rudder control required frequent adjustments to keep the plane on the desired heading. The rudder gyro seemed to drift off the heading faster than it should.

When they had burned well over 1,400 pounds of their fuel, it was time to reduce the engine power as Johnson recommended for the second three hours of cruise. After they finished resetting the engines, the Eclipse fuel flow meters read a little over 25 gph each. The total was very close to the 51 gph that Johnson had predicted.

Manning had climbed up on the tanks and crawled forward to work the controls of the Bendix receiver over Earhart's head. When he returned to the rear cabin, she could hear him transmitting to Pan American in Alameda for a radio bearing on the plane. At the same time, Noonan used the octant to get a celestial fix at 7:17 P.M. PST. He shot the star Sirius out the left cabin window and the planet Venus out of the right.

At 8:35 P.M. PST they reported to Pan American that they were approximately 600 miles out of San Francisco and making about 170 mph.

All through the night, Noonan took star sights every couple of hours to fix their position. Earhart was constantly busy monitoring the flight and engine instruments, adjusting the autopilot, switching the complicated fuel tank system, keeping the plane in trim, and logging events in her notepad. This was all accomplished in a cockpit where the roar of the engines was so loud that conversation was all but impossible.

After three hours the indicated airspeed was above 130 mph again, and they had burned over 2,300 pounds of the fuel. The Electra was starting to fly like a good, stable airplane. They had finally caught up with the recommended altitude where they were supposed to be flying, and it was time to reduce the power to Johnson's charted value for the third three hours of cruise at 8,000 feet.

At 12:00 midnight PST Manning sent their position, by voice on 3105, as latitude 31 degrees north, and longitude 139 degrees 49 minutes west. Manning got no answer from Pan American in Alameda, but for the first time Pan American on Oahu heard the plane, though the message was garbled by static. NMC, the Coast Guard radio station in San

Francisco, copied the message and forwarded it to Pan American Airways in Alameda.

Manning told Earhart they were ahead of their dead reckoned time and were now making 180 mph. She wrote in her notes that she hoped he knew what he was talking about.

At a quarter after the hour, Manning switched the Bendix receiver to band 2 and tuned to 640 kilocycles for radio station KFI in Los Angeles. He turned off the CW (BFO) switch used to receive Morse code so there would not be a carrier squeal and he could receive voice signals from the radio broadcast station. KFI came in clearly. The announcer gave the weather from the SS *Monterey* and a message from Bill Miller requesting their average true airspeed and last star fix.

At 12:53 PST Manning reported on 3105 kilocycles, "All is well." He had switched the Bendix receiver back to band 4 and tuned to receive Pan American on 2986 kilocycles. The CW switch was also turned back on so he could receive their Morse code signals. However, he didn't hear them and decided to try sending on 6210 kilocycles. Manning transmitted on 3105, telling Pan American that he was going to repeat the transmission on 6210 kilocycles. He had Mantz crank the transmitter to 6210. When Mantz was finished cranking, Manning transmitted the report again. There was still no answer. Manning didn't hear them reply, but Pan American had received his signals.

Johnson's telegram had recommended they climb to 10,000 feet after having cruised for nine hours. So far, when adjusted for their extra weight at takeoff, his power and fuel consumption predictions had worked very well. The true airspeed in cruise had averaged pretty close to the targeted 150 mph, and the total fuel burn of about 530 gallons was reasonably close. Applying climb power sometime after 2:00 A.M., they took only a few minutes to rise and level off at their final altitude of 10,000 feet.

Shortly thereafter the engines began to cough and run rough from carburetor icing. They immediately enriched the mixture and turned the carburetor heat on. After a few moments the engines smoothed out again.

When they finished re-leaning the mixtures, an audible beat could be heard in the cockpit from the sound of the propellers turning out of unison. (If two propellers turn at exactly the same speed their sound is a steady drone with no vibration. If one propeller is turning faster than the other, a rhythmic sound accompanied by a rhythmic vibration can be detected by the pilots. The farther the propellers are out of synchronization, the faster the rhythmic beat.) Earhart reached to adjust the propeller controls to bring the beat to a stop. The right propeller would not react to movement of the right propeller control. She could only adjust the left propeller to bring it into synchronization with the right propeller, which was stuck at 1,600 rpm.

This was the same situation as when she was flying over Oklahoma. The right propeller was stuck, so to speak, like an automobile stuck in high gear. The advantage in having a twin-engine plane over the oceans was to be able, if one engine failed, to get enough power out of the other to continue flying. If the left engine should fail, with the right propeller stuck they might not be able to get enough power out of the right engine to make it to Honolulu. Their bird was wounded.

Manning had come up forward on the tanks again. He told them Noonan was going to take some sights and asked them to hold the plane steady. He then switched the Bendix receiver to receive radio broadcast station KGU in Honolulu. KGU had agreed to stay on the air all night for the flight, and Manning could hear them broadcasting music. At 2:05 A.M. PST Pan American heard the plane report direct communication with KGU.

At 2:07 A.M. PST Noonan had finished shooting Polaris and Capella. He plotted the celestial fix on his chart. After making some measurements and calculations he consulted with Manning, who came forward over the tanks to tell Earhart they were way ahead of their dead reckoned flight time. They would have to slow the plane as much as they could. At their present speed they were going to get to Honolulu before daylight. They reduced the manifold pressure and let the indicated airspeed decline until it was steady at 120 mph. Earhart wrote on her pad that they were burning less than 20 gph per engine at 10,000 feet.

Mantz climbed out of his seat up onto the plywood on top of the tanks. He crawled aft into the cabin to stretch. This gave Earhart a chance to be alone in the cockpit for a while. To change her position she moved over into the right seat. Later, when Mantz returned from the cabin, he found it even more difficult to get down off the tanks than it was to get up on them. He finally worked himself into the empty left seat, and everyone was relieved by the break.

At 1:30 A.M. Hawaiian Standard Time, Manning sent their position as latitude 27 degrees 42 minutes north, and longitude 149 degrees 40 minutes west. About 650 statute miles from Honolulu, they had reduced their speed to 137 mph. He got an acknowledgment from Pan American in Honolulu that they had received the message.

In between messages they occasionally tuned to KGU and listened for weather reports or other information from ships on their route. Doing this meant switching the receiver bands, tuning, and turning the CW switch on and off, but it was reassuring to know that the weather was good in Honolulu and was forecast to remain that way.

The temperature was slowly warming as they headed to Hawaii, and so the air was growing less dense. The true airspeed was approximately 140 mph, and the fuel burn for the two engines was about 38 gph. With a 15-knot (17.3 mph) tailwind, they were flying over four miles for every gallon of fuel burned. They couldn't have hoped for anything better.

Earhart had never run into the problem of flying her plane too fast before. (It is axiomatic that, everything else being equal, if you experience stronger-than-expected tailwinds, you will arrive early. Conversely, if the headwinds are stronger than expected, you will arrive late. To arrive at the desired time the pilot must adjust the airspeed.) Within the confines of her airplane and engine limits, Earhart could go only so slow without danger of stalling, and only so fast without running out of gas before she got there.

Noonan had calculated from the 1937 *American Nautical Almanac* the time of twilight and sunrise in Honolulu. He used an improvised bamboo fishing pole to pass the message forward to the cockpit. He had written down that the sun would rise at about 6:08 A.M. HST. His estimated time of arrival was 5:45 A.M. HST, about the same time as the beginning of civil twilight, when there would be enough light for them to land.

Manning called Pan American for another bearing, and at the same time Noonan took a final sight on the star Vega. Manning transmitted a little longer than usual for the bearing. Suddenly the generator ammeter went to a negative reading. Pan American answered with a true bearing of 39 degrees from Mokapu Point. Noonan crossed it with the line of position he had obtained from Vega for a final fix at 4:50 A.M. HST. The generator was out, but they still had the ship's battery and the backup battery to keep the electrical equipment operating for the remaining hour until landing.

Manning came forward on the tanks and reached over Mantz's head to tune the Bendix receiver to the Makapuu radio beacon. Makapuu was a low-frequency marine beacon they would pass a few miles before coming to Diamond Head. Noonan wanted them to use the Bendix radio direction-finder to keep the radio homing beacon 10 degrees off the starboard bow. After Manning had tuned the receiver and the loop coupler control, he switched to the "loop" position and had Earhart rotate the loop until the signal she heard from the beacon faded to its weakest level. Then she rotated the loop back and forth on each side of the point where the signal was weakest to narrow down the direction of the minimum signal. They looked at the index pointer on the loop azimuth ring to read the bearing relative to the nose of the plane. It read 005 degrees, which meant the radio beacon at Makapuu was 5 degrees to the right of the aircraft's nose.

Noonan wanted them to keep the beacon 10 degrees off the starboard bow, or in flying terms, 10 degrees to the right of the aircraft's nose. Mantz turned the plane 5 degrees to the left, and again Earhart rotated the loop handle back and forth to obtain the minimum signal strength from Makapuu. This time when she checked the index on the loop it read 010 degrees. Now the radio beacon was 10 degrees to the right of the nose, just as Noonan wanted. Manning had tuned the Bendix control box, because it was in front of the pilot on the left side and Earhart was in the copilot's seat. When she had turned the loop for the minimum signal, it was the first time she had actually used the Bendix radio direction-finder.

At about 5:10 A.M. HST Noonan told them they were approximately 80 miles out and could begin their descent. He reminded them to continue checking the Makapuu radio beacon and to keep it 10 degrees off the starboard bow. Mantz, flying in the left seat, lowered the nose to start down, while Earhart handled the mixtures and throttles to adjust the power in descent. She continued to move the loop back and forth, making sure that the signal was minimum when the pointer index was at 010 degrees.

The clouds were scattered, and Earhart could see the dark outline of the mountainous island off to the right. It was just starting to get light enough to make out the details of the terrain when at 5:40 A.M. HST they saw Diamond Head ahead and slightly to the right.

Mantz added power with the throttles to maintain 1,500 feet as they passed Diamond Head and turned toward Honolulu and Pearl Harbor. The beach at Waikiki was in plain view, and the outlines of buildings could easily be seen in the morning twilight. They passed Honolulu at about 5:47 A.M. and continued northwestward toward the Army base and Wheeler Field.

The route took them over the Navy installations near Ford Island and the East Loch of Pearl Harbor. Earhart knew that low flying was prohibited in these areas. She hadn't gotten in trouble in 1935 when she had violated these airspaces, but Mantz was flying directly through them again.

The switches for the landing lights were on the front panel; Mantz switched them on as they neared the field. With the generator inoperative the two landing lights put a heavy drain on the battery. The electric motors for the landing gear and flaps would increase that load tremendously. In case a go-around was required during the landing there might not be enough power remaining in the battery to retract them. At the very least, the retraction rate was going to be slower than normal.

The ground had risen rapidly and they were only about 500 feet high when Mantz dipped across Wheeler Field from the southeast. He wracked the plane up into a steep bank to make a tight circle of the field in view of the waiting people. Earhart yelled, "Don't! Don't!" Mantz must have forgotten that the right propeller was disabled. He should have been making a conservative approach to the airport. They had to avoid any situation that might create the need for full power from the right engine. It was foolhardy to be showing off with a partially disabled plane. Mantz reduced the bank angle and flew a normal flight pattern from there on.

Earhart checked that the gas selector was turned to the proper tank for landing and that the mixtures were rich. She put the landing gear down while they were flying on the downwind leg. Normally they would have wanted the propellers set to low pitch for landing, but she had to leave them where they were. If Mantz added power with the throttles, and the propellers were at different pitch angles, he would get unequal power from the engines. Asymmetric power could turn the plane from its desired path.

As they were about to turn onto the base leg, Earhart put the wing flaps partway down. After making the left-hand base leg, Mantz turned to the final approach path, and Earhart put the flaps all the way down for the landing. Mantz had a little too much airspeed as he crossed the edge of the field and put the plane down, main wheels first. The plane's extra speed and the washboard roughness of the field caused it to bounce heavily back into the air. With the power off, the drag slowed the plane to the proper three-point speed; they came down solidly without bouncing again.

The wheels of the Electra touched the soft, grassy runway at 5:55 A.M., just 15 hours, 47½ minutes after taking off from Oakland. Earhart deserved to feel the flush of achievement. She realized they had broken the old speed record to Honolulu by more than an hour.

Mantz turned around at the end of the field. He followed the Army crew's guidance to the apron of the 75th Service Squadron. He turned in line with the hangar's entrance but didn't stop in front, as was customary and expected. Instead, he startled the crew by continuing until the plane was completely inside the hangar before shutting down the engines.

Spectators, photographers, reporters, radio announcers, and Army personnel all crowded around Earhart and her three companions. Lt. Col. John C. McDonnell, commander of Wheeler Field, presented each of the four fliers with the traditional lei. Bill Cogswell of the Pan Pacific Press Bureau, Amelia and G.P.'s representative in Hawaii, presented second leis to Earhart and Mantz. Then Chris and Mona Holmes, their hosts in Honolulu, added a third and fourth lei over Amelia's head. Amelia wouldn't allow any pictures to be taken until Manning and Noonan lined up with them.

When the photo session was finished, Wilber Thomas, the Pratt & Whitney engine representative for Hawaii, approached Amelia, accompanied by First Lieutenant Kenneth A. Rogers, station engineering officer for Wheeler Field, and First Lieutenant Donald D. Arnold, engineering officer of the Hawaiian Air Depot at Luke Field. They wanted to know what maintenance and servicing the Electra required, and to offer their help to Earhart in any way possible. She thanked them for the offer and told them that, since Mantz was her technical representative, they should handle all the particulars of aircraft servicing directly with him.

Mantz briefly described the mechanical problems. He related that for the last six or seven hours coming into Honolulu they had not been able to change the pitch of the right propeller; it probably needed greasing. The generator had not shown a positive charge during the latter part of the flight, and he was sure they would find that the generator control box was the problem. They could replace it with a control box from the spare parts kit. He wanted all the spark plugs of both engines replaced with brand-new ones. The instrument light on the pilot's panel was too bright when flying at night and needed to be dimmed.

Mr. Thomas and Lieutenant Rogers assured him they would get started immediately and personally supervise all servicing. Lieutenant Arnold said he would stand by in case assistance was needed from the Hawaiian Air Depot. Master Sergeant Biando, Horace Waters, and the other specially selected men from the 75th Service Squadron rolled the work stands across the hangar floor to the Electra.

Amelia gave the reporters factual highlights of the flight from Oakland. The flight had taken 15 hours and 48 minutes. There was still over

4 hours' fuel remaining when they landed, enough for at least another 600 miles of flying. With the tailwind at the end of the flight, they had approximately 700 miles in reserve. The average true airspeed they had flown was just over 144 mph. The overall average tailwind had been just under 11 mph.

Colonel McDonnell whisked the fliers off to his quarters where they could rest, freshen up, and have something to eat before meeting with reporters. Earhart would be able to file her personal story with the *Tribune* syndicate before talking at length with the other reporters.

It wasn't very long before Amelia pushed open the front screen door of the McDonnell residence and faced the photographers, reporters, and radio announcers on the front porch. The interview was reported as follows:

> The flight, she told them, was very uneventful; the plane performed perfectly. Comparing it with the West–East flight from Wheeler Field she had made to Oakland in January 1935, she would say the night seemed to be longer. She told them she hoped to make a daylight landing on Howland Island. That meant they would have to take off again late today or early tomorrow.
>
> She told the press that Mr. Mantz would remain in Hawaii, Mr. Noonan would continue to Howland, and Captain Manning would go on as far as Darwin, Australia. From there she would continue the rest of the flight around the world alone. Obviously tired by the long flight, she edged continuously toward the door as the interviewers continued their barrage of questions.

When the interview ended, Amelia retreated back into the house and prepared to leave with Chris and Mona Holmes for their Waikiki Beach home. She looked forward to revisiting the estate where she and G.P. and Paul and his former wife, Myrtle, had previously enjoyed themselves in 1935. Mantz would enjoy this visit with his new fiancée, Terry Minor.

It took the better part of an hour for the cars to drive from Wheeler Field to the Holmeses' residence at Waikiki. The estate of Christian R. Holmes, heir to the Fleischmann Yeast fortune, and his wife, Mona, the daughter of a senator, was located on Kalakaua Avenue at Queen's Surf, a magnificent setting.

After reading the cablegrams waiting for her, Amelia offered her apologies and retired to her room. She had to get some sleep if they were to leave for Howland that evening.

She placed a telephone call to G.P. in Oakland to exchange the latest information. When the connection was made she told her husband how well the flight from Oakland had gone. She was impressed with Noonan's ability as a navigator and told G.P. they knew exactly how well they were progressing at every moment. Noonan had developed special procedures that allowed him to compute a celestial fix for an airplane in 6 minutes, when normally it would take Captain Manning or any ship navigator 30 minutes to do the same thing. It was completely different from the dead reckoning she had done across the oceans before. During the last few hours she had even reduced speed, because Noonan said they would arrive before daylight. She wished that Noonan were going with them all the way to Australia.

G.P. told her it was reported that Paul Mantz had landed the airplane in Honolulu. He reminded Amelia that even when she piloted with her mechanic, some people claimed he was the one really flying the plane. It would be better in the future if she was alone in the cockpit for take-offs and landings. Amelia said she understood and would be the only one in the cockpit when they left that night for Howland Island. She would talk to Noonan about continuing on the flight, at least as far as Australia.

Amelia awoke and went to the lanai, where she found Paul dancing with Terry Minor to Hawaiian music. Harry Manning and Fred Noonan had apparently just come down before her, and were talking to Mona and Chris Holmes. After greeting her hosts, Amelia filled a glass with fresh pineapple juice before preparing to relax in the sun on the lanai.

When there was a break in the music, Amelia asked Paul if the plane was serviced and if he had obtained the weather forecast. He said that no one had called yet, but he was going out to Wheeler Field to check on things right away. She asked him to let her know if they were going to be able to take off that night or not.

It was not yet three o'clock when a maid came to Amelia and said there was an officer from the Coast Guard asking to see her. He apologized for the intrusion and introduced himself as Warrant Officer Henry M. Anthony, communications officer for the Hawaiian section. Lieutenant Commander Frank T. Kenner, commander of the Hawaiian section, and Commander G. T. Finlay, commanding officer of the U.S. Coast Guard cutter *Shoshone* at Howland Island, requested information regarding the radio communications and services desired by Mrs. Putnam for her flight from Howland Island to Lae, New Guinea. Amelia told him that Captain Manning would supply all the necessary information.

As Manning entered the parlor Henry Anthony rose to attention and introduced himself. He repeated the cutter *Shoshone*'s request for communications information regarding the flight from Howland to Lae. Manning told Anthony that they could use Morse code or voice to transmit on 3105 and 6210, but for long range he said they could usually get through better with Morse code. On 500 kilocycles they used Morse code exclusively. He had sent a message from Oakland outlining the times and frequencies for their *Shoshone* contacts. Anthony acknowledged that they had received the information. Manning told Anthony they would contact the *Ontario* on 500 kilocycles and would use 3105 at night and 6210 during the day to contact Lae. It was sometimes difficult to key the Morse code properly in bumpy air, and he had found ten to fifteen words per minute to be a good average code speed for sending and receiving messages. Anthony, who was taking notes, acknowledged that he now had a good understanding of the plane's radio equipment and how they would operate it.

Anthony told Manning that the Coast Guard cutter *Shoshone*'s radio call sign was NRUV. The Navy had positioned the 174-foot minesweeper USS *Quail* halfway between Honolulu and Howland Island. The *Quail*'s call sign was NIKQ, and its radio could not operate above 3000 kilocycles. For their flight from Howland Island to Lae, the 175-foot oceangoing tug USS *Ontario* was now on station at the midpoint; its radio call sign was NIDX. The *Ontario*'s radio could not operate above 1000 kilocycles.

Manning answered that they would work with the *Quail* and the *Ontario* using Morse code on 500 kilocycles. Anthony assured him that all of the ships would be monitoring 500 kilocycles and, if requested, would send the distinctive MO Morse signal on 375 kilocycles for the plane's radio direction-finder to take bearings on. The *Taney* (another Coast Guard cutter), the *Shoshone*, Navy radio NPM in Honolulu, and the Coast Guard monitoring station NMO in Honolulu would also be continuously monitoring 3105 and 6210 kilocycles.

Manning informed Anthony that they would normally send a position report on the hour and make an operation normal contact on the half hour. If the ship would send the weather 5 minutes before those times, it would allow him to make sure his receiver was tuned properly. It would also give him nearly 25 minutes of uninterrupted time for other work in between the radio schedules.

If the plane is not heard by the *Shoshone* 6 hours after our departure from Honolulu, he said, have them call us from 1 to 6 minutes and 31 to 36 minutes after the hour until contact is made as described in our earlier message. Anthony replied that they had received that information earlier, and he would advise the *Shoshone* to send their weather synopsis at 25 and 55 after the hour. Manning's detailed information to the Coast Guard communications officer on how the Coast Guard ships were to make radio contact with the Earhart plane would be passed three months later to the Coast Guard cutter *Itasca* and would lead to utter confusion.

Manning reported to Earhart that all of the arrangements for the radio had been made and were in order. They called the Fleet Air Base to check on the Howland Island winds and weather. Using the information he had been given, Noonan calculated the flight time for the 1,900-mile trip to Howland Island would be about 11½ hours. Even if they flew as slowly as they could, it would still take only 12 hours to get there. This was a puzzle to Earhart, because she wanted to arrive at the island during daylight.

Howland Island was about 18 degrees west of Honolulu. They would lose a little more than an hour of apparent sun time en route. The time for sunrise at Howland Island would be over an hour after the time for sunrise in Honolulu. They would either have to take off in the dark to keep from arriving at Howland before daylight, or delay their departure until the next morning and make it an all-daylight flight. Earhart decided to wait until Mantz called before making a decision.

It was after two o'clock when Mantz arrived at the 75th Service Squadron hangar at Wheeler Field. He walked over to where Mr. Thomas of Pratt and Whitney and the Army officers were standing by the Electra on the hangar apron. He learned that Thomas and the Army officers had found the right propeller hub nearly dry and had had to pump in a lot of lubricant when servicing it. Apparently the propeller had left Oakland in that condition. When they inspected the propeller there were no telltale streaks of leaking lubricant anywhere on the propeller hub or blades.

The reason the generator became inoperative was a blown current limiter fuse. In the generator control box they had found the maximum current set at 60 to 70 amps. This was too much amperage for their generator, and the extra heavy load caused the fuse to blow. They had reset the control boxes to the correct maximum current of 45 amps and had put the spare control box back into the kit. It appeared they had been using too much current at times during the flight. Miss Earhart might consider ways to reduce the number of electric devices being used at the same time, they suggested. Mantz remarked that they had held the key down on the transmitter for a long time for Pan American to take radio bearings, which might have caused the problem. They would use caution and turn off all unnecessary electrical equipment when using the transmitter.

Thomas had cleaned and re-gapped the electrodes of the spark plugs and put them back in the engines. The instrument bulb in the cockpit had been painted white to reduce the glare.

Mantz decided to do a run-up of the engines to check everything out. He closed the aft cabin door from the outside and went up over the wing into the cockpit to start the engines. After priming the engine with fuel he yelled "Clear right" from the little cockpit window and engaged the starter on the right engine. Within seconds the whine of the electric starter was replaced with the roar of the right engine coming to life. He then repeated the procedure to start the left engine. He tested both engines and propellers, and a few moments later shut them down and emerged from the cockpit shaking his head.

The right propeller was still frozen solid, and the pitch would not change even the slightest degree. He called Earhart and told her that the right propeller had not been fixed. There was no chance they could get off before dark. She told him that the weatherman had given them tailwinds again, and with the flight time to Howland Island estimated to be less than 12 hours, they might want to make a morning takeoff anyway.

They pushed the plane back into the hangar, where Sergeant Biando supervised the removal of the right propeller. It was then taken to the propeller room and partially disassembled. The propeller was found to be very badly galled, and the blades were frozen solid in the hub.

Mantz had resisted removing the propeller from the engine as long as he could, but there was no other way to find out what was wrong. Unfortunately, once the propeller was removed the plane should be test-flown before another heavyweight takeoff was attempted. He was well aware that during takeoff a problem easily handled at normal weight could turn disastrous when the plane was grossly overloaded. (Flying an overloaded plane is a very serious business—so serious that in all but exceptional cases it is now prohibited by law.)

After careful examination, Thomas and Biando both agreed that the hub had probably been nearly dry when the plane had left the mainland. The frozen blades had resulted from the lack of lubrication or the use of an improper lubricant. They had previously noted that there was no sign of any leaking lubricant. Everything was very clean and grease-free when they started the inspection.

Mantz decided that if that had been the case, it was possible the left propeller had not been lubricated and might be damaged as well. The only safe thing to do was to remove both propellers, inspect them fully, and repair them if necessary. Lieutenant Rogers suggested that Mantz ask Lieutenant Arnold to take the propellers to the Hawaiian Air Depot at Luke Field for overhaul. Arnold said he had a crew of men standing by for just such an emergency. They went back to the plane and the mechanics removed the left propeller. By four o'clock, both propellers had been delivered to the Hawaiian Air Depot at Luke Field for repair.

Mantz called Earhart in Waikiki to tell her that they were overhauling both propellers. He wasn't even sure they would be ready in time for her to depart in the morning. As there was nothing more he could do on the plane, he asked her to tell Terry he would be back from the field in an hour.

Thanking Rogers and his men for their work, Mantz told them he would call later that evening to advise them about a test flight and to say when Miss Earhart would be leaving for Howland Island. He left for Waikiki and a needed rest.

Amelia, Terry Minor, Fred Noonan, and Harry Manning were all waiting on the lanai when Mantz arrived back about four o'clock. Sitting on the arm of the couch by Terry, he told them of the problems with the propellers, and about the overload on the generator causing the fuse to blow. Since there was no chance for them to take off that night, they considered how late they could leave in the morning and still get to Howland Island before dark. He needed to get some sleep.

It was 6:30 when Mantz appeared again. It was getting dark, the sun having set about 20 minutes before. It was a beautiful and romantic evening in Hawaii, complete with moonlight shimmering on the Pacific waters off Waikiki Beach.

They had a light and informal dinner with Chris and Mona in the dining room, with temporary relief from the telephone. At the end of dinner the maid announced that Mr. Mantz had a call from a Lieutenant Arnold at Luke Field.

Arnold told him that they had completed taking apart the right propeller. It was necessary for them to use hot kerosene to accomplish the disassembly. Because of the seriousness of the right propeller's condition, it was decided to overhaul both propellers. Barring unexpected trouble, they could have the propellers back to Wheeler Field by two in the morning, and the plane would be ready for a test flight by daylight.

Mantz then told Amelia that everything should be fixed by early morning. If the plane was test-flown by seven o'clock, maybe she could get off by eight or nine. They would put on the final fuel load after the test flight. Everyone agreed that 825 gallons was a suitable fuel load.

Mantz phoned Standard Oil and requested that they be at Wheeler Field by seven o'clock in the morning. He asked for 100-octane fuel but was informed that it was not available. After the test hop, if everything checked okay, they could gas the plane and go. He then called Lieutenant Rogers to advise him of the early morning test flight and the possible departure for Howland Island at about eight or nine o'clock.

6 : THE CRASH

AT HONOLULU

I was still dark when Earhart was awakened at 4:30 A.M. on Friday, March 19. She had slept soundly and was oblivious to the heavy rain showers that occurred during the night.

Earhart bathed quickly and was ready before five o'clock. She went down to the dining room and was drinking her second glass of pineapple juice when Mantz came in. He took two or three gulps of coffee and was ready to go to Wheeler Field. Mantz spoke to her about the overnight rain, which concerned him because the plane was going to be heavy for takeoff. If the grass at Wheeler Field was too soft they might fly over to Luke Field, where they could fuel up and take off from a hard surface.

They left the residence and arrived at Wheeler Field a little before six o'clock. Lieutenant Arnold was waiting at the hangar when they arrived. He reviewed with them the propeller work that had gone on during the night. Earhart told him that they were thinking about using Luke Field for the Howland takeoff.

It was already light enough for them to inspect the field. Recent construction projects had required digging trenches across the takeoff and landing area. The excavations were very noticeable; as they drove down the runway they could feel the car sink into the wet ground when they crossed them. A damp mist was still in the air, and low clouds obscured the western Waianae Mountains. They decided to move the plane to Luke Field. It would be too late this morning to take off for Howland Island in any case.

It was already seven o'clock when they arrived back in Waikiki. Earhart updated Manning and Noonan on the details of the early morning visit to Wheeler Field and their decision to use Luke Field. Paul Mantz invited Terry and Chris to go out to Wheeler Field with him when he test-flew the Electra. He would probably be ready to leave in a couple of hours if they wanted to come.

It was almost ten o'clock when Chris, Terry, and Paul left Waikiki for Wheeler Field. As they passed Aiea, Chris pointed out Ford Island, located in the middle of Pearl Harbor; Luke Field was on the island. Chris explained that the Army Air Corps and the Navy Fleet Air Base shared it equally.

A few minutes later they arrived at Wheeler, and the driver parked by the 75th Service Squadron hangar. The Electra was on the flight line with a Standard Oil truck waiting alongside. Lieutenant Rogers came out of the hangar as soon as he saw them. As Standard Oil could not supply 100-octane fuel, Mantz asked Rogers to have the 100-octane gas they had pumped from the right to left main tank pumped back into the right main again. Earhart would save the 100-octane for takeoff at Howland Island. After the 100-octane was back in the right main wing tank, Mantz directed the Standard Oil fuel truck to add 87-octane to the left main tank, to be used for takeoff on the test flight.

Mantz told Rogers that if the plane checked okay on the test flight, he would land at Luke Field so that he could inspect the surface of the runway to see if it was suitable for a heavyweight takeoff. If he found it satisfactory he would not return, and Miss Earhart would take off for Howland Island from Luke Field.

While the truck finished fueling, Mantz called the operations officer at Luke Field and told him of his plans. Chris Holmes instructed his driver to wait for an hour to see if they returned. If they didn't come back, he was to drive to Luke Field and pick them up.

When Standard Oil had finished fueling, Mantz gave the plane a preflight inspection, then went up into the cockpit, closed the overhead hatch, and started the engines.

It took 10 minutes of running the engines before he was satisfied that everything was okay. He came out of the cockpit and looked around the engine nacelles and landing gear for any signs of oil leaks. There were none, but he did notice a problem with the oleo struts, the oil-and-air-filled shock absorbers on the landing gears: the right one was extended 4 inches, while the left one was extended only a little over 2 inches. He had the mechanic let air out of the right oleo air valve until it was extended the same amount as the left one.

Happy that everything was as it should be, he helped Terry and Chris into the plane for departure. They taxied to the far end of Wheeler Field for takeoff. At about 11:15 Mantz applied power for takeoff. The relatively light plane accelerated rapidly and seemed to spring into the air after only a short run. He retracted the landing gear and reduced engine power as the plane was already up to a thousand feet.

Pearl Harbor was just ahead, and Paul pointed off to the left in the distance, where Diamond Head was already visible. They passed the Aloha Tower where the passenger liners docked, and could see the traffic on the streets of downtown Honolulu. The Royal Hawaiian and Moana Hotels were at the beginning of Waikiki Beach. They could actually see the surfers on their surfboards. Chris was disappointed that there wasn't anyone outside the house as they went by his Waikiki estate. Mantz rocked the Electra's wings, but no one came from the house.

Paul gave Terry and Chris an air tour by circling around the entire island of Oahu. They finally came full circle back to the entrance to Pearl Harbor. Mantz checked the wind sock at Luke Field for landing, and they touched down about twelve noon. They were guided to the service apron in front of the final assembly hangar on the Army side of Luke Field.

Mantz told the waiting Army officers that the depot had done a wonderful job overhauling the propellers. They had never worked as well before as they did on the test flight. He asked Lieutenant Arnold if he had anyone who could look at the Sperry autopilot. The autopilot rudder control had drifted off course faster than he thought it should when they were flying from Oakland. Arnold said he would have the instrument mechanics look at it.

Checking the plane after landing, Mantz found that the right landing gear's oleo strut extension was now $2^1/_8$ inches, and the left was $2^5/_8$ inches. The right strut valve core was found to be leaking. He asked Lynn V. Young, a mechanic assigned to help him, to replace the valve core and pump air into the right oleo strut until it matched the extension of the left strut at $2^5/_8$ inches.

Mantz instructed Young and Fred Wood, the chief civilian depot inspector, on fueling the tanks. The plane was to be fueled directly from the Standard Oil Company truck, through a chamois-lined funnel that fit all of the gas tank filler necks and allowed the tanks to be filled without much spillage. The chamois filtered out any contaminants that might be in the gas.

Mantz explained to Arnold that Miss Earhart would be taking off about eleven o'clock that night or at dawn the next morning, depending on the weather. He would let him know before ten o'clock what her decision was. Chris, Terry, and Paul left for Waikiki at about 1:30, and it was after two when they got back to the Holmeses' residence.

Mantz reported that the plane was ready to go. He had checked the 3,000-foot runway at Luke Field, and it would provide a firm surface for takeoff in all weather conditions. Right now they were gassing the plane to 825 gallons. They could leave that night or in the morning, as far as the airplane and the airfield were concerned.

Amelia asked Fred Noonan if he would stay with the flight after Howland Island, at least as far as Australia. Noonan thought about it for a moment and accepted the offer. He wondered aloud if it might not be easier and cheaper for him to continue all the way. He would get home quicker by staying with the flight than by getting off in Australia. Amelia said she would have to have G.P. check the diplomatic clearances before she could make a decision. Manning would be co-navigator and radio operator. Amelia asked them both to remain at the navigation station in the cabin for landing and takeoff.

Noonan composed a Globe Wireless cablegram to send to Mrs. Martinelli, his fiancée, in Oakland: "LEAVING 1:30 AM YOUR TIME STOP AMELIA HAS ASKED ME TO CONTINUE WITH HER AT LEAST TO DARWIN AUSTRALIA AND POSSIBLY AROUND THE WORLD STOP WILL KEEP YOU ADVISED STOP TRIP AROUND THE WORLD WILL BE COMPLETED BEFORE I CAN RETURN FROM AUSTRALIA STOP . . . I LOVE YOU FRED"

A little after three o'clock a phone call came for Mantz from Luke Field. The Standard Oil truck was having trouble fueling the plane. In 40 minutes it had succeeded in delivering only 15 gallons through the chamois filters because of a suspected contaminant. Arnold had stopped all fueling until Mantz could be notified. The representative from Standard Oil was there and wanted to talk directly to Mantz. Paul had a lengthy conversation with him about the problem and decided to return to the field to sort it out. He requested Arnold to hold any further fueling until he arrived to personally supervise it.

At 4:15 Mantz arrived back at the final assembly hangar. He had the Standard Oil representative pump some gasoline from the truck through the chamois filter. A deposit of sediment was found. The Standard Oil man insisted that the dirt had already been in the chamois and did not come from his fuel. Mantz went into the plane and got a new chamois skin, and repeated the test. Again the filter showed sediment. Mantz requested that the plane be fueled with Air Corps gasoline. Permission was given by the Luke Field operations officer.

Shortly after five o'clock Lieutenant Arnold called for the fuel truck. By seven o'clock they had added 515 gallons. That brought the total in the tanks to 825 gallons. The mechanics took about 20 minutes to clean all the fuel strainers. By 7:30 the plane was refueled and placed under guard in the final assembly hangar with the doors locked.

Mantz immediately returned to Waikiki. Earhart, Manning, and Noonan were in the study talking about the Howland Island weather forecasts when he arrived. The reports indicated that the weather would be better if they arrived at Howland Island late tomorrow afternoon. Earhart thought they should delay their departure until early the next morning. Noonan agreed, preferring an all-daylight flight that would arrive at the island an hour or so before dark. That settled it.

Mantz called to advise Lieutenant Arnold of their decision. Arnold told him that there were no ferry services direct to Luke Field until 6:15 A.M. They would have to take a boat to the Fleet Air Base side of the field instead.

At 3:30 the next morning, a light rain was still falling as Chris Holmes drove them to Pearl Harbor. It had showered heavily all night. The rain must have soaked the grass at Wheeler Field, softening the turf even more. Earhart was glad they had changed the takeoff to the hard-surface runway at Luke Field.

They wound their way through the wet and deserted streets of Honolulu in the early Saturday morning darkness of March 20. It was after four when they arrived at Pearl Harbor to board the boat for the Fleet Air Base dock on Ford Island. They crossed the harbor to Ford Island and, after docking at the air base, proceeded to the weather station to pick up the weather charts and forecasts.

The flight forecast was for an average 15 mph tailwind. Noonan asked Earhart if she still wanted to be able to return to Honolulu after 8 hours. Amelia said that she did. Noonan pointed out that the 15 mph tailwind during the 8 hours outbound would turn into a 15 mph headwind coming back. It would take nearly 10 hours to return to Honolulu after flying only 8 hours outbound. They would need fuel for a total of nearly 18 hours.

Earhart decided to put on an additional 75 gallons, for a total load of 900 gallons. Mantz noted that with the extra gas the plane would be only about 450 pounds lighter than at Oakland.

They crossed the field over to the Army final assembly hangar, where Lieutenant Arnold had already moved the Electra out onto the run-up apron. Amelia greeted Lieutenant Arnold as he came toward them. "My goodness," Amelia said, "none of you people have had a moment's rest." Lieutenant Arnold told her the men had volunteered and were glad to help.

Newspaper reporters were beginning to arrive by 4:45. Mantz went to finish the fueling. By five o'clock it was completed, and he began a thorough preflight inspection of the plane.

Flashlight in hand, he inspected all of the control surfaces for security, freedom of movement, and damage. He gave special attention to the landing gear struts and tires. Checking closely for fuel and oil leaks, he made sure at the same time that all access panels and scupper covers were tightly secured. He shone his light on the pitot tubes, which furnished airspeed data, to check that nothing was obstructing their openings. Finally, he pushed with his foot against each of the wheel chocks to make sure they were firmly in place. Satisfied with the visual inspection, he was ready to do a run-up check of the engines. Arnold stationed a fire guard to stand by with a fire extinguisher while the engines were started.

After about five minutes of warming the engines, Mantz ran each of the engines at higher power to check for proper operation. When he was finished, he shut down the engines and opened the overhead hatch. Amelia had been watching from the hangar. As he came out of the cockpit she walked across the apron to meet him. Everything was in good shape. He was going to check the nacelles and landing gear for any oil leaks that might have occurred during the run-up. Earhart climbed up onto the wing to enter the cockpit.

It was almost 5:30 when she entered the cockpit through the overhead hatch. Looking out the windshield at the landing area, she could see that it was still wet from the last rain shower.

Earhart asked them to turn on the floodlights for a takeoff toward the southwest. A few moments later the floodlights came on, bathing the whole landing field in a soft, uneven light. She studied the layout of the field through her cockpit window for a few minutes and decided it would be best to wait for more natural light before departing. They shut the floodlights off, and her eyes slowly began to readjust to the dark. Mantz said they would guide her to the far end of the field with flashlights, so she wouldn't have to use the landing lights.

The dim outlines of tanks and buildings around the field were becoming visible in the early morning twilight. Earhart told Mantz to get Manning and Noonan aboard as there would soon be enough light to start up and taxi out. Manning and Noonan entered the navigator's compartment through the rear cabin door. Earhart started both engines in less than two minutes, and signaled for the wheel chocks to be pulled. After receiving an all-clear signal, she slowly started taxiing to the northeast end of the runway. She left her landing lights off, following the flashlights of Mantz and Lynn Young, who preceded her along the Navy side of the runway.

It was now 5:40 A.M. The sky was broken to overcast at three to four thousand feet. A light drift of wind from the southwest barely fluttered the wind sock on building number 78. The atmospheric visibility was good. There was sufficient daylight for the spectators to see her plane dimly at the far end of the runway. The horizon was quite bright toward the south. The smoke from two dredges at the mouth of Pearl Harbor was plainly noticeable. The buildings and various objects were distinguishable in the gray dawn, but there was insufficient light to permit photography without flashbulbs.

Earhart swung the Electra around at the end of the landing mat and stopped. The plane was lined up slightly to the right of the white line painted down the center of the runway. With the engines throttled back to idle she checked that Manning and Noonan were ready. They had themselves as far forward against the tanks as possible and were ready to go. It would have been helpful to have the experienced pilot Manning in the cockpit, but to ensure getting the piloting credit she would have to do this herself. Earhart made one last scan of the engine gauges, checking that all pressures and temperatures were normal. She reset the directional gyros to match the compass reading, and at 5:45 she advanced the throttles until the engines were running at about half power. Then she released the brakes and advanced the throttles for full power. The plane slowly gathered speed as Earhart held back pressure on the control yoke to keep the tail wheel firmly on the ground. Her left foot was holding in the left rudder, as the plane tended to drift slightly toward the right.

George H. Miller, a civilian mechanic at Luke Field, had walked down and positioned himself about in the middle of the flying field to be on hand in case of any mishap. He had worked on the plane engines earlier and was interested in watching Earhart apply power to start her takeoff roll. Now it seemed to him that the left engine was turning over a little faster than the right engine, and the plane was taking its course slightly toward the right of the field, where he was standing.

In the cockpit Earhart's left hand gripped the control yoke, applying elevator and aileron forces as needed. Her right hand was on top of both throttles so she could immediately respond if either engine should malfunction. With her feet on the left and right rudder pedals, she pushed them to keep the plane going in the proper direction. (Until near flying speed is reached, the engines, mounted off-center out on the wings, have more power to turn the plane off course than the rudders have to keep it going straight.)

While her hands and feet were busy, Earhart's eyes were carrying the heaviest workload. (The vision pilots depend on to keep from crashing is seriously handicapped in poor light. Recognition, depth perception, azimuth change, and other visual clues are all markedly degraded.) Her eyes were shifting rapidly from one light level inside the cockpit, reading instruments at close range, to a different light level outside, looking at distant objects. This imposed a handicap and made it difficult for her to obtain solid visual references while guiding the plane down the runway.

The plane was accelerating nicely with its heavy load. As the tail lifted up into flying position, the thought crossed Earhart's mind that in another ten seconds they would be up and on their way. Without the tail wheel on the ground it seemed that the plane was drifting farther to the right of the center line. Earhart pushed the left rudder pedal hard, all the way to the stop, to try to guide the plane back to the center. Still the plane continued its drift to the right. It was obvious that the plane would run off the right side of the runway before it became airborne. Earhart did the only thing she could do, easing the left throttle back to remove some of the power from the left engine. This temporary reduction in power would help the rudders in getting the plane straight with the runway again. At that moment the right wing seemed to drop slightly. Earhart was distracted as her attention was drawn to the sensation of motion. The first thing she thought of was the right oleo or the right tire letting go. A glance at the left engine's manifold pressure showed the power was reduced. When she looked back outside after the moment's distraction, the plane had already started a long, persistent left turn.

Major Phillips Melville, Luke Field's operations officer, was standing near the southwest end of the field. As he described the accident later, from his distant vantage point the Electra appeared to be gaining speed quickly. He could see the wing tips wobble slightly as the plane ran over some unevenness of the mat. Suddenly it began veering to the left with increasing speed, in the initial stages of a ground loop. The plane swung around and tilted with its right wing tip almost scraping the mat. The right landing gear suddenly collapsed, followed shortly by the left gear, and the plane slid in an abrupt left-hand skid on its belly. A shower of sparks spurted from between the airplane and the mat.

As George Miller reported it, when the Electra was about a hundred yards away from where he was standing at midfield, he noticed that the right engine seemed to surge and take a quick hold. At once the plane changed its course from turning to the right and began to make a sharp left turn for a quarter circle. At this point the right wing seemed to settle toward the ground and the left wing went upward. The left wheel was off the ground and remained in that position for about fifty or sixty feet before the right running gear gave way and let the plane come down on its undercarriage. The tire blew out under the excess pressure just as the plane settled down on its right side.

Earhart turned off the power with the throttles as the plane rose up on its right wheel in its uncontrolled ground loop to the left. After both landing gears had collapsed, the plane continued to slide and turn on its belly until it finally came to a stop 1,200 feet from where it had started, facing in the direction from which it had come.

With deliberate calm Earhart shut off the ignition and master switches and opened the overhead hatch. She stood up on the pilot's seat with her head and shoulders out of the cockpit. The fire truck was right behind her. She watched as it pulled up on the left side of the plane.

Even before the plane had come to a stop, Lieutenant Arnold had grabbed Chris Holmes by the arm and they had run to Arnold's car. They sped toward the plane, stopping on the runway a couple hundred feet short of the crashed Electra.

The firemen extended a fire hose to the fuselage, but miraculously there was no fire.

Lieutenant Arnold and Chris Holmes arrived at the plane just as Earhart exited from the cockpit. Chris helped her as she came down off the left wing.

Amelia asked, "What happened?"

Men gathered all around the plane. When the cabin door was opened they found Manning just inside, with Noonan at the navigator's table methodically folding up and putting away his charts. Except for a slight bruising of Manning's right elbow, no one was hurt.

The officer of the day quickly established a guard detail around the airplane, and everyone was warned that there was to be no smoking. He tried to move the press photographers away, but Earhart intervened and said to let them come.

Mantz arrived and immediately began inspecting the plane for damage. A crowd was already gathering, so Lieutenant Arnold led Earhart, Holmes, Manning, and Noonan to his car on the runway.

As they walked back down the runway to the car they stopped at intervals to examine the marks the tires had left on the mat. Earhart remarked that the right track was much wider than the left. When they were all seated alone in the car, she began to talk to the crew, reconstructing what had happened. Lieutenant Arnold summarized the event in his report to the Army investigation board:

[Amelia said] "The ship functioned perfectly at the start. As it gained speed the right wing dropped down and the ship seemed to pull to the right. I eased off the left engine and the ship started a long persistent left turn and ended up where it is now. It was all over instantly. The first thing I thought of was the right oleo or the right tire letting go. The way the ship pulled it was probably a flat tire."

Noonan remarked, "This is a piece of G.D. bad luck."

Amelia replied, "Yes, it is a little bit disappointing."

Manning was non-committal.

"Well," Noonan said, "when you're ready to fly again, I'll be ready to go along."

They returned to the airplane for a closer inspection, and the press began firing questions from all sides.

"You ran through bunches of grass didn't you?"

She answered, "The runway was perfect. The grass had nothing to do with it. I am sure of a structural failure."

"Of course now you will give up the trip?" a reporter asked.

Amelia shook her head, "I think not."

Earhart talked with Mantz about the damage to the plane. He told her it looked pretty bad. The right wing was damaged, and the right engine and nacelle were being held to the wing by only two bolts. The right oil tank had burst and spilled oil on the runway. The fuel filler neck had been torn open and had spilled gas. It was a miracle there hadn't been a fire. He told her they would need to check further before he could assess the total damage.

Chris Holmes invited them back to his home in Waikiki. Mantz said he would call her as soon as he finished inspecting the plane. Earhart took a glance in the direction of the reporters and agreed to leave.

Mantz asked Lieutenant Arnold if there was a room in the hangar where they could store the equipment from the plane for safekeeping. Arnold offered the final assembly tool room, where everything could be kept under lock and key. He would arrange for a truck and a guard to help Mantz move everything from the plane. Manning went into the rear cabin and retrieved the bubble octant. He wanted to keep the octant in his possession, as the Navy would hold him personally responsible for its return.

After picking up Terry, Lieutenant Arnold drove everyone to the Navy boat dock, where they departed for Honolulu. Mantz went to the hangar to send a cable to G.P.

It took only a minute for him to compose the cable: "AMELIA IN CRACK-UP WHILE ATTEMPTING TAKEOFF. TIRE BLEW OUT. ONE WHEEL OFF. OIL DRIPPING ON RUNWAY. NO ONE HURT. AMELIA CALM, COLLECTED." He telephoned it to the cable office and immediately returned to the runway to further inspect the damage to the plane.

Earhart arrived at Waikiki around seven o'clock. Mantz was already on the phone and wanted to talk to her. He told her that the plane wasn't as badly damaged as he had at first thought. They were defueling the plane preparatory to moving it from the runway to the hangar. But he did think that they would have to ship the plane back to the factory at Burbank to do the repairs.

Earhart asked how long he thought it would take to prepare the plane for shipment, and how long the factory would take to fix everything. Mantz estimated that the plane could probably be ready for shipment in two or three days. The factory could take another two or three months to do the job after that. The important thing was that the plane was definitely repairable, not a total loss.

Earhart then asked him about the propellers and the engines. Mantz answered that all four propeller blades were damaged and curled at the tips, but that was a good sign. It indicated there probably wasn't any sudden stoppage to cause the failure of major internal parts of the engines.

Earhart was getting ready to put in a transpacific call to talk it over with G.P. She would call Mantz back when she was finished.

G.P. sounded concerned when he asked Amelia how she was. She told him that she was not hurt, and the boys were fine too. "Only our spirits are bruised."

G.P. told Amelia that it would be fine with him if she called off the world flight, but she replied that she wanted to keep going. The harder question was whether they could raise the additional money it would take to make the repairs. If she wanted to try again, G.P. said, he would go to work on raising money right away.

In the meantime she wanted to know if she should issue a press release about the crash, or would G.P. do it. G.P. told her that he had more outlets and could do it for her. In the meantime, he continued, "Write your personal story of the crash for the *Tribune;* get it filed as soon as you can."

Amelia told G.P. that she was sorry for the mess the crash had caused. But G.P. told her that as long as she wasn't hurt, it didn't matter.

Earhart returned to the lanai and asked if they could book passage for the five of them on the SS *Malolo* to Los Angeles for that day's noon departure. A call to the passenger booking office of Castle and Cook quickly arranged for the passage and delivery of the tickets.

Earhart asked Mantz if he could arrange to have the plane prepared for shipment so they could all sail on the *Malolo* at noon. He replied that he thought he could, but she would probably have to sign some paperwork and releases before they sailed. Earhart said she would be available and began to write her article for the *Tribune* syndicate.

In less than half an hour the maid interrupted, saying Mr. Mantz was on the phone again. He told Earhart that he had arranged for the Army Air Corps to finish crating the plane and equipment for shipment. Also, he had made arrangements with a local shipping company, Young Brothers, to move the airplane from Luke Field by barge for shipment on the next transport to the harbor at San Pedro. She would have to write a letter to the commanding officer of the Hawaiian Air Depot at Luke Field guaranteeing payment for the Army to do the work. Mantz asked her to send the letter along with the car when it came to pick him up.

It was after eight when Earhart finished the article and phoned it in to the news desk. Bill Cogswell from the Pan Pacific Press Bureau said he would pick her up about 10:30 and drive her to the *Malolo.* She finished the letter to the commanding officer of the Hawaiian Air Depot and sent it along with the car to Luke Field.

Amelia then called G.P. in Oakland again to tell him of the arrangements for shipping the plane and to let him know that they would all be leaving on the SS *Malolo* at noon. She wanted to know how the press on the mainland was reporting her crash. G.P. told her that everyone understood what could happen if a tire blew out at 70 miles an hour in a car. They were treating the crash sympathetically.

Amelia told him that, after thinking about, she wasn't so sure it was a blown tire. "I know witnesses said the tire blew. However, studying the tracks carefully, I believe that may not have been the primary cause of the accident. Possibly the right shock absorber as it lengthened may have given way."

Regardless of the cause, G.P. responded, he would start contacting all of the sponsors and preparing them for her need of financial help to get the ship repaired. He told her he was on his way to Los Angeles, and would be home the next day if she needed him. He was very happy they would be returning shortly. He would meet the ship via the pilot boat before it even docked.

The crumpled airplane lying on the runway at Luke Field was an embarrassment to all concerned. Financially, it was a major setback for the Putnams. The cost of repairing and rescheduling the world flight was beyond their means. Previous benefactors would have to be asked again to help pay the bills. It would be disastrous if bad publicity brought discredit on anyone whose future help they would need. They had to find a way to resume the world flight.

Mantz got back a few minutes before ten o'clock. Cogswell arrived, and after a snack was served they loaded both cars. By 10:30 they were on their way to the ship for boarding.

Band music lent a festive mood to the crowd of passengers and their friends jammed around the wharf area of Pier 11 where the *Malolo* was boarding. Earhart's party moved through the throng, carrying what little luggage they had. Mona and Chris stopped to buy leis for everyone from the flower girls on the dock.

The purser met them at the head of the gangway and had them escorted to their cabins.

In a brief interview, Earhart assured reporters she would be back as soon as her plane was ready.

The group had been in Amelia's stateroom for only a few minutes when a long blast of the ship's siren signaled 30 minutes to sailing. It was time for Chris and Mona to leave. All of the travelers had heartfelt thanks for the wonderful Hawaiian hospitality that they had received.

With blasts from the ship's whistle and the band playing "Aloha Oe," the *Malolo* slowly pulled away from the dock. Amelia and Fred stood at the ship's rail watching Oahu slowly recede toward the horizon. They followed the custom of removing the leis from around their necks and tossing them into the sea. Legend had it that if a lei floats toward the island you will be sure to return. Amelia definitely wanted to return. She watched the wave from the ship's wake wash over her leis, but it was impossible to tell which direction they were taking.

7 : PREPARING FOR THE
SECOND WORLD FLIGHT

T HE SS *Malolo* rounded Point Fermin early Thursday morning, March 25, 1937. Only a few passengers were on deck as the Matson liner slowed at the entrance to Los Angeles Harbor. A boat came alongside the ship to transfer the harbor pilot. Following the pilot up the Jacob's ladder onto the ship was Amelia's husband.

G.P. went directly to Amelia's cabin. He brought her up to date on the interrupted flight. Reporters would be interviewing her when they docked. Because she had been out of direct contact with the press since leaving Honolulu, G.P. told her the story had run its course, but he was sure they would ask her about the crash. A blown tire or a landing gear failure with the heavy overload had been generally accepted as the cause. They knew the Electra was being shipped to Los Angeles and would arrive at the Lockheed factory by the end of the following week.

Before she met with the press, G.P. wanted to confirm Amelia was happy having only Fred Noonan along when the flight resumed. She thought Harry Manning did an excellent job operating the radios but believed she could do what was needed. She would simply revert to the radio procedures she had used when flying the Vega from Honolulu to Oakland in 1935. She had transmitted her messages at one time and received the replies from a broadcast station later. Even when Manning was working the radios during the flight to Honolulu, Amelia had received most of her information by listening to the regular broadcast stations KFI and KGU. The extra instruments, radios, and electrical equipment installed on the flying laboratory were overloading the plane's generator. Not having both the transmitter and receiver working at the same time would reduce the electrical load.

Amelia told G.P. that she had talked to Manning, who was very gentlemanly about being replaced by Noonan when the flight resumed. He was returning to his ship in New York. Noonan was to be met by his fiancée, and Paul Mantz and Terry Minor were returning to Burbank. Everyone was to come to her cabin before they docked.

The tugboats were maneuvering the *Malolo* into the pier when Terry, Mantz, Noonan, and Manning arrived at her cabin. G.P. told them what the press had been saying about the crash. All questions about continuing the trip were to be referred to Amelia. Manning should explain that he must return to his ship; Noonan could tell them he would be navigating when the flight resumed. The *Malolo* finished docking, and they went to meet the press.

The reporters asked about the route that she would take when she made her next attempt at the world flight. She told them that she might have to change her entire plans for the route that she would follow. She had worked them out on the assumption that she would make the flight this month. A delay of another month might result in climatic conditions that would compel a different itinerary.

As G.P. had predicted, they asked about the accident. Amelia told them it was probably a mechanical failure of some kind that wouldn't have happened if she had been doing ordinary flying. She had several tons more weight aboard the plane than it was intended to carry.

They collected their belongings and made their way off the ship to the waiting cars on the wharf. Manning left separately with Noonan and was never seen by Earhart again.

It took over an hour to drive from San Pedro to the San Fernando Valley. G.P. talked with Mantz on the way, suggesting that Mantz should capitalize on the publicity he was receiving in the newspapers. Now that everyone recognized his name, he might do well to change the name of his business from United Air Services to Mantz Air Services. They dropped Terry and Paul off; a few minutes later Amelia finally arrived home. It had been over two weeks since she had left for Oakland.

Elstrude and Fred Tomas, their maid and cook, were there to greet Amelia along with Amelia's young assistant, Margot de Carie. The house and grounds looked neat. Amelia felt good to be back again with her husband among familiar surroundings. There was work to be done and one more article to write, but at least she was in the seclusion and comfort of her own home.

A Western Union day letter arrived from Edward C. Elliott, president of Purdue University. In the wire Elliott affirmed the support of Purdue's Boilermakers' Guild for Amelia's flight. After lunch Amelia sat down at her desk in the study to write a final article about the world flight attempt. When she finished the article, she wrote a letter to Dr. Elliott, thanking him. She hoped to repair the plane and try again. Of course, she could not make any definite plans until it was examined by Lockheed engineers. She mentioned that the costs of repair, even more than time, would be the essence of her problem. She expected G.P. would be contacting him soon. With gratitude and greetings to Purdue, she signed it, "Sincerely yours, Amelia Earhart."

Amelia left the study, and on her way out to inspect the garden she picked up her antique copper watering can. She inspected the century plant and the rest of the garden, and was pleased to see everything was doing well in the rich valley soil.

In Honolulu Lieutenant Arnold was hard at work getting the damaged Electra ready for shipment on the SS *Lurline,* due to leave on Saturday. At 2:30 P.M. on Friday all property was officially signed for and placed in the care of Young Brothers Limited. There were fourteen boxes and crates plus the fuselage section. Altogether they were estimated to weigh 14,114 pounds.

The Hawaiian Air Depot's cost accounting department had maintained an accurate record of time and labor on all operations in which the depot was involved. Earhart would receive a bill for 1,079.25 hours of labor at a cost of $631.09, materials furnished costing $146.72, and eight days of airplane storage at $3.00 each for $24.00. When totaled with other expenses, the bill came to $1,086.10.

Young Brothers, acting as agents for the S. S. Bowman Company, loaded everything onto a barge and towed it from Pearl Harbor. It was taken to Honolulu Harbor, where it was loaded as deck cargo on the Matson liner *Lurline* early the next morning. The Putnams received a bill from the S. S. Bowman Company that included the Hawaiian Air

Depot's charges. For assembling the damaged plane for return to the United States and caring for all the details at Honolulu, the total cost was $4,100. In 1937 this was a considerable sum. Saturday morning, March 27, 1937, the plane was loaded onto the *Lurline,* and the Matson liner departed Honolulu for the mainland.

B ACK in North Hollywood Amelia had finished the last of several letters to sponsors and friends and had given reporters an interview they had requested. Word was received that her plane was on the *Lurline* and would arrive at the harbor on Friday. The Putnams could relax and enjoy the rest of the weekend at home. Monday would be soon enough to face problems of raising money and arranging for the repairs.

Fred Noonan and his fiancée, Mary B. Martinelli, decided to elope. They drove to Yuma, Arizona, where Fred's instantaneous Mexican divorce was legally recognized, which would not have been true in California. Fred was married to "Bee" Martinelli in Yuma on Saturday, March 27, 1937.

On March 30, G.P. dictated a letter to his secretary for Dr. Elliott. He wrote that the plane was due back to the factory on Friday. Shortly thereafter they would know fairly well the costs of repair. Tentatively, G.P. was estimating $30,000 would be required for everything from this point on.

Until the accident, G.P. said, the budget was working out almost exactly. Now, alas, that satisfactory situation had changed.

Here was how finances stood:

G.P.P. and A.E. had scraped up $10,000. Another stamp cover issue would earn $5,000, Bendix was probably good for $2,500, and Walker [an associate] $1,000. The total was $18,500.

Probably Odlum [another associate] would contribute up to another $5,000. Tactically G.P. would prefer to keep this help in reserve. Perhaps Bendix might increase his support.

Did Dr. Elliott suppose any of the Purdue friends who had so generously helped before would care to help further? G.P. knew that they had done their share—and more. But if another $5,000 could be arranged from them, it would be tremendously helpful. G.P. was sure that would mean a definite matching by Floyd Odlum—and that would just about button it up. Regardless, he and Amelia would be no less appreciative of the initial generosity which made possible purchase of the plane.

G.P. asked Dr. Elliott to please let him know frankly.

• •

F RIDAY, April 2, the Electra was off-loaded in San Pedro Harbor and picked up by the Smith Brothers Trucking Company. The width of the fuselage caused problems on the city streets, and the plane didn't actually arrive at the Lockheed factory until Saturday afternoon.

Earhart sent off a congratulatory telegram to her longtime friend and fellow pilot Louise Thaden. The Harmon Trophy had been presented to Thaden in New York when she was honored as the outstanding woman flier of 1936. She had also won the 1936 Bendix Air Race. When Earhart completed the round-the-world flight, she would be a leading contender for the trophy in 1937.

On Sunday, a couple of hundred miles away, Fred Noonan and his new bride, Bee, were driving on the Golden State Highway near Fresno, California. It was April 4, and Fred was celebrating his forty-fourth birthday. Unfortunately, he had a head-on collision with another car. Fred was slightly bruised in the crash, and Bee suffered a severe laceration on her knee. The investigating policeman cited Fred on a charge of driving in the wrong lane of traffic.

Back home in North Hollywood, Amelia and G.P. expected to learn in a few days the estimated cost to repair the Electra. Once they knew that, they could calculate their ability to pay. Only then could they determine whether any of the changes and improvements she would like to make to the plane were financially feasible.

Lockheed's assistant chief engineer, James M. Gerschler, was responsible for all repair and modification work that was done at Lockheed. He had each individual shop foreman arrange to clean, inspect, and report on the damaged parts of the plane. No work could be accomplished before Mr. Gerschler approved the repair or modification. If a repair was approved, an engineering order was issued to the shop, with a copy to the inspection department. Inspectors oversaw all shop work to make sure it was in accordance with the engineering order and accomplished to the highest standards.

After analyzing the reports of damage, Gerschler issued six pages of orders specifying the drawings, part numbers, and descriptions of the repairs to be made to the plane. Before the orders were issued, the Putnams were notified that the cost of the repairs would be approximately $12,500. Amelia and G.P. authorized Lockheed to go ahead.

Amelia talked to the Sperry autopilot company about how the plane wandered off the desired heading. They sent a factory representative to make modifications and new connections to the autopilot rudder control unit designed to keep the plane on a steadier course.

G.P. called radioman Joe Gurr and asked if he would work after hours to repair the radio installation while Lockheed was making the structural repairs. Except for testing the radios for proper operation, almost all of his work involved repairing antennas that had been damaged in the crash.

All the antennas under the fuselage, including the trailing wire, had been destroyed in the crash. Earhart and Gurr discussed the cost of repair, as well as the weight and drag, of the trailing wire that had been installed so Captain Manning could send Morse code signals on 500 kilocycles. Manning was no longer available, and neither Earhart nor Noonan knew Morse code well enough to use it. Joe Gurr believed that trailing wire antennas were mechanically unreliable anyway. To back up the trailing wire he had previously installed a 500-kilocycle loading coil to load the fixed antenna. They could switch to the fixed antenna for 500 kilocycles, though tuning the transmitter through the loading coil absorbed a lot of radio energy, and the signal would be weak. Gurr believed he could improve the signal strength by revising the loading coil and making the top antenna longer, but first he must remove all of the radios and check them for damage.

Earhart decided to remove the trailing wire altogether. She wanted to be able to transmit voice on 3105 and 6210. She didn't understand much about the antennas, but if they could have a signal on 500 kilocycles without the trailing wire, that would be fine. When Gurr was finished he would contact her and show her how to operate the new antenna installation.

The Lockheed men continued working to get the plane ready to fly again.

In its normal passenger configuration, an Electra had an escape hatch over the wing on the right side of the cabin. This was the only exit on the right side of the plane, but because of the fuselage fuel tanks it was covered over on Earhart's plane. In January two new windows had been installed in her Electra, one in the cabin entrance door and one in the right sidewall of the lavatory compartment. During repairs it was decided to make an exit of the window in the lavatory compartment by replacing it with an aluminum hatch. Not only did this provide an escape route, the hatch could be opened on the ground for cabin ventilation.

Mantz followed G.P.'s advice and decided to change the operating name of his company to Paul Mantz Air Service, Ltd. He and Earhart often visited the Lockheed plant to watch the progress on the repairs. A brand-new right wing was being fabricated and would be painted to match the left wing, which was being repaired. New wing tips were being installed on both sides, with new single navigation lights attached at their very tip.

Pacific Airmotive reported that the engines had been completely disassembled and inspected. No damage had been done to any of the internal parts. After reassembly, the engines would be tested and returned to the plane. All of the parts and tolerances would match those of a brand-new engine.

Hamilton Standard Propellers reported that both of the propeller hubs were found to be in good condition. All four of the individual propeller blades would be changed. There were several recommendations for frequent inspections and servicing of the propellers to prevent future problems. The changes were made to provide better lubrication and prevent future sticking or freezing of the propeller blades.

By the end of the first week, inspection of the critical and complex wing center section between the two engines was completed. Lockheed found the critical parts to be undamaged. Everything was progressing as planned. In another month the Electra would be ready to fly again.

Working after hours, Joe Gurr took considerable time to satisfy himself that the radios were all in good condition. He then tried to keep the 500-kilocycle frequency without a trailing wire. Gurr had the antenna mast on top of the fuselage moved as far forward as possible. This lengthened the antenna, which he hoped would make it more efficient. It would not radiate as well as a trailing wire, but perhaps well enough for Earhart to use it for a limited range. He tuned the transmitter's output through the loading coil to the new longer antenna on top of the plane. It was an electrically inefficient arrangement, but Gurr hoped it would work satisfactorily. He believed the longer antenna on top of the plane would make a great deal of difference in the amount of radio energy it would emit on 500 kilocycles.

Nothing was said to Paul Mantz regarding responsibility for the accident, but he was removed as technical adviser. He was in St. Louis and not even notified when Amelia left Burbank for Miami on the second world flight attempt.

In New York, on April 12, G.P. wrote a five-page letter to G. Stanley Meikle of the Purdue Research Foundation in Indiana. An annual meeting of the Purdue Foundation board was coming up, and G.P. wanted to be sure Mr. Meikle had all of the latest information available to him for that meeting. G.P. was still $10,000 short of the amount needed to complete the round-the-world flight. The Purdue Foundation's support could be crucial to those efforts.

In the letter G.P. listed in detail the approximately $63,000 in expenses the flight had incurred up to the date of the accident on March 20. He also detailed the sources of the $74,500 Earhart had in hand, or was assured, for the flight. She was still $5,000 to $10,000 short of having enough to cover the total costs and would be grateful for any help they could offer.

By late April everything was under control with the repairs. Amelia was able to get away from Burbank, and she joined G.P. in New York, where he was busy raising money. On Saturday, April 24, she made an appearance at Gimbel's Department Store to promote the sale of the second flight covers to stamp collectors. A week later on May 1, Amelia returned to Burbank.

In early May the airplane was really coming together. Joe Gurr supervised the reinstallation of the radio equipment and the hooking up of the new antenna system. When he was finished with everything, he would check out Earhart on the equipment.

The plane was coming together, but the money wasn't. G.P. still didn't have a commitment from any of the members of the Purdue Research Foundation. They were scheduled to have a board meeting on May 12. On May 6, G.P. wrote a letter to Josiah K. Lilly, Chairman of the Board of Eli Lilly Pharmaceutical Company in Indianapolis. Mr. Lilly was a wealthy benefactor of Purdue University. In the letter G.P. told Lilly that Amelia was completing final preparations for her second takeoff.

Because Mr. Lilly had been so extraordinarily friendly and helpful, Amelia had asked G.P. to write him about the world flight.

G.P. attached to the letter a copy of an editorial from the Springfield, Massachusetts *Union*. He told Lilly that it was characteristic of a great many such editorials. In one way or another they all said: "We're glad you've got the courage to carry on. Better luck next time."

Incidentally, he reminded Mr. Lilly any financial return or left-over money from this flight goes back into a permanent fund at Purdue.

The next evening G.P. telephoned Dr. Elliott at Purdue and talked with him about the letter he had sent to Mr. Lilly. He sent Dr. Elliott a copy of the Lilly letter, and also included a list of the thirty-eight major newspapers around the world that were going to be carrying AE's signed story of the flight. G.P. wrote that he had received a letter that morning from Admiral Leahy, Chief of Naval Operations, practically insisting that he provide the ships to be stationed half way between Honolulu and Howland and Howland and New Guinea, as was done the first time. Amelia had told him she did not want to put the authorities to that much trouble. This was a pleasant indication of the official attitude towards the flight.

There was nothing G.P. could do now but wait.

By the middle of May the Electra was rolled out onto the ramp at the Lockheed factory in Burbank, ready for functional ground testing of the repaired equipment.

Joe Gurr let Amelia know that the radio equipment was all installed; he was ready to show her the changes he had made. She met Gurr at the airplane, but she could stay only a limited time. He hurriedly told her how he had improvised the antenna loading coil to tune 500 kilocycles directly to the top antenna. It had yet to be actually checked in flight.

Gurr and Earhart entered the cockpit and put on headphones; he had her turn on the Bendix receiver. He asked her to tune in broadcast station KFI at 640 kilocycles. She very slowly cranked the band selector knob to band 2—400 to 780 kilocycles. She then turned the tuning knob until the dial read 640. As the station came in she had to turn the volume control down. KFI was a very powerful station and only a few miles away.

Gurr could tell from her hesitancy in tuning that she had not had sufficient time to become proficient at operating the Bendix receiver. He also wanted to make sure that she knew how to operate the radio direction-finder loop. He had her turn the direction-finder power switch on the loop control box to "ON" and then the loop selector switch to "R," for receiving. He explained that she must set the loop coupler frequency band selector to the same frequency as the Bendix receiver. Earhart turned the loop frequency band selector switch to "2" to match the band 2 selected on the Bendix receiver. But it was just a coincidence that band 2 on the loop coupler control box was suitable for resonating the direction-finder loop on 640 kilocycles. A listing of the five actual loop coupler frequency bands, covering from 200 to 1430 kilocycles, was written on the inside of the cover plate where Earhart couldn't see it. The only time she had ever used the direction-finder was going into Honolulu, when the low frequency of the Makapuu marine radio beacon was on band 1 of the Bendix receiver and the loop coupler was also set to band 1. The coincidence by which the Makapuu and KFI frequency band numbers happened to be the same on both the Bendix receiver and the loop coupler box was a classic human errors trap, a simple misunderstanding that would have tragic consequences.

By pure happenstance the first three bands of the radio receiver and the direction-finder loop were closely matched, and the direction-finder loop could obtain a bearing on bands 1, 2, and 3. However, the frequencies of the Bendix receiver's bands 4 and 5 were completely out of the design range of the direction-finder, and the loop could not process the signals to obtain bearings. But because both the loop coupler band selector and the Bendix receiver were marked with bands 1 to 5, Earhart thought she could take a radio bearing with her direction-finder loop on any signal between 200 and 10,000 kilocycles. She could not.

Without Manning, the information provided earlier by the Bendix representative, Cyril Remmlein, could not be conveyed to Earhart. None of the radiomen was aware of Earhart's mistaken assumption.

With Gurr's guidance she went through the steps of tuning and adjusting the loop. She eventually turned the loop to a position where the volume in her headphones dropped to a minimum. She stopped turning the loop when the volume was at the lowest minimum; the loop indicator was pointing toward KFI.

Earhart practiced taking the bearings until she felt she understood the process. Gurr explained to her that taking radio bearings on low-frequency radio beacons in the daytime would work well when she was close in. Radio beacons were mostly low power and not generally useful beyond a hundred miles. At night you could receive their sky waves farther away, but the bearings were not as reliable because the sky waves bounced unpredictably toward the loop from a variety of different angles, causing the reading to change. He believed the best stations to take radio bearings on were the broadcast stations. They were usually very powerful and could be received for two or three hundred miles. For really long range reception in the daytime, she would have to use the higher frequencies. Gurr mentioned that in the daytime his amateur station on 80 meters (3750 kilocycles) would generally reach only a few hundred miles. On 40 meters (7500 kilocycles), reaching over a thousand miles was not unusual. She would have to be very judicious in choosing the best frequency for radio direction-finding.

The available time was exhausted; Earhart had to leave for her other commitment. Before leaving, she posed with Gurr at the tail of the airplane. G.P. took a picture of the two of them together.

After studying the weather charts for the various locations on her route, Earhart decided to reverse her course. She would fly the Atlantic and African portions of the flight first. Her plan was to make a quick flight to Oakland, then return to Burbank all in the same day. This would serve as a crucial first test for the newly repaired plane. If those two flights went well, she would continue eastward across the country to Miami. By the time she reached Miami the plane and its equipment would have been well tested. She would know by then whether she should continue on around the world. If not, she would quietly return the plane to the factory in Burbank.

The plan was to avoid letting the press know that the flight was on again the moment she left Oakland. Amelia felt strongly that she could ill afford any more negative publicity. She wanted to delay committing herself publicly to the start of the flight until she was sure of the Electra's complete fitness.

Tuesday, May 18, turned out to be a very good day for the Putnams. G.P. was back home in North Hollywood when Lockheed called with the news that they were making a final test of the plane. It would be ready for delivery the following day.

In Indianapolis, Josiah K. Lilly dictated a letter to Dr. Elliott at Purdue: "Yes sir! I am quite willing to give $2,500 to the Research Foundation for the specific purpose of aiding Miss Earhart in her work. Will you be good enough to have Dr. Meikle tell me about when the remittance should go forward to the Foundation?"

Good as their word, Lockheed delivered the repaired Electra on Wednesday. The very next morning, May 20, 1937, Earhart quietly departed Burbank for Oakland.

Earhart never doubted that the crash in Honolulu was caused by some kind of mechanical failure. She saw no need to review throttle or other takeoff procedures with Lockheed. When the plane was delivered, she boarded the Electra with full confidence in her flying ability and resumed the world flight without hesitation.

8 : WORLD FLIGHT RESUMES—OAKLAND TO MIAMI

EARHART was in Oakland just long enough to pick up the philatelic envelopes she had left in Honolulu two months earlier. She made a short visual inspection of the plane before reentering the cockpit to take off for Burbank.

This would be the start of her second attempt to fly around the world. No announcement would be made. If Amelia was asked whether she was resuming the world flight, she would deny it, saying she was just testing her newly repaired plane.

Exactly five years ago she had taken off to become the first woman to solo the Atlantic, and ten years ago Lindbergh had flown from New York to Paris. At 3:50 P.M., Thursday, May 20, 1937, Amelia Earhart left Oakland, California, in an effort to become the first woman to fly around the world. The second world flight had begun.

The plane performed as if it were brand-new. When she landed in Burbank, shortly after 6:00 P.M., she knew it was ready to continue on to Miami. She parked it on the ramp by the Mantz Air Service hangar. Bo was to service the plane and to bring extra clothes with him the next day. They were flying east together for further tests of the plane.

WORLD FLIGHT–OAKLAND TO MIAMI
May 20–23, 1937

At home Amelia quickly packed the few clothes she would be taking. G.P. planned to fly with her as far as Miami, then go on to New York from there if she continued the world flight. He would remain in New York until Amelia was ready to leave Australia, when he would fly to Oakland to meet her on her return. He was still trying to find additional sponsors. They had had to mortgage the house in order to raise barely enough money for her expenses during the flight. The cash and American Express Travelers Checks that Amelia carried with her now would have to be spent judiciously.

Fred Noonan and Bee, now married for two months, were already at the hangar when Amelia and G.P. arrived the next afternoon. The Electra was on the ramp, and they began transferring the suitcases, thermos bottles, map case, and other equipment from their cars into the plane. A Mantz Air Service truck stood by on the ramp to run for any last-minute items they might need.

Amelia had a chance to talk to Bee while the men were loading the plane. Bee asked Amelia to encourage Fred to eat properly and drink lots of milk. She was worried because he was so thin. Amelia told Bee not to worry, as she was a great believer in proper nutrition. She would see that Fred ate well on the trip.

It was after two when Amelia, G.P., Fred, and Bo boarded the Electra to depart from Burbank. She had originally planned to fly nonstop to El Paso, Texas, but it was so late she decided they would go only as far as Tucson, Arizona. At 2:25 P.M. she took off from Union Air Terminal.

The sun was low in the west when they touched down at Tucson Municipal Airport, some 3 hours and 20 minutes after takeoff from Burbank. Earhart temporarily parked the plane at the airport office to arrange for hangar space. When she was restarting the engines to move the plane for servicing, the left engine backfired. The burst of flames set fire to accumulated excess fuel, and she immediately stopped the engine. She pulled the engine fire extinguisher handle, which discharged the Lux fire bottle automatically into the engine compartment and smothered the flames. There was no damage, and Earhart moved the plane to the municipal hangar. Bo had to replenish the extinguisher and clean the soot and extinguisher agent from the engine. The rest of the party retired to the Pioneer Hotel in Tucson.

They were up early because the plane was going to be heavy with fuel, and Earhart wanted to take off before the air temperature rose too high from the morning sun. Strong surface winds were blowing dust in west Texas, her destination, so she decided to bypass El Paso and fly nonstop to New Orleans. By 7:30 A.M. Saturday, May 22, they were airborne and on their way to New Orleans. It took about 8 hours and 40 minutes before they arrived at New Orleans's Shushan Airport. Again the sun was low in the western sky.

They stayed overnight at the airport hotel. After dinner, Amelia asked Fred where his wife was staying. Fred said she was still at the hotel in Hollywood but was planning to drive home to Oakland tomorrow. Amelia sent a Western Union telegram to Bee at the Hollywood Hotel: "JUST TO REPORT FRED DRANK TWO GLASSES OF MILK TODAY CHEERIO AE."

After a late Sunday morning breakfast, they left Shushan Airport for Miami, Florida. At 9:10 A.M. CST they took off and headed straight across the Gulf of Mexico toward Tampa Bay.

Fred was navigating and asked Amelia to stay at a low altitude. He wanted her to hold a constant heading on the compass and he would adjust it for drift as they flew 450 miles straight across the water to a landfall at Tampa, Florida. He would not be taking any celestial or radio fixes; instead he would keep track of the direction they flew right to the degree and would count up every mile they flew along that track. If they flew exactly 90 degrees (adjusted for wind and compass errors) east from New Orleans for one hour at 150 mph true airspeed, Fred would reckon that after one hour they were 150 miles due east (090 degrees) from New Orleans. (This is called navigating by dead reckoning, and it is how Earhart navigated to Ireland in 1932 and from Hawaii to California in 1935.)

At low altitude Fred could check the drift meter's indication against the actual surface wind that he could see on the water below. By having Amelia keep careful compass headings, Fred could check the accuracy of the compass on this easterly course. If they came directly on to Tampa, the compass would have zero deviation. If they ended up to the north or south of Tampa, he could measure the number of degrees the compass was off. The drift meter checked okay, but the autopilot, which was flying the plane, was swinging the plane back and forth through 30 degrees. The compass was never steady, and under those conditions Fred could not get a compass check.

Fred's dead reckoning along the track proved to be quite accurate. When they sighted the Florida coast west of Tampa, he was only one minute, or less than 3 miles, off his dead-reckoning estimate. That was after three hours and some 450 miles of navigating solely by dead reckoning across the waters of the Gulf. Fred's performance, at less than 1 percent error, was exceptionally good. Anything up to a maximum 10 percent of the distance traveled—45 miles in this case—could be considered a maximum reasonable error for dead reckoning.

Everyone acclaimed Fred's skill, and all aboard were very impressed. He graciously accepted their praise without mentioning that Pan American Airways pilots flew greater distances every day across the Caribbean navigating by dead reckoning. Unless there was a tropical depression or hurricane in the area, the trade winds were steady and dependable. Dead-reckoning navigation was not only easier in the tropics, but the benign atmosphere favored greater accuracy than pilots experienced in higher latitudes.

Amelia discovered another problem. Since taking delivery of the repaired plane, she had not used the Western Electric transmitter to call a radio station any great distance away. While they were out over the Gulf of Mexico she found that the distance her transmitter could reach was very limited.

At 3:04 P.M. EST Amelia touched down by mistake at Eastern's airport at Thirty-sixth Street in Miami. When she realized it was the wrong airport, she took off again and flew the plane over to the Miami Municipal Airport, where she had intended to land. Six minutes later, at 3:10 P.M. EST Sunday, May 23, while coming into the correct airport she misjudged her speed and height above the runway and made a very hard landing. The creak of metal could be heard all over the field as the plane came down with a thud.

She taxied the plane to the hangar and emerged to meet with reporters. Her first statement to them was, "I certainly smacked it down hard that time." She then turned to Fred and asked if that was the hardest letdown she had ever given him.

A reporter asked if she believed her round-the-world trip would be of scientific value, and she answered, no, not much. She was going for the trip. She was going for fun. Could they think of any better reason?

Arrangements had been made to keep the plane at a hangar. Bo stayed to look after the plane. Amelia, G.P., and Fred left for the Columbus Hotel.

Fred had to ask Bee to send him more money for his expenses on the flight. The trip was costing more than he had expected, and Amelia wasn't able to give him an advance.

The next morning Amelia was on the phone early to line up help for the work on the plane. The Sperry autopilot's rudder control needed attention, the radio transmitter wasn't putting out right, and Fred wanted the compasses to be swung for a deviation check. Amelia was also disturbed by the possibility that the hard landing she had made might have weakened the landing gear.

Pan American Airways agreed to send people from their Dinner Key maintenance base to the municipal airport to work on the plane. They would send an instrument mechanic to look at her autopilot, and a radio technician to check her transmitter. Amelia would return to the airport to meet them when they arrived.

Amelia drove the rented car, with G.P. and Fred as passengers, from their hotel to the airport. She parked in the shade of the hangar, where she could see Bo working by the plane.

His head was hidden up in the wheel well, but she knew it was Bo by the big block "AE" initials on the back of his coveralls. He was inspecting the landing gear with another mechanic, using flashlights and mirrors to look inside the dark and hidden areas. Amelia greeted them with "Good morning." Bo came out of the wheel well with a look of concern on his face.

He told her that so far they had not found any damage from the hard landing, but someone had scratched their initials on the steel strut of the landing gear. It was a highly stressed and critical area of the gear. The scratches could cause a concentration of load and possibly cause the gear to fail. Bo thought they should get Lockheed's opinion.

They went into the hangar office to place the call to Burbank. Amelia told the Lockheed technicians of the hard landing at Miami; the first question they asked was about the "G" loads of acceleration during the landing. Amelia had to tell them she didn't know. There wasn't an accelerometer in her plane, but this was the hardest landing she had ever made in it. They suggested installing a "G" meter to measure future accelerations.

Amelia put Bo on the phone. He told them about the scratches on the landing gear. They advised him to try to burnish and polish the scratches out. If the scratches were deep the strut might have to be replaced. When Bo got off the phone, he began right away to try to remove the scratches.

The Pan American mechanics from the Dinner Key base arrived to look at the autopilot and radio. Mr. Churchill, foreman of the instrument shop, had brought test equipment to check out the Sperry autopilot. Amelia described how the rudder control unit continuously swung the aircraft back and forth 15 degrees either side of the desired heading. The autopilot rudder had worked better before Sperry recently modified the connections to the rudder control unit.

Louis Michelfelder was sent from the Pan American radio shop to look at her radio. Amelia told him she was unable to transmit very far. She described to him the changes that had been made to the antenna system during the recent repairs. He immediately inspected the radio and antenna installations.

By midafternoon Bo reported there was no damage from the hard landing. They had successfully removed the scratched initials. Amelia was relieved not to have to face the major expense of replacing the landing gear strut.

Churchill could find nothing wrong with the autopilot in the plane, but he was going to take the rudder control unit into the shop for a bench check. Amelia asked him about getting an accelerometer instrument installed, and he told her he would arrange it.

Michelfelder asked Earhart how the 500-kilocycle channel had worked when she was transmitting. She told him that it had not been used since the new antenna was installed. She explained that neither she nor Noonan knew Morse code well enough to send and receive using it. The 500 kilocycles was only for an emergency. They could tap out "SOS" or just hold the key down to transmit for a radio bearing. Michelfelder responded that he would take the radios to the shop at Dinner Key for further checks. Once he was sure that the units were good, he would check that the antenna and loading coil were properly matched to the transmitter.

By late afternoon everything was being taken care of, and Amelia, G.P., and Fred returned to the hotel.

At the airport Amelia had told reporters that she greatly admired the transatlantic pilots Dick Merrill and Jack Lambie, who had recently flown a model 10-E Electra like hers on a round-trip between New York and London. They had returned from London with the first pictures of the coronation of King George VI. At the hotel a message was waiting inviting Earhart's group to attend the reception tonight for Merrill and Lambie. G.P. called to accept the invitation.

After dinner Amelia, G.P., and Fred were escorted to Bayfront Park for the reception. It seemed that all of Miami had decided to attend. The crowd filled all of the seats, aisles, and the outer rim of the park. It was estimated that between 10,000 and 15,000 people were there. Merrill and Lambie were presented with silver trophies by Mayor Williams on behalf of the city.

Earhart had little time to talk to Merrill and Lambie, but they did tell her that coming back from England they stayed low over the water at

1,500 feet. They maintained a constant indicated airspeed of 135 mph, and after all corrections had averaged a true airspeed of 140 mph. Merrill believed the 1,270 gallons of fuel onboard when he took off from England could have kept them going for at least 26 hours. The flight from England had actually taken approximately 24 hours. He still had a nearly full 97-gallon wing tank remaining when they arrived in New York.

Merrill's Lockheed 10-E had a fixed radio antenna on top very similar to Earhart's. Lambie, using voice and Morse code, was able to make radio contacts well over a thousand miles away. They had maintained a regular schedule at a quarter after each hour with Eastern Air Lines radio station WEEP in New York.

Back at the airport the next day, they learned that Churchill had thoroughly bench-checked the Sperry autopilot rudder unit and placed it back in the plane. Frederick Ralph Sias, Pan American instrument mechanic, came to install the accelerometer. He showed the "G" meter to Earhart, and they decided where to place it on the instrument panel.

Newspaper photographers took pictures of Earhart watching Bo and the mechanics work around the plane. Sias, an amateur photographer as well as an instrument mechanic, was especially interested in the cockpit. He took several pictures of the instrument-filled panels from different angles.

Earhart received word that the radios had tested well in the shop. Michelfelder would return the equipment to the plane and check the antenna installation. It was possible that the new antenna system wasn't properly matched electrically with the transmitter. He would readjust the antenna loading units to try to increase the transmitter's output.

Carl B. Allen, aviation editor for the *New York Herald-Tribune,* arrived in Miami to report on the flight preparations. Through Allen and the *Tribune* syndicate, Earhart announced that she had officially been on her round-the-world flight since leaving Oakland. Because of the changes in weather since March, she had reversed her course and would now fly from west to east over approximately the same equatorial route as was planned before.

Earhart told the readers that she would not attempt to use the code wireless set with which her plane was equipped when it took off from Oakland. She would depend entirely on voice broadcasts of her position on 3105 and 6210 kilocycles. She might take off for Puerto Rico and Africa on Sunday, but it was more likely she would depart Monday or Tuesday.

At the airport on Saturday they turned the airplane completely around, stopping at points to check the compasses. At the same time, Pan American radio technician Robert H. Thibert checked the accuracy of the radio direction-finder loop by taking radio bearings on broadcast station WQAM. Band 2 of the Bendix receiver and band 2 of the direction-finder loop coupler were both appropriate for WQAM's frequency. The loop pattern and deviation errors were normal. The direction-finder gave good bearings with a definite minimum when the loop was swung to point at the station.

The tail wheel of the Electra was raised up onto a wheeled dolly so the plane would be in flight attitude as it was rotated during the compass swing. Only the instrument and radio mechanics were in the plane. Unfortunately Earhart wasn't able to observe and talk with radioman Thibert as he checked the radio direction-finder. (When prototypes and untested equipment are newly installed on an airplane, they are notoriously unreliable. Even if the equipment is well designed and built, it has not yet been rigorously tested in the field. The new RA-1 receiver that Bendix had supplied was a perfect example of this. There was no manual for Earhart to study; she had to learn by trial and error.)

Though he tried most of the day, Michelfelder was never able to get the transmitter to tune properly to the antenna. He tried a different routing of the line from the transmitter to the antenna to shorten it, but the final tuning was still not satisfactory. He suggested she make a flight test the next day while local receivers monitored her frequencies. They telephoned WQAM and arranged for the station to monitor both 3105 and 6210 kilocycles while Earhart was making the test flight.

Michelfelder knew that some Pan American planes had fixed antennas similar to Earhart's. The range of their transmitters was a couple hundred miles with no more power than her Western Electric. The transmitter was checked and the antenna was a proven design. If she wasn't transmitting a good signal, the long antenna feed line must be causing the problem. They would have to shorten it.

Everyone agreed to meet at the airport and work on the plane. The first order of business was to check the plane and its systems. Amelia and Fred took off and flew along a half dozen test courses that Fred had laid out for Pan American several years before. He found the compasses to be performing about as accurately as it was possible to get them. Amelia tried to communicate with WQAM on both 3105 and 6210 kilocycles. Failing at that, she tried to reach the Bureau of Air Commerce airways station at the municipal airport. No one heard her signals. Finally, she turned on the autopilot to test the rudder control. It was still turning the plane back and forth just as before. An hour and a half later they returned and taxied up to the hangar where the Pan American technicians were waiting.

Fred reported that the compasses and navigational equipment checked okay, but Amelia had to report to the instrument mechanics that the rudder unit of the autopilot was still not right. They would have to remove the recent modifications to the rudder control connection. She asked them to replace the original installation and adjust it to meet her requirements.

Earhart told Michelfelder that she had been unable to reach anyone with the transmitter on either 3105 or 6210 kilocycles. Michelfelder believed that the long antenna feed line and loading coil would have to be removed. That would eliminate her ability to tune the transmitter to 500 kilocycles unless she installed a trailing wire antenna. He asked whether she wanted him to provide one.

Earhart decided she would scrap the 500-kilocycle channel. She told Michelfelder that since neither she nor Fred could use the Morse code key, the trailing wire antenna would be just one more thing to worry about.

The instrument mechanic removed the autopilot rudder unit, and Michelfelder began the work on the antenna feed line. They all hoped to be done in time for Earhart to test-fly the plane the next day. It would be Tuesday morning at the earliest before she could depart from Miami.

Amelia, Fred, Bo, and G.P. spent the rest of the day checking and loading the spare parts and supplies into the plane. When they were finished they returned for the night to the Columbus Hotel. While they were driving back, Fred sat on his glasses and broke them. He would have to have them replaced. Without glasses, he couldn't read the small print on his charts.

The next morning, Monday, May 31, was Memorial Day. At breakfast, Amelia told Fred they were going to the Dinner Key facility to thank all the Pan American people. If everything was ready, she wanted to take off early the next morning for San Juan. She planned to fuel the plane later in the day. They agreed to have 600 gallons onboard for the flight. Fred was to get his new eyeglasses, then meet them at Dinner Key.

G.P. and Amelia drove to the Pan American seaplane base at Dinner Key, arriving just before nine o'clock. They toured the maintenance facilities, talking to the various shop foremen and mechanics who had helped them so much over the last week. Fred came later with two new pairs of reading glasses.

Earhart was impressed with Pan American's shops and people. In talks with the crew who had been working on her autopilot she was convinced that it was in good order and would serve her on the flight. The radio technicians were as sure about her radio as the instrument mechanics were about her autopilot. When she transmitted on 3105 or 6210 kilocycles her transmitter would be working at maximum efficiency. The antenna installation was completely standard in design. They were sure it was tuned to match her transmitter's output and would radiate a good signal. Earhart decided that a further test flight was unnecessary. She would take off for San Juan, Puerto Rico. If the autopilot and transmitter proved satisfactory, she would continue to San Juan. If not, the flight would turn into another test flight and she would return to Miami.

G.P. asked about the status of the 500-kilocycle channel. It was explained that without the loading coil, the antenna was a complete mismatch. The transmitter could still generate the 500-kilocycle signal, but it was unlikely the antenna would radiate much of it. They were uncertain just how much output there might be. It was unpredictable. Somehow G.P. took this to mean that the usability of 500 kilocycles was dubious.

Pan American's meteorologist gave Earhart a favorable forecast for a flight to San Juan on Tuesday. They would be sending similar weather forecasts to her as long as she was flying over their routes. WQAM in Miami would broadcast them over the air. For her part, Earhart would send her position reports and brief messages on how things were going on the flight at 15 minutes before and 15 minutes after the hour. She would listen to WQAM on the hour to get any messages or updates. Such a relay through WQAM was necessary because Pan American's stations transmitted only by Morse code, which neither Earhart nor Noonan knew. Earhart collected a few spare parts to take with her on the flight before they left Dinner Key.

The U.S. Coast Guard Miami Air Station was located next door to the Pan American Airways facility. Earhart informed the Coast Guard of the radio procedures and frequencies she would be using when she left Miami. She would not try to communicate with any radio station but would broadcast her position at 15 and 45 minutes past each hour on 6210 kilocycles. She could also transmit on 3105 kilocycles. She told

George Palmer Putnam and Amelia Earhart at home in Rye, New York.

Amelia Earhart is greeted in Oakland, California, on January 12, 1935, upon being the first aviator to fly solo from Hawaii to California.

Captain Harry Manning, Earhart's original navigator, along with Earhart; Paul Mantz, her maintenance expert; and Fred Noonan, the navigator who replaced Manning for the around-the-world flight.

E arhart with Manning, who is holding a bubble octant, in February 1937.

E arhart and radio expert Cyril Remmlein examine a radio direction-finder loop and a coupler control box before installing them in Earhart's Electra.

E arhart signing commemorative envelopes carried on the "world flights"; at left, examples of the envelopes from the original and second takeoffs.

Mantz in the cockpit and Earhart and Noonan on the wing of the Electra just after the plane crashed while taking off from Luke Field near Honolulu on March 20, 1937.

Earhart in front of a map tracing the route of her planned Pacific crossing.

Radioman Joseph Gurr with Earhart at the tail of the Electra.

Pan American Airways mechanic F. Ralph Sias took this photo of the Electra's instrument panel about May 26 in Miami. Note the sharp-edged Bendix radio control box (upper left corner) mounted above where Earhart's head would be.

Earhart's Electra in the hangar at Darwin, Australia, on June 28.

Earhart coming down off the wing after landing at Lae, New Guinea, on June 29.

Barrels of aviation fuel stored in the shade of trees at Lae to prevent overheating.

Earhart taking off for Howland Island from the grass runway at Lae at 10 A.M. on July 2. This is the last known photograph of the Electra before it disappeared.

(Right, top) **H**owland Island, only half a mile wide and a mile and a half long—a flat, barren speck in the Pacific Ocean. This photo was taken from an altitude of 1,000 feet looking north-northeast toward the western shore, the view Earhart and Noonan were desperately seeking.

(Right, bottom) **T**he *Itasca* makes smoke as boats bring ashore a landing party to assist Earhart on her arrival. Note how the smoke lies on the surface and dissipates as it drifts away.

The U.S. Coast Guard cutter *Itasca* at a dock in Honolulu in 1936.

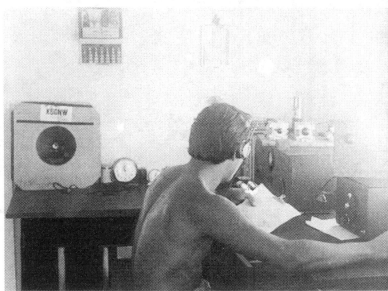

Amateur radio operator Yau Fai Lum, "K6GNW," on Howland Island, July 2, 1937. Daily radio schedules were maintained with Honolulu, Baker Island, and the *Itasca*.

A World War II Navy fighter plane, recovered in surprisingly good condition after 26 years in the Pacific, is washed down on the deck of a ship.

them her receiver would be used most of the time for taking radio bearings. Earhart said she would not attempt to use the "code wireless set" with which the plane was equipped when it took off from Oakland. This information was not included in the message later originated by the Miami Coast Guard Air Station, an oversight that would have tragic consequences.

After lunch Amelia, G.P., and Fred drove to the municipal airport to check on the Electra. The mechanics were still working on the plane; it would be late in the afternoon before they could finish. She arranged for Bo to fuel the plane and have it ready for takeoff at dawn. The hotel had been notified to wake them at 2:45 A.M.

At the airport the mechanics and technicians finished their work and returned to Dinner Key. It was late when Bo finally completed his last inspection. The Electra was fueled with 600 gallons of gas and ready to go. He had the plane put back into the hangar and locked up for the night.

In the morning they left the hotel and arrived at the Voelter hangar just after four o'clock. Earhart and Noonan's two suitcases were placed aboard the plane along with their maps, vacuum bottles of coffee, tomato juice, and ham and egg sandwiches.

At 4:30 they opened the hangar doors, and Bo rolled the Electra out onto the concrete apron that connected to the airfield ramp. The lights of an almost continuous string of autos could be seen on Ninety-sixth Street, heading west from N.W. Twenty-seventh Avenue, along the southern boundary of the field. Despite the early hour people were coming to see Amelia Earhart take off for a flight around the world.

Amelia and G.P. came out to the plane parked in front of the hangar. Amelia checked that the chocks were firmly in front of the wheels. It was still dark as she went up onto the wing and entered the cockpit. After closing the overhead hatch, she started the engines. When they were warm, she checked them carefully for about 20 minutes. No sooner had the propellers stopped than she came out of the cockpit to speak to Bo. During the check she had noticed that one of the cylinder head temperature gauges wasn't registering. Bo set about fixing the broken thermocouple wire. In less than a half hour he had completed the work, and the plane was ready to go.

Fred entered the cockpit first and moved over into the right seat. Amelia let herself down into the left seat. G.P. climbed up on the wing and talked to Amelia for a moment through the open hatch. Photographers' flashbulbs were popping as they took pictures of the moments before departure. G.P. came down from the wing, and Amelia started the engines again at approximately 5:40 A.M.

After checking that the cylinder head temperature gauge was working, Amelia signaled for the chocks to be pulled from in front of her wheels. She received an all clear signal before adding power to taxi toward the southwest corner of the field. Bo followed close behind in the car.

Dawn was fast approaching. It was already light enough for Amelia to see by the wind sock that the wind was now blowing from the northwest. She taxied across the south end of the field to the southeast corner so she could take off on the 3,600-foot diagonal runway directly into the northwest wind.

When Amelia stopped at the runway's end, Bo got out of the car and ran up to the plane. They had overgreased the constant speed propeller bearings. Grease was being splattered on the propeller blades. He checked that the grease was the source of the spattering and not an oil leak. He reassured Amelia that everything was okay, then returned to the car.

A few moments later Amelia applied power and began her takeoff roll. Only 2,000 feet and a little more than 25 seconds were required for her to lift the wheels off Miami Municipal's macadam runway. They were on their way to San Juan, Puerto Rico, at 5:56 A.M. EST.

It was a good thing Amelia had made the eastbound flight cross-country to Miami. The installation changes made in Burbank—Sperry's to the autopilot, and Gurr's to the transmitting antenna—had proven defective. The technicians from Pan American were able to undo the damage and correct the problems. The only thing she had lost was something she never really had, the ability to send a signal on 500 kilocycles. Now, with the Morse key completely removed, there was no practical way anyone could tap out a Morse code signal. Amelia had told the Coast Guard, Pan American, and the whole world through the press how she would be transmitting her positions. She was not sure she would ever know if anyone heard her or not.

At last she was on her way. The sturdy Electra was in perfect condition; its Pratt & Whitney engines tried and true. The propeller blades were changed and worked fine. She would lubricate them often and watch them carefully. The electrical overload lesson had been well learned going into Honolulu. Sitting next to her was one of the best aerial navigators in the world. She had crossed oceans before with a lot less in her favor. The world flight was looking good. Amelia couldn't help but be pleased.

G.P. stayed at the airport awhile, just in case Amelia and Fred should return. Once they were definitely on their way around the world, he had a lot of work to do. The Army, Navy, and Coast Guard must be notified and their efforts coordinated. Everyone must be in position before she started the dangerous Pacific crossing at the end of her trip.

9 : WORLD FLIGHT—
MIAMI TO DAKAR

The Electra cleared the power lines at the western end of the Miami airport by at least 50 feet. At 500 feet, Amelia banked to turn toward the southeast and San Juan, Puerto Rico. It took only 13 minutes to reach 3,500 feet, where she leveled off to cruise.

After setting the power, Amelia engaged the autopilot to check it, and, satisfied that all was well, sent her first radio report on 6210 kilocycles. Her transmitter was putting out a good signal and the message was received in Miami. She reported, "FLYING AT 3,500 FEET AND EVERYTHING OKAY." There was no equivocation of intent now. Amelia and Fred were off on a flight that would take them around the world.

Back at the Miami Municipal Airport G.P. had been waiting for the message that everything was okay. It was good news that no more work by the mechanics would be required. Already the bill for services from Pan American Airways totaled $665.

At 7:00 A.M. the plane was passing Andros Island in the Bahamas. They were bucking 25 mph headwinds, and Fred was keeping their course by looking out the window and matching the ground features to his map.

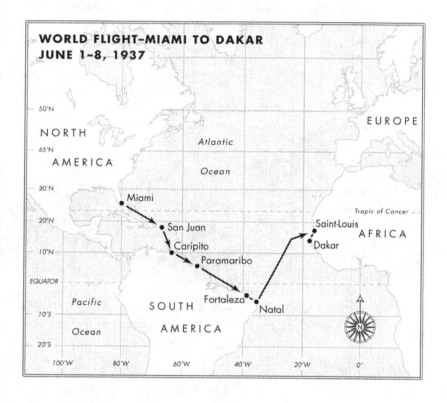

The Department of Commerce radio station at Miami last heard Amelia's radio at 8:45 A.M. EST, when she was estimated to be 410 miles from Miami. The radiomen at Pan American thought this was a surprisingly good daylight range for an aircraft's radiotelephone transmission on 6210 kilocycles.

After listening to a weather report from WQAM, Amelia tuned her receiver to around 1300 kilocycles. She could make out her name being mentioned on a Spanish language radio station. From now on, as she flew over the continents, until she reached Australia, foreign language broadcasts would be the rule.

Around noon Fred told Amelia that they were too far north and had her change the course to the right. They were flying over the ocean somewhere north of the Dominican Republic at the time. A little later, the shoreline of Puerto Rico appeared out of the haze. They followed along its north coast to the city of San Juan and the Isla Grande Airport.

The runway at Isla Grande was only 2,100 feet long, and there was construction on the field. Amelia brought the plane in low over the threshold and touched down about 1:30 P.M. EST. It had taken approximately 7 hours and 34 minutes to fly the 1,033 statute miles from Miami. To minimize the effect of the 25 mph headwind on their range, they had flown an average true airspeed of 161.5 mph. Their ground speed had averaged 136.5 mph.

Clara Livingston, a pilot friend of Amelia's from New York, was their host. She drove Amelia and Fred 20 miles from San Juan to her 1,600-acre plantation at Dorado for the night.

Early in the evening G.P. telephoned and talked to Amelia, but by eight o'clock they were all in bed with the alarm clocks set for 3:45 A.M.

It was still dark when they left the plantation for the San Juan Airport after 4:00 A.M. They arrived at the Pan American hangar before five o'clock, and the weather forecast was waiting for them. Headwinds of 25 knots, or 29 mph, were predicted all the way to Paramaribo in Dutch Guiana (now Suriname). Amelia would need as much fuel to make this flight as she had taken from Miami. The 2,100-foot runway at San Juan was too short for that. She decided they would have to stop at Caripito, Venezuela, to refuel.

The distance to Caripito was slightly more than 600 statute miles. At an airspeed of 161 mph it would take a little over four and a half hours. The Electra, now lighter than it had been out of Miami, climbed rapidly from San Juan to 8,000 feet, where Amelia leveled off to cruise. They flew across Puerto Rico on a course that would take them across the Caribbean Sea directly to their Venezuelan destination.

On the hour, Amelia turned on the Bendix receiver to listen for a weather broadcast from WQAM in Miami. She tuned the receiver but heard nothing.

From the south coast of Puerto Rico there were only clouds and sea for the next three hours. Fred would occasionally take a reading with the drift meter by sighting on the whitecaps on the waves far below. He would adjust their compass heading accordingly. If the drift meter indicated they were drifting to the right, he would compensate by changing the plane's heading an equal amount to the left. After more than 450 miles of dead reckoning, they made a landfall at Isla de Margarita just as Fred expected. As the island passed, a check of their overall ground speed indicated an 18 mph headwind. Amelia wrote in her notes: "Strong headwind, airspeed 160, ground speed 142, outside temperature 70 degrees."

Through the haze Amelia caught her first sight of South America and the Venezuelan coast. She flew across the Paria Peninsula and followed the river through the coastal mountain pass to Caripito's airfield. It was a well-equipped airport located in the heart of Venezuela's oil country.

Amelia touched down on the paved runway about 10:52 A.M. Venezuelan time, after an approximately 4-hour, 32-minute flight from San Juan. The plane was guided to park in front of the hangar. Amelia's fame had preceded her; a group of officials was on hand to greet them.

Amelia wanted to continue to Paramaribo, but the forecast was for strong headwinds and heavy rain showers. They expected tomorrow's conditions to be much improved, though the headwinds would persist. Even with the headwinds, they could have made Paramaribo before dark by using maximum cruise power, but Amelia decided against it. They left the airport and stayed overnight at the Standard Oil Company general manager's residence in Caripito.

Not being able to reach the next desired destination before dark was a problem that would constantly delay their progress. When she changed the direction of the world flight from westward to eastward, Amelia effectively shortened each period of daylight by two hours. At the equator, for each 900 nautical miles the Electra flew, the time of sunset would change by one hour. If she were flying west she would gain an hour of daylight, but by flying to the east she lost an hour.

Fred was so tired he went back to sleep when he was first awakened. It was Thursday, June 3, and the sun was already up when they arrived back at the airport. The headwinds were still predicted, but heavy clouds and rain showers were forecast for only the first half of the route. They were able to take off from Caripito at 8:48 A.M. Venezuelan time.

They flew across time zones so rapidly that there could be time zone confusion between Fred and Amelia. Fred eliminated this by referring to Amelia's cockpit clock, always set to the time in the time zone of their point of departure.

Out of Caripito, Amelia leveled off below the clouds. She flew southeastward along the shore dodging the heaviest of the rain showers. She was finally forced to climb to 8,000 feet. Headwinds cut their ground speed down to 132 mph. After they passed Georgetown, British Guiana (now Guyana), the weather improved and she was able to descend. The city of Paramaribo was located a few miles from the coast, along the Suriname River. They were to land at the Zandery Airport some 25 miles farther inland.

They touched down approximately 4 hours and 50 minutes after leaving Carapito. The local time at Paramaribo was 2:38 P.M. Dutch Guiana time. A director with a white flag guided Amelia to the parking area. She cut the engines and deplaned to meet the waiting Dutch and American officials.

Amelia told them she planned to leave in the morning for Fortaleza, Brazil, and would like to fuel the plane before leaving the field. The soldiers helped pump the gas from drums into the plane. After they finished, it took an hour by train to reach the city, where Amelia and Fred checked into the Palace Hotel. Pan American Airways employees stayed at the hotel, and Fred enjoyed visiting with his former associates.

On Friday, June 4, they were up and on the train heading to Zandery airfield before dawn. It was too early to get the new forecasts from Pan American Airways at Paramaribo. They would have to fly more than 1,300 miles to Fortaleza without current weather information. Airborne at 7:10 A.M. Dutch Guiana time, the Electra barely skimmed over the trees at the airport's edge. Amelia turned to head direct to Fortaleza.

Their route cut straight across the interior jungles of Dutch and French Guiana. Pan American Airways always flew along the coast, but Amelia and Fred's route took them across the mountains and jungle to the Amazon Basin of Brazil. They would not see the Atlantic Ocean again until after they had passed the Amazon River. Amelia would soon cross the equator into the southern hemisphere for the first time. They arrived at Fortaleza after a flight of about 9 hours and 20 minutes. It was approximately 5:00 P.M. Brazilian eastern time.

The manager of the airport was there to meet them. He put the extensive facilities of Pan American Airways at their disposal. Amelia decided to stay for an extra day to have work done on the plane. Sunday they would fly on to Natal, Brazil, where she planned to take off for the Atlantic crossing.

The overhead hatch had leaked when they flew through the rain showers out of Caripito. The Pan American Airways mechanics went to work giving the plane a complete check.

Amelia and Fred stayed at the Excelsior Hotel. The next morning after breakfast they went shopping. They bought some sponge rubber to seal the leaky cockpit overhead hatch and coveralls to wear when working on the plane.

After lunch they went to the airport to check on the plane. The mechanics continued their work while Amelia and Fred checked and reloaded the spares and equipment. The fuel was loaded for the short flight to Natal, and Amelia and Fred went back to the hotel. Fred picked up the charts they had used flying from Miami to Fortaleza. Amelia mailed her flight notes along with the charts back to G.P. in New York.

After dinner they both retired early to their rooms and wrote letters home before going to sleep. The plan was to leave as early as possible in the morning, because if the Atlantic weather permitted, they might continue through to Africa on the same day.

It rained heavily during the night, but Sunday morning, June 6, dawned bright and sunny. They checked out of the hotel and arrived at the airport shortly after six o'clock.

The Electra, lightly loaded for the flight of less than 300 miles to Natal, took off rapidly. They departed from Fortaleza at 6:50 A.M. Brazilian eastern time, or 0950 GMT. Amelia checked the engines and systems carefully en route to Natal, since the next flight would be across the Atlantic.

She flew along the coast and actually spotted the Parnamirio Airport before she saw the town of Natal. A heavy rain shower was fast approaching the field from the other direction. She landed just before the squall reached the field. As they taxied to the hangar, the tropical downpour hit with full force. Amelia shut the engines down just outside the hangar entrance. With the rain coming down in torrents, the mechanics and workmen pushed the plane into the hangar before Amelia and Fred deplaned. The flight had taken approximately 2 hours and 5 minutes.

Natal was the major jumping-off place for flights between South

America and Africa. Air France alone had two mail flights each week across the South Atlantic. Amelia conferred with the Air France meteorologists about the forecast to Dakar, French West Africa (presently Senegal). They told her she could expect headwinds of 20 mph for the first half of the trip. The worst of the weather would be near the equator about 800 miles out of Natal.

The Air France crews preferred to take off in the early morning hours before daylight so as to fly through the worst of the weather in the morning hours. Amelia decided to follow their lead by refueling and preparing her plane for an early morning takeoff. She would depart about three o'clock, so she alerted the people at the field of her intentions. With the plane fueled and ready to go, they left for the hotel in Natal.

They retired early and were awakened shortly after midnight. There was no moon, and a light rain was falling as they left the hotel for the Parnamirio Airport. Rain was still falling when they arrived at about 1:00 A.M. A photographer was there to take her picture. Amelia laughed when the powder in his old-fashioned flash pan got so wet from the rain that it wouldn't burn.

At the Air France meteorological office, they were briefed by the weathermen and given the latest forecasts. Amelia thanked the meteorologists and went to the hangar to get the plane ready for departure. Unfortunately, the wind at the airport was blowing directly across the long lighted runway. Amelia would have to use a shorter, unlighted grass runway if she wanted to take off into the wind.

Using flashlights, Amelia and Fred went to the runway and walked the length of it. They shined their lights in the dark to reveal landmarks that would guide them during the takeoff. Satisfied that the runway's grassy surface was suitable, with no obstructions or rough spots, they returned to the hangar.

They boarded the plane and taxied to the unlighted runway. It was very dark, but the landing lights in the nose of the aircraft allowed Amelia to make her way. When they were ready to go, she advanced the throttles to takeoff power. The plane accelerated steadily down the dark grass runway. The wheels left the ground of South America at 3:13 A.M. Brazilian eastern time, 0613 GMT. It was Monday, June 7, 1937. No woman pilot had ever made this flight before.

The weather predictions were accurate. They made their way toward Dakar, mostly flying through heavy rain in the early morning hours. Afterward, there were no celestial observations drawn on Noonan's charts, nor any mention in Amelia's notes about the sighting of Fernando De Naronha or any of the other islands along their way. They were holding the compass course to Dakar and dead reckoning their position along that course by estimating their ground speed. As they flew more and more miles they would be less and less sure of their position, and their area of uncertainty would grow larger.

At 7:15 A.M. Amelia broadcast on 6210 kilocycles, "ALL IS WELL, AND EVERYTHING IS GOING FINE." Amelia never knew whether anyone ever heard her messages, but Natal had received the report from a distance of nearly 600 miles. She tried listening to the Bendix receiver, but concluded that it was not functioning and was useless for navigation.

By 9:00 A.M., 1200 GMT, the rain was slackening, and the clouds were breaking up and thinning. They were coming to the northern edge of the equatorial zone of convergence that occurs near the equator in early June. (As June progresses, that is, the band of weather associated with the equatorial front follows the sun farther northward. By July, the worst of the weather is several hundred miles north of the equator.)

Contrary to what might at first seem true, the navigation of the flight into Dakar was actually more difficult than that of the flight into Howland Island.

AFTER more than six and a half hours and 950 miles of dead reckoning from Natal, the area of uncertainty would be a circle with a 95-mile radius around their dead reckoned position. Fred took his first observation of the sun at 1240 GMT. Their procedure was for Amelia to hand-fly the plane, keeping it as steady as possible, while Fred took his observations. (Aerial navigators use a bubble octant, as marine navigators use a sextant, to measure the angle of celestial objects in respect to the horizon. Because many times haze or clouds obscure the natural horizon, the bubble acts as an artificial horizon to tell a navigator when the octant is level. For greatest accuracy, it is important that the plane be flown smoothly without any changes in direction, speed, or altitude.)

The sun was directly in front of the plane, and Fred made the observations through the windshield from the copilot's seat. The result of a sun observation is a single line of position that is always perpendicular to the azimuth (direction) of the sun. Because the sun was directly in front of the plane, when Fred plotted the 1240 GMT sun line of position on his chart, it ran at right angles directly across their course and would indicate their speed. He knew only that they were somewhere along that sun line of position but not whether they were to the left or right of their course. (An observation made to either side, which will indicate if the plane is to the left or right of course, is called a course line.) A few minutes later Fred passed a note to Amelia reporting that they had averaged a ground speed of 147 mph since taking off from Natal.

Because Fred's sun observations would be accurate within 15 miles, the area of uncertainty is modified by eliminating all of the 95-mile-radius circle that is more than 15 miles either side of the 1240 GMT sun line of position. Thus the 1240 GMT area of uncertainty was 30 miles wide and 190 miles long, centered on the Natal-to-Dakar course.

About midway they passed the Air France mail plane *City of Montevideo*. It had departed Dakar at 3:00 A.M. with 617 pounds of mail, going in the opposite direction to Natal. It would have been useful if they could have exchanged information, but Air France, like Pan American Airways, operated exclusively by Morse code telegraphy.

The higher clouds were broken and the general visibility was good. The time was near when the sun would be at its highest, or what navigators call local apparent noon. Unlike maritime navigators, who can measure from a solid fixed horizon, an aerial navigator using the bubble horizon cannot easily determine accurately the exact time of the sun's zenith. A little before 1340 GMT, Fred asked Amelia to hold the plane steady for his sightings. At 1341 GMT, his average observation of the sun's elevation above the horizon was near 75 degrees. Its azimuth or line of direction was due north at 360 degrees. He plotted the resulting east–west 090–270-degree line of position at 7 degrees 37 minutes of north latitude. Because the sun was obliquely off to the left of their course to Dakar, the sun's line of position was neither a speed line nor a course line. Fred could be sure of neither their speed nor their course. They were just somewhere on the line 090–270. Fred moved the 1240 GMT speed line forward along their course about 150 statute miles to account for the distance the plane had traveled at 147 mph during the intervening one hour and one minute. (Where the advanced 1240 and 1341 GMT sun lines cross each other is called a running fix. Errors using this procedure reduce the fix's accuracy.) Under the circumstances, Fred could be only 90 percent certain of his position within a trapezoidal area measuring 30 by 60 miles. The 1341 GMT area of uncertainty was bounded 15 miles north and south of the 090–270 line, but because of the 150 miles traveled since 1240 GMT the boundary was 30 miles each side of the 1240 GMT advanced line.

Variations in window glass, bubble motion, atmospheric refraction, Coriolis force, semi-diameters, parallax, chronometer time, tabular errors, and a host of other variables conspire to make celestial navigation from an airplane as much an art form as a science. Because celestial observations are so predictably inaccurate, navigators' credentials are established by their judgment in determining the current area of uncertainty as well as their mechanical ability in taking a celestial fix.

Fred passed a note to Amelia saying they were a little north of course. At 11:15 A.M. Natal time, she changed the compass heading to 076 degrees. They were less than five hours from Dakar.

The flight settled into a routine. Fred took drift sights when the ocean was visible below. Amelia made notes in her stenographer's pad as events occurred.

They flew into some cumulus clouds, and heavy rain splattered onto the windshield. The rainwater mixed with the grease and oil that had previously been slung onto the glass by the propellers to make a smeary brown emulsion that Amelia couldn't see through.

While checking the fuel consumption rates, Amelia noticed that one of the Eclipse fuel flow meters was reading zero. It was inoperative, but there was ample fuel and it wasn't something she needed to worry about.

It was coming up on 1:30 P.M. Natal time, or 1630 GMT. The clouds had thinned, and Fred asked Amelia to hold the plane steady again. The average of the sights he took of the sun at 1630 GMT was near 44 degrees above the horizon. The sun's azimuth was 291 degrees. The line of position, at right angles to the azimuth of 291 degrees, ran reciprocally 021–201 degrees. Fred plotted the 021–201-degree line of position on his chart. Like the 1341 GMT sun line it was at an oblique angle to their course and neither a course nor a speed line.

He now had a line of position he could depend on within 15 miles, but since they had traveled approximately 450 miles along their dead reckoned course he could reasonably be anywhere 60 miles to the left or right of course. Fred could be only 90 percent certain that their position was somewhere within this 30-by-120-mile area.

The accuracy of navigation depends upon the ability of a navigator to periodically fix his position, and Fred had nothing since 1341 GMT. Because the last ten hours of the flight were all in daylight and there was no moon, Fred had been unable to fix his position.

At 1700 GMT, and again at 1800 GMT, Fred took more sun lines to follow their progress closely. Now, late in the afternoon, the sun's azimuth was holding nearly steady at 291 degrees, which produced the same oblique line of position 021–201 degrees. He decided to make his approach to Dakar from the south and use the sun line as a course line. He could change their course to Dakar by flying eastward until the course to Dakar became 021 degrees. He could only reckon the time when they would arrive at Dakar, but the sun lines would guide the plane with reasonable accuracy on a course heading directly toward it.

Dakar's Ouakam Airport was located at the western end of the Cape Verde Peninsula. If Dakar were on an island instead of connected to the African mainland by the peninsula, it would be exactly as if they were approaching an island in the middle of the ocean. They would fly until they were sure they were off to one side of the island, in this case to the south, then use the small amount of error accumulated from the recent sun line of position to guide their approach course.

Fred plotted the 1800 GMT line of position. A few minutes later he would have Amelia turn to intercept the 021 degrees true course that ran through Dakar. He calculated they would intercept that line in 36 minutes, at 1836 GMT. It was necessary to adjust the 21 degrees true course for local variation and drift. Fred added 18 degrees for the westerly variation and subtracted 3 degrees for the right drift. The final approach compass heading to Dakar would be 36 degrees.

Fred wrote a note and passed it up to Amelia clipped on the end of a bamboo pole. The note read: "3:36 change to 36 degrees. Estimate 79 miles to Dakar from 3:36 PM." The time was Natal time, to which Amelia's cockpit clock was set.

This was Fred's best estimate of their position, but they could be anywhere within the area of uncertainty. The Electra had traveled approximately 100 miles since the 1800 GMT 021–201, north–south sun line of position, and 820 miles since the 1341 GMT 090–270, east–west sun line. Their area of uncertainty was now bounded by 25 miles to the east and west, and 97 miles to the north and south. At 1836 GMT Fred could be only 90 percent certain they were somewhere within the 50-by-194-mile area centered on his dead reckoned point 79 miles from Dakar.

At 3:36 P.M. Natal time, 1836 GMT, Amelia turned the plane to a heading of 036 degrees on the compass. A few minutes later she turned the elevator control on the autopilot to drop the nose slightly downward. The plane picked up speed as she descended into the murky haze below. She adjusted the throttles and mixtures as they continued descending toward Dakar.

Fred must have judged that Amelia had done a good job of flying the headings when he wrote "79 miles to Dakar at 3:36 P.M." Under the circumstances, there was no way for Fred to know accurately their north–south position on the 021–201 Dakar line. Where they actually were, up and down the sun lines, depended on the accuracy of their dead reckoning navigation since his last fix at 1341 GMT. Fred obviously had a high degree of confidence in the Electra's compass.

He came forward over the tanks into the cockpit, bringing with him a chart of the coast of Africa near Dakar. The visibility in the haze was very poor; Fred estimated it to be no more than a mile. Under the circumstances, if they were to the west they could easily fly past Dakar without seeing it. It would be safer if they few eastward until they hit the coastline, then followed the shore to the airport. He had Amelia turn due east and hold the heading at 090 degrees.

After about 10 minutes they came over the coastline. It was a rather featureless area that ran northeast and southwest. Fred looked at his map for a coast that ran northeast and southwest. It became obvious that they had passed the Cape Verde Peninsula and were north of Dakar. After more than 12 hours in the noisy cockpit sitting right between the engines, they were both nearly deaf. Fred raised the map for Amelia to see as he pointed to the coastline north of Dakar. He indicated for her to turn right and head back to the south.

Amelia asked Fred, writing on the bottom of his earlier note, "What put us north?" Fred pondered the possibilities. The flight visibility had been very poor in the thick haze. They had passed more than 5 miles to the west of Cape Verde. Just the initial 15-mile possible error of the sun line could have caused that to happen. The sun line approach procedure itself was not at fault. The problem was the use of the line-of-position approach procedure in a situation where the reasonable error exceeded the visibility. That might explain what put them west, but it did not address the question of what had put them north.

They had actually passed Dakar's airport on the tip of the Cape Verde Peninsula at about 1841 GMT. Fred was about 66 miles north of his 1836 GMT assumed position. That was a total dead reckoning error of nearly 7 percent, still within the normal 10 percent error. Less than 5 degrees of unknown westerly compass deviation would account for the error. Fred had done nothing wrong, but just as Captain Manning had found when flying into Burbank, celestial navigation has limited accuracy. Radio direction-finder bearings were sometimes essential. It was too bad the Bendix receiver was not functioning and they didn't know Morse code. Amelia could easily have worked the French radio direction-finding station at Dakar to help Fred fix their position.

Fred did not know what had put them north.

The sun was only a few degrees above the horizon. It would be setting in little more than 20 minutes. Amelia knew there were suitable airports maintained by the French approximately every hundred and fifty miles along the coast north of Dakar. There was nothing for hundreds of miles to the south of Dakar. The visibility behind them was very poor, and it would soon be dark. Ahead to the north was an airport of some kind. To the south she could not be as positive of the outcome. Amelia decided it was best to turn left and continue up the coast toward the north. As it turned out, this was the wrong direction but the right decision. It was the safest thing to do.

In less than 20 minutes they were circling over an airport located on an island in the middle of a river. After a short time circling over the island, Fred pointed on the map to show Amelia that the island and river matched with the location of Saint-Louis, in French West Africa (now Senegal). They were only about 120 miles north of Dakar, but the sun was on the horizon. It would be dark before they could retrace their way.

Amelia brought the Electra down for a landing at Saint-Louis at approximately 7:35 P.M. local time, 1935 GMT. Including circling and the time to identify Saint-Louis, it had taken approximately 13 hours and 22 minutes to cross the Atlantic. Amelia Earhart was the first woman pilot to have flown from South America to Africa. She had piloted across both the north and south Atlantic.

Amelia wrote her dispatch about the Atlantic crossing and cabled it to the *Tribune* syndicate. The French cable company could not send it to New York collect. The charges were more than Amelia could continue to afford.

They went to the weather office to talk to the Air France meteorologist. If they were going to fly across the center of Africa they would fly to Dakar tomorrow. If not, and they decided to fly around the top of Africa, they would continue north from Saint-Louis.

The interior of Africa was having a hot spell. On a direct course across central Africa, the weathermen thought Amelia could fly south of the Sahara sandstorms and north of the monsoon rains. They did not believe it would be necessary for her to fly around Africa via the northern route.

Amelia and Fred were shown to rooms at the Air France quarters and retired for the night. It had been a long day. Amelia left the light on all night in her room to keep the mosquitoes and other creatures from venturing out.

The next morning, Tuesday, June 8, they were up at daylight. There had been no dramatic changes in the weather in the interior of Africa. Amelia considered taking off directly from Saint-Louis to Niamey, in French West Africa (now Niger) but decided against it. The Saint-Louis airfield wasn't as suitable for a heavyweight takeoff as the field at Dakar.

They thanked their Air France hosts and were soon ready to fly the less than 120 miles to Dakar. The lightly loaded Electra became airborne a little after 0900 GMT. Amelia turned southwestward, directly down the coast. In approximately 40 minutes they were over Dakar's Ouakam Airport on the western tip of Cape Verde. Amelia circled the field before landing into the wind at approximately 0953 GMT.

They were guided to park in front of the Air France hangar. After shutting the engines down, Amelia and Fred deplaned onto the ramp. Two invitations were immediately proffered to them: one, to stay at the mansion of the governor general; the other, to put the Electra's engines into the hands of the local Air France mechanics. Amelia gladly accepted both.

Using a lot of sign language, she informed the mechanics of the failure of the Eclipse fuel flow meter. She requested that the engines be given a 40-hour check and that the plane be thoroughly scrubbed down before they flew into the heart of Africa.

They stopped at the meteorological office for a briefing on the current and forecasted weather conditions between Dakar and Niamey. A low-pressure area was causing severe weather with thunderstorms and possible tornadoes bordering their route to the south and threatening Niamey as well. Amelia thanked the meteorologists, and left with Fred for the governor general's mansion.

The only reception of the trip so far was a lunch given by the Aero Club at Dakar. Amelia explained to her hosts that they had only slacks and shirts available to meet with kings or beggars.

Afterward, Amelia donned her coveralls and went to the hangar to write an article for the *Tribune* while watching the mechanics work on the plane. They had found the shaft of the fuel flow meter broken. It required fashioning a new one from scratch in the machine shop. The engine oil had been changed, and the whole plane was being scrubbed clean. They expected to be finished with the work so she could leave the next morning.

When she was finished writing the article she went to the French cable office and sent it to the *Tribune*. She wrote out another cable for delivery to G.P. in New York. She told him that she could not afford to cable the stories to the *Tribune,* and it was impossible to send them collect. She would omit them through Africa unless advised differently at Dakar. G.P. cabled right back to say that the *Tribune* was making arrangements for her to send the stories collect. He wanted to know her plans.

Fred wrote a letter to Bee telling her that the radio direction-finder was not functioning. He complained that the radio was useless and he didn't have any radio bearings going into Africa.

Tʜᴇ reduced visibility had rendered the celestial line of position approach ineffective. They had flown past Dakar in the haze and ended up to the north. If the radio direction-finder had been working, that would not have happened. Regardless, no one was fixing the Bendix receiver. Amelia and Fred were not hesitating to cross Africa with the inoperative radio direction-finder.

The weathermen said that the route to Niamey was still threatened with bad weather. They suggested she might bypass Niamey by going to Gao (located in present-day Mali), 200 miles farther up the Niger River. The distance to Gao was about 1,140 miles; the flight time would be about seven and a half hours.

When Amelia returned to the hangar, the mechanics asked her to run the engine to check the new fuel flow meter shaft. Everything worked fine on the run-up. Afterward they fueled the plane for departure. Amelia alerted the meteorological office that they would be coming out to the field about five in the morning for a dawn takeoff; then she and Fred returned to the governor general's residence. After a hot bath and early dinner, Amelia retired for a good night's sleep. This time her bed was large, modern, and mosquito free.

1 0 : W O R L D F L I G H T —

D A K A R T O S I N G A P O R E

It was getting to be their regular routine: wake up, dress, and leave for the airport before daylight. The European custom of a late and leisurely multicourse dinner was cutting into the few hours remaining for sleep.

When they arrived at Ouakam Airport, they went directly to the meteorological office to get their briefing. The weather had not changed. The more northerly route through Gao would get them to Fort Lamy in French Equatorial Africa (now Chad) without difficulty. Amelia and Fred thanked the weathermen for their help, then went to the hangar to prepare for departure.

They climbed into the cockpit just as the sun rose above the horizon. Amelia started the engines and taxied to the southeast end of the field. She stopped in position for a few minutes to check the engines before takeoff. Everything was ready for their departure. Thursday, June 10, 1937, the Electra lifted off at approximately 6:51 A.M. Dakar time.

A few hours earlier, halfway around the world in San Pedro, California, a message from the commander of the San Francisco division was

WORLD FLIGHT–DAKAR TO SINGAPORE
JUNE 10–20, 1937

transmitted to the U.S. Coast Guard cutter *Itasca*. The message, received at 0932 PST, June 9, directed the *Itasca* to be prepared on short notice to proceed to Howland Island, via Honolulu.

Though heavily loaded with fuel, the plane took off with little strain. Amelia made a sweeping left turn to circle back over the field. When they were over Ouakam Airport she turned to a compass heading of 100 degrees, direct to Gao. This would be the first of the four stops they would make across the interior of Africa.

The bright morning sun was off a little to the left but still glaring almost directly into her eyes. She leveled the plane a couple thousand feet above the ground. When the engines stabilized Amelia leaned the mixtures for cruise. The fuel flow meters were working perfectly.

As the hours passed and the sun rose higher in the sky, it was warm in the cockpit but not really uncomfortable. Fred calculated their ground speed when they passed over the Senegal River. The wind was actually helping them along. He estimated they would arrive at Gao before three o'clock.

Gao's military airport was located near the Niger River. Amelia spotted it easily. She circled the field once to check the wind before landing at 2:46 P.M. GMT. (Gao is located on the Greenwich prime meridian, the same line of longitude as London. The local time was Greenwich mean time [GMT], which today we call Zulu time, universal time, or coordinated universal time. GMT, GCT, Zulu, and coordinated universal time are all the same.)

Local officials and French officers were on hand to meet Earhart and Noonan at the Gao airfield. With French mechanics helping, they refueled and oiled the plane for the next morning's departure to Fort Lamy.

Up before daylight, they were served a breakfast of mushroom omelet and cocoa. With the plane already serviced they were ready for takeoff at first light. They planned to fly down the Niger River to Niamey but would land only if necessary. If everything was going well over Niamey, they would continue on to Fort Lamy nonstop. Amelia was off from Gao at 6:10 A.M. GMT, Friday, June 11.

The winds were forecast to be in their favor at the lower altitudes. Amelia leveled off the plane at about 2,000 feet above the Niger River, following it downstream on a southeasterly course. Fred estimated they would be over Niamey at about 7:45. Almost exactly on schedule, they flashed past Niamey. Amelia spotted the military airfield a couple of miles inland from the river. All was well. She flew past the Niamey air-field, turning easterly to continue on to Fort Lamy.

There was little to be seen after Niamey until Lake Chad came into view. The Fort Lamy airport was located along the Chari River just south of the lake. Amelia brought the plane down onto the fort's brick-paved runway at 1:48 P.M. It had taken them 6 hours and 38 minutes.

As Amelia pulled up in front of the only hangar on the field, drops of perspiration were already collecting on her forehead. Fort Lamy's com-mandant was there to greet them. After they moved the plane into the shade of the hangar they were invited to lunch at the commandant's quarters at the fort. Little work could be accomplished in the afternoon heat. It was suggested they leave the refueling until after sundown.

A comprehensive system of communications and direction-finding stations had been established stretching from South America to Aus-tralia. Aeronautical telegraphic radio stations were positioned to serve the wide-ranging French, British, Dutch, and Italian airlines that flew between their respective countries and their colonies. Strategic centers such as Dakar, Fort Lamy, Khartoum, and Karachi had radio direction-finding stations that could take bearings on aircraft. Captain Manning's Morse code and radio operating abilities would have been an invalu-able asset.

Earhart did not need better celestial navigation, which was inherently incapable of providing the accuracy she required. Her dire need was for improved communications and radio direction-finding. She had al-ready proved she could navigate across the Atlantic and the Pacific en-tirely by dead reckoning. Both of her earlier ocean conquests had averaged a dead reckoning course error of less than 3 percent over an average distance of more than 2,000 miles.

Saturday morning, June 12, Earhart and Noonan were to leave early. The chief meteorologist at the fort briefed them for their flight to Khar-toum, in Anglo-Egyptian Sudan. It was already getting hot as they left for the airfield.

During her preflight inspection, Amelia found that an oleo shock ab-sorber strut had leaked its air. The French mechanics looked for the cause and found that the air valve was leaking. A search through the plane's stored spare parts turned up a new valve, but once the valve was replaced, the mechanics had to refill the strut. This led to a new problem, because the fittings on the Electra were not metric. An adapter had to be made before the French pump could fill the strut. By 10:00 A.M. it was too late to take off and arrive at Khartoum before sunset. Amelia substituted El Fasher, 500 miles west of Khartoum, as their new destination.

They were airborne at approximately 12:24 P.M. for the 695-mile flight to El Fasher, also in Anglo-Egyptian Sudan.

Their route took them over a featureless landscape. Without the radio, a compass course and dead reckoning were their only guide. Great areas on their charts were blank, indicating that the topography was unknown or had never been mapped.

After a bumpy flight of about 4 hours and 6 minutes, Amelia landed at El Fasher. They were met by the governor of Darfur Province, who invited them to stay overnight at the governor's house. They would leave early in the morning to make the 500-mile flight to Khartoum.

Amelia wanted to arrive in Khartoum early enough to refuel and continue on to Massawa, in Eritrea on the Red Sea. As usual, they were up and at the airfield before daylight. They left El Fasher at approximately 6:10 A.M., Sunday, June 13.

Of the regions of Africa they had flown over, their charts from El Fasher to Khartoum contained the largest portions of unmapped territory. The city of Khartoum was located at the confluence of the White and Blue Nile Rivers, with the airport about a mile east of the railway station on the southeast edge of the city. Amelia circled the Khartoum Aerodrome before landing at approximately 9:25, about 3 hours and 15 minutes after takeoff.

This was Amelia's first attempt to "gas and go" on the trip since leaving Oakland. With the cooperation of customs and health officials, everything went smoothly. The refueling crew pumped the gas as fast as they could in the hot morning sun, and the fliers were ready to leave in little more than an hour. Again, the sun turned the cockpit into a veritable sauna as they departed Khartoum at 10:50 A.M. bound for Massawa, on the east coast of Africa.

They passed to the north of Asmara, the capital of Eritrea, situated on a 7,000-foot-high plateau. Italy had recently overthrown the Ethiopian government, and the country was now occupied by Italian military forces. A few minutes later they crossed the spectacularly steep edge of the mountains that descended to sea level near the Red Sea. It was less than 30 miles from the edge of the mountain cliffs to the Italian military airfield on the coast. Because Amelia preferred to have about 65 miles to comfortably and efficiently descend from 10,000 feet to sea level, she had to follow a snakelike course to extend the 30 miles into something nearer the desired 65 miles.

It was 100 degrees Fahrenheit on the ground when they landed at Otumlo Airdrome at 2:40 P.M. on Sunday. It had taken about 2 hours and 50 minutes from Khartoum. Massawa had a deserved reputation as the hottest place in the world.

They were greeted by Italian air officers and given accommodations in the nearby military quarters. The 100-degree heat at the time of their arrival was described by their hosts as a relatively cool day. They were told that later in summer the daily high temperatures could rise above 120 degrees Fahrenheit.

The mechanics changed the oil and completed a general inspection of the plane in preparation for the long flight to India. About 300 miles down the Eritrean coast was the Makaaca Military Airdrome at Assab (now Aseb), Eritrea. Assab's runway was 500 feet longer than Massawa's, and it was nearly 300 miles closer to Karachi. Amelia decided to go to Assab for the takeoff to India.

They had learned about taking off in the midday heat at Fort Lamy and Khartoum. Amelia departed Massawa in the relative cool of early Monday morning, June 14, at 7:30 Eritrean time. She leveled off at 4,000 feet and leisurely followed the coast of the Red Sea to Assab. In a little over two hours they came to the Italian military field. She circled the area, taking note of the hills to the south and east of the airport. If they were going to make their departure at night she would need to know the surrounding obstructions. They touched down at Assab at approximately 9:56 A.M.

It was already hot as they deplaned to meet the Italian officers waiting to greet them. Fred was able to hold limited conversations with the men using a combination of Italian, Spanish, and English.

That evening Fred wrote a letter to Bee describing how he had told one of the officers that he was married to a girl of Italian-American descent. He wrote about their flight across Africa and said it was easier to navigate across oceans than uncharted jungles and deserts. The maps were incomplete and occasionally misleading. Sometimes, he wrote, he wouldn't have bet five cents on the accuracy of their assumed position.

A preliminary forecast along the route to Karachi, India (today Pakistan), predicted good weather for the flight of over 1,900 miles. Fred calculated that at 150 mph it would take them just under 11 hours to fly to Gwadar and 13 hours to reach Karachi. Because they were flying eastward, they had approximately 11 hours between the time of sunrise at Assab and sunset at Karachi.

Amelia decided to leave Assab before daylight, around 3:30 in the morning. They would fly at least as far as Gwadar, in Baluchistan (Pakistan). If there was enough daylight remaining when they were over Gwadar she would try to make it through to Karachi.

At 3:30 in the morning it would be pitch black with no illumination of the terrain or horizon. A greatly overloaded aircraft taking off from a minimal 3,800-foot dirt runway into a black hole required that high performance standards be met fully by equipment and pilot. There was no margin for failure or error.

They were up before 2:30 and wasted little time starting and checking the engines. Satisfied with the engine run-up, Amelia taxied to the end of the field to begin the takeoff. Using takeoff power, the heavy Electra slowly gained enough speed to fly off at approximately 3:15 on Tuesday morning, June 15.

In the black of night Earhart climbed on instruments from Assab to 6,000 feet, on a compass heading of approximately 120 degrees. Even with no moon, after her eyes became accustomed to the dark, she could faintly see Perim Island as they flew overhead. She turned eastward to follow along the southern coast of the Arabian peninsula. As she passed Aden, it was just getting light enough for her to see the outlines of the harbor.

They continued eastward, following the advice she had received from her friend Viscount Jacques de Sibour to stay well offshore. Fred kept track of their position by noting the points of land and an occasional island. He advised Amelia that they were making a ground speed of about 160 mph.

Amelia was having trouble with the fuel flow meters again. To ensure that the engines were properly supplied with gasoline, she would set a small alarm clock to warn her when a tank was due to run dry.

When it was time for them to climb to 8,000 feet, Amelia richened the mixtures and advanced the engines to climb power. In a few minutes the Electra was level at 8,000 feet. Amelia allowed the plane to accelerate to about 135 mph before reducing to cruise power. After the engines had stabilized, she attempted to adjust the mixture for best fuel economy on the left engine by setting the desired reading on the Cambridge exhaust analyzer, but the analyzer had failed. She leaned the mixture the old mechanical way, by slowly reducing the amount of fuel flow until the engine began to run rough, then slightly richening the mixture until the engine ran smooth again.

When Amelia attempted to lean the mixture on the right engine, the Cambridge analyzer on that side did not respond. It appeared to be inoperative too. She placed the mixture in rich and waited a couple of minutes before trying again. This time, when she attempted to adjust the right engine mixture control, it had no effect on the exhaust analyzer or the fuel flow meter. Regardless of what she did the mixture was stuck in rich. The right engine was gulping fuel at a much higher rate than normal because of the rich mixture, and she could do nothing about it.

With both the Cambridge exhaust analyzer and the Eclipse fuel flow meter systems working improperly, it was difficult for her to judge how well they were doing. She made an assessment that even with the right engine burning excessive fuel, they had enough to reach Gwadar. They would make a new judgment then. In the meantime she adjusted her airspeed for maximum economy to conserve the fuel they had.

At Gwadar, they found they had both sufficient daylight and fuel reserves to continue on to Karachi. Fred estimated the 300 miles would take two hours. They should arrive about seven o'clock Karachi time.

On schedule the city of Karachi came into view. Amelia skirted north of the prohibited area that surrounded the city and harbor. She followed the river for about eight miles to the Drigh Road Civil Aerodrome in Karachi. They touched down at 7:05 P.M., completing the first flight ever made from Africa across the Red and Arabian Seas direct to India. It had taken approximately 13 hours and 22 minutes.

When the plane was parked at the ramp, Amelia recognized the first familiar face she had seen since leaving Puerto Rico. Viscount Jacques de Sibour had flown to Karachi to assist her at the midpoint of the world flight. When the propellers came to a stop, she hurried to greet him.

Mr. and Mrs. Markley, of the Standard Oil Company, offered to host Amelia and Fred while they were there. Sibour told Amelia that G.P. had called from New York; she could speak with him when they got into town.

A telephone call was put through to G.P. in New York. Amelia was able to talk to her husband for the first time since Puerto Rico. The *Herald-Tribune* made a stenographic record of their conversation.

[G.P. asked] "How do you feel?"
[Amelia answered] "Swell! Never better."
   "How's the ship?"
   "Everything seems O.K. There's been a little trouble with the fuel-flow meter, but I think they'll cure that here."

"How long will you stay in Karachi?"

"Probably only one day. I want everything checked thoroughly. Wednesday, with luck, we'll shove off."

"Where to?"

"Probably Calcutta."

"How about this report you're going to be quarantined?"

"I don't think so. Every one is being most awfully nice to us."

"How's Fred?"

"Fine."

"Are you the first person to fly from the Red Sea across Arabia to Karachi?"

"I hadn't thought of that. I'll try to let you know. *[Pause]* Jacques de Sibour is here and he says he thinks this is the first non-stop flight across to India."

W HILE they were sleeping in Karachi, the U.S. Coast Guard cutter *Itasca* arrived in Honolulu from San Pedro, California, on its way to Howland Island to act as guard ship for the Earhart flight.

The next day, the coal-fired navy tug *Ontario* left Tutuila Naval Station, American Samoa. It was en route to act as the Earhart guard ship at a point halfway between Lae, New Guinea, and Howland Island.

A FTER breakfast the next morning, Viscount Sibour drove them back to the airport. Amelia described to the mechanics the problem she was having with the right mixture control, the fuel flow, and the Cambridge system. She asked that they give the plane a complete check. The mechanics from Imperial Airways were to change the oil, install new spark plugs, and make any repairs needed to put the plane back in perfect condition. (This would have been an excellent time to have someone look at the Bendix receiver, but there is no record of any mention of the radio.)

Everything was going well except for the work on the Cambridge analyzer. There were no spare parts for it in Karachi. The Imperial Airways mechanics were not familiar with the system, so the Royal Air Force sent over two of their instrument mechanics. After checking the system over, the Royal Air Force men said they had no replacement parts either and there was nothing more they could do.

Amelia retrieved the philatelic covers from the nose compartment of the Electra, while Fred collected all of the charts they had used since Fortaleza. They took them to the Karachi post office. Amelia had the 8,000 postal covers stamped while she packaged her notes with the used charts to be mailed to G.P. in New York. She also sent a radiogram to his cable address, "GEPEPUT," in New York: "ESTIMATE ONE WEEK KARACHI LAE, LOVE."

Viscount Sibour drove them back to the aerodrome, where the Imperial Airways mechanics advised Amelia that the plane was ready to go except for the Cambridge analyzer. She would have to leave with it inoperative.

Later that evening Amelia sent another cable to G.P.: "FUEL ANALYZER OUT ASCERTAIN FROM CAMBRIDGE INSTRUMENT IF POSSIBLE GET REPLACEMENT OR IF ANYONE AVAILABLE TO REPAIR HESITATE ATTEMPT PACIFIC WITHOUT CABLE CALCUTTA."

Fred wrote a letter to Bee before going to sleep. He told her he expected to be back home in about two weeks, around the end of June. They were making some minor adjustments to the plane and engines in Karachi. There was no trouble; everything was perfect. The Markleys' home was nice and cool, a relief after the heat of Africa. He closed by telling Bee how much he missed her.

Amelia and Fred arrived at the Karachi airfield just after six o'clock Thursday morning, June 17, and departed at about 7:25 for Calcutta, India.

Except for an encounter with soaring eagles at 5,000 feet, the flight was uneventful. Fred was able to navigate by pilotage. He looked out the window, identifying cities, rivers, mountains, and railways as they made their way over Allahabad and across India. They just escaped another rain shower as they descended onto the soggy, wet grass of Dum Dum Aerodrome at about 4:45 P.M. Calcutta time. When the wheels touched down a huge spray of water came up from the saturated turf. The grass was too soft for the plane to take off with a heavy load of fuel. With the field that wet, it would be impossible to make a direct flight to Bangkok or Rangoon. Amelia decided they would probably have to make a fuel stop at Akyab, Burma. (Akyab is now Sittwe; Burma is Myanmar.)

It was hard for her to predict accurately just how much fuel they would burn without the Cambridge exhaust gas analyzer. Amelia wasn't confident she could adjust the mixtures to the extremely low settings that were recommended by Lockheed's Kelly Johnson, if she had to revert to the old system of leaning the mixtures without instruments.

A cable from G.P. was waiting for Amelia at Calcutta in response to hers from Karachi the night before. It read: "KLM USES CAMBRIDGE CABLING AMSTERDAM HEADQUARTERS TO ARRANGE CALCUTTA SUPPLY NEW ANALYSIS CELL IF NECESSARY WHICH BELIEVE FAULTY STOP IF UNAVAILABLE ALONG ROUTE SATURDAY PLANE FROM AMSTERDAM COULD FLY WHATEVER REQUIRED TO SINGAPORE STOP NAVY ASSUMING LAE TWENTYFOURTH PROCEEDING ACCORDINGLY STOP ACCEPT TRIBUNE PHONE TEN AM EDT TOMORROW GIVING STORY RAPIDLY OVER PHONE CONVERSING ME LOVE"

Amelia received the telephone call from G.P. that evening. After filing her story, G.P. told her the KLM Dutch affiliate in Bandoeng, Java (Bandung, Indonesia), could fix the Cambridge analyzer.

They would get off from Calcutta as early as possible for either Akyab or Rangoon (Yangon), Burma. From there, if possible, she would try to make Bangkok, Siam (Thailand), on the same day.

While they were sleeping, moderate monsoon rains continued through the night.

The next morning Amelia inspected the takeoff area at Dum Dum airfield, and found it much softer than she desired. They had lost the race to get across India and Burma before the monsoon rains began. A light fuel load was all that she dared carry out of the soggy field. There was not enough fuel to make Rangoon, so she would fly to Akyab, Burma.

When they were ready to leave, Amelia taxied to the far northeast corner of the aerodrome. The Electra's big tires were partially sinking into the sodden grass as she slowly moved into takeoff position. She was using every foot of the field available. Amelia applied takeoff power and released the brakes. Everyone held their breath as the plane very slowly gained speed. She held the plane on the ground to the very edge of the southwest boundary of the field. Then she pulled it off, barely clearing the row of trees just beyond. They were airborne at 7:05 A.M., Friday, June 18. The takeoff from Calcutta's waterlogged field was much too close for comfort. Lightening the fuel load had saved their lives.

Amelia leveled off at a low altitude beneath the clouds. They headed east across the delta at the mouth of the Ganges River. When they came to the east shore of the Bay of Bengal, near Chittagong, she turned southward to follow the coast to Akyab. They landed at the Akyab airfield at approximately 10:00 A.M. Burma time. Immediately upon deplaning Amelia started the refueling process in preparation for flying on to Bangkok, or at least to Rangoon.

The forecast was for thunderstorms and rain showers. Amelia and

Fred thought they might skirt underneath the weather and sneak through. They departed Akyab after noon but ran into extremely heavy rain and had to turn back. Fred gave her compass headings to fly as he navigated by dead reckoning back to the Akyab airfield. After flying for 2 hours and 6 minutes they arrived back around 2:30 P.M. They would have to wait until the next morning before they could try again. For the first time in over a week they would be staying overnight in a downtown hotel.

They returned to the airfield early Saturday morning, June 19, and took off at 6:30. Soon after leaving Akyab, they found the weather was just as bad as it had been the day before, or worse. They were not going to be able to fly visually below the clouds. For the second time they returned to Akyab, landing at 7:37 A.M.

Amelia and Fred agreed they should climb to an altitude higher than the coastal mountains. They would then fly through the weather, cutting directly over the mountains to Rangoon. They took off at about 8:42 A.M., leaving Akyab for the third time, and climbed through heavy turbulence and rain to 8,000 feet before turning to cross the mountains. Fred navigated by dead reckoning toward the great Irrawaddy River Valley that ran from Mandalay to Rangoon. The autopilot did most of the flying while Amelia closely monitored the engines and instruments. When Fred calculated they were clear of the mountains, they began their descent to get below the clouds.

A few minutes later, through breaks in the clouds, they could see the valley floor below. They let down below the clouds where the visibility was good enough for them to stay clear of the local showers. Then they followed the valley to the airfield at Rangoon. As soon as they landed, a heavy rain shower covered the airfield. While they waited for the rain to abate, Amelia wrote a dispatch for the *Tribune* syndicate. When it became clear that the rain was going to continue for quite a while, Amelia decided to accept an invitation from the American consul, Mr. Austin Brady, to stay overnight.

The next morning they returned to the airport before five o'clock. Amelia hoped to make it all the way to Singapore in one day. They were airborne at 6:30 on Sunday morning, June 20, 1937.

Their route took them across the Gulf of Martaban to the city of Moulmein. Amelia knew that flying over the rugged terrain of Burma and Siam was a serious business. A little more than a year before, Sir Kingsford-Smith had disappeared in this very area trying to break the London-to-Australia record in his plane the *Lady Southern Cross*.

At Moulmein, she climbed to 8,000 feet to be above the tallest peak in the Dawna Mountain Range. They repeated their success of the day before by flying across the mountains to the broad plain that led southward to Bangkok. The flight took only 2 hours and 43 minutes. It was 9:13 A.M. when Amelia landed at Bangkok's Don Muang flying field.

They refueled and completed the customs formalities in record time, to depart from Don Muang in a little over an hour. At approximately 10:27 A.M. in Bangkok, they were airborne for the 900-mile flight to Singapore.

The weather improved considerably as they proceeded southward from Bangkok down the coast of the Malay Peninsula. About two hours out of Bangkok they came to the narrowest part of the peninsula. Amelia crossed to the western shore of the peninsula, where the weather was clear as they continued southward toward Singapore. The monsoon was definitely behind them. The weather was better, but one of the fuel flow meters had failed again.

Less than six and a half hours after leaving Bangkok Amelia came to the new Kallang Airport at Singapore, landing on the large circular airfield at 5:25 P.M. Singapore time. The new multimillion-dollar airport had been in operation for only a week. Because the Electra had been in Africa less than nine days before, the Yellow Fever Flag was being flown at Kallang for the first time. Insects carrying yellow fever were easily transported from continent to continent by aircraft. Aircraft arriving from an infested region were sprayed, and a yellow flag was flown to warn of the possible infestation and quarantine.

As Amelia and Fred deplaned, Mr. and Mrs. Monnet B. Davis greeted them. Mr. Davis, U.S. consul general in Singapore, offered to be their host while they were there. It took two and a half hours to service the plane before they could leave with the Davises for the night. There was no time for social activities. After a bath and dinner, Amelia apologized for her unsociability and went to bed. They were to be awakened before daylight for an early flight to Bandoeng, Java.

11 : WORLD FLIGHT—
SINGAPORE TO LAE,
NEW GUINEA

THE next morning, Mrs. Davis served Earhart and Noonan a breakfast made mostly of Malayan fruits. Afterward, Mr. Davis drove them to the Kallang Airport. They were relieved to have the monsoon weather behind them. From here on they would only have to contend with the reliable and predictable weather of the equatorial tropics. In the twilight before dawn they entered the plane for the 630-mile flight to Bandoeng, Java, in the Dutch East Indies.

They left Singapore on Monday morning, June 21, at 6:17. Earhart gave priority to the transport traffic and didn't take off until after the skyliners of Qantas and KLM had departed.

Out of Kallang she turned to a course that would take them across the Singapore Strait to the islands along the coast of Sumatra. She leveled at cruising altitude and manually adjusted the engine mixtures for best fuel economy. They were heading for Bandoeng, where the inoperative instruments could be repaired in the shops of the Dutch East Indies airline, KNILM.

The East Indies airline flew Douglas DC-2 airliners, and the government had purchased the Martin company's model 139W twin-engine

bombers. Both types of planes were equipped with American instruments, so Bandoeng had the only instrument shop on Earhart's route capable of fixing the American Cambridge and Eclipse instruments. If at all possible, she wanted those to be operative for the 2,556-mile flight from Lae to Howland Island. After a month of flying since leaving Oakland, she had a good idea of the Electra's fuel consumption. She believed that for a safe crossing of the Pacific the fuel control instruments must be operative.

They flew over the city of Batavia (Jakarta), continuing straight across the mountains to Bandoeng, which was located on the relatively cool high plains in the center of the island of Java. Within 30 minutes Earhart was circling the long rectangular field, checking the wind sock before landing. They touched down about 4 hours and 20 minutes after leaving Singapore.

Local time in Java was kept on the nearest half hour relative to Greenwich mean time, as in Singapore, Honolulu, and Howland Island. It was approximately 10:37 A.M. Java time, or 0307 GMT. During Earhart's final flight, as insignificant a detail as it may seem, the fact that the local time was on the half hour would lead to a serious misunderstanding.

Earhart was guided to the civilian end of the field, where she parked on the ramp in front of the airline hangar. After they finished the customs, immigration, and public health formalities, her first priority was to get the mechanics working on the instruments.

An American field engineer for the Martin company, Francis O. Furman, introduced himself and offered his services while they were at Bandoeng. He was an experienced mechanic who had performed engine overhaul work for the U.S. Navy. The Martin bombers at Bandoeng had Cambridge exhaust analyzers similar to the Electra's. The DC-2s based there were equipped mostly with American instruments, including Sperry autopilots. Furman recommended they stay at the Grand Preanger Hotel, where he was living.

The airline mechanics were briefed on the work Earhart wanted done. Furman helped as she explained her problems to the instrument mechanics. She told them she wanted to continue to Port Darwin, Australia, the next day. They wasted no time in getting to work.

The airport office informed her that there was a telephone call from her husband in New York. She told G.P. of the expected delay in Bandoeng to fix the instruments and said she was not sure whether she would be able to depart for Darwin on Tuesday or Wednesday morning. They talked about coordinating with the Navy and Coast Guard the necessary weather reports and facilities she would need for the flights from Lae to Honolulu via Howland Island. The Navy and Coast Guard ships wanted to know the times and frequencies they were to use for communications and homing signals. Amelia told G.P. she would send them full particulars before she left Darwin.

During lunch, Noonan asked Furman about getting precise time checks for his chronometers. It was critical that his time be as accurate as possible, because he would be using celestial navigation over the Pacific. He wanted to make daily checks of the exact time so he could rate any error his chronometers might have. Noonan explained that each four seconds of error was equal to a nautical mile. Furman said he would find out how to get the time checks.

At the KNILM hangar, the mechanics had found the Cambridge analyzer sampling tube broken where it connected to the engine exhaust. They would replace the broken tube, then check to see if the analyzer worked properly. The fuel flow meter malfunction was a mechanical problem that required that parts be replaced. After they found, or made, the replacement parts, it would take several hours to make the repairs. The Electra would not be ready to leave by morning. Furman returned to the Preanger and apologetically informed Earhart of the work that had to be done.

He told Noonan that he could get a radio time check for his chronometers at the airfield. Every day at 8:30 A.M. (0100 GMT) a time signal was broadcast from the Malabar, Java, radio station. If Noonan would come to the airfield before 8:30, the radiomen at the station would tune in the time signal for him.

L IEUTENANT H. F. MacComsey, captain of the U.S. Navy seaplane tender *Swan*, departed Pearl Harbor Monday morning, June 21, at 0600 HST for the Earhart guard station halfway between Howland Island and Honolulu.

I N Bandoeng, west of the international date line, it was Tuesday morning. After breakfast, Furman drove Earhart and Noonan to the airport. Noonan went to the radio station to set his chronometer while Earhart went to the hangar. The mechanics were making progress, but they had to wait until the exhaust stack was repaired before they could run the engine to check their work. Maintenance believed the plane would be ready for departure early Wednesday morning. This was the first time the fliers had spent two nights in the same place since Karachi.

When Earhart and Noonan arrived at the airfield before dawn Wednesday morning, the mechanics were still working on the accessory section of the engines. They were having difficulty repairing the engine exhaust stack where the Cambridge analyzer sampler tube had broken. The mechanics needed more time. Earhart decided to delay the takeoff until the early morning hours on Thursday.

A full moon shone brightly as Amelia and Fred made their way from the hotel to the Bandoeng airfield around 3:00 A.M. on Thursday. Fred calculated that at 150 mph, it would take a little over seven and a half hours to fly the 1,130 statute miles to Koepang, on the island of Timor. They hoped to continue on to Port Darwin the same day. At 3:45 A.M. they entered the Electra; Amelia started the engines and warmed them for a check. She carefully tested the Cambridge fuel analyzers and the Eclipse fuel flow meters. The analyzers were okay, but one fuel flow meter was not. The mechanics took hours to discover the problem and more hours to fix it. By then it was too late to fly to Koepang before dark. Amelia changed their destination to Surabaya, which was only 360 miles away, and departed Bandoeng about two o'clock in the afternoon Thursday, June 24.

WHILE Amelia and Fred were en route to Surabaya, the Coast Guard cutter *Itasca* arrived off Howland Island. It was 2100 hours, Wednesday evening, June 23.

THE uneventful flight to Surabaya took about 2 hours, 35 minutes, and Amelia landed at approximately 4:35 P.M. Java time (0905 GMT).

Amelia placed a telephone call to G.P., who was on a flight to Oakland at the time. His plane was on the ground refueling in Cheyenne, Wyoming.

She told G.P. of the delay and that she expected to fly to Howland Island on Sunday and Honolulu on Monday, then arrive in Oakland Tuesday or Wednesday. That would put them in Oakland on June 29 or 30. The *Herald-Tribune* reported their telephone conversation:

G.P.P.—"Is everything about the ship O.K. now?"
A.E.—"Yes. Good night, Hon."
G.P.P.—"Good night. . . . I'll be sitting in Oakland waiting for you."

These were the last words spoken between G.P. and Amelia.

The next morning, Earhart and Noonan were up at four. She wanted to take off for Koepang on Timor Island before dawn. There would still be moonlight to light their way before they went out over the Timor Sea. She hoped to make it on to Darwin, Australia, the same day.

After the Surabaya officials cleared her flight, she started the engines to leave. During the engine run-up she discovered the fuel flow meter was inoperative again. She shut the engines down and placed a telephone call to Furman in Bandoeng.

She asked his advice about how to fix it. He could only suggest she return to Bandoeng. It was the only place in the region with the men and facilities to solve the problem. After she had already been delayed four days, it must have taken a tremendous amount of self-control for Earhart to return to the KNILM shops. She knew that fuel management was critical to the Pacific crossing and the instruments must be working.

They took off from Surabaya at six o'clock, Friday morning, June 25, spending only two and a half hours on the return flight. At Bandoeng, the mechanics were ready to go to work. They removed the cowling, and Furman looked carefully at the wiring for the fuel flow meter system. He found one wire had broken. A careful examination revealed that the earlier broken sampler tube had allowed hot exhaust gases to leak onto the wires, causing them to become brittle. The brittle wires were easily broken by engine vibration and would have to be replaced. Unfortunately, the job could not be completed in time for her to leave that day.

THE U.S. Navy seaplane tender *Swan* arrived at its assigned Earhart guard station halfway between Honolulu and Howland Island on Thursday afternoon, June 24, at 1500 hours. The U.S. Navy tug *Ontario* had reached its station halfway between Lae and Howland the evening before. The three Earhart guard ships (the *Itasca* was at Howland Island) were now all in position and waiting for her flight.

AT that point Earhart, Howland Island, and the three ships were operating with their individual clocks set in five different time zones and their calendars on two different days and dates. Two were set in zones where the whole hour came at the same time as the Greenwich whole hour; two had their clocks set a half hour different from Greenwich time; the fifth, Earhart's, was variable and changed with her movements. With the international date line in the middle of the assembled ships and stations, the system was all but incomprehensible. Any requirement that an action be timed to occur on the hour as opposed to on the half hour, at a quarter before the hour as opposed to a quarter after the hour, or at any specific number of minutes before or after the hour, was wide open to misinterpretation. Regardless, this was the system that Earhart and the ships were to use when communicating with each other. (As a direct result of Earhart's flight such procedures were changed, and the Greenwich time and date were adapted for all distress communications.)

Amelia went to the cable office to send the *Tribune* the story of their return to Bandoeng. An incoming cablegram was there for her from Richard Black, her liaison or representative aboard the *Itasca*. It had been sent via the governor of American Samoa and Amalgamated Wireless to Amelia Earhart Putnam at Darwin or Bandoeng, Java.

> QUOTE ONTARIO NIDX TRANSMITTER 500 WATTS FREQUENCY RANGE 195 TO 600 KCS EITHER CW OR MCW PERIOD NO HIGH FREQUENCY EQUIPMENT ON BOARD STOP SWAN NIJP CAN TRANSMIT ONE HALF KILOWATT BETWEEN 195 AND 600 KCS AND BETWEEN 2000 AND 3000 KCS PERIOD ALSO CAN TRANSMIT 100 WATTS 600 TO 1500 KCS AND FROM 3000 TO 9050 KCS PERIOD 35 WATTS VOICE AVAILABLE 350 TO 1500 KCS AND 3000 TO 9050 KCS STOP PLEASE CONFIRM AND DESIGNATE SIGNALS DESIRED FROM ONTARIO ITASCA AND SWAN WITHIN THESE RANGES BEST SUITED TO YOUR HOMING DEVICE STOP ITASCA CAN GIVE ANY FREQUENCY DESIRED STOP INFORMATION FROM TUTUILA AND SUVA INDICATE DELAY AT LEAST FOUR HOURS IN MESSAGES BETWEEN LAE AND ITASCA STOP BLACK

Mr. Black told Earhart the radio capabilities of each of the guard ships, *Ontario, Swan,* and *Itasca,* and asked her to select a frequency and type of transmission within each ship's listed capabilities that was best suited for her radio direction-finder. He also warned her that messages sent between Lae and the *Itasca* would take at least four hours to get through.

Before leaving the airfield for the Preanger Hotel, Earhart copied the frequency bands of the Bendix receiver on the back of the old Calcutta flight forecast. She hadn't used the receiver enough to have memorized the frequency ranges of the individual bands. In selecting homing frequencies she would not want any of them to be at the end of a band, in order to be able to tune above and below the frequency. All this required a lot of study before she could compose an answer to Black's cable. She would have to remember all the things she had been told about radio direction-finding.

Saturday morning, Furman informed them that the plane would be ready for Earhart to check the flow meter about nine o'clock. The mechanics had made the new wires a little longer so the wires could make a bigger loop where they attached to the flow-meter generator. This would help keep the engine vibration from breaking the wires. The mechanics had also annealed the analyzer exhaust sampler tube so it would not break again.

They arrived at the airfield early enough for Noonan to get his time check. Earhart filed the cablegram she had prepared for Mr. Black on the *Itasca:*

SUGGEST ONTARIO STAND BY ON 400 KILOCYCLES TO TRANSMIT LETTER N FIVE MINUTES ON REQUEST WITH STATION CALL LETTERS REPEATED TWICE END OF EVERY MINUTE STOP SWAN TRANSMIT VOICE NINE MEGACYCLES OR IF I UNABLE RECEIVE READY ON 900 KILOCYCLES STOP ITASCA TRANSMIT LETTER A POSITION OWN CALL LETTERS AS ABOVE ON HALF HOUR 7.5 MEGACYCLES STOP POSITION SHIPS AND OUR LEAVING WILL DETERMINE BROADCAST TIMES SPECIFICALLY STOP IF FREQUENCIES MENTIONED UNSUITABLE NIGHT WORK INFORM ME LAE STOP I WILL GIVE LONG CALL BY VOICE THREE ONE NOUGHT FIVE KCS QUARTER AFTER HOUR POSSIBLE QUARTER TO BT EARHART

The frequency and type of signal Earhart wanted each ship to transmit for her radio direction-finder ranged from 400 to 9000 kilocycles. She also instructed the ships when to send the homing signals.

An unintended implication was sent to the *Itasca* with these instructions. The *Itasca*'s message said that the *Ontario* had no high-frequency radio equipment on board. Earhart requested the *Ontario* to transmit the Morse code "N" signal when she needed. But she would have to transmit to the *Ontario* using Morse code on 500 kilocycles. In her message she unintentionally suggested to the *Itasca* that she had the capability to do so.

Among her other requests, Earhart asked that the *Itasca* transmit a letter "A" homing signal on the half hour on 7500 kilocycles (7.5 megacycles). She also said that she would give a long call using voice on 3105 kilocycles at a quarter after the hour, and possibly at a quarter to the hour. But, as already explained, Earhart and the ships were all in different time zones, some of which differed by a half-hour, rendering instructions about half- and quarter-hours meaningless.

It was after 10:00 A.M. by the time Earhart could run the Electra to check the fuel flow meter. She ran the engines very carefully, checking both the Cambridge and the Eclipse systems. It was too late again for Koepang, so she checked the weather for a flight back to Surabaya. They took off just before noon, Saturday, June 26. All told, it had been five days since their first arrival in Bandoeng, and the delay had consumed a great deal of Earhart's dwindling supply of money.

This time, as she approached the airfield at Surabaya all the instruments were working properly. Nothing should keep them from going on to Koepang and Darwin the next day. They landed at 2:30 in the afternoon and arranged for an early morning departure.

The next morning they left the hotel early, but it took longer than expected to clear with the local officials. Strong headwinds were forecast for the 780-mile flight to Koepang. Fred estimated it would take nearly six hours. It was 6:30 A.M. Sunday, June 27, when they departed Surabaya.

Bucking the headwinds, they leveled off and headed down the Lesser Sunda Islands toward Koepang Airport on Timor Island. After several hours Earhart descended from cruise altitude to the airfield located near the western end of Timor. She circled the field, noting from the wind sock that there was also a strong surface wind blowing. She carefully maneuvered the plane to land directly into the wind at 1:30 P.M., an hour behind their planned schedule because of the headwinds.

Earhart taxied over to the only building on the airfield. They deplaned hurriedly to refuel and be off to Darwin.

Earhart met with the local officials and was given a message that had been sent from the Darwin radio station regarding frequencies and schedules. She informed the Koepang officials she wanted to take off for Darwin as soon as possible; she needed only to add a couple hundred gallons of gas.

In an hour they were ready to go, but Noonan calculated that with the headwinds it would take over three and a half hours to make the 520-mile flight. It was already 2:30 P.M. in Koepang, or 0630 GMT. He estimated the sun would set at Port Darwin at 0900 GMT. They could not make it to Darwin in time.

They stayed overnight at the Government Rest House, rising early Monday morning, June 28, to make the flight to Australia. They departed Koepang at 6:30 A.M.

Earhart rounded the southwestern tip of Timor Island, heading 104 degrees straight for Darwin on the other side of the Timor Sea. She leveled off to cruise at 7,000 feet and stabilized the engines at cruise power. With deliberate precision, she leaned the mixtures with the Cambridge analyzer. She cross-checked the consumption with the fuel flow meters to confirm that everything was okay. Earhart must have felt good about the delay they had endured to make sure the instruments were working right.

Less than three hours later they could see the broad expanse of Bathurst Island ahead to the left. The coast of Australia came into view. About 65 miles out, Earhart started their descent into Darwin. Although it was not a large city, its strategic location in the Northern Territory of Australia made it an important transportation hub. If one expected a relaxed atmosphere at an airport in such a remote location, it would be a pleasant surprise to find Darwin being operated correctly, efficiently, and unerringly by the book.

She circled the large airport before landing at approximately 11:26 A.M. Darwin time, and parked in front of the airport administration building.

The public health inspector, Dr. Curruthers, found Earhart's vaccination certificates improperly certified, lacking an official U.S. Public Health stamp. He made inquiries of any symptoms of fever, headaches, nausea, or diarrhea that Earhart or Noonan might have had. Dr. Curruthers was apprehensive because they had recently traveled extensively through areas of yellow fever, smallpox, malaria, and cholera. He would allow them to go to the Gordon's Hotel Victoria, but they must report to him any symptoms that might suddenly appear. Dr. Curruthers would cable the Australian director general of health regarding the improper certification stamp and inform Earhart of the director general's decision.

Customs and immigration were next. As there were no passengers or cargo, the procedures were relatively simple to clear the plane and its crew into Australia. After the official work was completed, Earhart received greetings from the airport administrator and representatives of the Northern Territory government. She was informed that a number of telegrams and messages were waiting for her in the airport office.

Walter A. Dwyer, chief meteorologist at Darwin, and Norman W. King, mechanic for Qantas Airways, offered their assistance. Sergeant Stanley Rose introduced himself as head of the aeronautical wireless telegraphy and radio direction-finding unit. As discreetly as possible, Sergeant Rose, who had waited until last to speak with Earhart, inquired why she had not contacted the Darwin direction-finding unit while flying across the Timor Sea. He had sent full particulars as to frequencies and schedules to her at Koepang. Earhart acknowledged that she had received them, but she had thought they were only advisory in nature. He informed her that the Australian radio rules for aircraft communications were mandatory.

Sergeant Rose pressed her for details of how she would conduct communications during the flight to Lae, New Guinea. After some hesitation, Earhart admitted that her receiver had not been working properly since she had left the United States. Rose told her he would have a look at the receiver to see if he could find out what was wrong.

Earhart told the Qantas mechanic, Norman King, that the left landing gear shock absorber strut was low, and King pumped air into the strut to level it with the other one.

She requested the Vacuum Oil Company to add 438 U.S. gallons (365 imperial gallons) of Stanavo 87-octane gas to the tanks. Fred figured it would take them just over eight hours at 150 mph to fly to Lae. If they burned about 54 gallons per hour they would arrive at Lae with the same amount of fuel reserve as when they arrived at Darwin. The right main wing tank had previously been fueled with 100-octane gas and still contained some gas. It was not to be touched: the 100-octane fuel was being saved in case they needed more than normal power from the engines. It must not be diluted with any of the 87-octane gas.

Sergeant Rose believed he had found the problem with the Bendix receiver. He told Earhart he would be back in a few minutes with a replacement for a fuse he found had burned out. He wanted to check further but would wait until they were through fueling before he ran the radio dynamotor for a test.

When Rose returned, Earhart went with him into the cockpit to check the Bendix receiver. They put on the headsets, and he tuned in a local radio station that came in loud and clear. He explained that he had replaced a blown fuse in the receiver's power supply and showed her how to replace the fuse if it should ever burn out again. He would supply her with spare fuses.

Sergeant Rose asked Earhart what radio schedules she would keep on the flight to Lae. She told him she would use voice to transmit on 3105 kilocycles at 15 and 45 minutes after the hour and would listen for Darwin to respond a couple minutes later. Rose explained that it was preferred that there be no transmissions during a three-minute silent period starting at 15 and 45 minutes, so she agreed to transmit at 18 and 48 minutes after the hour when working Australian stations. A message would be sent to Lae so they would be listening for her too. And before she left in the morning he would bring her some spare fuses to carry on the plane.

Amelia and Fred went to the airport office and picked up all the cables and letters waiting for them there. They asked Mr. Dwyer, the meteorologist, to prepare a flight forecast to Lae for an early morning departure.

Amelia signed her name on the face of a couple of letters that a Mr. Crome of Sydney had sent to Darwin for return. She pushed the envelopes over to Fred and he signed them too. This was to be the only time that both of them signed any of the covers that people had sent to them during the trip.

Amelia picked up a duplicate of Black's cable from the *Itasca* that she had received in Bandoeng, along with two other cables from the *Itasca*. One was dated June 23 at 1550 hours and had been sent before the *Itasca* received Amelia's message from Bandoeng. It requested that twelve hours before her departure from New Guinea, the *Itasca* be fully informed of her desires. The *Itasca* would notify the *Swan* and *Ontario,* and they would conform to whatever she wanted as to frequencies or radio schedules. The cable cautioned that communications via Port Darwin were very slow.

The second message, dated June 25 at 1935 hours, was from Lieutenant Daniel A. Cooper and described Howland Island's airfield.

Months before, a box of spare parts and equipment had been sent to Darwin from the United States. Amelia asked if the spares were there. The shipment was brought to the plane, and Amelia and Fred set about sorting out what they wanted to keep from the items they would ship back home. At the same time the navigational charts they had used from Karachi to Darwin were collected for mailing back to G.P.'s office in New York.

Earhart and Noonan went to the hotel and cleaned up before going to meet C. L. A. Abbott, administrator of the Northern Territory. They had to decline Mr. Abbott's invitation to other social events because they were to leave very early in the morning.

At the Gordon's Hotel Victoria Amelia found a note from Dr. Curruthers stating that a vaccination exemption had been granted directly by the director general of health in Australia.

After dinner in the hotel dining room, they left a wakeup call for about 4 A.M. Malaria was a very serious threat in that part of the world and it was necessary to sleep with mosquito nets covering their beds.

By 5:30 the next morning, at the Darwin airport office, Mr. Dwyer was predicting headwinds along their route, with towering cumulus buildups over New Guinea. The cumulus cloud activity over the mountains would intensify as the day progressed.

A hint of dawn illuminated the eastern sky as Amelia and Fred left the Darwin airport office. They walked across the ramp toward the illuminated hangar that housed the Electra, standing fueled and ready for the eight-hour flight to Lae.

They had repeated this scene at least twenty-five times since leaving Miami and had flown 130 hours in the process. For the last twenty-eight days they had been flying the plane, fueling it, or working on it. They must have been tiring of the constant tension.

Sergeant Rose handed Earhart the spare fuses and told her he would be listening at the direction-finder station for her signals.

The plane was easily rolled out of the hangar down a slight incline onto the ramp. It was getting light enough for Amelia to inspect the plane without using a flashlight. Everything was okay, and Fred was first up on the wing. He gave Amelia a hand up as they went to enter the cockpit.

They were getting the routine down pat. Amelia set the cockpit for engine start. The right engine started almost immediately, roaring to life with a deep rumble of power from its exhaust. She repeated the procedure for the left engine. In less than a minute both engines were running. A quick check of oil and fuel pressures showed all was normal. Amelia gave the signal for the mechanic on the ground to pull the chocks from in front of her wheels. They were ready to taxi.

Amelia slowly taxied to the takeoff end of the field. After checking both engines, she lined up with the runway for departure and began the takeoff run, setting the throttles for 34.5 inches of manifold pressure. The Electra gained speed as they roared down the 2,400-foot runway, becoming airborne from Darwin at 6:49 Tuesday morning, June 29, 1937.

Amelia turned to climb on a heading of about 069 degrees direct to New Guinea. The sky up ahead was clear. The sun glared almost directly into her eyes.

She leveled at cruise altitude and accelerated to cruise airspeed. After the power had stabilized at cruise, Amelia leaned the mixture of each engine with its Cambridge analyzer.

At approximately 7:18 A.M., Amelia transmitted her first radio report to Darwin. She announced on 3105 kilocycles that all was okay and they were cruising on course to Lae. In Darwin, Sergeant Stanley Rose received her signal clearly. She was about 60 miles from Darwin at the time, and the radio direction-finder bearing showed she was on the proper course toward Lae. Sergeant Rose transmitted to Earhart the radio bearing he had taken on her signals.

Fred followed their course by pilotage as they flew over the Van Diemen Gulf just north of the Australian shoreline. Navigating en route by pilotage was not going to be difficult, but crossing over New Guinea to Lae on the far shore was going to be tricky. The mountains that ran the length of New Guinea rose to over 15,000 feet. In the afternoon, the clouds covering the mountains would reach much higher.

At about 7:48 A.M. Amelia sent another message on 3105 kilocycles. Sergeant Rose could still hear her fairly well at the direction-finder station. By then the aircraft was about 135 miles east of Darwin.

Fred could get a good visual fix to check their ground speed as they passed the Goulburn Islands. From there, they flew a course of approximately 068 degrees across the Arafura Sea to Papua New Guinea.

About 8:18 A.M. Earhart transmitted another message on 3105 kilocycles that all was okay. Sergeant Rose received the message in Darwin, but the signal strength was poor and weak. Earhart was about 210 miles from Darwin and her signal was fading. Rose was not surprised that he did not hear any more of her signals.

When they were three hours out, Amelia reduced the engine power as the load of fuel lightened. She was leaning the mixtures when she found that on the right engine the Cambridge analyzer and carburetor air temperature gauges were inoperative. She finished leaning the mixture manually and cross-checked the consumption with the Eclipse fuel flow meter. They had brought along a spare Cambridge analyzer cartridge from Bandoeng. They could change it at Lae and hope that would fix the problem.

A couple of hours passed before New Guinea came into view ahead to their left. Actually, the first thing they saw was the towering cumulus cloud cover above the mountainous interior of New Guinea. (The mountains of Papua New Guinea rival the Rocky Mountains in the United States and the Alps in Europe for sheer ruggedness and height, waiting to trap an unwary pilot.) Amelia and Fred worked their way eastward along the shoreline of the Gulf of Papua, carefully pinpointing their position. They passed Cape Blackwood to the point on the coast where they would turn northward to cross the island. Their mapmaker, Clarence Williams, had selected a relatively low and narrow section of the mountains over which to fly.

The cumulus clouds ahead were very tall, and if they had to fly on instruments they would have to navigate by dead reckoning. It was 71 miles from their southern starting point on a heading of about 006 degrees to the Markham River Valley on the other side. After 71 miles, Amelia would turn toward Lae, letting down below the clouds over the valley. This was the same as they had done between Akyab and Rangoon, only these mountains were much higher and the Markham valley much narrower.

Amelia richened the mixtures and applied power to climb. She had to climb above 11,000 feet to keep in the clear as they threaded their way between the towering clouds over the mountains. At the high altitude Amelia noticed the right engine fuel pressure was fluctuating below normal, but she smoothed it out with a few strokes of the wobble pump, a hand-operated device supplying fuel under pressure to the engine.

The autopilot was on, and Amelia carefully monitored the compass heading while Noonan kept a close check of the elapsed time. The Sperry gyro horizon instrument was showing the right wing was low, but Amelia could see that the wings were actually level with the true horizon. She continued on the course over the mountains to cross the island of New Guinea.

Fred indicated that the dead reckoning time he had allotted had elapsed. Amelia turned to a heading of 073 degrees, hoping to fly parallel down the Markham valley. It was time to descend carefully into the clouds that blotted out the terrain. They were trusting the dead reckoned position to place them over the valley, not into the mountains. Fred knew it was a good bet, because after 71 miles they could reasonably be only a maximum of 7 miles off. Even so, with their existence at stake they could not help feeling apprehensive.

Through a break in the clouds they could see the expanse of the river valley below. With relief, Amelia increased the rate of descent to get below the cloud base. She followed the Markham River to the shore of the Huon Gulf. They spotted Lae Airport at the edge of the coastline a little north of the river.

They touched down on the 3,000-foot grass runway at approximately 3:02 P.M. Lae time, or 0502 GMT, after flying about 7 hours and 43 minutes. (It was Tuesday afternoon, June 29, and they were now in the "minus 10" time zone. Anywhere in the minus 10 time zone one would subtract 10 hours to get GMT. If it was 12 noon in Lae, it would be 0200 GMT.)

Earhart and Noonan were now poised for the longest flight of the trip. They endured the delay in Bandoeng to ensure that the Cambridge and Sperry fuel management systems would be operative, specifically for the 2,556-mile flight from Lae to Howland. Despite reports in the press that the Electra had a range of 4,000 miles, Earhart knew from flying the trip thus far that the practical range of her Electra with full tanks was closer to 3,400 miles. With the almost constant headwinds, she had been required to fly faster than the optimum 150 mph no-wind true airspeed, and her hourly fuel consumption had increased accordingly. (Since leaving Miami, on the few occasions when it is possible to reconstruct the fuel consumption, the Electra had averaged burning 54 gph while flying at a true airspeed of 157 mph—all made with fuel loads less than 950 gallons.) Earhart was right to be apprehensive, considering the great distance and correspondingly heavy fuel load required on the next leg.

Since leaving Bandoeng, the Electra had flown approximately twenty hours. Already the Cambridge exhaust analyzer on the right engine was inoperative, and Earhart noted five other non-routine malfunctions for the mechanics to fix at Lae. Since Earhart left Oakland for Honolulu in March, she had never flown ten hours without a failure of at least part of a propeller or an electrical or fuel mixture control system.

Once the airplane and its systems were in good working order, there were three minimal requirements Earhart and Noonan would have to satisfy before they started across the Pacific. The forecasted winds aloft would have to indicate they could make the 2,556-miles flight safely; the weather in the vicinity of Howland Island would have to be suitable for taking celestial observations; and Fred would need a time check to set his chronometer exactly to the second. The chronometer had to be exactly set because with every second of time the stars and sun move across the surface of the earth at a phenomenal speed—at the equator, more than 1,000 mph; and with every second of time the navigator's celestial position moves exactly the same amount. Thus Noonan's chronometer had to be set with utmost precision.

12 : PREPARING FOR THE LAE-TO-HOWLAND FLIGHT

A<small>T</small> the remote airfield, cut out of the jungle brush at Lae, New Guinea, customs and public health officials were standing by to clear the plane and its crew on arrival.

Eric H. Chater, general manager of Guinea Airways at Lae, and Mrs. Chater welcomed Amelia and Fred to New Guinea. While talking with Amelia, Mrs. Chater invited her to their home for dinner. Mr. Chater told Amelia that Harry Balfour at the radio station had many messages for her. Chater introduced James A. Collopy, district superintendent of the Australian civil aviation agency in New Guinea, who had come from Salamaua, a few miles across the Huon Gulf, to offer assistance.

Chater then introduced Frank Howard, manager of the Vacuum Oil Company, who would see to the fueling of her plane. The first thing Earhart wanted was to get the mechanics working on the Electra. She explained the maintenance problems she had noted on the flight from Darwin to Edward "Ted" Finn, chief engineer for Guinea Airways. They would move the plane into the hangar, and the mechanics would get to work on it right away. Chater then took Amelia and Fred over to the

Guinea Airways radio station and introduced them to Harry Balfour, the sole operator of the station. Except for occasional mail deliveries, this one-room radio station was the only way Lae could communicate with the outside world. Balfour handed Earhart several cablegrams that had arrived earlier, mostly congratulatory telegrams from Australians and duplicates of earlier messages from the *Itasca*.

There was one new message from the *Itasca*. It had been sent to Lae at 0910, June 28, through the governor of American Samoa. "8028 FOL-LOWING FOR AMELIA EARHART PUTNAM LAE QUOTE ITASCA TRANSMITTERS CAL-IBRATED 7500 6210 3105 500 425 KCS CW AND LAST THREE EITHER CW OR MCW PERIOD ITASCA DIRECTION FINDER FREQUENCY RANGE 550 TO 270 KCS PERIOD REQUEST WE BE ADVISED AS TO TIME OF DEPARTURE AND ZONE TIME TO BE USED ON RADIO SCHEDULES PERIOD ITASCA AT HOWLAND ISLAND DUR-ING FLIGHT 0910"

This message confirmed that the *Itasca* had received Amelia's list of frequencies and that its transmitters were already tuned and ready for her flight. The "CW" and "MCW" references did not make it clear that the *Itasca*'s transmitter on 3105 kilocycles was the only transmitter on board capable of transmitting voice signals. Earhart apparently had this information, as she never asked the *Itasca* to transmit voice on any fre-quency other than 3105. The same is true for the statement that the *Itasca*'s direction-finder could take bearings only on frequencies be-tween 550 and 270 kilocycles. Apparently Earhart also knew that the *Itasca* had set up a radio direction-finder at Howland capable of taking bearings on 3105 kilocycles.

Earhart intended to answer the *Itasca*'s message when she had a bet-ter estimate of their departure time.

The Lae station was privately operated by Guinea Airways to main-tain communications among the airfields at Lae, Salamaua, Bulolo, and Wau. The main New Guinea territorial administration was headquar-tered nearly 400 miles away in Rabaul, on the island of New Britain. A district headquarters at Salamaua, a little over 20 miles across the Huon Gulf, was where Mr. Collopy was stationed. The Salamaua radio station, operated by Amalgamated Wireless Australasia (AWA), maintained peri-odic schedules with the main regional AWA radio station at Rabaul. Mes-sages between Lae and Salamaua were scheduled to be exchanged only four times each day—at 6:00 A.M., 10:00 A.M., 2:00 P.M., and 6:00 P.M.—and at those times Balfour would contact the AWA station at Salamaua.

The cable service was very expensive. A cable to the naval radio sta-tion in American Samoa cost 56 cents per word, including address and salutation. In 1937 that was a lot of money; a few hundred more words and Earhart's travelers checks would be gone.

Earhart asked if she could make a telephone call to the United States and was told there was no telephone service from New Guinea. The radio operators at the AWA stations, using radio telegraphy, provided the only means of communicating with the outside world.

Balfour had been listening on the radio for Earhart to call while she was flying from Darwin but had not heard her. He showed her the message he had received from Vacuum Oil Company at Darwin. The message listed her receiving and transmitting frequencies as 36.6 meters. Earhart told Balfour her transmitter operated only on 3105 (96.6 meters) and 6210 kilocycles. The message from Darwin had transposed the "9" to a "3" and listed an erroneous frequency.

Earhart picked up the other messages Balfour was holding for her and told him that she would be writing some dispatches for him to send. They returned to the hangar, where Finn already had mechanics working on the plane. Earhart told Chater and Finn that she hoped to leave the next day if possible. She stayed at the hangar to watch the mechanics continue their work.

To get the philatelic covers she was carrying stamped and canceled at Lae, she spoke to Alan E. Roberts, assistant district officer, who supervised the Lae post office. He took the covers to the post office to have them stamped and assured her the envelopes would be ready by morning.

Amelia and Fred checked into the only hotel in Lae, the Hotel Cecil, located along the shoreline a few hundred feet north of the airport. The owner, Mrs. Flora Stewart, welcomed them in the lobby.

About an hour later, Chater came to take Earhart to his home for dinner. When they left, Fred was in the bar having a drink with Collopy and Bertie Heath, a pilot from Guinea Airways. Collopy asked Fred why he wasn't going with Amelia to dinner at Chater's. Fred told him it was his night off, and besides he hadn't been invited. He had been flying on the trip for more than a month, and this was the first time he had been able to relax with the boys since he had left California. Collopy bought Fred a scotch whiskey with water, while he and Bertie Heath each had a beer.

Collopy and Heath were very interested in Noonan's pioneering flights on the Pan American Clippers. Fred told them of his early sailing days as a youth, and how he had decided to quit the sea and get into aviation. In 1929, while he was living in New Orleans, he had taken flight training at the Texas Air Transport SAT division, in Chalmette, Louisiana. In January 1930 he was issued his limited commercial pilot's license.

In mid-1930 Fred went to work for the New York, Rio & Buenos Aires Line just before it was absorbed by Pan American Airways. Before long he became chief navigator at Pan American Airways and was developing their plans to start flying across the oceans. During the four years before they were ready, Fred was navigator on all the survey flights across the Pacific to Asia.

Fred asked Bertie Heath about the flying he did for Guinea Airways. Heath replied that he mainly flew back and forth to primitive jungle airstrips up in the mountainous interior of the island. He flew a single-engine German Junkers airplane and carried everything from parts to people. The flights were short and he would sometimes make several round-trips in a day. If you liked flying in mountains, Heath said, there was a lot of job security in New Guinea.

It was Heath's turn to buy the drinks. It was about the third scotch whiskey for Noonan.

The conversation turned to the upcoming flight to Howland Island. What did Fred think about crossing 2,556 miles of ocean that had never been flown over before? Fred told them he was not apprehensive about the flight. He did not consider the small size of Howland Island a problem. With Pan American Airways he had navigated more than a dozen flights to Wake Island, which was not much bigger.

Heath left, and it was near twelve before Noonan and Collopy decided to call it a night. When Fred got up to leave the bar, the scotches affected his equilibrium. He staggered as he made his way across the lobby toward the stairs. Collopy steadied him as they climbed the stairs to his room. Noonan was in too great a hurry to lie down on his bed. He had forgotten about the ever-present mosquito netting and descended onto the net, flailing his arms at the unexpected contact. The commotion woke Amelia in the next room. She called out through the thin walls, asking if it was Fred. His loud shushing of Collopy not to answer made more noise than the collapsing mosquito net had. With Collopy's help, Fred finally got into bed, with the netting in place. He fell sound asleep almost instantly.

It was still dark when Earhart awoke Wednesday morning, June 30, and prepared to go to the radio station, which Balfour was to open just before six o'clock. She wanted to be there early to pick up any messages and to cable an answer to the message she had received from the *Itasca*. She hoped they could leave for Howland Island by noon, depending on the progress the mechanics had made on the Electra, the weather to the island, and what condition Fred was in when he woke up.

Earhart left the hotel and walked briskly in the morning air to the radio station. Balfour was busy getting the morning weather reports from the goldfields. When he was finished, Balfour handed over the only message he had received for her during his six o'clock schedule with Salamaua.

The message was from Oakland, filed the night before, June 29, at 10:24 P.M.: "AMELIA EARHART LAE / CONGRATULATIONS SPLENDID PROGRESS FLIGHT STOP OUR THOUGHTS AND BEST WISHES CONTINUE WITH YOU OVER REMAINDER OF ROUTE / BOARD OF PORT COMMISSIONERS"

It was ironic that a congratulatory cable was the only message to get through. Earhart asked if she could send a direct wire or some other type of message that could go directly to the United States. Balfour explained that all messages had to be relayed through Rabaul. Depending on the time that a message was received at Rabaul, she could get an answer back at Lae in anywhere from 1 to 16 hours. It depended entirely on the timing of all the radio schedules between the stations.

Earhart did not know—and we know only in hindsight—that Rabaul had 24-hour-a-day contact with Sydney, Australia, which in turn had 24-hour-a-day-contact with San Francisco and London. Messages could be relayed in a few minutes from Rabaul to San Francisco and vice versa. This was why only the Oakland message got through in a timely manner; it had bypassed the naval communications system, having been sent direct from San Francisco by commercial radio to Sydney. This was the strange mix of military and commercial communication systems that was confounding Earhart's attempts to exchange timely information. Without weather forecasts and winds aloft reports, she could not leave for Howland. The original concept that everything had to be routed through the governor of American Samoa was an impediment to Earhart's attempt to fly eastbound from Lae. Naval Radio Tutuila in American Samoa, situated in the backwaters of the Pacific, had infrequent communications schedules with the Australian stations and was a major bottleneck in her communications. Captain Manning had originally made this communications plan in California when they were to fly westbound.

Earhart told Balfour that she hoped to leave at midday if the flight forecasts arrived in time and Noonan could get a time check for his chronometer off the radio before they left. Balfour told her that getting a time check in the daytime would be very difficult. The Australian radio time signals were sent on 600 meters (500 kilocycles). It might not be possible to hear a signal on that low a frequency until sometime after dark. She hadn't known that the time signals were low frequency and usually heard only at night.

Earhart left a message to answer all the questions in the *Itasca* cable she had received on arrival. Balfour filed it at Lae at 6:15 A.M., June 30, which was 2015 GCT, June 29. The message was handled routinely through the commercial and naval communications system; it would be over nine hours before Captain Thompson on the *Itasca* received her message and took action.

The cable read: "COMMANDER USS ITASCA PLAN MIDDAY TAKE OFF HERE PLEASE HAVE METEOROLOGIST SEND FORECAST LAE HOWLAND SOON AS POSSIBLE IF REACHES ME IN TIME WILL TRY LEAVE TODAY OTHERWISE JULY FIRST REPORT IN ENGLISH NOT CODE ESPECIALLY WHILE FLYING STOP WILL BROADCAST HOURLY QUARTER PAST HOUR GCT FURTHER INFORMATION LATER" (In the last sentence of this message Earhart specified that she would be using GCT—Greenwich time zone—for her communications schedules.)

Captain Thompson did not have the capability to send a weather forecast in answer to Earhart's request. He sent the following message via "NPU" Tutuila radio to her at Lae: "8029 FOLLOWING FOR AMELIA EARHART PUTNAM QUOTE REFERENCE YOUR MESSAGE HAVE NO AEROLOGIST ABOARD HAVE REQUESTED FORECAST FROM FLEET AIR BASE COMMA PEARL HARBOR FOR HOWLAND TO LAE THOUGH DOUBTFUL IF OBTAINABLE WILL FORWARD HONOLULU HOWLAND FORECAST AS INDICATED UNQUOTE 1830"

Tutuila forwarded the message to Suva, in the Fiji Islands, during its next radio schedule at 0930 GCT, June 30, and Suva passed it on to Rabaul. By then it was about 8:00 P.M. in Rabaul. The message could not be delivered to Earhart in Lae until six o'clock the following morning, July 1.

While these messages were being routed around the Pacific, Earhart went to the hangar to ask Finn whether he thought the plane would be ready by midday. He told her the work was going well, but they had found that an air scoop between two cylinders on the port engine needed repairing. Midday or any time that day would be unlikely.

Earhart and Mr. Howard from Vacuum Oil Company discussed refueling the aircraft. She told him they had not received a flight forecast and hadn't figured the fuel load yet. A departure that day seemed unlikely.

Back at the station, Earhart told Balfour she hadn't expected messages to be delayed so long. She wanted to know if the *Itasca* could make direct radio contact with the Lae radio station. Balfour said he had an eight-tube superheterodyne shortwave receiver that could cover the 25-meter (12,000 kilocycles) marine frequencies, but he could transmit only on 46 meters (approximately 6522 kilocycles). If he had a scheduled time to listen for the *Itasca* he could try to make contact. Earhart composed two messages.

One was to Richard Black on the *Itasca:* "BLACK ITASCA VIA TUTUILA ACCOUNT LOCAL CONDITIONS PLAN START JULY 1ST 2330 GCT IF WEATHER OKEH STOP WILL ITASCA TRY CONTACT LAE DIRECT ON 25 METERS LAE ON 46 SO CAN GET FORECAST IN TIME PARTICULARLY INTERESTED PROBABLE TYPE PERCENTAGE CLOUDS NEAR HOWLAND ISLAND STOP NOW UNDERSTOOD ITASCA VOICING THREE ONE NOUGHT FIVE WITH LONG CONTINUOUS SIGNAL ON APPROACH CONFIRM AND APPOINT TIME FOR OPERATOR HERE TO STAND WATCH FOR DIRECT CONTACT"

So far as is known, no one at Lae ever received a reply to this message.

The second message was addressed to G.P. in Oakland: "PUTNAM TRIBUNE OAKLAND CALIF RADIO MISUNDERSTANDING AND PERSONNEL UNFITNESS PROBABLY WILL HOLD ONE DAY HAVE ASKED BLACK FOR FORECAST FOR TOMORROW YOU CHECK METEOROLOGIST ON JOB AS FN MUST HAVE STAR SIGHTS STOP ARRANGE CREDIT IF TRIBUNE WISHES MORE STORY"

The next radio contact between Lae and Salamaua wasn't scheduled until 10 o'clock. Earhart asked Balfour if under the circumstances there was some way to speed up the process. She had to know the weather and winds en route before they could plan the flight. Balfour said he would try to contact Salamaua and ask the radio operator to maintain a continuous watch on Lae's frequency while the station was open.

Howard suggested he send a message to Chief Wireless Inspector Twycross at Rabaul, asking him to contact the islands along her route. If she was not going to leave until tomorrow, there was enough time for them to furnish her with individual local winds and weather. Earhart said she would appreciate any information she could get. Howard wrote out a message: "TWYCROSS RABAUL AMELIA EARHART WOULD BE GRATEFUL IF YOU COULD OBTAIN WEATHER REPORTS BY ABOUT TEN AM FIRST JULY FROM NARAU OR OCEAN ISLAND TARAWA AND RABAUL ALSO FOR YOUR INFORMATION HER PLANE KHAQQ WILL TRANSMIT ON 6210 KCS QUARTER PAST EACH HOUR ON HER FLIGHT ACROSS TO HOWLAND ISLAND VACUUM"

By now Earhart had been in Lae for nearly 18 hours. So far, she had not received any forecast for the winds or the Howland weather, nor did she have a time check for Noonan's chronometer. She must have been disappointed.

Amelia returned to the hotel. Fred was in the dining room when she came in for breakfast. He asked whether she had received a flight forecast. She told him nothing had come in yet, and it didn't look as if they would be able to leave today. After breakfast, they both went to the radio station. Balfour told them there was no reply to her messages yet, but Salamaua would be monitoring Lae almost continuously. Noonan asked for a time check, but there was so much local radio interference it was impossible to receive the time signals. He would have to come back later.

While talking to Balfour, Earhart mentioned that the radio receiver in the Electra seemed to have a lot of static too, and she wondered if something could be wrong with her receiver. Balfour suggested they meet at noon in the hangar and he would check it. At the same time he would calibrate her receiver to the frequency of Lae's radiotelephone transmitter on 6540 kilocycles, or about 46 meters.

Noonan and Earhart went to the hangar to straighten out some of the equipment in the plane. When Roberts returned the stamped postal covers, she put the envelopes back in the nose compartment. At noon Balfour arrived. They turned on the power to the Bendix receiver, and Balfour tuned it to a land station on 500 kilocycles. Even inside the hangar, he was able to receive satisfactorily on the long-wave 500-kilocycle band of the receiver. He then tuned the receiver to 6540 kilocycles, the frequency of his radiotelephone transmitter at Lae. The receiver checked okay.

The mechanics were still working on the engines. It was going to be a while before they could finish.

After lunch, Noonan went to try again for a radio time check and Earhart returned to the hangar to see what progress was being made on the plane. Finn reported that repair to the air scoop was taking extra time. The instrument mechanic had just finished cleaning and oiling the Sperry gyro horizon. He would work next on the temperature gauge in the carburetor air scoop. They were just about finished replacing the right fuel pump. He estimated they would be ready for her to run the engines at about four o'clock.

The mechanics were still greasing the propellers, but the instrument mechanic had finished fitting a spare adapter plug to the carburetor air temperature gauge line. A new cartridge had been installed for the Cambridge analyzer on the right engine, and a thermocouple connection had been repaired. Clean spark plugs had been fitted to both engines. As soon as the engine cowlings were replaced, the Electra would be ready for a ground test.

Howard had his assistant, Robert W. "Bob" Iredale, fill the oil tanks with 60 gallons of Stanavo 120 engine oil. Before he was finished, Iredale checked that all screens and filters were properly reinstalled.

By five o'clock the work was finished, and workers pushed the Electra out of the hangar. Earhart started the engines to check the systems, paying special attention to the items that had been repaired. She shut down the engines and reported to Finn that the right fuel pressure was too low.

The mechanics removed the new fuel pump. Then they took the original pump into the shop to grind the valve seat to remove unevenness. In less than an hour the original fuel pump was back on the engine and ready for another ground check. This time when she ran the engines both fuel pressures were good. It was so late she would delay the test flight until early morning. If Noonan was able to get his chronometer set, they would fuel the plane and depart for Howland Island at 9:30 the next morning. Howard reminded her that all fuel had to be pumped into the tanks by hand, which might take a couple of hours. She assured him she would have the test flight completed by seven o'clock.

Earhart went to the radio station, where Balfour and Noonan were still trying to get a time check. No messages had arrived, so she returned to the hotel. When no messages for Earhart came at the 6:00 P.M. schedule with Salamaua, Balfour closed the station. Noonan walked back to the hotel as dusk settled over the Huon Gulf.

After cleaning up, Fred went down to the public rooms, where Collopy was having a beer before dinner. Collopy invited Fred to join him for a drink, but Fred said that he had had quite enough the night before. Amelia came down to the lobby and they joined her there.

Amelia asked Collopy what the prevailing winds were at Lae Airport in the mornings. He told her that the Guinea Airways pilots usually expected the heavier cool air off the mountains to flow down the Markham valley from the northwest early in the morning. Later, as the sun heated the air in the interior, the cooler air over the Huon Gulf would start to flow onshore and the wind would shift to the southeast.

Fred told Amelia that they had been unable to get a radio time check, but Balfour was confident he could work out something in the morning. Collopy said he would get in touch with Rabaul if necessary;

they might be able to help. Amelia told Fred they would be making a test flight first thing in the morning.

It was still dark when Fred opened his eyes at the sound of the persistent knocking on his door. When Amelia came downstairs, Fred walked with her to the radio station. It was just after 6:00 A.M., Thursday, July 1.

Balfour was already at work making his morning contacts. He handed Earhart several messages and informed her that authorization had come through for her to send press messages to the *Tribune* collect. One message was a flight forecast from Lae to Howland that had come from Pearl Harbor. At last they had a forecast of the winds en route. Fred could now calculate the time and fuel required for the flight to Howland Island. The forecast was from the Fleet Air Base at Pearl Harbor. Navy aerologist Lieutenant Arnold E. True had sent the message the evening before.

The weather was predicted to be generally average, with a headwind of a little less than 12 mph. With that amount of headwind, if they maintained an optimum-range true airspeed of about 155 mph, they would have a ground speed of about 143 mph. At 143 miles per hour it would take them a few minutes less than 18 hours to travel the 2,556 statute miles to Howland Island. That was almost an hour longer than the original no-wind flight plan calculated by Clarence Williams. They would need every pound of fuel the Electra could lift off from the 3,000-foot grass runway at Lae.

A message from Tutuila dated June 29 at 1410 GMT gave a coded report of the *Itasca*'s weather, the Howland Island weather, and the winds aloft. The actual winds blowing at 5,000 feet were stronger than those forecasted by Lieutenant True for their flight from 175 degrees east longitude to Howland Island.

G.P. had sent another message from San Francisco the afternoon before via Tutuila: "8029 REQUEST FOLLOWING BE FORWARDED TO EARHART AT LAE QUOTE REQUEST APPROXIMATE TIME YOUR TAKE OFF FROM LAE SIGNED PUTNAM UNQUOTE IT IS REQUESTED THAT THE ANSWER WHEN RECEIVED BE FORWARDED TO ONTARIO AND ITASCA FOR INFORMATION 1235"

Earhart filed the answer with Balfour for transmission. "BLACK ITASCA TUTUILA RADIO ASK ONTARIO BROADCAST LETTER N FOR FIVE MINUTES TEN MINUTES AFTER HOUR GMT FOUR HUNDRED KCS WITH OWN CALL SIGN LETTERS REPEATED TWICE END EVERY MINUTE STOP PLAN LEAVE BY TEN THIS MORNING NEW GUINEA TIME EARHART"

Earhart wanted to finish the test flight so the men from Vacuum Oil could start the slow process of fueling the plane. She told Balfour that she would be taking off shortly and would call him on 6210 kilocycles after she was airborne. She would listen a minute or two after she completed her call for his radiotelephone answer on 46 meters. She also requested that he give her a long dash, since she would be testing the radio direction-finder on the Lae station.

It was not obvious, even to a professional radioman such as Balfour, that the Bendix radio direction-finder loop was incapable of taking bearings on 7500 kilocycles. Balfour had inspected the equipment the day before and now was going to send signals for Earhart on 6540 kilocycles. Balfour, like Earhart and others, thought that the five frequency bands that were labeled on the receiver and on the loop coupler box meant that the direction-finder loop could take bearings on all the receiver frequencies.

Earhart went to the Electra, where local people had gathered to watch the test flight. After starting the engines she taxied the short distance from the hangar to the southeast end of the field by the shoreline. She took off into the wind toward the northwest, and became airborne at 6:35, Thursday morning, July 1.

As she crossed over the northwest end of the airport, she could see the dense growth of scrub trees at the end of the runway beyond the clearway. It was a solid 10-foot-high growth that would destroy any plane that ran into it. The other end of the runway ran right to the edge of a 20-foot bluff at the water's edge.

She made a left turn and flew out over the Huon Gulf. Leveling off, Earhart pulled the power back to cruise and waited for the engines to stabilize. With relief, she saw that the Cambridge analyzer worked when she leaned the right engine carburetor mixture. The Sperry gyro horizon was showing the wings level, and both carburetor air temperature gauges were now working. Amelia selected the number 4 cylinder head temperature on the right engine to see if it was fixed. A check of the other instruments, including the fuel pump pressure gauges, showed everything normal. The Electra was in good condition.

Earhart turned on the transmitter. While the tubes were warming up she made sure the frequency was cranked to transmit on 6210 kilocycles. She called Lae and asked Balfour to transmit a long signal so she could take a radio bearing with the direction-finder. The Lae signal came in very loud when Balfour came on the air. Earhart turned the volume down before turning the direction-finder coupler on. She switched the coupler band switch to 5 and tuned for the loudest signal.

She then switched to get a minimum with the direction-finder loop. The signal was very strong, and she turned the loop completely around several times without finding any point where the signal fell off to a lower volume. She thought it must be that she was too close and the Lae station too powerful for the loop to get a minimum signal.

She turned the receiver off and headed back to Lae for landing. The wind sock showed that the wind was still coming from the northwest, flowing down from the interior, when she landed at 7:05.

Eric Chater and Ted Finn were waiting in front of the hangar as she taxied back. Earhart noticed that they had the barrels of gasoline in position to fuel the plane. She told them that everything had checked okay, that they had done a swell job of getting the plane ready to go. She was planning to take off at 9:30 and wanted to get the fueling started.

Noonan went to the radio station to try again for a time check. Earhart went with Chater over to where Howard and Bob Iredale were standing by the barrels of gasoline. Iredale had been in New Guinea long enough to learn the local pidgin English dialect. He would translate Earhart's instructions to the workers to make sure they were carried out properly.

Earhart told them that she would be using full throttle to obtain all available power from her engines for takeoff. This required that 100-octane gas be used to prevent detonation. She had about half a tank of 100-octane gas in the right main wing tank that she had been saving for just such a necessity. It must not be diluted with 87-octane fuel under any circumstances.

They would start by filling the left main wing 97-gallon tank and both the left and right 102-gallon wing locker tanks. The tank capacities were all in U.S. gallons; they would have to divide the U.S. figures by 1.2 to obtain the capacities in imperial gallons. Earhart was going to work out the final fuel requirements with Noonan at the radio station. Before they finished with the wing tanks, either she or he would be back to direct the loading of the remaining fuel.

When Amelia came into the radio station Fred told her that they still couldn't get a time check but were expecting to be able to get one at 11:00 A.M. At eight different times each day, Australian stations "VIS" Sydney, "VIP" Perth, "VIM" Melbourne, and "VIA" Adelaide would alternate sending a time signal on the low-frequency band of 500 kilocycles. Balfour, at Lae, was unable to receive any of the low-frequency signals clearly enough in the daytime for a time check. The stations were so far away that interference blanked them out.

In Bandoeng Fred had used the Dutch East Indies station located at Malabar, Java, to set his chronometers. In contrast to the Australian stations, the Dutch station "PLO" at Malabar sent only one time signal a day in the high-frequency band of 26.22 meters (11,440 kilocycles). Balfour was confident that they would be able to receive the high-frequency signal at 8:30 A.M. Java time (11:00 A.M. Lae time) and obtain a time check.

Balfour asked Earhart if she had received Lae's signal. She replied that she was unable to get a minimum with her direction-finder loop because the Lae station's signal was too powerful and too close. No one questioned the Bendix direction-finder's ability to work on the high frequencies.

Earhart asked how her signal had sounded. Balfour reported that her transmitter was working satisfactorily, but the carrier wave on 6210 was rough. He advised her to pitch her voice higher to overcome the distortion caused by the rough carrier wave.

Earhart and Noonan decided to take all the gas they could carry. She would order all the tanks to be filled except for the right main wing tank, which contained the 100-octane. They would leave at 9:30 A.M. if Noonan got a time check for his chronometer. Earhart told Howard to fill all but the one tank with the Stanavo 87-octane fuel. She cautioned them to make sure each tank was completely full. It was impossible to overfill or rupture a tank, since the fuel tank venting system would vent any excess fuel overboard. Dick Merrill had recounted how his full Electra had vented the excess gas overboard when it expanded in the heat of the day in Southport, England. There should be only limited expansion of the fuel anyway, because the gas in the barrels was probably already warmed to 75 degrees.

A Guinea Airways single-engine Junkers plane landed to the northwest and taxied back to park by the hangar. Earhart wondered when the surface wind might turn around and start blowing onshore from the southeast. With all the gas they were carrying they would weigh over 15,000 pounds on takeoff. If at all possible she wanted to take off toward the water of the gulf, but she couldn't afford to have any tailwind. A headwind versus a tailwind would demand that the Electra accelerate more on the ground to reach adequate airspeed and would require many hundreds more feet of runway. She could only hope that the wind would reverse.

Earhart watched closely as Bob Iredale and the Vacuum men slowly hand-pumped the gas out of the steel barrels to fill each of the fuselage tanks.

Noonan came to the plane shortly after eight o'clock with a couple of messages. The first was a report of weather conditions at Nauru Island; the second was a coded weather report from the guard ship *Swan.*

While they were watching Iredale, Earhart asked Howard to send a departure message to Black on the *Itasca* after their takeoff, to advise him of their departure time and their expected 18-hour flying time to Howland.

When Iredale was finished, Howard had Earhart sign for the 654 imperial gallons (785 U.S. gallons) of Stanavo 87-octane gas. Now the Electra had 1,100 U.S. gallons of fuel aboard. All tanks except one were full at 9:00 A.M. as the plane sat in the morning air outside the Guinea Airways hangar.

Earhart and Noonan went to the radio station to try again to get a time check. They would be ready to depart in another hour, in order to arrive at Howland Island at dawn. Balfour told her there was a Burns Philps company ship, the *Macdhui,* in the vicinity. He would ask the Salamaua operator to contact the ship and see if they could give them an accurate check of the time. But the ship, when contacted, proved unable to relay an accurate time check. They had no choice but to wait until 11:00 A.M. for the Malabar signal.

At about a quarter to eleven they returned to the radio room. Balfour reported that he had had no luck trying to contact the *Itasca* or the *Ontario,* and no new messages had come in. The Malabar station, on 11,440 kilocycles, came on the air at 10:50 A.M. with good signal strength, announcing that all stations should stand by for the time signal. However, no time signal came, though they waited until well past the allotted period. Then Malabar reported there was a fault on the line from the observatory, and they were unable to transmit the signal.

Earhart stepped outside to look at the wind sock on the hangar, which indicated the wind was still coming from the northwest. She returned to the radio station and wrote a message for Balfour to send via Tutuila to the *Itasca:* "BLACK ITASCA—TUTUILA RADIO DUE LOCAL CONDITIONS TAKE OFF DELAYED UNTIL TWENTY ONE THIRTY GMT JULY SECOND STOP ANY FORECAST LAE HOWLAND BEFORE THEN APPRECIATED NOTIFY ONTARIO CHANGE BT EARHART"

Balfour said he would keep trying to get a time signal and would continue to listen for the *Itasca* and the *Ontario.* He didn't hold out much hope until after dark.

Earhart and Noonan returned to the plane, where they found Collopy sitting in the shade under the wing. Fred told him they were delaying until tomorrow morning at 9:30. Collopy inquired about the fuel and oil onboard for the flight and the problems associated with taking off that heavy. They knew the 3,000-foot grass runway at Lae was minimal. They would need a bit of headwind to have any margin of safety. It would be best to take off in the coolest part of the morning, because every degree of temperature increase would lessen the air density and thus require more takeoff room. They had to arrive at Howland Island in the daytime because they needed the sunlight for visibility. If they left Lae before 9:30 A.M. they would get to Howland before sunrise.

Every mile per hour of wind, every degree of temperature, every foot of runway, and every pound of weight was critical. Everything was balanced on the edge of what was possible. Earhart and Noonan had control over only one thing, the weight. They would need every pound of fuel, but ounce by ounce they could remove everything that wasn't absolutely necessary for the flight.

They worked over the plane from tail to nose, removing all items not essential to flying to Howland Island. Flares and smoke bombs, spare parts, extra maps, books, tools, suitcases, clothing, and personal belongings were all removed, to be given to people at Lae or shipped home. They packaged the three books that listed the world marine navigational lights, broadcast stations, and coast and ship stations. Earhart included for shipment the new fuel pump, a used set of spark plugs, and both their suitcases full of their personal effects.

On the way back to the hotel for lunch, Earhart stopped by the radio station and gave Balfour all the charts, facility lists, and reference items they didn't feel were worth the expense of shipping. Balfour had not received any additional messages, nor had he had any luck hearing a time check. Earhart said they would come back later in the afternoon.

At the hotel during lunch, Amelia and Fred talked with the owner, Mrs. Stewart. Amelia asked her how long she had known the flight was coming to Lae. Mrs. Stewart said for many months, ever since they had stored the barrels of gasoline under the trees across from the hotel. The expansion of the gasoline in the heat of the day, and its contraction during the night, had caused the closed barrel ends to "pong" like a chorus of Caribbean steel drums. Noonan explained that the expansion of the gasoline changed the volume, but not the weight. A gallon—a specific volume—weighs less when it is warm than when it is cool. For accuracy, Pan American always adjusted the fuel for temperature and calculated the total aircraft's fuel in pounds, not by the number of gallons on board.

That afternoon Amelia and Fred did a little local sightseeing. When they returned, Amelia went to her room to compose a dispatch to the

Tribune. The long article started with a quote from *Hamlet:* "DENMARK IS A PRISON . . . LOCKHEED STANDS READY FOR LONGEST HOP WEIGHTED WITH GASOLINE AND OIL TO CAPACITY" and ended, "WE SHALL TRY TO GET OFF TO-MORROW THOUGH NOW WE CANNOT BE HOME BY FOURTH OF JULY AS HAD HOPED EARHART"

When she was finished she walked over to the radio station. Balfour accepted the message for dispatch. He told her he had arranged with both Salamaua and Rabaul to stay on tonight during the Sydney and Adelaide time signals at 9:00 and 10:30. All three stations would be try-ing to get the time check for her. Earhart said they would be back be-fore nine o'clock and would bring the chronometer.

The conversation was interrupted by a message from Salamaua. It was from Lieutenant True at the Fleet Air Base in Pearl Harbor, origi-nated on June 30, 1220 HST, and relayed via Naval Radio Tutuila.

Heavy cumulus clouds were forecasted about 250 miles east of Lae. Earhart was warned to avoid their centers, as they could frequently be dangerous. After reading the message, she left to go back to the hotel.

She found Fred and showed him the latest message from Pearl Har-bor. Fred made some calculations. The headwinds in this message were a little stronger than in the earlier forecast, now averaging nearly 15 miles per hour. That called for a slightly higher optimum-range air-speed of 156 mph, with an average ground speed of about 141 mph. It would now take them just a few minutes more than 18 hours to make the 2,556-mile flight to Howland.

After dinner, Fred collected the chronometer and met Amelia to go to the radio station. The lights were on, and Balfour was already there with the receiver tuned to 500 kilocycles, listening for Sydney. The problem was not purely one of radio propagation, as the signals from Sydney could usually be heard at night on 500 kilocycles with little dif-ficulty. The problem was that many other stations could be heard trans-mitting at the same time on 500 kilocycles. There were so many different signals on the air at the same time that it was impossible to read the Sydney time signal with certainty.

The 9:00 P.M. Sydney signal came on, but the interference was so heavy they were unable to get the time signal at Lae. Balfour checked with Rabaul, but they hadn't gotten it either. They would stand by again for the Adelaide time signal due at 10:30. Mr. Twycross at Rabaul had arranged for a message to be sent out at 10:20 P.M. from all Australian coastal stations. It requested all shipping to keep radio silence for ten minutes during the transmission of the Adelaide time signal.

Complete silence prevailed during the Adelaide time signal, and Fred was finally able to check that his chronometer was exactly three seconds slow. They thanked Salamaua and Rabaul for their extra effort and cooperation.

Amelia and Fred returned to the hotel and retired before eleven o'clock. The clerk knocked on their doors at 5:30 Friday morning, July 2.

Collopy was having morning tea with Fred when Amelia came down.

They took their few remaining belongings from their rooms and met in the lobby to pay the bill and leave for the airfield. Chater was there with his car to take them to the hangar so they could check the plane and prepare for departure.

Fred loaded the thermoses and lunches into the cabin, and Amelia did a thorough preflight inspection, covering every inch of the Electra. By 7:30 she was satisfied that the plane was ready. She took a small package from the cabin before going with Fred to the radio station.

Balfour was looking at one of the radio facility charts Earhart had given him, while listening to Morse code coming from one of his receivers. He was sorry he had not had this information before. There were many high-frequency time signal services available in the Pacific that he just hadn't known about. He was very knowledgeable about the stations and radio circuits that he worked with every day, but knew little of the facilities and procedures outside his own system.

Balfour was listening to station "FZS 3" in Saigon, French Indochina, on 9620 kilocycles. It was getting ready to send a time signal at eight o'clock. When Fred checked his chronometer with the Saigon time signal, he found it was still exactly three seconds slow.

Earhart handed the package she had brought from the plane to Balfour in appreciation for his help while they had been at Lae. Balfour opened the paper and inside was a 32-caliber handgun with a small box of ammunition. He was very pleased and thanked her for the gift.

When they had arrived at Lae, Balfour had told Earhart that radio stations had scheduled times when they contacted each other. She didn't exactly comprehend what he meant. She had a full slate of radio schedules herself. Starting on the hour at 00 minutes she would listen for the *Itasca*; at 10 after the hour she would listen for the *Ontario*; at 15 after she would transmit to the *Itasca*; at 18 after she would transmit to Lae; at 20 after she would listen for Lae; at 30 after she would listen for the *Itasca* again; and at 45 after, if she had time, she would transmit to the *Itasca*.

With all of those radio schedules, Earhart suggested that Balfour should come along on the flight and work the radio for her. He declined, saying that as much as he might like to fly off with them to Howland Island, he'd probably find himself in hot water with both Mr. Chater and Mrs. Balfour.

If Earhart only had to work the radio, she might have been able to set up more schedules with the *Itasca*. Regular transport planes carried full-time radio operators, engineers, and copilots to assist the pilot. Earhart had to do everything herself over a very long, arduous pioneering flight. As it was, four schedules each hour devoted to the *Itasca* was probably too much.

Amelia and Fred waited until after nine o'clock for a message or late flight forecast to come in, but nothing arrived, so they left the radio station for the hangar. A glance at the wind sock showed the wind had swung around to the southeast and was blowing onshore.

Most of the European population at Lae had come down to the field to see them off. Sid Marshall, the Guinea Airways chief pilot, was filming the scene with his 16 mm movie camera.

It had taken three days but they were finally ready to leave. The torturous delays waiting for everything to be right for departure had been wearing. After six weeks of herding the *Electra* and its reluctant instruments around most of the world, Amelia must have felt that it would be all downhill from here. Three more flights—Howland, Honolulu, and home.

Fred climbed up onto the wing and extended his hand to give Amelia a boost up. Though it wasn't quite ten o'clock, the aluminum skin was already hot to the touch. They made their way forward to the overhead cockpit hatch. Fred lowered himself through the hatch and shifted over into the right seat. Amelia soon followed. Lowering herself down into the left pilot's seat, she closed the overhead hatch and started the Electra's engines for departure.

At about five minutes before 10:00 A.M., Earhart added power to the engines to start the Electra slowly taxiing away from the hangar area toward the far northwest end of the runway. It took more power than usual to keep the heavy plane rolling up the slight slope of the runway.

It was getting very hot in the cockpit by the time they arrived at the far end of the field and she completed her checks. They were ready for takeoff. Earhart applied full power.

Howard and Collopy watched from in front of the hangar as the Electra labored down the runway, slowly gaining speed. They could see the rudder movement as Earhart maintained directional control with her feet pushing rapidly on the rudder pedals. The plane passed the smoke bomb at the halfway point. There were only 500 yards remaining to the edge of the cliff at the Huon Gulf. Almost imperceptibly, the plane was moving faster and faster as the roar of its engines grew louder.

Fifty yards before it reached the edge of the field the Electra became airborne. Frank Howard noted Earhart had taken off at exactly 10:00 A.M. (0000 GMT). He watched as she held the plane close to the water, accelerating straight ahead. Still low on the horizon, it went several miles before turning to head toward Howland Island. Howard went to the radio station to send a departure message to Black on the *Itasca*, as Earhart had requested.

Balfour was busy in the radio station copying messages when Howard arrived. One message was a new flight forecast from Lieutenant True at the Fleet Air Base, Pearl Harbor. Nauru Island had sent their current weather and winds aloft, and later Howland Island sent theirs as well. The winds forecast by Lieutenant True, and the upper-air soundings of the actual winds aloft from both Nauru and Howland, showed stronger headwinds over the route than reported earlier. Instead of the slightly less than 15 mph headwind previously forecast, the average headwind was about 26.5 mph. With the stronger headwind, the plane's optimum-range true airspeed would increase from about 156 mph to approximately 160.5 mph, and it would make an average ground speed of only about 134 mph. Earhart and Noonan didn't know it, but instead of a few minutes more than eighteen hours, it was going to take them more than nineteen.

Balfour transmitted the new Fleet Air Base forecast and Nauru Island winds by radiotelephone to Earhart just after 10:20 A.M., 11:20 A.M., and 12:20 P.M. Local interference prevented him from receiving acknowledgment that she ever received the latest wind information.

Howard wrote out the departure message for Balfour. It read: "URGENT BLACK ITASCA TUTUILA RADIO AMELIA EARHART LEFT LAE TEN AM LOCAL TIME JULY 2ND DUE HOWLAND ISLAND 18 HOURS TIME VACUUM"

13: THE *ITASCA* AND HOWLAND ISLAND

A LITTLE over two weeks earlier, just before noon on Tuesday, June 15, 1937, Commander Warner K. Thompson, captain of the U.S. Coast Guard cutter *Itasca*, stood on the wing bridge as he conned the gleaming white 250-foot vessel into Honolulu Harbor. The *Itasca* had traveled from Los Angeles to Honolulu to act as guard ship for the upcoming Amelia Earhart flight into Howland Island.

The next morning, Captain Thompson conferred about Earhart's flight with USN Rear Admiral Orin G. Murfin, commandant of the Fourteenth Naval District. USCG Lieutenant Commander Frank T. Kenner, commander of the Coast Guard's Hawaiian section and previous captain of the *Itasca,* also attended. Captain Thompson received orders to proceed to Howland Island to provide communication and other services for Earhart. The *Itasca* was also to carry out a routine quarterly resupply mission of the Line Island colonists on the same cruise. Because Captain Thompson had never made a Line Island trip before, Kenner would accompany the ship on the cruise.

To establish sovereignty, the United States had colonized three islands along the line of the equator. Four young Hawaiians lived on

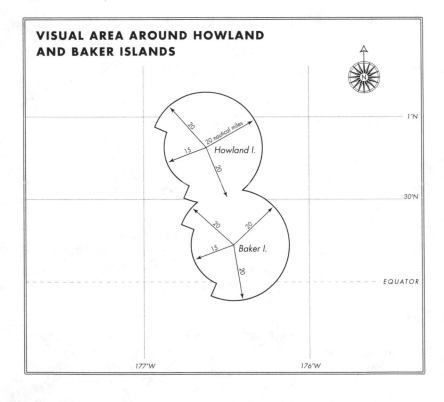

VISUAL AREA AROUND HOWLAND
AND BAKER ISLANDS

each of the so-called Line Islands—Howland, Baker, and Jarvis—as colonists. Their original sponsor had been the Department of Commerce, but in 1936 the Department of the Interior took over management of the islands. The Coast Guard provided a ship to resupply the islands every three months.

Earlier, during the voyage to Honolulu, Captain Thompson had requested information regarding any radio schedules the *Itasca* was to have with the Earhart plane. The commander of the San Francisco division informed him that no radio schedules had been arranged. The report added that on Earhart's previous flight, her plane was equipped with a 50-watt transmitter that could transmit on 500, 3105, and 6210 kilocycles. Earhart's receiver covered all frequencies, and her direction-finder covered from 200 to 1500 kilocycles. All transmissions were made by key, using Morse code, though it was possible for her transmitter to send voice signals. The communications were handled by Pan American Airways, with Earhart working on 3105 and Pan American sending on 2986 kilocycles.

This official message was important to the radiomen of the ship, because they used the dots and dashes of Morse code almost exclusively for their transmissions. The 500-kilocycle frequency was universally used for making radio contact between ships and was also a very reliable frequency for radio direction-finding. The message told the communication personnel on the *Itasca* that communication with Earhart would be easy. Unfortunately, the message was outdated and inaccurate.

Earlier in the year, G. P. Putnam had designated Richard B. Black, a field representative in Honolulu for the Department of the Interior, to be Earhart's representative aboard the USCG cutter *Shoshone* during the March flight. Black was now serving the same function aboard the *Itasca*.

On Wednesday morning, June 16, the *Itasca*'s officer of the deck noted receiving four drums of aviation gasoline and a high-frequency radio direction-finder for delivery to Howland Island. In March, Earhart had requested that a high-frequency radio direction-finder be set up on Howland Island. Black, along with Lieutenant Daniel A. Cooper, U.S. Army Air Corps, arranged for an experienced U.S. Navy radioman to accompany the Navy high-frequency radio direction-finder to Howland Island, to operate the direction-finder during the Earhart flight. When Captain Thompson learned of this arrangement, he overruled it for the reason that the Coast Guard had sufficient radiomen to perform its work.

The *Itasca*'s chief radioman, Leo G. Bellarts, was actually the only seasoned operator on the *Itasca*, the other three operators being relatively inexperienced radiomen third class. Captain Thompson requested that the Coast Guard Hawaiian Section temporarily assign a radioman first class to help Chief Bellarts, but none of the first-class radiomen stationed in Honolulu was assigned. Instead, the dry-docked Coast Guard cutter *Taney* transferred Radioman 2nd Class Frank Cipriani for temporary duty to the *Itasca*. The communications officer aboard the *Itasca*, Ensign William L. Sutter, welcomed whatever help he could get, whether first or second class.

The *Itasca* continued to load supplies and stores for the voyage. On Thursday, June 17, they received eighteen #486 radio batteries from the Department of the Interior. Four boxes of spare parts for Miss Earhart's plane also came aboard.

Friday morning, June 18, Richard Black received a message from Mr. Putnam that had been relayed to Black by Ruth Hampton, Assistant Director, Department of Interior, Washington, D.C. The message stated that Earhart would broadcast by radiotelephone at a quarter after the hour and a quarter to the hour. She would broadcast on 6210 during daylight and 3105 at night. She also had 500 but it was of dubious usability. Earhart wanted to know what frequencies the *Itasca* and the Navy vessels would be using to transmit to her. It was suggested that the Coast Guard and Navy coordinate so that helpful weather information could be broadcast to Earhart on the hour and half hour after her takeoff from Lae. Putnam asked the *Itasca* to forward the Howland weather forecast to Lae via the *Ontario* prior to her takeoff. He concluded by informing them he would ask Earhart to take an aerial photograph of Howland Island.

Three crucial pieces of information in this message were never understood by the radiomen of the *Itasca:* First, the use of 500 kilocycles was dubious. Second, Earhart would only be broadcasting, using radiotelephone, at a quarter after and a quarter to the hour. Third, she would be listening only when the Navy ships and the *Itasca* broadcast on the hour and half hour. These broadcasting times were misinterpreted by the *Itasca* as being what radiomen commonly refer to as *schedules,* the keystone of orderly and dependable radio communications: the agreement of a radio operator to be on certain frequencies, at a certain time, ready to send and receive messages—for example, the arrangement between Balfour at Lae and Radio Salamaua at 6:00 A.M., 10:00 A.M., 2:00 P.M., and 6:00 P.M. All the broadcast times in subsequent messages were misinterpreted as schedules. The communications personnel on the *Itasca* never understood that Earhart did not receive directly after transmitting. This fact would prove so confounding to the *Itasca*'s radio operators that they would never grasp why Earhart wasn't hearing them. In the midst of preparing for departure, Captain Thompson, Ensign Sutter, and Black would not have a chance to review Putnam's message until later at sea.

Even though the ship was moored in Honolulu Harbor, the radio room still maintained communications with the commander, San Francisco division, via the USCG radio station NMC. On Friday, June 18, a message from the commander, San Francisco Division, addressed to the commander, Hawaiian Section, with information to the *Itasca*, was originated at 0921 PST. It reported that the *Itasca*'s transmitter was apparently faulty and directed that the radio electrician investigate and make necessary adjustments prior to sailing.

Warrant Officer Henry M. Anthony, communications officer and radio electrician for the Hawaiian section, came to the *Itasca* to investigate the report. He tested the 500-watt T-16-A high-frequency telegraphy transmitter for proper keying of its "continuous wave" (CW) Morse code signals.

For a radio operator to receive CW Morse code signals, the receiver must have a beat frequency oscillator (BFO), which must be switched on. The T-16 on the *Itasca* could not transmit radiotelephone signals. It was designed exclusively to transmit high-frequency CW Morse code between 4,000 and 18,100 kilocycles.

If Earhart was listening for a voice transmission on the hour or half hour and the *Itasca* transmitted a CW Morse code signal, she would not hear it because, while receiving voice, she would have the BFO of her receiver turned off. (On the Bendix receiver the beat frequency oscillator switch was not even labeled "BFO"; it was labeled "CW," "on," and "off.") If a CW signal was strong, Earhart might hear a *whoosh* sound as she tuned for a voice signal. With the CW switch on she would hear a voice signal, but it would be accompanied by a constant squeal.

While Warrant Officer Anthony was on the *Itasca*, he talked with Ensign Sutter and Chief Bellarts. He provided them with copies of the same information and messages that he had supplied to the cutter *Shoshone* in March. Anthony told them of the meeting he had had in Honolulu three months earlier with Earhart and Captain Manning to discuss Earhart's radio equipment, and how they would handle the radio schedules while she was in flight. The detailed radio information that Captain Manning had given to him in March was now passed along to the *Itasca* as firsthand confirmation of Earhart's capabilities and mode of operation. It was, of course, no longer accurate.

But Anthony's report was consistent with the earlier message Sutter had received from the San Francisco division. It reinforced the belief that Earhart would use Morse code for her radio schedules and that 500 was available. The three crucial points of misunderstanding were now firmly entrenched in the consciousness of the men responsible for the *Itasca*'s communications.

Last-minute supplies were still coming aboard Friday morning, June 18, along with the Department of Interior island personnel and Army, Army Air Corps, and Navy men assigned to be at Howland to assist the Earhart flight. The duty officer logged them aboard as they came up the gangway onto the ship. There were airplane mechanics, pilots, photographers, news reporters, colonists, relatives, and friends who were authorized as guests for the cruise.

At 1600 HST, Friday afternoon, June 18, the *Itasca* slipped her mooring from Pier 12 and made her way out of Honolulu Harbor bound for Howland Island.

After the first night at sea, several people spent part of Saturday, June 19, meeting to develop plans for Earhart's arrival at Howland. Richard Black had been aboard the cutter *Shoshone* in March and could confirm the information given by Warrant Officer Anthony. But the message that Earhart might not be able to use 500 kilocycles was disturbing. If correct, it would automatically follow that the *Itasca*'s low-frequency radio direction-finder, which could take radio bearings only on frequencies between 270 and 550 kilocycles, was also of dubious value. Radio direction-finding to guide Earhart into the island was a significant part of the *Itasca*'s mission, and the crew had no experience with the Navy's high-frequency unit. Therefore, this problem urgently needed attention.

Ensign Sutter was responsible for the communications plan, but he still did not know the frequency Earhart wanted the *Itasca* to transmit on for her homing device. Mr. Black wrote a message for the ship to send by commercial telegraphy service to Mr. Putnam.

Buried in the text of this message were subtle, almost imperceptible changes from what Putnam had stated in his June 18 message. Putnam's remark about "500 kilocycles being of dubious usability," was changed to "also try five hundred close in." Putnam, as a writer and publisher, might be expected to use words with some precision. *Dubious* does not mean *close in*. This may have been an attempt to clarify "dubious usability," but it was an interpretation of the *Itasca* crew's.

A message was sent to the governor of American Samoa at 1430 HST, requesting the frequencies available on the Navy ships *Swan* and *Ontario* for transmission of signals to the homing device on Earhart's plane.

At 1400 on Sunday all ship's clocks were set back by one half hour. The ship was now using the plus 11 hour time zone and thus was a half hour behind Honolulu.

On Monday communications personnel tried to find out whether NPU, Naval Radio Tutuila, Samoa, could make direct contact with the Australian radio station VJQ in Salamaua, New Guinea. The governor of Samoa told them this was not possible. All messages had to be relayed through Suva in the Fiji Islands, with a delay of 4 hours expected for the message to be relayed from Suva to Salamaua. Naval Radio Tutuila had only three schedules with Suva on weekdays, and one schedule on Saturdays and Sundays. They were trying to arrange for two more weekday schedules, but Suva Radio was completely closed for 8 hours every night. Salamaua had only four schedules a day with Lae, and Lae was closed for 12 hours every night. It was unlikely that a question sent to or from Lae would receive an answer on the same day. Traffic was delayed so long that when the answer came back, no one could be sure what question it was answering.

On Tuesday, June 22, at 1400 all ship's clocks were set back yet another half hour in accordance with a new time zone. (For convenience, from now on we will call this *Itasca* ship time (IST).) They were now 1 hour behind Honolulu (HST).

The *Itasca* was due to arrive at Howland Island early on the evening of June 23. Black sent a message to Earhart via the governor of American Samoa requesting her to state which frequencies they were to transmit on for her homing device. He included a list of frequencies that the *Ontario, Swan,* and *Itasca* could provide. In the case of the *Swan,* only 35 watts of power were available to transmit a radiotelephone signal.

In addition to Black's message, the *Itasca* sent a message via Naval Radio Tutuila to Earhart at both Darwin and Lae, asking her to give at least 12 hours' notice of her radio requirements before she left New Guinea. They warned that communications were slow between the *Itasca* and Darwin.

Wednesday evening, at 1930 IST (*Itasca* time), the light on Howland Island was sighted at a distance of 8 miles. The *Itasca* moved to a position west of the island, where Captain Thompson stopped engines at 2100 IST to drift until daylight.

Most of the day on Thursday, June 24, the *Itasca* was transferring supplies to Howland Island. The *Itasca*'s regular 1300 IST weather report was combined with Howland Island's 1200 HST weather and upper air observations into one message. The surface wind at Howland Island was out of the east at 15 mph, and the wind aloft at 10,000 feet was blowing out of the east at 34 mph.

Black sent a message to Ruth Hampton at the Department of the Interior in Washington. He told her that they had transferred all the supplies to Howland Island and asked her to tell Putnam that the ships were in position on their stations. He wanted Putnam to keep them informed of Earhart's movements.

The *Itasca* drifted all night to the west of Howland Island. Friday morning, June 25, at 0504 IST, the ship laid course for Baker Island, sighting it at 0740 IST. By 0850 IST they were lowering boats to transfer the Department of the Interior colonists and supplies to the island. In a little over two hours all boats were secured back on the ship. At 1112 IST the *Itasca* departed Baker Island on a gyro compass course of 346 degrees to return the approximately 40 miles to Howland Island.

A message came from the San Francisco division to the *Itasca* stating that Mr. Putnam was now in Oakland. Putnam said that Earhart would voice her positions at 15 and 45 minutes past the hour. There was no reference to Earhart trying "500 close in." Putnam had failed to grasp the significance of this earlier message. The *Itasca* was informed again that Earhart's radio direction-finder operated in a range from about 200 to about 1400 kilocycles. They were to adjust their transmitter for possible voice transmissions to Earhart on 3105 kilocycles. Chief Bellarts would have to calibrate the T-10 transmitter on 3105 kilocycles and make sure it operated correctly.

At 1320 IST, Howland Island was sighted. Less than an hour later the *Itasca* stopped engines and drifted to the west of the island. Boats were lowered to move personnel to and from the island.

A very long message regarding Earhart arrived in the *Itasca*'s radio room on Saturday morning, June 26, from the commander of the San Francisco division; it was addressed for action to the *Itasca*. The information was represented as having been received from Earhart on that date.

The message informed the *Itasca* that Earhart's direction-finder bands covered the frequencies of 200 to 1500 and 2400 to 4800 kilocycles. The *Itasca* was to choose any frequency not near the band ends to send as a homing signal for Earhart's direction-finder. San Francisco Division suggested that they select a suitable frequency, keeping in mind the uncertain characteristics of the high frequencies. They recommended the *Itasca* use the low frequencies of either 333 kilocycles or 545 kilocycles. The *Itasca* should run tests with other stations in the area to determine which frequency was best. They were to advise Earhart at Lae, via Tutuila, which frequencies they had selected for her direction-finder. The *Itasca* was to inform her that they would be sending continuous signals after they believed her direction-finder was in range.

The message continued: "SHE BROADCAST ON QUARTER AFTER AND QUARTER BEFORE HOUR ON 6210 AND 3105 KILOCYCLES PERIOD AM ADVISING EARHART THAT ITASCA WILL VOICE RADIO ON 3105 ON HOUR AND HALF HOUR AS SHE APPROACHES HOWLAND PERIOD"

The message ended by directing the *Itasca* to send a priority message to San Francisco when they determined that the T-10 radiotelephone transmitter was satisfactory for use on 3105 kilocycles.

San Francisco was advising Earhart that the *Itasca* would be using radiotelephone to call her on 3105 kilocycles on the hour and half hour as she approached Howland. Chief Bellarts would have to report the results of his tuneup of the T-10 transmitter on 3105.

It appeared that all the previous information the *Itasca* had received about the frequency range of Earhart's radio direction-finder was wrong. The new message quoted Earhart saying she could take radio bearings on frequencies as high as 4800 kilocycles. Yet the San Francisco division suggested that they try 333 and 545 kilocycles because of the uncertain characteristics of high-frequency direction-finding.

That afternoon a message came to the *Itasca* via Naval Radio Honolulu NPM, transmitting the message Earhart had sent before leaving Bandoeng for Surabaya on June 26. She requested that the *Ontario* send "N" on 400 kilocycles for five minutes with call letters repeated twice at the end of every minute, and the *Itasca* send "A" and call letters on 7.5 megacycles (7500 kilocycles) on the half hour. She requested the *Swan* to transmit to her by voice on 9.0 megacycles (9000 kilocycles). If she was unable to receive the *Swan* on 9.0 megacycles, they were to be ready to send on 900 kilocycles. If the frequencies were unsuitable for night work, they were to inform her at Lae. She concluded the message by stating she would give them a long call by voice on 3105 kilocycles at a quarter after and possibly at a quarter to the hour.

Nowhere is 500 kilocycles mentioned. Other than the homing signals, all transmissions mentioned were to be made using voice. The message indicates that Earhart understood that the *Ontario* could not transmit except by Morse code, and then only on frequencies below 600 kilocycles. She could copy (i.e., transcribe) an "A" and an "N" in Morse code. Those two letters were repeated continuously by all low-frequency radio range stations in the United States, and were heard over and over by pilots flying the radio ranges. She asked the *Ontario* to transmit on request in Morse code the letter "N" on 400 kilocycles. The *Ontario*'s call letters (NIDX) and the *Itasca*'s (NRUI) could be recognized if they were repeated and she knew in advance what Morse code signals to expect. She could write out the individual dots and dashes to match with the signals if necessary.

In the case of the *Swan* she picked two frequencies: 9.0 megacycles (9000 kilocycles) and 900 kilocycles. Both of these were within the frequency limits of the *Swan*'s voice transmitter. She specifically requested the *Swan* to transmit using voice and made no mention of any Morse code letter for the *Swan* to transmit. The transmitting power of the *Swan* was reduced to only 35 watts when transmitting radiotelephone, which meant that the range of the *Swan* transmitting 35 watts of voice by ground wave on 900 kilocycles in the daytime would be unreliable for much more than 100 miles.

Though the *Itasca* never informed Earhart of its radiotelephone capabilities, the message indicates that she had that information. She had selected 3105 kilocycles for the *Itasca* to transmit radiotelephone, with no specification of day or night. This subtle but important fact explains why, on her flight to Howland Island, Earhart in the daytime stayed with 3105 until the end. She knew the *Itasca* could not transmit voice on 6210 kilocycles. (She would switch to 6210 at 0843 IST on her flight to Howland Island to make a final desperate broadcast of her plight.)

San Francisco, in its earlier message, stated it was advising Earhart that the *Itasca* would use radiotelephone on 3105 on the hour and half hour as she approached. With the exception of the low-powered portable T-22, the only transmitter the *Itasca* had available for radiotelephone transmissions was the T-10. The General Electric 200-watt model T-10 transmitter was designed for transmissions between 2000 and 3000 kilocycles. They hoped to stretch the T-10 a little beyond its design limits to send spoken messages on 3105. When the T-10 was transmitting voice, its power would probably be reduced to less than 100 watts, so the range of the *Itasca* transmitting voice by ground wave on 3105 in the daytime would be unreliable much beyond 200 to 300 miles.

Earhart also requested they transmit the Morse code letter "A" on 7.5 megacycles on the half hour. The only transmitter capable of 7.5-megacycle (7500 kilocycles) transmissions was the 500-watt T-16, which was a dedicated CW-only transmitter. This caused a conflict for the radiomen on the *Itasca* because Earhart now requested they send "A's" with the T-16 transmitter on 7.5 megacycles on the half hour, while San Francisco had them scheduled to be voicing on 3105 with the T-10 transmitter. The two transmitters shared the same antenna; a knife switch overhead in the radio room selected which of the transmitters was connected to the antenna. They could not use both transmitters at the same time. The information was contradictory and confusing.

Captain Thompson was uneasy. He was receiving information from his superiors in San Francisco that differed from what Earhart was telling him. He sent a message at 1705 IST, June 26, to the commander, San Francisco Division, with information to the Hawaiian section. Captain Thompson reported to the commander that he considered the present relationship of the division and the *Itasca* communications unsatisfactory and potentially dangerous to Earhart's contacts and other vital schedules. He urgently requested that the *Itasca* be given complete communications independence.

The *Itasca* received an answer from the commander at 2255 PST: Captain Thompson's request had been granted. The responsibility for communications with Earhart was squarely placed on his shoulders from that moment on.

Early Sunday morning, June 27, a message came to the *Itasca* from Earhart via RCA Radio Manila; it was the same message they had received the afternoon before via Naval Radio Honolulu. Captain Thompson now felt secure that he knew what Earhart was requesting.

At 0600 IST the *Itasca* moved up to Howland Island. Boats were lowered to take the work parties ashore to prepare for Earhart's arrival. They had decided to put up a tent near the intersection of the runways, where they would install the Navy high-frequency radio direction-finder. The canvas walls of the tent, invisible to the radio waves coming to the direction-finder's loop antenna, would protect the radio from the sun, wind, and rain. A 35-ampere-hour battery, normally used on the *Itasca*'s 5-inch gun, was hooked up to the direction-finder to provide operating power.

Using small charges of TNT, they made several efforts to move the birds off the runways onto the north end of the island. The work party cleared and filled in the west end of the east–west runway, adding several hundred feet to the length that could be used for takeoff.

Later, Captain Thompson sent a message to the commander in San Francisco with information to the Hawaiian section: "6027 SWAN ON-TARIO ITASCA ON POINT STATIONS ASSIGNED AND COMMUNICATION FOR FLIGHT SATISFACTORY PERIOD DIRECTION FINDER INSTALLED ON HOWLAND PERIOD GENERAL OPINION HOWLAND AIRFIELD USABLE PERIOD LARGE BIRDS APT TO BE PROBLEM PERIOD ITASCA LANDING ORGANIZATION SET IN CASE CRASH PERIOD FIRE COMMA SURF RESCUE COMMA ARRANGEMENTS COMPLETE PERIOD ORGA-NIZED FOR DAY OR NIGHT ARRIVAL BUT STRONGLY RECOMMEND DAYLIGHT AR-RIVAL 1420" The captain had determined that everything was in readiness for Earhart's flight.

Ensign Sutter completed his communication plan and organization of radio personnel for the Earhart flight and posted it in the radio room. As on the *Shoshone* in March, a printed form titled the "Synopsis of Weather for Radio Room" was prepared. It indicated that the weather was to be sent at 25 and 55 minutes past the hour while Earhart was in flight.

By 1840 IST the *Itasca* was drifting 8 miles to the westward of Howland Island for the night. Sunday had been a busy day.

Monday morning, June 28, at 0558 IST the *Itasca* started engines to stand up to Howland Island. All hands were called at 0600, and the island was sighted at 0633. As the ship maintained its position just off the western shore of Howland, at 0910 IST the *Itasca* sent a message to Earhart at Lae via the governor of Samoa. They informed Earhart that their transmitters were calibrated to 7500, 6210, 3105, 500, and 425 kilocycles CW, and the last three either CW or "modulated continuous wave" (MCW). The *Itasca*'s direction-finder frequency range was 550 to 270 kilocycles. They asked to be notified of the departure and zone times Earhart would use on her radio schedules. They concluded by stating the *Itasca* would be at Howland Island during her flight.

On Tuesday and Wednesday, June 29 and 30, the *Itasca* exchanged messages about weather and communications with Earhart while they waited for word of her departure from Lae.

Thursday, July 1, the *Itasca* sent the ship's 1200 IST weather report and Howland Island's 1300 HST weather and upper-air observations combined into one message to Earhart at Lae. The weather observations were taken at the same time, but Howland Island was using the 10+30 hour time zone—the same as Hawaii standard time—while the *Itasca* was using the 11+30 hour time zone: the two were one-half mile apart, but one hour different in time. The Howland surface wind was northeast at 14 mph, and at 9,000 feet it was east-northeast at 31 mph.

Earhart was already en route to Howland, but the *Itasca* would not learn that fact for several hours.

That evening at 2130 PST, the commander, San Francisco Division, sent the following message to the *Itasca* with information to the *Swan* and *Ontario:* "8012 UNITED PRESS REPORTS EARHART TOOK OFF AT NOON LAE TIME 2130" The message was inaccurate, but it was the first indication the *Itasca* had that Earhart had left Lae.

In the *Itasca*'s radio room Radioman 3rd Class Thomas J. O'Hare was standing watch with NMC San Francisco, NPM Honolulu, and NPU Tutuila, American Samoa. At 1900 IST, another radioman came on watch to monitor and handle transmissions to and from Earhart. There were now two radio logs, one for the ship's radio traffic and the other for the aircraft.

At 1905 IST, boats number 1 and 3 were sent to Howland Island with Radioman 2nd Class Frank Cipriani to man the high-frequency radio direction-finder. Cipriani was given instructions to monitor 3105 kilocycles and to keep a radio log. He was to take radio bearings on all of Earhart's signals, then report them to the *Itasca* on 2670 kilocycles using the portable T-22 transmitter/receiver.

Less than an hour later, at 1955 IST, the *Itasca* received a message from Lae via Naval Radio Tutuila: "URGENT BLACK ITASCA TUTUILA RADIO AMELIA EARHART LEFT LAE TEN AM LOCAL TIME JULY 2ND DUE HOWLAND ISLAND 18 HOURS TIME BT VACUUM"

It was 0725 GCT July 2, and Earhart had been in the air for 7 hours and 25 minutes when the *Itasca* finally received the message from Lae of her departure. Earhart's estimated time of arrival at Howland was calculated to be 1800 GCT or 0630 IST, a few minutes after sunrise.

Captain Thompson was confident the *Itasca* was ready to guard the Earhart flight. They had the capability to bring her to the island with the radio direction-finders if necessary. She would be taking radio bearings on their 7500-kilocycle transmissions, while Cipriani would be taking radio bearings on her 3105-kilocycle transmissions. When the plane got close in, Earhart would transmit on 500 kilocycles so the *Itasca* could take radio bearings with the ship's very accurate direction-finder. There were three independent ways for Earhart to be guided to the island. It would have been hard for Thompson to imagine how anything could go wrong.

But the Coast Guard radiomen aboard the *Itasca* expected that Earhart would call them as scheduled, at a quarter before and a quarter after each hour, to communicate and exchange information. As Friday,

July 2, began, the men in the *Itasca*'s radio room listened for the first message to come from Earhart. The *Itasca* was east of the international date line and would be experiencing the Friday morning sunrise in a few hours. To those west of the international date line it was already Friday evening.

It was early in the morning before the first signal was heard. At 0245 IST, in a low monotone voice, Earhart was heard to report "cloudy and overcast." Her signal, at strength 1 to 2, was barely heard and mostly unreadable.

One hour later, at 0345 IST, Earhart came on again. This time she called the *Itasca* with the following message: ". . . OVERCAST—WILL LISTEN ON HOUR AND HALF HOUR ON 3105" (repeated). Her signals were at strength 2. The radiomen could make out only some of what she said.

At 0453 IST the *Itasca* heard Earhart's voice say the words "partly cloudy." Her volume was at strength 1, barely heard to unreadable.

The next time they heard her transmission was near sunrise. From that point onward, during the daylight hours, every signal the *Itasca* received from Earhart came in stronger than the one before. She was getting closer and closer to the island.

The *Itasca*'s small radio room became the focus of attention as ship's officers Thompson, Kenner, and Sutter, along with news reporters James Carey of Associated Press and Howard Hanzlik of United Press, crowded around the doorway to listen to Earhart. Her transmission came in so strong that Chief Bellarts was able to turn on a speaker so everyone could listen to her messages.

The executive officer, Lieutenant Commander. L. H. Baker, departed the ship with the shore party at 0610 IST. He was in charge of the mechanics and other personnel who were on the island to assist Miss Earhart on her arrival.

At 0614 IST, Earhart reported about 200 miles out. She asked them to take a bearing on her 3105 signal and report back on the hour. Her signal strength was 3, or poor reception. She was readable but with difficulty. Radioman O'Hare was working Honolulu when Chief Bellarts took the antenna from O'Hare on the hour GCT (0630 IST) to transmit to Earhart using CW (code) on 7500 kilocycles. The simplest of booby traps had ensnared the hapless radiomen. Earhart's "on the hour" was their "on the half hour." If Earhart had listened on the hour GCT for the *Itasca* to send her a radio bearing on 3105, she would have heard nothing.

Captain Thompson ordered the *Itasca* to start making smoke. In

March, Earhart had requested as a daylight signal that the ship make smoke as they approached. The idea was for a column of smoke to rise high in the air as a distinctive visual signal that could be seen for many miles. Unfortunately the smoke came out of the *Itasca*'s stack and settled down onto the water, spreading out more like a smoke screen than a smoke signal. The murky smoke lay on the water, slowly drifting to the west in the light easterly wind.

At 0645 IST, Earhart reported approximately 100 miles out. She asked them to give her the bearing of her 3105 signal on the half hour. Her signal strength was 4, or fair reception. She could be read easily. Again, the radiomen interpreted that Earhart wanted a call "in a half hour" instead of "on the half hour." From 0700 to 0703 IST (1830 to 1833 GCT) the *Itasca* was transmitting to Cipriani on Howland Island. He reported that the battery powering the Navy high-frequency direction-finder was low. It was impossible for him to get a bearing on Earhart's signals.

At 0715 IST, exactly thirty minutes after Earhart's request, the *Itasca* transmitted with voice on 3105. Unfortunately, this was Earhart's time to be transmitting. If Earhart did transmit a message at that time, the *Itasca*'s transmission blanked it out. Nothing was reported having been heard from Earhart at that time.

At 0742 IST, she reported that she should be on them but could not see them. Her gas was running low and she had only one half hour left. She told them she was not hearing them on her radio and reported that she was flying at altitude 1,000 feet. The signal strength was 5, or good reception. She was loud and must have been nearby.

At 0758 IST, she reported she was circling. She asked them to transmit on 7500 kilocycles either now or on the scheduled time on the half hour. They responded immediately on 7500 kilocycles, and Earhart heard their signals. She tried to take a bearing on the 7500 signal but couldn't get a minimum. Her signal strength was 5 plus, or very good reception. She was very loud and sounded even closer than before. Every signal the *Itasca* had received since 0615 IST was stronger than the one before.

Earhart completed her message at 0803 IST by asking the *Itasca* to take a bearing on her and answer with voice on 3105. She sent long dashes, each a vocalized "Dahhhh," for them to take bearings on. They did not get a bearing, and they transmitted at 0815 IST with voice on 3105, again during her transmission period. If she transmitted a message, the *Itasca* had blocked it again. Nothing was reported heard from Earhart during her 0815 IST scheduled transmission time. In fact, Captain Thompson later noted Earhart was never heard reporting at a quarter after the hour, except at 0615, and mildly rebuked her for not maintaining the agreed-upon schedules.

The radiomen had tried everything they could think of to get in contact with Earhart. When they found out she was in flight, they started sending the weather reports by CW (code) on 7500 kilocycles at 25 and 55 minutes after the hour. NMC in San Francisco had even told them to slow down the Morse code speed to ten words per minute for Earhart.

Every time they had heard Earhart they had answered immediately, usually with Morse code. At 0715 and 0815 IST they had transmitted voice messages on 3105—during Earhart's transmission time. They knew something was wrong. Earhart didn't seem able to hear the *Itasca*'s transmissions. Earhart's receiver, or the antenna system for the receiver, might be bad. Or maybe the *Itasca* was just not transmitting a signal Earhart could hear during the periods when she was listening.

Chief Bellarts switched the T-16 transmitter to 12,600 kilocycles to send a message to NMC San Francisco.

Without warning, Earhart came on the air at 0843 IST with a signal strength of 5, or good reception. She was loud, at the same strength that she had been an hour earlier at 0742 IST when she reported that she must be on them. For the first time, her signal was not quite as strong as the preceding signal had been. She reported that they were flying on the line of position 157–337, and she would repeat the message on 6210 kilocycles. They were flying north and south on the line. She told them to wait and listen on 6210 kilocycles.

Nothing was ever heard from Amelia Earhart again.

Evidently, as Earhart was cranking her transmitter to change from 3105 to 6210 kilocycles her fuel supply ran out and she was forced to ditch her plane into the sea.

It was indeed tragic that the *Itasca* radiomen did not know that neither Earhart nor Noonan could understand Morse code. That simple misunderstanding negated over 90 percent of the *Itasca*'s efforts to establish two-way radio communications. In addition, because the *Itasca* was using code exclusively when transmitting on 500 and 7500 kilocycles, over 90 percent of the ship's total transmission time was of no value to Earhart. During the entire two and a half hours that Earhart was in range, the *Itasca* transmitted a spoken message on 3105 only once, at 0730 IST, and then only for one minute, within a three-minute period after the hour or half hour. The only time Earhart ever acknowledged receiving a transmission from the *Itasca* was the 7500-kilocycle

Morse code signals they had sent at 0800 IST. Hoping she might answer again, they called repeatedly using Morse code on 7500 kilocycles. Unfortunately all this effort was wasted. Probably because it seemed illogical and contrary to their normal procedures, the radiomen of the *Itasca* could not comprehend that Earhart was listening for them to transmit voice messages only on the hour and half hour. Inexplicably, they did just about everything *but* transmit voice on 3105 at those scheduled times. Whether these were the reasons for the *Itasca*'s inability to reach Earhart by radio, or whether there was a malfunction of the Electra's receiving apparatus, it makes little difference. The results were the same. She did not receive any of the *Itasca*'s radiotelephone signals on 3105.

Earhart was busy running the engines, managing the fuel, flying the airplane, looking for the island, conferring with Noonan, and making decisions. She put on the headphones to listen only a few minutes out of each hour. Though it had been repeated in message after message that Earhart transmitted at one time and received at another, this was never understood by the men on the *Itasca*.

Radioman 2nd Class Frank Cipriani had begun operating the high-frequency direction-finder on Howland Island at ten o'clock the night before. Operating the direction-finder all night had depleted the battery. By the time Earhart was in range, the unit wasn't working properly, and Cipriani could not take a bearing on her signal. She did not transmit on 500 kilocycles, so the *Itasca* was never able to take a bearing with the ship's direction-finder. She could not get a minimum on 7500 kilocycles with her Bendix. As improbable as it was, all three direction-finders failed to provide Earhart with any guidance to the island. Both Earhart and Cipriani, without proper training or manuals to guide them, had operated their direction-finders inappropriately, and effectively rendered them useless. Human factors had played a major part in this tragic outcome.

If Radioman Cipriani, Lieutenant Commander Baker, or anyone in authority had thought to borrow batteries from the Department of the Interior island colonizers, they could have gotten the direction-finder working again. True, they couldn't pass information to Earhart, but it would have been of great value to the *Itasca:* Earhart and Noonan's possible survival would depend heavily on the direction Captain Thompson chose to start the search for the downed Electra.

The final flight of Amelia Earhart and Frederick Noonan had ended. The greatest search effort ever mounted by the U.S. Navy was about to begin.

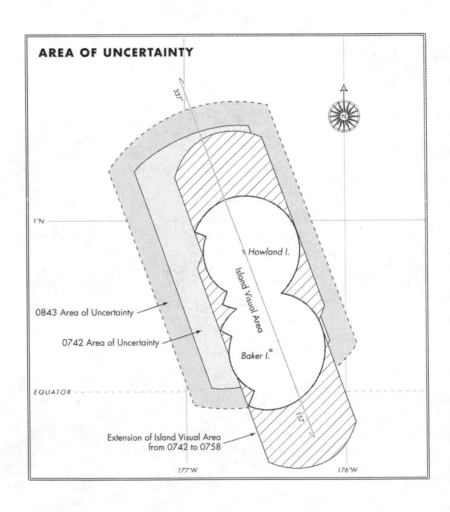

AREA OF UNCERTAINTY

337°

N

1°N

Howland I.

Island Visual Area

0843 Area of Uncertainty

0742 Area of Uncertainty

Baker I.°

157°

EQUATOR

Extension of Island Visual Area
from 0742 to 0758

177°W   176°W

The men planning the search did not know why Earhart had run out of fuel at 0843. Captain Thompson, who personally heard Earhart say on the radio she was running low on fuel with only a half hour left, believed her. But those far removed from the scene heard other voices and were not so sure.

14: THE SEARCH

FOR EARHART

A FTER Earhart's last transmission at 0843 IST, the *Itasca*'s radiomen called almost constantly on 500, 3105, and 7500 kilocycles asking her to answer. She never responded.

Radioman Cipriani called the *Itasca* from Howland Island and was told to get the high-frequency direction-finder working at all costs. But its battery was dead and he could not comply.

A coded message was dispatched to the commander of the San Francisco division reporting that Earhart was overdue on her flight to Howland Island. They were to pass the information to Washington, D.C., interested government agencies, and all military departments.

Captain Thompson hurriedly met in his cabin with Lieutenant Commander Frank T. Kenner and Richard B. Black to get their individual assessments of the situation.

The *Itasca*'s executive officer, Mr. Baker, and the Earhart landing party were recalled from Howland to make preparations to search for the downed Earhart plane.

After his meeting, Captain Thompson based his decision of where to begin the search on two items of information: Earhart's last transmission

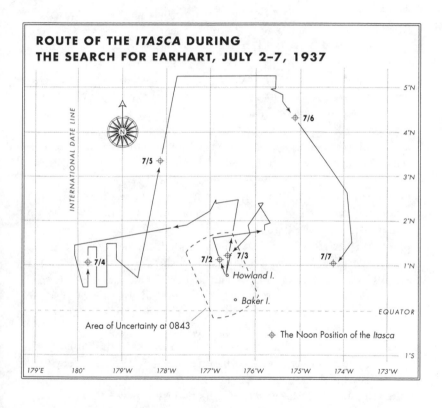

**ROUTE OF THE *ITASCA* DURING
THE SEARCH FOR EARHART, JULY 2–7, 1937**

INTERNATIONAL DATE LINE

N

5°N
4°N
3°N
2°N
1°N

7/6

7/5

7/4

7/2 7/3

7/7

Howland I.

Baker I.

EQUATOR

Area of Uncertainty at 0843

The Noon Position of the *Itasca*

1°S

179°E   180°   179°W   178°W   177°W   176°W   175°W   174°W   173°W

said she was on the line of position 157–337; also, because Baker Island lay to the southeast, Earhart was more likely to the northwest. This reasoning was reinforced by the visual observation that the weather was clear to the south and east, but heavy cumulus clouds were visible in the distant north and west.

At 1015 IST, Captain Thompson sent the following message to the commander, San Francisco Division, with information to the Hawaiian section: "6002 EARHART CONTACT 0742 REPORTED ONE HALF HOUR FUEL AND NO LAND FALL POSITION DOUBTFUL CONTACT 0646 REPORTED APPROXIMATELY 100 MILES FROM ITASCA BUT NO RELATIVE BEARING PERIOD 0843 REPORTED LINE OF POSITION 157 DASH 337 BUT NO REFERENCE POINT PRESUME HOWLAND PERIOD ESTIMATE 1200 FOR MAXIMUM TIME ALOFT AND IF NON ARRIVAL BY THAT TIME WILL COMMENCE SEARCH NORTHWEST QUADRANT FROM HOWLAND AS MOST PROBABLE AREA PERIOD SEA SMOOTH VISIBILITY NINE CEILING UNLIMITED PERIOD UNDERSTAND SHE WILL FLOAT FOR LIMITED TIME 1015" (The visibility reported, number "nine," is the highest on a scale of one to nine and indicates an actual visibility of more than 20 nautical miles.)

Three minutes later, at 1018 IST, the *Itasca* sent a message to the Hawaiian section in Honolulu suggesting the Navy be requested to send a seaplane to help with the search. There were 1,600 gallons of aviation gasoline and 95 gallons of lubricating oil now available on Howland Island for the plane.

Captain Thompson knew that time was a critical element in a rescue effort. He decided not to wait any longer to start the search. At 1040 IST the *Itasca* got underway from Howland Island on a course heading 337 degrees. He would go to the northwest, right up the line of position 157–337 that Earhart reported she was flying on north and south.

Every vantage point on the ship was taken by eager, hawk-eyed young sailors. They searched the sea in all directions as the *Itasca* made its way toward the northwest at 16 knots. Watch standers were kept continuously in the crow's nest. Four men were posted with binoculars on the wing bridges. The watch officers themselves were intently scanning the waves, hoping to be the first to spot Earhart's plane or life raft. The weather was cooperative, with visibility remaining excellent.

The radio room was busier than ever. The ship-to-shore circuit was alive with messages to and from the *Itasca,* almost all of them about Earhart. The operator of the ship-to-airplane circuit continued to call Earhart on every available frequency whenever a transmitter and the antenna were available.

The incessant calls of the *Itasca,* calling KHAQQ and Earhart by name, were being broadcast indiscriminately to most of the Pacific and a good part of the world. Dozens of people, having just heard the name "Earhart" or "KHAQQ" over their receiver, sent reports of having heard her. Some even claimed to have messages sent in Morse code by Earhart, or messages of her reported position where no land or island existed. It took a while for these dozens of reports and messages to make their way through channels to the controlling agencies. In the meantime, the world press was reporting that signals were being heard from Earhart. Officials responsible for conducting the search found it impossible to ignore the messages and reports when they arrived.

At 1940 EST (1310 IST) July 2, in Washington, Secretary of the Navy Claude A. Swanson originated a message to the commander of the Fourteenth Naval District, with information to the commander in chief, U.S. Fleet, Fleet Air Base, Pearl Harbor; the commandant, U.S. Coast Guard; and the commander, Air Base Forces: "0002 USE AVAILABLE NAVAL FACILITIES TO CONDUCT SUCH SEARCH FOR MISS EARHART AS IN YOUR OPINION PRACTICABLE 1940"

This set in motion what was to be, to that time, the largest search ever conducted for an aircraft lost at sea. The actions taken in the next few hours bore remarkable testimony to the ability of the U.S. Coast Guard and Navy personnel to respond quickly. Most successful rescues at sea are made in the first 24 hours. Every hour of delay decreased the likelihood of a favorable outcome.

The Coast Guard was in contact with Putnam in San Francisco. If the Electra had ditched, they needed information about Earhart's emergency radio, life rafts, and buoyancy. Putnam placed a call to the Lockheed factory in Burbank. Lockheed was able to give them most of the information, but the direction-finder and Bendix receiver had not been installed by the factory radio technicians. Putnam thought of the United radioman, Joseph Gurr. He was able to reach Gurr by telephone at his home. Gurr told him that with battery power and the antenna on top of the plane, he believed it was possible the plane could still transmit when on the water.

The commander, San Francisco Division, sent a message to the *Itasca* at 1910 PST (1540 IST): "8002 POSSIBILITY PLANE MAY ATTEMPT USE RADIO ON WATER AS RADIO SUPPLY WAS BATTERY AND ANTENNA COULD BE USED ON TOP OF WING PUTNAM AND LOCKHEED STATE POSSIBILITY OF FLOATING CONSIDERABLE TIME EXCELLENT AND THAT EMERGENCY RUBBER BOAT AND PLENTY OF EMERGENCY RATIONS CARRIED ON PLANE 1910"

Gurr's belief that it was possible for Earhart to transmit from the plane after it had landed on the water lent credibility to the radio messages reported coming from Earhart. The information was not corrected until Monday morning when the Lockheed radio technicians returned to work.

The *Itasca* made the following comment in its report: "This information formed the basis of the *Itasca*'s search at sea until the information was contradicted by Lockheed on about 5 July. The *Itasca* assumed the plane would float 9-hours or so. The *Itasca* kept listening on 3105 and 500. The probability of the plane being able to use radio gave credence to the numerous false amateur position messages. Arrival of the Navy plane on 3 July, it was hoped, would expand search efforts. As long as radio use was possible the search was not a hopeless affair. The *Itasca* steadily called the plane."

The Navy dispatched a PBY Catalina flying boat—number 6-P-3, radio call sign 62C—with Lieutenant Warren W. Harvey and seven crew members, from Pearl Harbor at 1923 HST. The Navy seaplane tender *Swan*, with 10,000 gallons of aviation fuel aboard, was ordered to leave its Earhart guard station halfway between Howland and Honolulu and proceed to Howland Island. The *Itasca* was ordered to return to Howland Island by daybreak of July 3 to act as a seaplane tender for the inbound PBY until the *Swan* arrived. The U.S. Navy battleship *Colorado*, in Pearl Harbor on a summer ROTC cruise, was ordered to make preparations to sail as soon as possible. The *Colorado* would bring its float-mounted scout planes to help with the search for Earhart.

In the meantime, the *Itasca* had gone up the line of 337 degrees from Howland Island for approximately 55 statute miles. At 1355 IST it turned to a course of 080 degrees to search the area eastward about 55 miles north of Howland. The *Itasca* continued on the course of 080 degrees until after sunset. Covering a 15-mile swath along its course, the *Itasca* had thoroughly searched a 2,000-square-mile area during daylight. After dark it searched with negative results as far as 120 miles northeast of Howland, using searchlights. The *Itasca* returned to Howland, sighting the island 10 miles ahead at 0710 IST.

At 2030 Samoan time (2000 IST), Tutuila radioed to Wailupe Naval Radio and the *Itasca,* also informing the Hawaiian section and the commander, San Francisco Division, that the British cruiser *Achilles* had heard a station say "KHAQQ" a couple of times and ask for dashes if they were heard. The *Achilles* heard two dashes from a station at 0620 GMT (1850 IST), more than 11 hours after Earhart's last transmission.

The HMS *Achilles,* radio call GVBK, was a British cruiser on a goodwill visit in the Pacific, presently en route from Tutuila, American Samoa, to Honolulu. After many messages and much information was exchanged between the *Itasca* and the *Achilles*, they determined that it was the *Itasca* that the *Achilles* had heard.

Lieutenant Harvey in the PBY seaplane ran into bad weather in the zone of equatorial convergence about 500 miles before reaching Howland Island and had to return to Pearl Harbor.

Captain Thompson sent a message to the Hawaiian section at 0800 IST saying he was drifting off Howland Island under orders of the commandant of the Fourteenth Naval District. The Navy plane was apparently returning to base. It was imperative that the *Itasca* resume the search.

The Hawaiian section replied at 0956 HST, with information to Fleet Air Base in Pearl Harbor and the San Francisco division, as follows: "6003 NAVY PLANE REPORTS RETURNING PEARL HARBOR DUE BAD WEATHER ITASCA RESUME SEARCH ALL POSSIBLE SPEED ADVISE IF YOU CONCUR 0956"

At 0930 IST the *Itasca* departed the island on course 002 degrees to search directly to the north of Howland. At 1015 HST the Hawaiian section asked the *Itasca* how long its fuel would allow it to continue searching at full speed. They would advise the *Itasca* later if they could replenish it at sea.

A little over an hour later the *Itasca* answered that they could continue scouting until 0800 of July 5. At that time they would have to proceed to Honolulu or have fuel available at Howland Island. Captain Thompson did what he could to conserve fuel without diminishing the search effort.

The *Itasca* continued on its way north for about 80 statute miles, then at 1400 IST turned to a course of 030 degrees. They held the 030-degree course for about 38 statute miles, then turned to the west on a course of 262 degrees at 1605 IST. They continued generally westward, searching the sea about 115 statute miles north of Howland, for any sign of the Earhart plane.

In the meantime the battleship *Colorado*, under the command of Capt. Wilhelm L. Friedell, departed Pearl Harbor to join in the search effort at 1300 HST Saturday afternoon.

The *Itasca* received a message from the commander, San Francisco Division, originated at 2350 PST: "8003 FOUR SEPARATE RADIOMEN AT LOS ANGELES REPORTED RECEIVING EARHART VOICE THIS MORNING AND VERIFY QUOTE 179 WITH 1 POINT SIX IN DOUBT UNQUOTE POSITION GIVEN AS QUOTE SOUTHWEST HOWLAND ISLAND UNQUOTE ABOVE HEARD ON 3105 KCS

AND CALL OF PLANE DISTINCTLY HEARD AND VERIFIED ACCORDING TO AMA-
TEURS 2350"

As the *Itasca* radio transcripts summarized later: "With the information that the plane could probably use its emergency transmitter on
water this message could not be ignored. The position placed Earhart
nearly on the line of flight and about 200 miles short of Howland. This
caused diversion of ITASCA from the *probable northwest sector.* However, a searching vessel cannot assume information as faked or false
and pass up investigation particularly when the probable sector is only
probable. The ITASCA therefore, proceeded to the westward of the report area and searched 2000 square miles on 4 July without result."

In response to the Los Angeles radiomen's report, Captain Thompson had left the area where Earhart was most likely down. He calculated that Earhart's plane would drift to the north and west. The *Itasca*
took up a course that would put it just to the west of the international
date line at sunrise on Sunday morning, July 4. This, he estimated,
would put the ship in front of the drifting plane as reported by the Los
Angeles radiomen. From there, the *Itasca* would work its way eastward
across a broad front. Following Captain Thompson's calculations, a few
minutes before sunrise the *Itasca* turned to a course of 178 degrees to
cut south across the path of the drifting plane. All day Sunday it cut
south, then north 60 miles, back and forth, advancing its path about 15
miles farther east at every turn.

During the day the *Itasca* was informed that the Navy would send
the aircraft carrier *Lexington* from San Diego to cooperate with the
Itasca and *Colorado* in the search for Earhart. The *Lexington* had to refuel in the Hawaiian Islands before it could proceed to the South Pacific, but because of the *Lexington's* deep draft, it would have to refuel
at Lahaina Roads, located off the leeward side of the island of Maui.
This would require reversing the course of the Navy tanker *Ramapo,*
which was presently steaming westward away from the Hawaiian Islands toward Guam. The *Ramapo* was under the direction of Admiral
William D. Leahy, chief of naval operations, in Washington, and he
would not be available until office hours resumed on the morning of
Tuesday, July 6.

Captain Thompson on the *Itasca* was relieved to receive a message
from the *Colorado* suggesting he continue scouting. The *Colorado*
would refuel them at sea on Thursday, July 8, and wanted to know
how much fuel the *Itasca* would require.

After sunset on Sunday, the *Itasca* expended over a dozen pyrotech-
nic flares and rockets for test purposes and to attract Earhart's atten-

tion. It was probably of no value to the search, but a fireworks display in the middle of the Pacific was not entirely inappropriate on the Fourth of July.

The *Itasca* slowed during the night to conserve fuel for daylight search operations. They continued the search at night, using the ship's searchlights every 15 minutes to sweep the waters about them. At daylight they would be able to finish searching the remainder of the area around 200 miles west of Howland.

The commander of Destroyer Squadron 2, Captain Jonathan S. Dowell, sent a message to the commandant of the Fourteenth Naval District, with information to the commander in chief, U.S. Fleet, the chief of naval operations, the *Colorado,* and the *Itasca.* The *Lexington* group was leaving San Diego and would refuel at Lahaina Roads before proceeding to search duty assigned. They expected to arrive at Lahaina at 1400 hours on July 8.

Chief Bellarts came to the *Itasca* radio room to call Howland Island. He exchanged messages with Frank Cipriani, through the amateur station K6GNW, from around 2216 to 2240 IST and told him to keep the high-frequency direction-finder in use, especially at night. Honolulu was apparently getting Earhart signals. He told Cipriani to keep Baker Island on alert and to send any plane data to the *Itasca* through Howland Island. He was told to use the Department of Interior batteries if he had to, get the direction-finder in operation on 3105 and take bearings, and keep a log. The captain expected results.

When a chief petty officer tells a radioman second class that the captain wants results, he's going to get results—good, bad, or as in this case, bordering on the outlandish.

Frank Cipriani opened the station and, using a pocket compass, took a magnetic bearing on an unknown continuous carrier signal that was not on Earhart's frequency. No call sign was given, and the frequency was slightly above 3105 kilocycles. In less than an hour, at 0035 HST, he had taken a radio bearing and reported back to the *Itasca* the results they expected.

The radio bearing Cipriani reported was of no value to the Earhart search. A radio bearing on an unknown, continuous carrier, off frequency, can be taken by any operator at any time on any day, and is meaningless. It was reported to placate his superiors, but unfortunately the radio bearing was widely disseminated as evidence that Earhart might be down somewhere to the north-northwest or south-southeast of Howland.

A message to the *Itasca* from the Hawaiian section, originated at

0242 HST (0142 IST), related that three radiomen at Navy Radio Wailupe had heard a Morse code signal from a station that read "281 NORTH HOWLAND CALL KHAQQ BEYOND NORTH DONT HOLD WITH US MUCH LONGER ABOVE WATER SHUT OFF." The keying was extremely poor and the phrases were fragmentary, but it was copied by three operators. (No one knew that the Morse code sending key had been removed from the Electra in Miami because neither Earhart nor Noonan knew the code well enough to communicate with it.)

There were three ships within a few hundred miles of this position. The British steamer *Moorby,* Captain T. Hill in command, was en route from Vancouver, British Columbia, to Sydney, Australia. The *Moorby,* radio call GYSR, had a single radioman, Mr. J. Harris, aboard. The British ship was approximately 100 miles from the reported position, located 281 miles north of Howland Island. The *Swan* was to the northeast and the *Itasca* to the southwest.

The *Itasca* radio transcripts report:

> This message received by three (3) Wailupe operators on 3105 and yet not received by ITASCA, MOORSBY [sic] and other listening agencies was probably a faked message originating in the Hawaiian Islands. However, Howland, on night 4 July, did get a bearing on some signal. At the time of its receipt ITASCA was 200 miles west of Howland searching down the 4 authenticated amateur reports. The position was in poor form and the message contained useless information but the report required immediate check up.
>
> The ITASCA had difficulty reaching MOORSBY due to that vessel having a one operator watch. The USS SWAN was to the northeast of the position and was requested to stand toward it. On the night of 5 July at dark three searching vessels converged on the position 281 (miles) north of Howland.

The *Itasca* sent off the following message to the *Swan:* "6005 OFFICIAL INFORMATION INDICATES EARHART DOWN 281 MILES NORTH OF HOWLAND SUGGEST YOU SEARCH AS INDICATED PERIOD ITASCA PROCEEDING 0255."

The *Moorby* received the following from the *Itasca:* "EARHART PLANE APPARENTLY DOWN 281 MILES NORTH OF HOWLAND ISLAND AND YOU ARE CLOSEST VESSEL IF YOU CAN DIVERT SUGGEST SEARCH THAT VICINITY ITASCA PROCEEDING AND WILL ARRIVE THIS AFTERNOON COMDR ITASCA."

The *Itasca* had not even finished investigating the "200 miles west of Howland" report, and it was already off to check on the new "281 miles north" report. All day Monday, the fifth, the *Itasca* steamed on a gyro course of about 13 degrees at 160 rpm, making 16.5 knots toward the reported position of Earhart.

The commander, San Francisco Division, sent a message at 1525 PST to the *Itasca* and the *Colorado:* "OPINION OF TECHNICAL AIDS HERE THAT EARHART PLANE WILL BE FOUND ON ORIGINAL LINE OF POSITION . . . THROUGH HOWLAND ISLAND AND PHOENIX GROUP PERIOD RADIO TECHNICIANS FAMILIAR WITH RADIO EQUIPMENT ON PLANE ALL STATE DEFINITELY THAT PLANE RADIO COULD NOT FUNCTION NOW IF IN WATER AND ONLY IF PLANE WAS ON LAND AND ABLE TO OPERATE RIGHT MOTOR FOR POWER PERIOD NO FEARS FELT FOR SAFETY OF PLANE ON WATER PROVIDED TANKS HOLD AS LOCKHEED ENGINEERS CALCULATE 5000 POUNDS POSITIVE BUOYANCY WITH PLANE WEIGHT 8000 . . ."

As observed in the *Itasca* radio transcripts:

This message changed whole search problems and virtually eliminated all intercepted radio traffic ideas (unless the plane was on land).

The message arrived at a time when three ships were checking the 281 report.

Until this time the ITASCA had considered *plane had emergency radio capable of transmitting on water* [emphasis in original].

At 1300 the *Itasca* did not muster the men for roll call because of the search. Just after dark they turned due east to sweep eastward along latitude 5 degrees 30 minutes north, to the point 281 miles north of Howland.

Several hundred miles away aboard the battleship *Colorado,* the radio room was keeping a constant watch on 3105 kilocycles. As the *Colorado* search report described events:

At 2132 on the night of the 5th the listeners in the radio room of the COLORADO were startled to hear on the plane frequency, the words, "Earhart from ITASCA did you send up a flare? If you did send up another. Please go ahead."

At 2140 the following was received, "Earhart Plane from ITASCA, we see second flare, we are coming for you, we are starting toward you."

At 2145, "We see your flare and are proceeding towards you," these reports continued to be broadcast by the ITASCA, and apparently to a listening world, the position 281 miles north of Howland Island in which the ITASCA, SWAN and MOORBY were searching was the correct position. It was therefore with great sadness that the following was received shortly thereafter, "Report in error, objects sighted are apparently meteors. Howland reported same effect." And the SWAN verified the opinion by reporting sighting meteors at the time the ITASCA was believed to be sighting a flare from the Earhart Plane.

On the 6th of July, 1937, the Commandant, Fourteenth Naval District was directed to take charge of all Naval Forces based Pearl Harbor and those in the search area. The Coast Guard Cutter, the ITASCA was further directed to operate under Commandant, Fourteenth Naval District. The Commandant, Fourteenth Naval District, directed the Commanding Officer, U.S.S. COLORADO to take charge of Naval and Coast Guard Units in the Search Area and coordinate the Earhart Search Unit, until the arrival of Commander Destroyer Squadron Two. . . .

A message was received from Mr. Putnam stressing the Phoenix Island Group and stating that headwinds aloft had been much stronger than expected for the flight. Again it was stated that the Lockheed Aircraft Engineers stated that the radio could not operate unless the plane was on land. It was further suggested by Mr. Putnam, that a plane from the COLORADO investigate the Phoenix Island Area. The possibility that the position 281 miles north of Howland was in error and might have been south and southeast was also considered. A third report also stated that a strong signal had been heard and a man's voice calling the ITASCA. A fourth signal report stated "Position 281 miles north of Howland, drifting northwest." This report was definitely known later to be a false report.

The commanding officer of the *Colorado* therefore decided to hold to his original decision, that of searching to the southeast of Howland. As the *Colorado* search report continued:

He would modify it by searching the land areas of the Phoenix Group with his planes, prior to the large water areas. Large areas of intervening water, of course would be covered at the same time.

Accordingly at 0800, Tuesday, the ship's head was changed to 205 degrees true and speed increased to eighteen point three knots (18.3). Arrangements were made in answer to a request from the ITASCA for a rendezvous with that ship at 0600, the 7th of July, for the purpose of fueling the ITASCA and provisioning her from the COLORADO. The SWAN was directed to search to Latitude 0 degrees, Longitude 175 degrees West.

At day break, Wednesday, 7 July, the ITASCA met, fueled and provisioned from the COLORADO.

During the refueling, Captain Thompson was able to confer with Captain Friedell about why he had originally searched to the northwest of Howland Island on the morning of July 2. Friedell had not known that the sky was clear to the south and east that morning, which would not restrict Noonan's ability to navigate or take celestial observations if he were east or south. If the sky had been clear when Earhart could not see Howland, Noonan could easily have fixed their position by taking celestial observations of the sun and moon.

The *Colorado* search report concluded: "Upon completion the ITASCA was directed by the Commanding Officer of the U.S.S. COLORADO to proceed to a point 0 degrees–20 minutes South latitude, Longitude 178 degrees West, and from there to search a sector, eastward and south from a line bearing 157 degrees from that point and to search to the eastward a distance of 120 miles."

Back in the Hawaiian Islands, the aircraft carrier *Lexington,* commanded by Capt. Leigh Noyes, arrived at Lahaina Roads on Thursday morning at 1146 HST and waited there for the tanker *Ramapo* to arrive the next day. The *Lexington* search was delayed for a day because the tanker *Ramapo* was under the orders of Admiral Leahy, and he was not available over the long Fourth of July weekend. Orders to turn her around were finally issued by Admiral Leahy at 0945 EST when his office reopened Tuesday morning.

Immediately after the *Lexington* arrived at Lahaina, the commander of Destroyer Squadron 2, the commanding officer of the *Lexington,* and two officer assistants flew to Pearl Harbor for a conference with Admiral Murfin, the commandant of the Fourteenth Naval District, and Captain Whiting, the commander of the Fleet Air Base in Pearl Harbor.

The *Lexington* group analyzed all the available information about Earhart's flight to determine her most likely landing point. They determined that the Electra's most economical airspeed in still air was 130 knots (150 mph), and with optimum carburetor adjustment the plane would burn 45.8 gallons per hour. At a true airspeed of 140 knots (161 mph) it would burn 53 gallons per hour. The Electra had 1,100 gallons of fuel onboard prior to departure from Lae. At 130 knots (150 mph) the tanks would have run dry after 24 hours and 1 minute; at 140 knots (161 mph), the tanks would have run dry after 20 hours and 45 minutes.

They correctly assessed that Earhart had encountered stronger headwinds than she had anticipated. After their study, the *Lexington* group concurred with Captain Thompson that Earhart had come down to the northwest. They decided to plan their search from "the most probable landing point, 23 miles northwest of Howland Island."

The *Colorado* meanwhile spent Thursday, July 8, advancing southward toward the Phoenix Islands. It catapulted its float scout planes to search for reported reefs, sandbars, or the Earhart plane. Though the visibility was excellent, nothing was sighted. The *Colorado* search report described this effort:

> At 0700 on the morning of 9 July in Latitude 3 degrees 54 minutes South, Longitude 174 degrees-46 minutes West, the COLORADO launched her planes in the direction of McKean Island. Upon locating McKean and searching the vicinity, the planes continued to Gardner and then to Carondelet Reef before returning to the ship in Latitude 4 degrees-30 minutes South, Longitude 174 degrees-24 minutes West. After the vain search for Reef and Sand Bank and for Winslow Reef it was to be expected that the other Islands did not or might not exist. They were however, all located by the planes and although they were not in the exact charted position they were seen from a considerable distance and the planes had no difficulty in locating them.
>
> McKean Island showed unmistakable signs of having at one time been inhabited. On the northwest side of the Island there appeared buildings of the adobe type. No one was seen on either Gardner Island or McKean Island.
>
> Carondelet Reef was under water but plainly could be seen from the planes at a distance of 10 miles.

After recovering the planes from the morning flight, the *Colorado* continued on course toward Hull Island. At 1400 the planes were launched to search the waters in front of the ship and to locate Hull Island:

> As the planes approached Hull Island natives were seen running out of their huts and waving clothes at the plane. Lieutenant Lambrecht, the senior aviator and in charge of the flight, landed for the purpose of asking if the inhabitants had seen or heard of the Earhart Plane. A European Resident Manager of the natives came out in a canoe to meet the plane. He and his natives were astonished and excited in seeing the three planes. The Resident Manager asked where the planes were from and when informed Honolulu, nearly upset the

canoe in his excitement. It was necessary to explain to him that the planes had not come direct but had arrived by the battleship COLORADO which was relatively close by. The Resident Manager said that there was a radio on the island, however, he knew nothing of the Earhart flight and created doubt of his having ever heard of Miss Earhart herself. Neither he nor his natives had seen or heard a plane. The planes returned to the ship in Latitude 4 degrees 33 minutes South, Longitude 173 degrees 08 minutes West.

After recovering its planes the *Colorado* began making its way toward Canton Island. It was now more than seven days since the Electra had vanished.

In the Hawaiian Islands at Lahaina Roads, at 1515 HST, Friday, July 9, Captain Noyes got the *Lexington* underway at 18 knots for the search area in the vicinity of Howland Island. The *Lexington* was to meet the destroyers *Drayton, Lamson,* and *Cushing* at "point origin"—latitude 2 degrees, 30 minutes north, longitude 177 degrees west—at daybreak on 13 July. "Point origin" was approximately 100 miles north-northwest of Howland Island.

In the Phoenix Islands aboard the battleship *Colorado,* at 0700 Saturday morning, July 10, Captain Friedell launched the planes to search Sydney, Phoenix, Enderbury, and Birnie Islands. Three hours and fifteen minutes later the *Colorado* recovered the planes. Friedell wrote:

Sydney was the only Island which showed any signs of recent habitation and in appearance was much the same as Gardner Island. It had the usual shallow lagoon which in this case was large enough for a seaplane to make a safe landing. Phoenix and Birnie Islands had the appearance of a lagoon, but the latter Island being very small. Enderbury had a lagoon but it was very shallow.

When the planes were recovered, the SWAN was taken alongside and refueled and provisioned. Upon completion of fueling the SWAN was directed to search in a northwest direction across the open water north of the Phoenix Group enroute Latitude 2 degrees South, Longitude 175 degrees West.

The COLORADO at 1445 in Latitude 03 degrees-22 minutes South, Longitude 175 degrees-45 minutes West launched planes for a search to and of Canton Island. This island was located and carefully searched by the planes. It was the largest of any of the islands searched. Its lagoon was deeper than those of the other islands but was crossed with coral reefs in such a manner that it would be dangerous to land except at two places, one at each end of the island. At the western end there remains the shacks and scaffolding erected by the recent eclipse expedition. When the planes were recovered, the course was set at 350 degrees to take the COLORADO to a rendezvous at 0700, 12 July, with the destroyers approaching the search area with the LEXINGTON Group.

The rendezvous to refuel the destroyers *Drayton, Lamson,* and *Cushing* was made by the *Colorado* on schedule Monday morning, July 12. They departed to meet the *Lexington* at "point origin" 100 miles north-northwest of Howland. The *Colorado* was detached from the search group and directed to return to the West Coast.

Captain Friedell concluded his report with the following paragraph: "As this is written the LEXINGTON Group is approaching the Search Area and will be able to conduct an extensive search over a large water area. The COLORADO has, however, covered the land area within a radius of 450 miles of Howland Island, and definitely ascertained that the Earhart plane is not on land within the region unless on an unknown, uncharted and unsighted reef."

The *Colorado* had determined that Earhart's plane was not in the Phoenix Islands, but the Gilbert Islands, which were under British Administration and control, had not been searched. The *Lexington* group commander, Captain Dowell, directed the *Swan* and *Itasca* to proceed to Onoatoa Island and Arorai Island respectively. The *Swan* would visit the southern Gilbert Islands and the *Itasca* the northern. Authorization to search for any sign of Earhart on any of the islands in the group was obtained through the Department of State.

No U.S. ship or plane ever came within several hundred miles of any of the Marshall Islands or other Japanese territory. The Japanese government was notified of the search for Earhart and cooperated by directing all ships and stations under its control to be alert for any sign of the missing plane or fliers.

After talking to the chief resident on Nukunau, the *Swan* was able to make radio contact on 500 kilocycles with station ZCC on Beru (Peru) Island. The Gilbert Island radio network was alerted to the presence of the search ships looking for the missing plane. Operated by the London Mission Society, ZCC radio relayed through the *Swan* that all contacts with the other islands for information about Earhart were negative.

The *Lexington* arrived at "point origin" at 0636 Tuesday, July 13, 1937. Captain Noyes launched sixty planes to begin the search for Earhart eleven days after she had disappeared.

Five days later, at 1648 Sunday, July 18, the *Lexington* recovered the last plane and terminated the search. The *Itasca* had been released to return to Honolulu via Howland Island, and the *Swan* was also released to return to Pearl Harbor. Captain Noyes steered the *Lexington* on a great circle course that would take them direct to San Diego.

Captain Dowell transferred his pennant to the destroyer *Lamson,* and the *Lexington* group search organization was terminated. The *Lamson, Drayton,* and *Cushing* would stop in Pearl Harbor for refueling. The *Lexington,* after passing near the island of Oahu, would continue on to San Diego alone.

The *Lexington* group had searched a total of 262,281 square miles. Its findings were summarized in the last sentence of the final report: "No sign nor any evidence of the Earhart plane was discovered."

In hindsight, we can conclude that 90 percent of the value of the search was over when the *Itasca* began chasing radio reports from a plane that could not transmit. Of all the reported positions, messages, radio bearings, dashes, continuous carriers, and garbled signals, not one was ever authenticated to have originated from Earhart. It took three days before Lockheed informed the Navy and Coast Guard that Earhart's transmitter could not work on the water. By then, the *Itasca* was out of position 281 miles north of Howland. There would be no immediate attempt to complete the search in the probable northwest quadrant, where Earhart most likely went down.

When Captain Friedell of the *Colorado* rendezvoused with the *Itasca* at daybreak on Wednesday, July 7, and was able to confer directly with Commander Thompson, he became aware for the first time of the emotional content of Earhart's final messages. He learned then that the men listening on the *Itasca* believed Earhart when she said she was running low on fuel and had only a half hour left. From the strength of her radio signals, Captain Thompson believed Earhart came down within 100 miles of Howland.

Friedell also learned that the weather on Friday morning was such that Earhart could have easily seen the island *except* from the northwest, where cloud cover would limit Noonan's ability to establish his position. To the south and east of Howland the weather was clear. If they had been to the south or east, Noonan would have been able to obtain additional sun and moon positions at will. They would never have flown away from their only safe haven. The hypothesis of Noonan being lost to the south and east of Howland, blindly following an earlier sun line in the wrong direction, was unsupportable.

Regardless, Captain Friedell had had several good reasons to continue his search of the Phoenix Islands. The consensus among Navy officials who met at Pearl Harbor was that stronger winds than normal in the region had probably carried the plane to the southeast of Howland. These opinions led Captain Friedell to concur that southeast of Howland was the most likely area to search, and he had already positioned his ship to do so. The world press was alive with reports of radio signals from Earhart. If any of the reported signals were authentic, the plane would have to be on land. Finally, Mr. Putnam had requested that they check the Phoenix Islands.

That the *Lexington* should have begun its search eleven days after Earhart had disappeared was extremely optimistic.

A short time after running out of fuel and ditching, the Electra would have filled with water and sunk to the ocean floor. Like the *Titanic,* the Electra was there, but it rested then, and it rests now, on the bottom, hidden from the searching eyes intently scanning the surface above.

1 5 : EXAMINING

THE EVIDENCE

W E know more today about the tragic disappearance of Amelia Earhart than anyone in 1937.

To begin, we know that Earhart ran out of fuel. Captain Thompson heard Earhart's voice on the radio saying she was running out of fuel. He heard the tone and concern in her voice build as the situation became more desperate. Here is how he put it when he wrote to Admiral Waesche on October 18, 1937: "I was personally present in the radio room during the last hour she was on the air and heard all of her transmissions, as she was coming in very clearly on the loud speaker. From the time she had apparently reached the end of her dead reckoning run until she finally ceased transmitting her voice rose constantly in pitch and quite evident tension. Up to the last hour she seemed to be very cool and her voice was well modulated and apparently normal, but towards the end I could distinctly notice an inflection of tension coming into it and decided increase in the pitch as though she was talking under a great deal of stress or emotion."

Just an hour and a half after her last communication, he had sent this message to the San Francisco division: "EARHART CONTACT 0742 RE-

PORTED ONE HALF HOUR FUEL AND NO LANDFALL . . . " Less than thirty minutes later the *Itasca* departed Howland Island to search to the northwest on the line 157–337 degrees.

Seven other people who listened to the same broadcasts from Earhart confirmed Thompson's account: Department of Interior representative Admiral Richard Black, Lieutenant Cooper, Ensign Sutter, Chief Radioman Bellarts, Radioman 3rd Class Galten, Radioman 3rd Class O'Hare, and United Press correspondent Howard Hanzlik. Three of the seven had contemporaneously written records of what Earhart said about her fuel at 0742 IST.

Chief Bellarts had Galten's original *Itasca* radio log, which stated: "Gas is running low." O'Hare had a copy of his radio log, and it said: "Running out of gas only 1/2 hr left." Hanzlik's handwritten notes stated: "Gas is running low have half hour supply left."

In theory Earhart should have had more fuel remaining. Until recently it wasn't possible to say conclusively why she ran out of gas. But now we know, thanks to Mr. Hugh Leggatt, manager of communications for Placer Dome Inc. Eric Chater mailed an eight-page Amelia Earhart report on July 25, 1937, to M. E. Griffin of Placer Management Ltd. in San Francisco. Chater was general manager of Guinea Airways on Lae, and observed the Electra's takeoff for Howland Island. The report was subsequently lost and the information in it could not be recreated because of the untimely accidental death of Mr. Chater at Lae. The report was found again in 1992 by Mr. Leggatt. It supplies the information needed to determine Earhart's airspeed during the flight, and thus, her fuel consumption.

The Chater report confirms that Earhart's plane was fueled to 1,100 U.S. gallons the day before departure. But because of the 88-degree daytime temperature at Lae, which would affect the 87-octane fuel's density, the 1,100 gallons onboard were reduced by expansion and venting to an equivalent 1,092 standard 6-pound U.S. gallons. (At higher temperatures fuel expands and weighs less per gallon.) All performance figures for the Electra were based on fuel weighing 6 pounds per gallon. Aircraft engine fuel burn rates are calculated by the pound, not by the gallon. Earhart had 1,092 standard 6-pound U.S. gallons onboard.

Earhart reported, at 0418 GCT, that she was flying at 140 knots (161.1 mph). An average of the forecasted winds and actual reported winds aloft over the route was 26.5 mph. Earhart reported at 0718 GCT that the wind was 23 knots (26.5 mph). The distance from Lae to Howland

Island, via the route they actually flew, was approximately 2,573 miles, and they took 19 hours and 12 minutes. Her average ground speed was 134 mph. When the 26.5 mph headwind is added to the ground speed, her average true airspeed calculates to be 160.5 mph. According to data from the Lockheed Model 10 Flight Manual, with a headwind of 26.5 mph the correct true airspeed for maximum range is 160.5 mph. This is very close to the airspeed Earhart confirmed with her 0418 GCT message.

Calculating from the information supplied by Kelly Johnson, we can say that with 1,092 standard 6-pound gallons onboard, at a true airspeed of 150 mph, Earhart would have run out of fuel in 22 hours and 29 minutes. But Earhart flew at an airspeed of 160.5 mph. This increased her ground speed from 123.5 mph to 134 mph, an increase of 8.5 percent. If the maximum range remains constant, it is a mathematical certainty that an 8.5 percent increase in ground speed will result in an 8.5 percent increase in hourly fuel consumption. The 160.5 mph fuel endurance works out to 20 hours and 34 minutes.

During actual flight, altitude deviations, speed variations, turbulence, rain, power settings, fuel mixture settings, carburetor ice, bugs, oil, dirt, and literally thousands of flight control movements may conspire to shorten the actual flight time. None of them add endurance, and all accumulate to shorten the time from the calculated maximum. Earhart had flown the Electra within 1.7 percent of the predicted values to make the fuel last for 20 hours and 13 minutes.

Lockheed was well aware of the differences between predicted and actual flight results. Their contracts guaranteed only that the Electra's range and endurance performance would come within 5 percent of the published values. Even to meet the 5 percent level of performance Lockheed knew that a flight had to be carefully controlled. (Lockheed even stipulated to customers that all flight tests to substantiate performance guarantees were to be conducted by the company at the factory and that if the first test didn't come within 5 percent of the predicted performance, Lockheed had the option to keep trying and conduct additional tests.)

Earhart's fuel economy performance was excellent. Her early losses in flying at uneconomical density altitudes may have been partially recouped by flying at maximum endurance speeds while searching during the last hour. However it averaged out, she had done well. This fact is more than a confirmation that Earhart ran out of fuel at 0843 IST, it is a vindication of her reputation as a pilot. She had operated the Electra correctly and efficiently.

Having determined beyond any reasonable doubt that it ran out of fuel at approximately 0843 IST, can we say where the Electra was at 0843?

Captain Thompson believed Earhart was within 100 miles of Howland when her fuel was exhausted at 0843 IST. He based this on the strength of her radio signal at 0843, while transmitting with only 50 watts of power. The radiomen on the *Itasca* knew from their operating experience that the strength of a radio signal is inversely proportional to the distance it has traveled.

The men of the *Itasca* believed that Earhart could not be more than 100 miles from Howland, based on their interpretation of the strength of her last radio signal at 0843 IST, which was the same strength as her 0742 signal. At 134 mph ground speed, during the 1 hour and 28 minutes between 0614 and 0742 the Electra would have traveled approximately 196 miles. Remember the maximum distance Sergeant Rose was able to hear Earhart's radio signals when she was flying from Darwin to Lae. If Earhart's 50-watt transmitter could be heard only at signal strength 3, on 3105 in the daytime across 250 miles, and if Earhart was flying toward Howland as she reported, she could at the most be only 54 miles from Howland at 0742 and 0843.

So where did the Electra ditch?

There is no uncharted island, rock, shoal, reef, sandbar, or water less than 30 feet deep within 350 miles of Howland Island. The inescapable conclusion is that shortly after 0843 IST, Earhart was forced to ditch the plane somewhere within 100 miles of Howland Island.

Noonan's navigation and Earhart's radio and fuel management duties were completed. The aircraft must now be brought down on the water. Two devices on the Electra would have played major roles in their chances for survival.

The importance of wearing a shoulder harness in a crash is obvious today, but in 1937 the Electra was not equipped with them. That is bad enough, but a photograph of the cockpit taken by F. Ralph Sias in Miami shows something even worse. The remote control box for the Bendix receiver was located exactly at eye level. The sharp corner and edge of the box were in front of Earhart's forehead. In a crash landing, a more lethal location can hardly be imagined.

For all practical purposes water is not compressible. If you hit it fast with a flat, stiff object, it can be compared to concrete. (Think of the difference between a nice clean headfirst dive and a belly flop.) The empty Electra was very light and its stall speed was very low. This would have allowed Earhart to touch down, or more correctly splash down, at the relatively slow speed of somewhere around 60 mph. That would give the water time to flow out of the way and not seriously damage the plane. The only areas of high pressure would be on the underside of the belly and wing. Unfortunately these are areas of particular concern.

If you were to study carefully photographs of Earhart's Electra showing the flat surface area under the fuselage and wing, you would see five large round openings. These are dump valves designed to allow the rapid dumping of fuel out of the tanks in an emergency. A latch kept each from opening, with levers in the cockpit to allow the latches to be opened wide. The fuel would then dump rapidly out through the openings. But the design of the dump valve latching mechanism, and the thinness of director chute sheet metal, indicate they were not designed to withstand the high-impact forces of compressed water hitting them during a water landing.

In a letter to the commandant of the Coast Guard Captain Thompson wrote, "As regards the search, I was very sanguine up to the time the Lockheed people stated that her plane could not possibly be landed without crashing and sinking."

The fuel dump valves could have become scuttling valves that filled the tanks rapidly, sinking the Electra in a very short time. Even if somehow the dump valves did not fail, the fuel vent lines would fill the tanks with seawater, and the plane would sink. There is no question that one way or another the Electra was going to find its way to the bottom, and probably before much time had passed.

After sixty years, it is still there. It is lying quietly on the ocean floor in the deep water near Howland Island. It can be found, and it can be recovered.

Of course the area within 100 miles of Howland Island encompasses 31,416 square miles. Is there a way to reduce significantly the size of the search area without drastically reducing the probability of success?

16: SOLVING

THE MYSTERY

ELGEN Long began flying in the U.S. Navy during World War II. One operation that Elgen will never forget was the patrol flights in PBY Catalina flying boats out of Canton Island, in the Phoenix group. One sector of the patrol visited both Baker and Howland Islands almost exactly six years after Earhart's disappearance. The outlines of the runways constructed on Howland in 1937 were still visible. It was always a daylight flight, and there were usually only sun lines available for updates, but the fliers never experienced any trouble finding Howland or Baker Islands. Of course they had the advantage of knowing the islands' true position and were trained in the best of the techniques developed earlier by pioneers like Earhart and Noonan. Navy fliers were taught to navigate just as Noonan had done with chronometer and octant, drift sight and compass, dead reckoning between fixes or sun lines. They seldom became lost, but when their position was in doubt they simply adjusted the area of uncertainty.

Today there are satellite, inertial, and electronic navigation. A Global Positioning System can furnish a pinpoint fix within a few meters. The area of uncertainty concept is becoming a lost art, though it remains

EARHART'S AREA OF UNCERTAINTY AT
HOWLAND ISLAND, FRIDAY MORNING, JULY 2, 1937

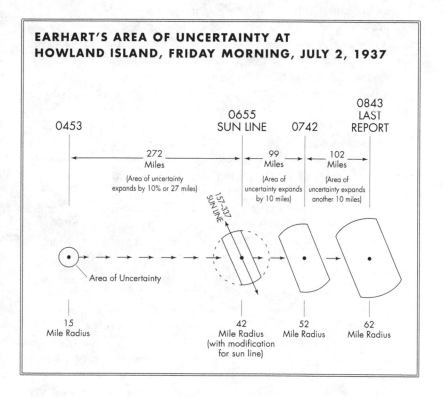

valid. In fact, all of us who go to work every day use a similar concept when we leave home in the morning. When we start, we know about how long it will take us to get to work. Accordingly we leave a number of minutes early so as to arrive on time. If we have an unusual delay en route we realize immediately we are going to be late. We don't have to wait until we get to our destination to know this. It is the same with pilot or navigator. Depending on how the flight has progressed, they have special knowledge of their navigational accuracy, and know how late they are going to be before they actually arrive.

From previous experience a pilot or navigator will allow for the maximum error that might reasonably be expected nine out of ten times. They are 90 percent certain they will be within that maximum area, and are in fact usually closer.

Let's use an extreme example to illustrate the point. When Noonan left Lae to fly the 2,556 miles to Howland Island, he would be 90 percent certain, if he dead reckoned all the way, that at the end of eighteen hours he would be somewhere within 256 miles (10 percent of 2,556) of Howland. If he got a positive visual fix when they were 500 miles out of Howland, he would be 90 percent certain that at his estimated arrival time they would be within 50 miles (10 percent of 500) of the island. There is only one chance in ten that they would be farther away. The 256-mile and 50-mile circles around Howland are the navigator's area of uncertainty. The area of uncertainty is dynamic; it changes with every navigational event.

The chart shown makes a graphical presentation for clarification. The graphic coincides with an assumed approach Noonan might have chosen to Howland Island, so that we can demonstrate the *area of uncertainty* concept and apply it to Earhart's last flight at the same time.

The hypothetical chart starts at 0452 IST (1622 GCT), when Noonan takes a celestial fix to get a position. The time 0452 IST was selected solely to prevent any doubt about sky conditions. We believe that at 0452 the stars were visible, because Earhart reported by radio it was "partly cloudy" at 0453 IST.

If Noonan had wanted, or needed, a fix he could have taken one. It would be unreasonable to believe otherwise. Actually he would have preferred to wait another 30 or 40 minutes before taking his morning star fix, and very well might have. If he had, the final area of uncertainty would be smaller at 0843 IST. The hypothetical chart is drawn to illustrate the concept. Earhart may actually have been well to the north or south of the depicted position. Later, however, we will examine evi-

dence that Noonan had indeed determined his position accurately before daylight.

The chart is drawn with the position of Noonan's 0452 IST celestial
fix represented by the small dot in the center of the circle. A celestial fix
taken from an aircraft is affected by many variables that prevent it from
being absolutely accurate. Noonan wrote that he found that they were
generally accurate to within 10 miles. Our experience agrees with this
assessment.

Noonan was one of the most experienced aerial navigators in the
world. He enjoyed a reputation for competency that was earned over
many years as chief navigator with one of the premier airlines of the
world. His latter-day detractors have nothing to say about his navigational abilities, but only allude to character flaws, such as intemper-
ance, which are not pertinent to the area of uncertainty. Noonan was
very experienced, knowledgeable, practiced, tested, and adept at taking celestial observations. It is entirely realistic to assign a 90 percent
probability to the assertion that any sighting or fix Noonan took was accurate to within 15 miles.

We are not stating that it was impossible for Noonan to take a celestial observation more than 15 miles in error. We are saying that if he
did, it would be unusual, and we can be confident that nine times out
of ten he would not. We can draw a line 15 miles away from that line
or fix to denote the far edge of the area of uncertainty. So, at the point
of Noonan's 0452 IST fix we circumscribe a circle with a 15-mile radius,
to enclose the area of uncertainty. This is the *start fix*, the circle from
which we begin our calculations.

From 0452 IST to the next navigational event Noonan and Earhart
would use dead reckoning to make their way toward Howland Island.
Just as she had done when flying across the Pacific from Honolulu to
Oakland in 1935, she used the compass to keep on the desired course.
The conditions under which Earhart and Noonan were operating were
almost ideal for accurate dead reckoning. The winds were steady in
both direction and velocity. Normal flight conditions existed in tropical
weather, and the equipment was tested and familiar to the experienced
crew. These all argue for a much better than average dead reckoning
performance, but they are impossible to quantify.

The next navigational event, after Noonan took the celestial fix at
0452 IST, was a sun line of position 157–337. We assume it was taken 2
hours and 3 minutes later, at 0655 IST. The Electra had traveled approximately 272 miles since Noonan had taken the celestial fix at 0452 IST.

The maximum dead reckoning error would equal 10 percent of that 272 miles, or 27 miles. This additional 27-mile error is added to the 15 miles of radial error at the starting fix, for a total now of 42 miles. The new, updated area of uncertainty is drawn around the point of the dead reckoned position on the 0655 IST sun line. It is a circle with a radius that has increased to 42 miles.

But we must modify the 0655 IST area of uncertainty circle to account for the accuracy provided by the new sun line. Within the 42-mile circle, 15 miles to either side of the 0655 sun line we draw lines that represent the maximum 15-mile error of a celestial observation. We then eliminate all of the 42-mile circle that is beyond those lines. Our circle now begins to look more like a rectangle with its north and south ends curved with a 42-mile radius. Noonan's area of uncertainty is now 15 miles east and west of the 0655 IST sun line, and 42 miles north and south of his dead reckoned point on the line 157–337. The situation is similar to that at Dakar, when Noonan could determine his position from the sun lines to the east and west quite accurately, but had to rely on 820 miles of dead reckoning to determine the north and south component.

An assumption was made in the previous paragraph that Noonan took a sun line of position 157–337 degrees at 0655 IST. He could have taken the line of position at any time between sunrise and when they began their descent, as long as it was before the azimuth changed from 067 degrees. A prudent navigator under these circumstances would delay making the final observation as long as practicable. Observations of the sun are less affected by unknown variations in atmospheric refraction the higher the sun is above the horizon. Very low observed altitudes are less reliable, and Noonan would have waited to let the sun rise higher. He would also have waited until they were closer to their destination, to minimize the distance they would have to navigate by dead reckoning. It is possible he waited until 0715 IST and was 45 miles closer to Howland when he made this observation. This, of course, would reduce both the east and west dimensions of our 0742 IST area of uncertainty by 4 miles. The 0655 IST time was selected for the navigational model because, like the selected 0452 IST fix time, it is a conservative choice.

An interesting deduction we can make about Noonan's actual sun observation, regardless of when he took it, is that the sun line correlated well with his previous fix. The sun line was taken sometime after Earhart had radioed to the *Itasca* her "approximately 200" and "100 miles out" reports, and those reports were based on Noonan's earlier navigation. The sun line provided Noonan with a good speed line to measure their progress toward Howland. The sun line must have agreed well with his previous fix, because his arrival time at Howland did not change much from what we can deduce from the earlier 200 and 100 estimates. It confirms that Noonan was not experiencing any difficulty in fixing his position during the latter part of the flight as he navigated steadily toward Howland Island.

The next navigational event occurred at 0742 IST, when Earhart announced they should be on Howland Island but could not see it. They had run on dead reckoning until their position was the same as where they thought Howland Island was located. In doing so they had traveled approximately 99 miles since taking the sun line at 0655 IST. Ten percent of the 99 miles traveled adds an additional 10 miles to the possible dead reckoning error. All edges of the area of uncertainty are moved 10 miles outward. As can be seen in the chart previously shown, at 0742 IST it is 25 miles wide on each side of the 157–337 advanced line. It has curved ends of 52-mile radius, capping the 104-mile length of the line. The whole 0742 IST area of uncertainty is centered on the position where they believed Howland Island to be.

This brings us to a new piece of evidence. Howland Island is actually about 6 statute miles *east* of the position shown on Earhart's chart. Noonan's whole approach was biased by that amount to the west; thus the area of uncertainty is not actually centered on Howland Island. It is centered on their dead reckoned position for the island, about 6 miles to the west of the actual island. This may not seem to be a significant distance, but when you realize their visibility eastward may have been reduced to 15 nautical miles by the early morning sun, the mismapping of the island becomes more important. The 6 statute miles represent about 35 percent of 15 nautical miles. If Earhart was to the west, those 6 miles would reduce her chances of finding Howland Island by more than a third. That makes the importance of the 6-mile displacement dramatically clear.

The 0742 IST area of uncertainty is very informative. It tells us that we can be 90 percent certain that the Electra at 0742 was a maximum distance from Howland Island of 31 miles to the west, 19 miles to the east (this represents the 6-mile mismapping adjustment), and 52 miles to the north and south. Anything else, while possible, would be unreasonable.

While we have Earhart's flight progress frozen at 0742 IST, let's add some additional information to the area of uncertainty. We have examined the boundaries within which there is a 90 percent probability the Electra *must be*. Now, let us examine the areas within those same boundaries where the Electra *could not be*.

The visibility at the time was excellent at Howland and Baker Islands. It is theoretically possible for someone flying at 1,000 feet to see a coral island from a distance of 39 nautical miles. However, sighting a low-lying island is more likely from a distance of 20 nautical miles. This can easily be reduced to 15 nautical miles if the viewer is looking into a glaring sun. On the chart shown at the opening of chapter 13 we have drawn 20-nautical-mile circles around Howland and Baker Islands except to the west-southwest, where the viewer would be looking toward the sun. There we have drawn 15-nautical-mile sections. The areas adjacent to the islands within those lines represent the visual area where a viewer would see either Howland or Baker Island. It represents an area where the Electra *could not be* at 0742 IST. We believe Amelia Earhart when she said, "We must be on you, but cannot see you."

The visual area where the plane *could not be* at 0742 IST is extended by their movements between 0742 and 0758 IST. We know, because Earhart's radio signal increased in strength between 0742 and 0758 IST, that Noonan had turned in the correct direction toward Howland when he intercepted the advanced line of approach 157–337. That means during those 16 minutes the Electra was either actually to the north of Howland and flying 27 miles southward 157 degrees, or was actually to the south and flying 27 miles northward 337 degrees. North or south, imagine Earhart's position as being 27 miles on the line above or below the 20-nautical-mile visual circles around Howland and Baker Islands at 0742 IST. In either case, during the next 16 minutes the plane would have entered the visual circles; Earhart would have sighted one island or the other. Not only is the visual area extended 27 miles to the north and south, but the area where the Electra *could not be* at 0742 IST is extended as well.

Earlier it was alluded that experienced navigators could make reasoned judgments as to the accuracy of their past performance based on subtle nuances that cannot be quantified. Noonan obviously made one at 0758 IST. He interrupted their progress, and Earhart began to circle after traveling 16 minutes and approximately 27 miles beyond his estimate for Howland Island. At that time, with excellent visibility, Noonan could see an additional 20 nautical miles in front of them. Noonan made the judgment that, after flying 27 miles and being able to see 23 statute miles farther ahead, they had passed Howland. Noonan, who was there experiencing the situation, was literally willing to bet his life that his dead reckoning was not off by more than 50 miles along the 157–337 track. Inasmuch as he was within the area of uncertainty, he was probably right.

On the chart shown near the end of chapter 13 you can see the remaining area that is outside the visual area, yet still within the *area of uncertainty*. We can be 90 percent certain that at 0742 IST the Electra *must be* somewhere west of Howland within the remaining area. It is obvious that any dead reckoning errors that would put Earhart and Noonan off to the west were critical.

We possess information that Earhart and Noonan did not have, which might answer why they ended up to the west. The first fact, already reported, is that Howland Island is 6 miles east of the position plotted by Clarence S. Williams on the February 9, 1937, charts provided to Earhart. (Mr. Williams cannot be faulted, as his charts were completed before June 1937, when the first Hydrographic Office chart no. 1198 was issued showing the new position. The information up to that time was classified.)

Both the battleship *Colorado* and the carrier *Lexington* were directly under the command of the Fourteenth Naval District, which had previously received the island survey report. It is noteworthy that neither command was given the correct positions for Howland or Baker Island. Nor did any of the official search reports of the Army, Navy, or Coast Guard ever mention this discrepancy. It either was not known, or its relevance escaped those who knew.

A second piece of information that Noonan could not have known is that at both 0700 and 0800 IST the *Itasca* measured the surface wind to be out of the east at 4 to 8 mph. To an observer looking down onto the water from an airplane at 1,000 feet, a wind slower than 12 mph will not show whitecaps. Without whitecaps it is impossible to tell if the wind is anything but calm, and without a smoke bomb Noonan could not obtain a drift sight. Unknown to Earhart and Noonan, the wind was relentlessly pushing them an average of 6 miles farther to the west each hour.

When they were closest to the island, with their strongest radio signal at 0758 IST, the island's true position and the east wind alone would have put them nearly 9 miles to the west. That would be true even if Noonan was exactly correct in all other calculations and Earhart flew perfect courses. By 0843 IST, the undetectable 4-to-8-mph east wind would compound the island's 6-mile position error and place the Electra 10 to 14 miles to the west, very close to the maximum distance from which the island could be seen. A small additional error of 2 or 3 miles might cause them to miss the island completely. Celestial navigation from an airplane cannot guarantee that kind of accuracy. Without radio direction-finding, the successful outcome of the flight depended as much on luck as on Noonan's skill.

Though it does not affect our deductions, there is an additional piece of information that we can add to the chart to complete the picture of the overall situation that existed on July 2, 1937. The *Itasca* departed Howland at 1040 IST on a course of 337 degrees to search to the north. By 1355 IST the *Itasca* had searched an area 15 miles wide from Howland Island approximately 55 miles northward. At that point the ship turned eastward to search till dark on a heading of 080 degrees.

We must make a final adjustment to the boundaries of the area of uncertainty for the dead reckoning errors that may have accumulated between 0742 and 0843 IST. At maximum endurance airspeed the distance traveled would be approximately 102 miles. All boundaries are extended an additional 10 miles outward. The 0843 IST rectangular area of uncertainty becomes 70 miles wide, with its 124-mile length capped with 62-mile-radius curved ends. At 0843, the Electra was within 62 miles to the north or south of Howland, and within 29 miles to the east and 41 miles to the west. We have determined that the Electra is within the area of uncertainty, to the west of the visual areas of Howland and Baker Islands. If this approximately 2,000-square-nautical-mile area is searched, there is a 90 percent probability that the Electra will be found within it.

Every signal received from Earhart from 0615 to 0758 IST was stronger than the one before. After sunrise, when communication is no longer possible over the highly efficient gray line (a band, surrounding the earth, that occurs where daylight and darkness meet), the high level of solar radiation in 1937 would effectively prevent sky wave radio propagation on 3105 kilocycles. Earhart's radio transmissions had traveled entirely over water to the *Itasca* by radio ground waves. The strength of those signals would be related to the distance they had traveled.

At 0742 IST, Earhart's signal was logged at strength 5, good reception. The listeners all agreed that 16 minutes later at 0758 IST the signal was noticeably stronger, and the signal was logged as strength 5, very good reception. We know that between 0742 and 0843 IST the Electra was flying north and south on the line 157–337. Because the signal got stronger, the plane was closer, and Noonan had turned correctly toward the island. Forty-five minutes later, Earhart's signal strength had diminished to return to the same strength it had been at 0742 IST. It was logged again at strength 5, good reception. The strength of the 0843 signal indicates the plane was no farther from Howland Island at 0843 than it had been at 0742 IST. The men on the *Itasca* made the same observation.

The maximum distance the Electra could have been from Howland, yet still be within the area of uncertainty at 0742 IST, was 52 miles. The signal strength analysis suggests that at 0843 the Electra was still somewhere within 52 miles of the island. Even more important, it confirms that Earhart was still searching in the vicinity of Howland, and not flying off in some other direction. We believe Amelia Earhart when she said, "We are flying north and south on the line of position 157–337." It matters little how Earhart and Noonan died. It is the truth of their lives that contains the heart and meaning of their message. The simple truth of their lives is obscured by the mystery that surrounds their death.

THE idea of recovering Earhart's Electra was first proposed in 1973 by the commanding officer of the U.S. Navy bathyscaphe *Trieste II*, Lieutenant Commander Malcom G. Bartels. Commander Bartels told of the discovery and recovery of a World War II Navy fighter plane that had ditched twenty-six years earlier off the coast of San Diego. Although submerged in 3,400 feet of water, the plane was in marvelous condition. In very deep water there is little or no free oxygen, ultraviolet sunlight, or coral growth. With the temperature near freezing, even inner granular corrosion and galvanic action are slowed. Aluminum is relatively stable in those conditions. An aircraft's structure would remain well preserved in comparison to a ship's steel or wood hull.

How deep is the ocean where the Electra rests? What are the geological and topographical conditions of the ocean bottom there? How large an area must we search in order to have a reasonable probability of finding the plane?

No bathymetric map of the ocean bottom around remote Howland Island was available until 1989. Then the Scripps Institution of Oceanography was able to do accurate bathymetric mapping of the area north and west of Howland. The results showed the search area to be favorable for a sonar search. At an average depth of 17,250 feet, the bottom consists mainly of 100 feet of sedimentation lying over the bedrock. If the bottom had consisted of rugged mountains and ravines, a sonar search would have been difficult if not impossible. But approximately 93 percent of the area mapped was a featureless abyssal plain, well suited for a search by sonar sensors to find a lonely aircraft target.

There are no active volcanoes upwind of the search area to cause significant fallout, or mighty river deltas emptying mud to cover the Electra. Sedimentation accrual rate is minimal and measured in very small amounts over thousands of years. After sixty years the plane should be covered with only a light dusting, something like what you might find on an automobile parked too long in a garage. The remoteness of Howland Island is a two-edged sword. It adds to the mobilization costs, but makes the search easier. Infrequent visits by ships, and no World War II battles or aircraft losses reported in the area, means less litter on the ocean floor, which minimizes the problem of false sonar targets and eases the target verification task.

Previous analysis made no attempt to quantify any probabilities, except for the 90 percent ascribed to the whole 2,000-square-mile area of uncertainty. If we divide the whole search area into smaller search sections, statisticians can calculate and assign the probability of finding the plane in any one of them. In the planning phase, the development of probability maps will be one of the tools used to select objectively the most promising areas to search first. This of course would improve the odds of finding the plane during an early phase. From what we consider a conservative analysis, the whole area must be searched to obtain 90 percent certainty of success.

There are two different means to effect a sonar search in deep water. One is by towing a sonar device on the end of a very long cable behind a ship. The other is to use an autonomous unmanned vehicle (AUV). The towed systems, which have been around for several decades, are mature systems with fairly well defined capabilities. The largest ocean area ever searched commercially was the 1,400-square-mile search for the ship *Central America*. A towed sonar system was able to pinpoint the exact location of the 100-year-old wreck in the North Atlantic.

A towed system uses the towing cable to supply power to the sonar unit near the bottom. The sonar information from the sensors is sent back up the cable to recorders on the ship. Several limitations to a towed system severely curtail its capabilities in water over 17,000 feet deep. The cable must be towed very slowly to prevent mechanical strumming, and to keep it from flying up away from the bottom. The slow speed hinders the tow ship's ability to keep steerage on an exact course when there are unfavorable winds or seas. To prevent voids in the search area, any deviation in course necessitates an increase in the overlap of the adjacent search pattern, in typical "lawn mowing" style. Lower-frequency sonar search units, with wider swath capabilities, minimize the number of tracks required.

The Autonomous Unmanned Vehicles (AUV) have the advantage in deep water of not requiring or being hindered by a cable. The AUV can travel at any speed selected to optimize the sonar's target search scenario. The AUV also has the capability to stop, investigate, and photograph a target in just a few minutes, for example, right in the middle of a search pattern. Acoustic data links can transfer the sonar and video signals through the water to the ship in near to real time. When you consider that it could take several hours just to turn a towed cable around to look at something, the tremendous advantage the AUV has in this regard is readily apparent.

There are also limitations. An AUV is dependent on its own power sources. The capacities of its batteries or other power source define how long it can continue on a mission. Deepwater AUV technology is still relatively new. The dependability level that will come with more operational experience is still not well defined.

Equipment redundancy, spares, and equipment repair facilities available on-site in midocean are all part of the equation. It would be a pity to have a system fail before completing the search. Just the cost of getting the ship, people, and equipment out there and back is a significant portion of the overall expense.

We have known for twenty-five years that the solution to the Earhart mystery lies on the ocean floor under 17,000 feet of water. Only recently have improvements in the computer analysis of sonar signals and the full activation of the Global Positioning System (GPS) turned the 2,000-square-mile search into a practical endeavor. Though the cost of a search has dwindled to a third of what it was a decade ago, it will still cost around two million dollars.

Of course there are risks. There would be no adventure if it were a sure thing. It is the unknown that will make the recovery of the Electra so exciting.

What will we find inside? Is there impact damage to the fuel dump valves that would have filled the tanks with seawater immediately? Is the emergency equipment still there? Is there damage to the Bendix remote control box in front of Earhart? Are the stamped envelopes still in the nose compartment? Are there any signs of remains? There are dozens of questions that can be answered only by recovering the plane.

The recovery of the Electra from the ocean floor will require equipment and personnel completely different from the search effort. Fortunately, the recovery phase does not require any new or untested technologies. If used wisely, expert aid from competent individuals and institutions can help keep the costs down. Academic and commercial organizations are available to help with a wide array of useful know-how.

Amelia Earhart was an early symbol of women's emergence as individuals in their own right, and a pioneering advocate of women's having careers other than as wives and mothers. Fred Noonan, as navigator of the Pan American Airways China Clipper, was a role model for thousands of young Americans aspiring toward careers in aviation. They were both on the leading edge of society in the 1930s, blazing trails for a generation of women and men to follow. Though they lost their lives prematurely, they succeeded beyond their wildest dreams in making their lives count for something of value.

Amelia's haunting question to Fred at Dakar remains unanswered: "What put us north?"

When the Electra is found, we may be able to give Earhart the answer she deserves.

APPENDIX

FLIGHT LOG FOR EARHART'S AROUND-THE-WORLD FLIGHT

FROM	TO	DATE	TIME	FLIGHT TIME
Oakland	Burbank	5-20	1550	2:15
Burbank	Tucson	5-21	1425	3:20
Tucson	New Orleans	5-22	0730	8:40
New Orleans	Miami	5-23	0910	5:00
Miami	Miami	Two Flights		2:00
Miami	San Juan	6-1	0556	7:34
San Juan	Caripito	6-2	0650	4:32
Caripito	Paramaribo	6-3	0848	4:50
Paramaribo	Fortaleza	6-4	0710	9:20
Fortaleza	Natal	6-6	0650	2:05
Natal	Saint Louis	6-7	0313	13:22
Saint Louis	Dakar	6-8	0905	:52
Dakar	Gao	6-10	0651	7:55
Gao	Ft. Lamy	6-11	0610	6:38
Ft. Lamy	El Fasher	6-12	1224	4:06
El Fasher	Khartoum	6-13	0610	3:15
Khartoum	Massawa	6-13	1050	2:50
Massawa	Assab	6-14	0730	2:26
Assab	Karachi	6-15	0313	13:22
Karachi	Calcutta	6-17	0725	8:20
Calcutta	Akyab	6-18	0705	2:27
Akyab	Akyab	6-18	1224	2:06
Akyab	Akyab	6-19	0630	1:07
Akyab	Rangoon	6-19	0842	2:30
Rangoon	Bangkok	6-20	0630	2:43
Bangkok	Singapore	6-20	1027	6:28
Singapore	Bandoeng	6-21	0617	4:20
Bandoeng	Surabaya	6-24	1400	2:35
Surabaya	Bandoeng	6-25	0600	2:30
Bandoeng	Surabaya	6-26	1154	2:36
Surabaya	Koepang	6-27	0630	5:30
Koepang	Darwin	6-28	0630	3:26
Darwin	Lae	6-29	0649	7:43
Lae (Test Flight)	Lae	7-1	0635	:30
Lae	[near] Howland I.	7-2	1000	20:13

Note: Times are based on best available data for the year 1937.

THE ELECTRA'S FUEL CONSUMPTION

FLIGHT TIME	AMOUNT OF FUEL USED (GALLONS)	BURN RATE (GPH)
1 hr.	100	100
3 hr., 5 min.	235	65
6 hr., 5 min.	415	60
9 hr., 5 min.	568	51
12 hr., 5 min.	697	43
22 hr., 29 min.	1092	38

Note: Engine start, taxi, takeoff, and climb consume an extra amount of fuel, hence the high burn rate in the first hour. Afterward, burn rate decreases as the weight of fuel on board decreases, other flying conditions more or less constant.

Source: Lockheed *Horizons,* May, 1988; C. L. "Kelly" Johnson telegrams March 11 and March 13, 1937, regarding Earhart's Hawaii-to-California flight, as modified.

In March 1937 Kelly Johnson wired to Earhart the performance predictions for her Electra with a fuel load of 900 gallons flying at 150 mph to Honolulu. This information is shown in the fuel analysis chart above. To calculate the Electra's time to dry tanks on the morning of July 2, we must adjust the 900-gallon Honolulu flight performance figures to reflect Earhart's fuel load of 1,092 gallons out of Lae in July.

Regarding the chart it should be noted that, when an aircraft is heavier—everything else being equal—fuel will be consumed at a higher rate. In this case, the fuel over 900 gallons will be consumed at 65 gph. To reflect an approximate 342-pound weight reduction made in the aircraft's equipment and crew between March and July, it is necessary to adjust the aircraft's zero fuel weight by 342 pounds. Accordingly, after the first hour, the 342 pounds reduces to 135 gallons, the amount to be consumed at 65 gph. From that point, the aircraft's weight is equivalent to the March Honolulu flight, and the chart is in alignment with Lockheed's performance predictions.

NOTES

DOC: Department of Commerce
DOI: Department of Interior
DOT: Department of Transportation
EC: Eric H. Chater
EE: Dr. Edward C. Elliott
EHCR: Letter from Eric H. Chater to
  M. E. Griffin, dated July 25, 1937
ELM: *El Mundo* (San Juan, Puerto
  Rico)
EM: Elgen and Marie Long
FAA: Federal Aviation Administration
  (records at ACB and ARB)*
FG: Frederick A. Goerner
FN: Frederick J. Noonan
GOAS: Governor of American Samoa
GP: George P. Putnam
HAD: *Honolulu Advertiser*
HM: Harry Manning
HSB: *Honolulu Star-Bulletin*
IBA: Interview by authors (recorded
  on audio or video tapes)
IRL: USCG Cutter *Itasca* radio logs
IRTEF: *Itasca*—Radio Transcripts
  Earhart Flight
ISL: USCG Cutter *Itasca* ship's
  logbook
JC: James A. Collopy
JG: Joseph H. Gurr
LAC: Lockheed Aircraft Corporation*
LACH: *Lockheed Horizons*
LAT: *Los Angeles Times*
MDN: *Miami Daily News*
NADC: National Archives, Washington,
  D.C. (includes repositories at
  Suitland, Maryland, and College
  Park, Maryland)**
NASB: National Archives, San Bruno,
  California**
NASM: National Air & Space Museum
NDM: *New York Daily Mirror*
NHLA: Natural History Museum of Los
  Angeles County*
NHT: *New York Herald-Tribune*
NLA: National Library of Australia*

NMC: USCG Radio San Francisco
NOX: *Northern Standard* (Darwin,
  Australia)
NPM: U.S. Navy Radio Honolulu
NPU: U.S. Navy Radio Tutuila,
  American Samoa
NSWL: New South Wales Library*
NYT: *New York Times*
NZM: Chester W. Nimitz Museum*
OKT: *Oakland Tribune*
OPE: *The Post Enquirer* (Oakland)
OSL: USS *Ontario* ship's logbook
PAA: Pan American Airways
PCO: Personal collection of . . .
PDI: Placer Dome Inc.*
PEB: *Providence Evening Bulletin*
  (Rhode Island)
PM: A. Paul Mantz
POPA: *Popular Aviation*
PUL: Purdue University Libraries
  Special Collections*
PW: Lt. Comdr. P. V. H. Weems
RB: Richard B. Black
RW: Rear Admiral Russell R. Waesche
SECN: U.S. Secretary of the Navy
SECS: U.S. Secretary of State
SFC: *San Francisco Chronicle*
SLRC: Schlesinger Library, Radcliffe
  College*
SMH: *Sydney Morning Herald*
  (Australia)
SRCO: Search Report of USS *Colorado*
SRIT: Search Report of USCG Cutter
  Itasca
SRLX: Search Report of the *Lexington*
SRNCG: Search Report of the U.S. Navy
  and Coast Guard, July 2–18,
  1937
SSL: USS *Swan* ship's logbook
SST: *Singapore Straits Times*
TFB: *The Fresno Bee* (California)
TMH: *The Miami Herald*
TXO: *The Sind Observer* (Karachi,
  India, present-day Pakistan)

* See Archives, Section I.
** See Archives, Section II.

UOW: University of Wyoming,
American Heritage Center*
USACR: U.S. Army Crash Report of
Earhart at Luke Field
VM: O. Vernon Moore

WEC: Western Electric Corporation
(Bell Laboratories)*
WM: William T. Miller
WT: Commander Warner K. Thompson

CHAPTER 1: TRAGEDY NEAR HOWLAND ISLAND

13 *The heavily loaded plane:* Lae Airport Chart No. 20/1935. PCO JC, Melbourne, Australia.

13 *Soon they would take off:* Letter from JC to Civil Aviation Board, Aug. 28, 1937. PCO JC.

13 *The Electra, nearly 50 percent:* Amelia Earhart, *Last Flight,* page 223.

13 *1,100 gallons of fuel:* EHCR, page 5, PCO PDI.

15 *Fred Noonan, at age forty-four:* Marriage Record of FN, July 11, 1927, Jackson, MS.

15 *They passed the smoke bomb:* Sid Marshall film of Earhart takeoff from Lae, N.G. NLA.

15 *The force required:* Sid Marshall film of Earhart takeoff from Lae, N.G. NLA.

15 *She relaxed some of the pressure:* Sid Marshall film of Earhart takeoff from Lae, N.G. NLA.

15 *They were off the ground:* Letter from JC to Civil Aviation Board, Aug. 28, 1937. PCO JC.

15 *The seven seconds required:* LAC Report 466, page 4. LAC.

16 *After they were safely:* Chart by CW dated February 9, 1937. NASM.

16 *Fred wrote down:* Time zone at Lae minus ten, and EHCR page 7. PCO PDI.

16 *Having calculated that the flight:* Message from Vacuum to RB, July 1, 1937, IRTEF, page 36. NADC.

16 *they had to time their arrival:* Sunrise Howland Island 1747 GCT, July 2, 1937. "Distant Suns."

16 *Harry Balfour, the Guinea Airways:* EHCR, page 7. PCO PDI.

16 *The messages indicated:* EHCR, page 7. PCO PDI.

16 *Earhart's radio schedule:* EHCR, page 8. PCP PDI

16 *and to listen for Lae:* EHCR, page 7. PCO PDI.

16 *In addition, for more than four:* EHCR, page 8. PCO PDI.

16 *She reported "HEIGHT 7,000 FEET:* EHCR, page 8. PCO PDI.

17 *Amelia reported the change:* EHCR, page 8. PCO PDI.

17 *She reported "HEIGHT 10,000 FEET:* EHCR, page 8. PCO PDI.

17 *The worst had happened:* LAC Model 10 Flight Manual, pages 7 and 8. LAC.

17 *Lae heard nothing:* EHCR, page 8. PCO PDI.

18 *Again, the geographical position:* From Lae to S 4.33–E 159.7 is 848 statute miles. At 134.5 mph Earhart would be there at 0618 GCT.

18 *Her signals on 6210:* EHCR, page 8. PCO PDI.

* See Archives, Section I.

18   *(For every wind component:* LAC Model 10 Flight Manual, IAS for Maximum Range, page 35a. LAC.

19   *Even with a helping headwind:* Sid Marshall film shows smoke blowing from southeast to northwest. NLA.

19   *no more 100-octane available:* EHCR, page 5. PCO PDI.

19   *It would be dark:* Moonrise, July 2, 1937. "Distant Suns" (computer program).

19   *As Earhart continued:* EHCR, page 8. PCO PDI.

19   *closer to the optimum altitude:* LAC recommended 8,000 feet. CJ telegram, 1200P, March 11, 1937. PUL

19   *The sun had set:* Sunset, July 2, 1937. "Distant Suns."

19   *the Navy guard ship* Ontario: OSL, July 2, 1937. NADC

19   *Navy auxiliary tug was not equipped:* Message RB to AE, June 23, 1937, 2230GMT. NASB GOAS NPU.

20   *Earhart had requested by cablegram.* Message AE to RB, "ASK ONTARIO TO . . . etc," IRTEF, page 32. NADC

20   *her Western Electric transmitter:* Western Electric manual 13C transmitter. WEC.

20   *At 0910 GCT she may have listened:* Lae to USS *Ontario* 1291 statute miles. At 134.5 mph pass *Ontario* at 0936 GCT.

20   *The tug was running short:* OSL, July 3, 1937. NADC./and Message 0101/1120, July 1, 1937, IRTEF, page 33. NADC.

20   *"A SHIP IN SIGHT AHEAD:* Cable 1000PM, July 3, 1937 CONSL Albert M. Doyle, Sydney, to SECS. NADC.

21   *Amelia must have welcomed:* Moonrise GCT, July 2, 1937. "Distant Suns."

21   *At 1415 GCT, Earhart transmitted:* Radio transmission from AE 0245-0248 IST. IRTEF, page 39. NADC.

21   *The 26.5 mph headwind:* LAC Model 10 Flight Manual, IAS for Maximum Range, page 35a. LAC.

21   *They could rationalize:* Federal Air Regulations 91.22. DOT FAA.

21   *At 1515 GCT, Amelia turned on her transmitter:* Radio transmission from AE 0345 IST (1515 GCT). IRTEF, page 40. NADC.

22   *Nautical twilight would begin:* Nautical Almanac, July 2, beginning of nautical twilight. 1937 *Nautical Almanac.*

22   *Standard procedure was for Amelia: Amelia Earhart, Last Flight,* page 61.

22   *Eight minutes late:* Radio transmission from AE 0453 IST (1623 GCT). IRTEF, page 40. NADC.

22   *A celestial fix at 1622 GCT:* Position at 1622 GCT directly interpolated from position of SS *Myrtlebank* at 1030 GCT and Earhart reporting should be on Howland Island at 1912 GCT (0742 IST).

23   *Meanwhile, to ascertain:* AE "must be on you" at 1912 GCT (0742 IST). IRTEF, page 42. NADC.

23   *At a total of 40 gph:* AE "1/2 hour left" at 1912 GCT (0742 IST). IRTEF, page 42. NADC.

23   *This transferred every remaining drop:* Fuel System Diagram, LAC Drawing No. 42681, March 10, 1937. LAC.

23   *The Itasca transcribed:* AE radio transmission 1744 GCT (0614 IST). IRTEF, page 41. NADC.

23 *She gave them a moment:* AE radio transmission 1745 GCT (0615 IST). IRTEF, page 41. NADC.

24 *She sent the following:* AE radio transmission 1815 GCT (0645 IST). IRTEF, page 41. NADC.

24 *The sun was about 7 degrees:* Azimuth and elevation of the sun at 1825 GCT, July 2, 1937. "Distant Suns."

24 *After many years of aerial navigation:* Letter from FN to PW, May 11, 1935. Published May, 1938, POPA.

26 *They had received no radio bearings:* SRLX, page 6. NADC.

27 *At about 1902 GCT:* SRCO, page 8. NADC.

27 *The sun was only 17 degrees:* Elevation of the sun at 1912 GCT, July 2, 1937. "Distant Suns."

27 *Also, the shiny aluminum surfaces:* Amelia Earhart, *Last Flight,* page 60.

27 *"KHAQQ CALLING ITASCA WE MUST BE ON YOU:* AE radio transmission 1912 GCT (0742 IST). IRTEF, page 42. NADC.

27 *It had been agreed by cablegram:* Message 8019/1340, IRTEF, page 10. NADC.

27 *Earhart probably chose:* LAC Model 10 Flight Manual, IAS for Maximum Endurance, page 35a. LAC.

28 *He judged the island:* AE radio transmission 1928 GCT (0758 IST). IRTEF, page 42. NADC.

28 *"KHAQQ CALLING ITASCA—WE ARE CIRCLING:* AE radio transmission 1928 GCT (0758 IST). IRTEF, page 42. NADC.

29 *"KHAQQ CALLING ITASCA WE RECEIVED YOUR SIGNALS:* AE radio transmission 1930-33 GCT (0800-03 IST). IRTEF, page 43. NADC.

29 *They decided to retrace:* "running north and south" 2014-16 GCT (0844-46 IST). IRTEF, page 45. NADC.

30 *Unfortunately there was nothing but noise:* Itasca on 7500 kilocycles at 2000 GCT (0830 IST). IRTEF, page 44. NADC.

30 *At 2013 GCT, with her voice pitched:* Letter from WT to COMDTCG RW, October 18, 1937. NADC.

30 *"WE ARE ON THE LINE OF POSITION:* AE radio transmission 2014-16 GCT (0844-46 IST). IRTEF, page 45. NADC.

30 *The stall speed of an empty Electra:* LAC Model 10 Flight Manual, Landing speeds, page 43. LAC

31 *The distance from Lae to Howland:* "First nonstop . . . 2504 mile flight" MDN, March 23, 1935, page 1.—"First Commercial Flight Alameda to Honolulu" . . . 2400 miles, OPE, April 17, 1935, page 1.

CHAPTER 2: IN THE SHADOW OF HISTORY

32 *Amelia Mary Earhart was born:* 1897 Baptismal Records, Trinity Episcopal Church, Atchison, Kansas.

33 *"deduces the correct answers:* Writings of Sarah Walton. Atchison College Preparatory School. AEAK.

33 *"There was little room for nostalgia:* Muriel Earhart Morrissey, *Courage Is the Price,* page 109.

34 *I remember well:* Amelia Earhart, *20 hrs. 40 min.: Our Flight in the Friendship,* pages 87–89.

35   *She wanted to arrange:* Amelia Earhart, *20 hrs. 40 min.: Our Flight in the Friendship,* pages 47–49.

35   *The Kinner Airplane and Motor Corporation:* Kinner Airplane & Motor Corporation passenger contract PCO EM.

35   *After signing the form:* IBA of Neta Snook Southern, July 12, 1975. PCO EM.

35   *Amelia soloed:* Amelia Earhart, *The Fun of It,* page 35.

36   *After soloing, she flew alone:* Amelia Earhart, *20 hrs. 40 min.: Our Flight in the Friendship,* pages 77–79.

36   *She appeared more comfortable:* IBA of Neta Snook Southern, July 12, 1975. PCO EM.

36   *The posters promised exhibitions:* D. D. Hatfield, *Los Angeles Aeronautics 1920–1929,* page 80.

36   *Miss Amelia Earhart, local aviatrix:* Amelia Earhart, *20 hrs. 40 min.: Our Flight in the Friendship,* pages 77–79.

38   *They continued their friendly relationship:* Muriel Earhart Morrissey, *Courage Is the Price,* pages 134–135.

38   *Without any serious accident:* Amelia Earhart, *Cosmopolitan Magazine,* January, 1929, page 163.

CHAPTER 3: THE LEGEND BEGINS

40   *The sponsors wanted an American woman:* Amelia Earhart, *20 hrs. 40 min.: Our Flight in the Friendship,* page 98.

40   *George Palmer Putnam II was born:* IBA of George Palmer Putnam III, May 22, 1976. PCO EM.

41   *"Boy Mayor of Bend:* James L. Crowell, "Frontier Publisher" (Master's Thesis), page 211.

42   *The copious notes and computations:* Nathaniel Bowditch, *American Practical Navigator* (AE's copy). PCO EM.

42   *The Fokker trimotor* Friendship: Amelia Earhart, *20 hr. 40 min.: Our Flight in the Friendship,* page 119.

42   The Story of the Titanic Disaster: Amelia Earhart, *20 hr. 40 min.: Our Flight in the Friendship,* page 151.

42   *Approximately twenty hours:* Amelia Earhart, *20 hr. 40 min.: Our Flight in the Friendship,* page 198.

43   *She would leave with:* Amelia Earhart, *The Fun of It,* page 89.

43   SS *President Roosevelt:* Amelia Earhart, *20 hrs. 40 min.: Our Flight in the Friendship,* page 209.

43   *Harry Manning was six months older:* IBA of Mrs. Harry Manning, circa 1978. PCO EM.

43   *He later received:* "Manning Gained World Fame," Scrapbook of HM. PCO Mrs. Harry Manning.

44   *It was the first solo flight ever:* Amelia Earhart, *The Fun of It,* page 89.

44   *She flew back to New York:* Amelia Earhart, *Cosmopolitan Magazine,* November, 1928, page 32.

44   *Now she was certified:* Amelia Earhart, *The Fun of It,* page 154.

45   *Of the four who did not finish:* D. D. Hatfield, *Los Angeles Aeronautics 1920–1929,* page 188.

45 *A divorce was granted:* Sally Putnam Chapman with Stephanie Mansfield, *Whistled Like a Bird,* page 164.

46 *On April 7, 1931:* Frank Kingston Smith, *Legacy of Wings: The Harold F. Pitcairn Story,* page 183.

46 *She arrived in Oakland:* "Flying Windmill Links Oceans." SFC, June 7, 1931.

46 *"sack of potatoes":* Amelia Earhart, *The Fun of It,* page 209.

47 *After they returned from Europe:* George Palmer Putnam, *Wide Margins,* page 299.

47 *The 2,477-mile flight:* "Miss Earhart sets mark from coast," NYT, August 25, 1932.

47 *the first nonstop transcontinental flight:* "Mrs. Putnam first woman to span U.S. non-stop alone," PEB, August 25, 1932.

47 *By early 1933 Amelia had sold:* Amelia Earhart, *Last Flight,* page 19.

48 *Earhart, Paul Collins:* James Haggerty, *Aviation's Mr. Sam,* page 28.

49 *She had made a good showing:* "U.S. and France share 1933 Feminine flying honors," PEB, December 13, 1933.

51 *By Friday afternoon:* "Leaves filed at 4:44 p.m. for Mainland," HSB, January 11, 1935, page 1.

51 *" 'AE,' the noise of your motor:* Amelia Earhart, *Last Flight,* page 27.

51 *"EVERYTHING IS FINE:* "Miss Earhart's story of flight is told in messages from plane," HSB, January 12, 1935, page 1.

52 *"FLYING ABOUT 8,000 FEET:* "Miss Earhart's story of flight is told in messages from plane," HSB, January 12, 1935, page 1.

52 *She could turn on her transmitter:* Amelia Earhart, *Last Flight,* page 32.

52 *The Vega landed:* "Lands at bay city airport at 11:01 a.m.," HSB, January 12, 1935, page 1.

53 *"FLYING AT 10,000 FEET:* "Aviatrix in try for record," OPE, May 8, 1935, page 1.

53 *Earhart had to be rescued:* "Amelia in record flight," OPE, May 9, 1935, page 1.

53 *G.P.'s cousin Palmer had declared bankruptcy:* George Palmer Putnam, *Wide Margins,* page 300.

CHAPTER FOUR: PREPARATIONS FOR THE WORLD FLIGHT

57 *By May of 1936:* Jean L. Backus, *Letters from Amelia,* page 190.

57 *Bo was born in Patterson:* IBA of BO, October 17–18, 1975. PCO EM.

57 *Right on schedule:* "Amelia hops in new ship," LAT, July 22, 1936.

58 *Richey had been the first woman:* "U.S. women in aviation: the 1930's," *Air & Space Magazine,* Winter, 1980, page 16. NASM.

58 *The Department of Commerce:* E. H. Bryan Jr., *Panala'au Memoirs,* page 1.

59 *For instance, Amelia had remained friends:* Amelia Earhart, *The Fun of It,* back flyleaf after page 218.

59 *Western Electric said they could modify:* WEC instruction bulletin No. 830 for Type 20B radio receiver. WEC.

60 *At a press conference:* "Amelia Earhart will fly around world in March," NHT, February 12, 1937, page 1.

60 *Cyril D. Remmlein:* "To whirl round the world" (photo caption), NDM, February 15, 1937.

60 *Earhart and Manning chose to have the receiver:* Daily Journal of BDX engineer VM, entry on February 15, 1937. PCO VM.

61   *They were able to:* [Earhart story], BST, February 21, 1937, page 1.

61   *As the others were deplaning:* Letter from JG to FG, May 3, 1982, page 2. NZM.

61   *There were no manuals:* Letter from JG to FG, May 3, 1982, page 2. NZM.

61   *From then on, Gurr was the person:* Letter from JG to FG, May 3, 1982, page 3. NZM.

62   *The radio direction-finder loop:* Letter from JG to FG, May 3, 1982, page 3. NZM

62   *Before Eugene Vidal resigned:* "Plans being completed for Amelia's world hop," OKT, March 2, 1937, page 1.

62   *At G.P.'s expense:* IBA of Vivian Maatta Sims, March 10, 1977. PCO EM.

62   *After passing the tests:* Personal scrapbook of HM, Radio License P-11-1695. PCO Mrs. HM.

63   *The new Bendix receiver:* BDX manual for RA-1 series receiver for aircraft, specifications, page 2. BDX.

63   *The receiver had five bands:* Earhart listed the frequency bands of her receiver on the back of India weather chart. They matched the bands listed in NM's journal exactly. PUL

63   *The limited space:* BDX RDF-2-A Navy radio direction finder instruction book, page 12. BDX.

63   *If Earhart or Manning tried:* IBA of Al Hemphill, BDX direction-finder engineer, May 21, 1976. PCO EM.

63   *This natural, seemingly harmless mistake:* IBA of JG, January 20, 1976. PCO EM.

64   *Kelly took several days:* LAC report No. 623, by CJ, March 10, 1937, pages 0–11. LAC

64   *Joe Gurr could test:* Letter from JG to FG, May 3, 1982, page 5. NZM.

64   *The plan was to have Manning:* "Earhart plane circles bay but aviatrix stays in L.A.," OKT, March 10, 1937, page 9.

64   *Even though it was not yet daylight:* Letter from JG to FG, May 3, 1982, page 6. NZM.

64   *In a few minutes the sun:* Sunrise for March 10, 1937. "Distant Suns" (computer program).

65   *A 26-day-old moon:* Moon position for March 10, 1937. "Distant Suns."

65   *The Navy tug* Ontario: GOAS NPU Messages 0110/1040 and 6010/1042, March 10, 1937. NASB.

66   *With room for only four people:* "Scared? No just thrilled, says Amelia of world hop," OKT, March 11, 1937, page 4.

66   *The commanding officer:* "She can do it, says examiner," OKT, March 11, 1937, page 1.

67   *"He told them that he wasn't worried:* "Scared? No just thrilled, says Amelia of world hop," OKY, March 11, 1937, page 4.

67   *The plan was to complete:* COMDT12ND, Comaer message 27th at 1155, February 27, 1937. NASB.

67   *They agreed to pay:* IBA of Theresa Minor Mantz, July 19, 1975. PCO EM.

67   *Amelia didn't want any announcements:* "Amelia plans to take off today on world hop; final weather report waited," OKT, March 14, 1937, page 1.

67   *He also reminded them:* Telegram from CJ to AE, 12:00 noon, March 11, 1937. PUL.

68   *The plane would send for the first two minutes:* COMSFDIV message 8013/0926, March 13, 1937. NASB.

69   *The arrangements for radio communications:* COMSFDIV message 8013/1320, March 13, 1937. NASB.

70   *Manning closed by telling:* "Amelia will take off on world flight tomorrow," OKT, March 13, 1937, page 1.

70   *QUOTE FOR CUTTER:* COMSFDIV message 8013/0905, March 13, 1937. NASB

70   *. . . CONTACT SAMOA NAVAL RADIO:* COMDT12ND, Comaer message 13th at 0935, March 13, 1937. NASB.

71   *Amelia met with reporters:* "Take-off time tentatively set for 2 p.m.," OKT, March 14, 1937, page 3.

71   *She told them:* "Take-off time tentatively set for 2 p.m.," OKT, March 14, 1937, page 3.

72   *No wonder Kelly had advised:* Telegram from CJ to AE 10:20 a.m., March 13, 1937. PUL

72   *"I am too old a hand:* "Storm again postpones Earhart hop," OKT, March 15, 1937, page 1.

72   *"All that remains:* "Storm again postpones Earhart hop," OKT, March 15, 1937, page 1.

72   *By cable, Amelia thanked:* "Storm again postpones Earhart hop," OKT, March 15, 1937, page 1.

72   *Amelia decided:* "Storm again postpones Earhart hop," OKT, March 15, 1937, page 1.

72   *Miller informed Ragsdale:* CMDT12ND message 1015/1927, March 15, 1937. NASB.

73   *Pan American was delaying:* "Amelia plans world hop tomorrow," OKT, March 16, 1937, page 1.

73   *With another day to dry out:* "Amelia plans world hop tomorrow," OKT, March 16, 1937, page 1.

73   *He would advise them again:* CMDT12ND message 8016/1057, March 16, 1937. NASB.

73   *The instrument was to be turned over:* CMDT12ND message 1016/1010, March 16, 1937. NASB.

73   *"Amelia's navigator seeks Mexico divorce:* "Amelia's navigator seeks Mexico divorce from wife," OKT, March 16, 1937, page 1.

74   *Altogether the takeoff path:* "Earhart ready to start trip around world," OKT, March 17, 1937, page 3.

74   *The tailwind:* "Earhart set for flight 'round earth," OKT, March 17, 1937, page 1.

74   *She wanted the motors in good shape:* "Earhart ready to start trip around world," OKT, March 17, 1937, page 3.

75   *He would fill the left and right:* Amelia Earhart, Last Flight, pages 57–58.

75   *Navy men helped:* "Earhart soars over Pacific from Oakland to Hawaii on first leg of world journey," OKT, March 18, 1937, page A.

75   *The Hawaii Clipper took off:* "Earhart soars over Pacific from Oakland to Hawaii on first leg of world journey," OKT, March 18, 1937, page A.

75   *The 4:00 P.M. weather report:* U.S. Weather Bureau observation, Oakland Airport, 4:00 p.m., March 17, 1937.

75   *The roar of the motors:* "Earhart soars over Pacific from Oakland to Hawaii on first leg of world journey," OKT, March 18, 1937, page A.

76   *The stopwatch registered:* "Earhart soars over Pacific from Oakland to Hawaii on first leg of world journey," OKT, March 18, 1937, page A.

76   *MISS EARHART OFFICIAL TAKEOFF:* USCG message 8017/2158, March 17, 1937. NADC.

CHAPTER 5: THE FLIGHT TO HONOLULU

77   *Opposite the Ferry Building:* "Earhart soars over Pacific from Oakland to Hawaii on first leg of world journey," OKT, March 18, 1937, page A.

78   *She would fly closer:* "Amelia Earhart on first leg of flight around world," LAT, March 18, 1937.

78   *He allowed the engines to stabilize:* Telegram CJ to AE 12:00 noon, March 11, 1937. PUL

78   *Soon Mantz had to increase:* Necessary indicated airspeed to maintain a true airspeed of 150 mph at 3500 feet altitude with ISA-5 temperature. Model 10E Flight Manual, LAC report 466. LAC.

78   *The fuel burn:* The power settings specified in CJ's telegrams were based on AE fueling to 900 gallons. AE added 47 gallons of fuel, making the aircraft heavier. Now, for CJ's specified power settings to be correct, AE must first burn off the extra fuel.

78   *The faster Electra soon left:* "Here is log of first lap of journey," OKT, March 18, 1937, page A.

78   *There were squalls:* "Here is log of first lap of journey," OKT, March 18, 1937, page A.

78   *Mantz put both mixture controls:* "Amelia credits success to skill of navigators." OKT, March 19, 1937, page 1.

78   *Again, the airspeed fell below:* Application of heat to carburetors decreases air density. Engine manifold pressure must be increased accordingly to compensate.

78   *Some of the squalls:* "Amelia credits success to skill of navigators," OKT, March 19, 1937, page 1.

78   *She decided to climb:* "Amelia credits success to skill of navigators," OKT, March 19, 1937, page 1.

78   *The indicators were showing:* Necessary indicated airspeed to maintain a true airspeed of 150 mph at 8000 feet altitude with ISA temperature. Model 10E Flight Manual, LAC report 466. LAC.

79   *After they burned off:* Power settings at 8,000 feet; telegram CJ to AE 10:20 a.m., March 13, 1937. PUL

79   *The total was very close:* Power settings at 8,000 feet; telegram CJ to AE 10:20 a.m., March 13, 1937. PUL

79   *He shot the star Sirius:* East-half of actual chart FN used Oakland to Honolulu, March 17–18, 1937. PUL.

79   *At 8:35 P.M. PST they reported:* "Here is log of first lap of journey," OKT, March 18, 1937, page A.

79   *Earhart was constantly busy monitoring:* AE's Electra fuel system diagram; drawing No. 42681, March 6, 1937. LAC.

79   *The Electra was starting to fly:* Amelia Earhart, *Last Flight*, page 61.

79 *Manning got no answer:* "Here is log of first lap of journey," OKT, March 18, 1937, page A.

80 *She wrote in her notes:* Amelia Earhart, *Last Flight,* page 61.

80 *The announcer gave the weather:* Amelia Earhart, *Last Flight,* page 61.

80 *Manning didn't hear them reply:* "Here is log of first lap of journey," OKT, March 18, 1937, page A.

80 *They immediately enriched the mixture:* USACR; exhibit "E", page 1. NADC.

81 *She could only adjust:* USACR; exhibit "E", page 1. NADC.

81 *At 2:05 A.M. PST:* "Here is log of first lap of journey," OKT, March 18, 1937, page A.

81 *He plotted the celestial fix:* West-half of actual chart FN used Oakland to Honolulu, March 17–18, 1937. PUL.

81 *Earhart wrote on her pad:* Amelia Earhart, *Last Flight,* pages 64, 65, and 69.

81 *He got an acknowledgment:* "Amelia sets record on Oakland-Hawaii hop in 15 hours 48 minutes,: OKT, March 18, 1937, pages 1, and A.

82 *Doing this meant switching:* "Amelia credits success to skill of navigators." OKT, March 19, 1937, page 1.

82 *The true airspeed:* "Amelia credits success to skill of navigators." OKT, March 19, 1937, page 1./and Amelia Earhart, *Last Flight,* page 65.

82 *With a 15-knot (17.3 mph) tailwind:* An indicated airspeed of 120 mph at 10,000 feet will produce a142 mph true airspeed. With a 17.3 mph tailwind a ground speed of 159.3 mph. At 38 gph AE would travel (159.3 mph/38 gph) 4.192 miles for each gallon of fuel burned.

82 *Noonan had calculated:* USACR; exhibit "M," item 92 (Nautical Almanac). NADC

82 *His estimated time of arrival:* Nautical twilight, civil, twilight, and sunrise at Honolulu, March 18, 1937. "Distant Suns" (computer program). Nautical twilight is the first or last hint of light in a dark sky, and is defined by the sun at 12 degrees below the horizon. In civil twilight there is just enough light for objects to be visible, and by definition the sun is 6 degrees below the horizon.

82 *Suddenly the generator ammeter:* Amelia Earhart, *Last Flight,* page 64.

82 *Noonan crossed it with the line of position:* West-half of actual chart FN used Oakland to Honolulu, March 17–18. 1937. PUL.

82 *Noonan wanted them to use:* Amelia Earhart, *Last Flight,* page 64.

83 *When she had turned the loop:* Amelia Earhart, *Last Flight,* page 64.

83 *At about 5:10 A.M. HST:* Amelia Earhart, *Last Flight,* page 66.

83 *It was just starting to get light:* Amelia Earhart, *Last Flight,* page 66.

83 *They passed Honolulu:* "Amelia sets record on Oakland-Hawaii hop in 15 Hours, 48 Minutes," OKT, March 18, 1937. Page 1. [Honolulu time 2½ hours earlier than Oakland time].

84 *She hadn't gotten in trouble:* Amelia Earhart, *Last Flight,* pages 25 and 26.

84 *The switches for the landing lights:* "Story of Amelia's flight," HSB, March 18, 1937, page 1.

84 *Earhart yelled, "Don't! Don't!":* Don Dwiggins, *Hollywood Pilot,* page 102.

84 *Mantz had a little too much airspeed:* USACR; exhibit "E," page 1. NADC.

84 *The plane's extra speed:* John Clayton. Amelia says: "It's all shining adventure." LAT, June 20, 1937.

84 *With the power off:* "Amelia sets record on Oakland-Hawaii hop in 15 Hours, 48 Minutes," OKT, March 18, 1937, page 1.

84 *The wheels of the Electra:* "Amelia sets record on Oakland-Hawaii hop in 15 Hours, 48 Minutes," OKT, March 18, 1937, page 1.

85 *He followed the Army crew's guidance:* USACR; exhibit "A," page 1. NADC.

85 *Instead, he startled the crew:* USACR; exhibit "A," page 1. NADC.

85 *Then Chris and Mona Holmes:* "Amelia and her three companions get welcome at Wheeler Field," photoraph number 4, HSB, March 18, 1937, page 6.

85 *Amelia wouldn't allow any pictures:* "Amelia sets record on Oakland-Hawaii hop in 15 Hours, 48 Minutes," OKT, March 18, 1937, page 1.

85 *He related that for the last six:* USACR; Board Proceedings, page 2. NADC.

85 *The instrument light:* USACR; exhibit "A," pages 1 and 2. NADC.

85 *Lieutenant Arnold said:* USACR; exhibit "E," page 2. NADC.

85 *Master Sergeant Biando:* USACR; exhibit "A," page 2. NADC./and IBA of Horace G. Waters, March 6, 1981. PCO EM.

86 *With the tailwind:* "Amelia credits success to skill of navigators." OKT, March 19, 1937, page 1.

86 *It wasn't very long:* "Flier resting after record (from page 1)," HSB, March 18, 1937, page 6.

86 *The flight, she told them:* "Flier resting after record (from page 1)," HSB, March 18, 1937, pages 1 and 6.

87 *She placed a telephone call:* "Flier delayed in Hawaii by ocean storms," OKT, March 19, 1937, page 1.

87 *Noonan had developed special procedures:* Frederick J. Noonan, "Navigating the Clippers," HAD, April 19, 1936. (Magazine Section).

87 *G.P. told her:* "Amelia is trim boyish figure," HSB, March 18, 1937, page 6.

87 *After greeting her hosts:* Amelia Earhart, *Last Flight,* page 67.

87 *Amelia told him:* IBA of Lt. Comdr. Henry M. Anthony, July 22, 1975. PCO EM.

88 *Anthony, who was taking notes:* IBA of Lt. Comdr. Henry M. Anthony, July 22, 1975. PCO EM.

88 *If the plane is not heard:* COMSFDIV message 8013/0905, March 13, 1937. NASB.

89 *Anthony replied that they:* "Synopsis of weather for radio room," personal scrapbook of Lt. Leo G. Bellarts (gift collection, College Park, MD) NADC.

89 *This was a puzzle to Earhart:* "Problem of flying speedy plane slowly was puzzle to Amelia," OKT, March 20, 1937.

89 *It was after two o'clock:* USACR; exhibit "A," page 2. NADC

89 *When they inspected the propeller:* USACR; Board Proceedings, page 2, and exhibit "A," pages 1 and 2. NADC

89 *They had reset the control boxes:* USACR; exhibit "A," pages 1 and 2. NADC.

89 *Mantz remarked that they had held:* Amelia Earhart, *Last Flight,* page 64.

90 *Thomas had cleaned and re-gapped:* USACR; exhibit "E," page 2. NADC.

90 *The instrument bulb:* USACR; exhibit "A," page 2, item 20. NADC

90 *The right propeller was still frozen solid:* USACR; exhibit "A," page 2. NADC.

90 *The propeller was found:* USACR; exhibit "A," page 2. NADC.

90   *Everything was very clean:* USACR; exhibit "A," page 2. NADC.
91   *By four o'clock, both propellers:* USACR; exhibit "E," page 2. NADC.
91   *He left for Waikiki:* USACR; exhibit "E," page 2. NADC.
91   *At the end of dinner:* USACR; exhibit "E," page 2. NADC.
91   *Barring unexpected trouble:* USACR; exhibit "E," page 2,/and exhibit "A,"
     page 2. NADC.
92   *He then called Lieutenant Rogers:* USACR; exhibit "A," page 2. NADC.

CHAPTER 6: THE CRASH AT HONOLULU
93   *If the grass at Wheeler Field:* "Problem of flying speedy plane slowly was puz-
     zle to Amelia," OKT, March 20, 1937.
93   *He reviewed with them:* USACR; exhibit "E," page 3. NADC
93   *thinking about using Luke Field:* "Problem of flying speedy plane slowly was
     puzzle to Amelia," OKT, March 20, 1937.
94   *They decided to move:* "Problem of flying speedy plane slowly was puzzle to
     Amelia," OKT, March 20, 1937.
94   *As Standard Oil could not supply:* USACR; exhibit "A," page 3. NADC.
94   *if the plane checked okay:* USACR; exhibit "D," page 1. NADC.
94   *If he found it satisfactory:* USACR; exhibit "A," page 3. NADC.
94   *While the truck finished fueling:* USACR; exhibit "D," page 1. NADC.
95   *He had the mechanic let air out:* USACR; exhibit "A," page 3. NADC.
95   *The relatively light plane:* USACR; exhibit "A," page 3. NADC.
95   *Mantz rocked the Electra's wings:* IBA of Theresa Minor Mantz, July 19, 1975.
     PCO EM.
95   *They were guided:* USACR; exhibit "D," page 1. NADC.
95   *They had never worked as well:* USACR; exhibit "D," page 1. NADC.
95   *He asked Lynn V. Young:* USACR; exhibit "E," page 3. NADC.
96   *The chamois filtered out:* USACR; exhibit "E," page 4. NADC.
96   *Chris, Terry, and Paul left for Waikiki:* USACR; exhibit "E," page 4. NADC.
96   *Right now they were gassing:* USACR; exhibit "E," page 5. NADC.
96   *"LEAVING 1:30 AM YOUR TIME:* IBA of BN, February 10, 1975. [Cable from FN to
     BN, March 19, 1937]. PCO EM.
96   *He requested Arnold to hold:* USACR; exhibit "E," page 4. NADC.
97   *Mantz requested that the plane:* USACR; exhibit "E," page 4. NADC.
97   *By 7:30 the plane was refueled:* USACR; exhibit "E," pages 4 and 5. NADC.
97   *They would have to take a boat:* USACR; exhibit "D," page 2. NADC.
97   *It had showered heavily:* USACR; exhibit "D," page 2. NADC.
98   *an additional 75 gallons:* USACR; exhibit "E," page 5. NADC.
98   *for a total load of 900 gallons:* USACR; Board Proceedings, page 4. NADC.
98   *Amelia greeted Lieutenant Arnold:* USACR; exhibit "D,' page 2./and exhibit
     "E," page 5. NADC.
98   *Lieutenant Arnold told her:* USACR; exhibit "E," page 6. NADC.
98   *By five o'clock it was completed:* USACR; exhibit "E," page 5. NADC.
98   *After about five minutes:* USACR; exhibit "E," page 5. NADC.
98   *Looking out the windshield:* USACR; exhibit "E," page 5. NADC.
99   *Mantz said they would guide:* USACR; exhibit "E," page 5. NADC.
99   *She left her landing lights off:* USACR; exhibit "E," page 5. NADC.

99   *The buildings and various objects:* USACR; exhibit "E," page 5. NADC.
99   *The plane was lined up:* USACR; exhibit "I," page 1. NADC.
99   *Then she released the brakes:* USACR; exhibit "H," page 1. NADC.
99   *Her left foot was holding:* USACR; exhibit "H," page 1. NADC.
100 *Now it seemed to him:* USACR; exhibit "F," page 1. NADC.
100 *(Until near flying speed is reached:* In multi-engine aircraft this is Vmc [velocity minimum control] speed.
100 *This imposed a handicap:* Harold P. Van Cott. Human Engineering Guide to Equipment Design, pages 47–61.
100 *As the tail lifted up:* Amelia Earhart, *Last Flight,* page 71.
100 *Earhart did the only thing:* Amelia Earhart, *Last Flight,* page 72.
100 *The first thing she thought of:* Amelia Earhart. "Aviatrix tells story of dismaying turn in events," [continued from page 1.] OKT, March 21, 1937, page 4.
100 *When she looked back outside:* USACR; exhibit "E," page 6. NADC.
101 *A shower of sparks:* USACR; exhibit "D," page 3. NADC.
101 *The tire blew out:* USACR; exhibit "F," page 1. NADC.
101 *After both landing gears had collapsed:* USACR; exhibit "I," page 1. NADC.
101 *She watched as it pulled up:* USACR; exhibit "E," page 6. NADC.
101 *Chris helped her:* USACR; exhibit "E," page 6. NADC.
102 *"What happened?":* Charles Moore. "Aviatrix and navigators sail for U.S." OKT, March 21, 1937, page 4 (continued from page 1).
102 *When the cabin door was opened:* Amelia Earhart. "Earhart is amazed by events grounding her, delaying tour," OKT, March 21, 1937, page 4 (continued from page 1).
102 *Except for a slight bruising:* USACR; exhibit "E," page 6. NADC.
102 *The officer of the day:* USACR; exhibit "D," page 3. NADC.
102 *He tried to move the press photographers:* "Earhart crashes on take-off; fliers uninjured; plane will be sent to U.S. for repairs," OKT, March 20, 1937, page 1.
102 *A crowd was already gathering:* USACR; exhibit "E," page 6. NADC.
102 *They returned to the airplane:* USACR; exhibit "E," page 6. NADC.
102 *"I think not":* USACR; exhibit "E," page 6. NADC,/and Amelia Earhart, *Last Flight,* page 73.
103 *It was a miracle:* Amelia Earhart. "Earhart is amazed by events grounding her, delaying tour." OKT, March 21, 1937, page 4 (continued from page 1).
103 *Earhart took a glance:* USACR; exhibit "E," page 6. NADC.
103 *He would arrange for a truck:* USACR; exhibit "E," page 6. NADC.
103 *He wanted to keep the octant:* Receipt for navy octant on SS Malolo stationery from FN to HM. PCO Mrs. Harry Manning.
104 *After picking up Terry:* USACR; exhibit "E," page 6. NADC.
103 *"AMELIA IN CRACK-IP:* "Flight will continue as soon as ship is repaired," OKT, March 20, 1937, page 1.
103 *The important thing:* Amelia Earhart. "Earhart is amazed by events grounding her, delaying tour." OKT, March 21, 1937, page 1.
104 *If she wanted to try again:* "Aviatrix calm in Luke Field takeoff crash," HSB, March 20, 1937, page 1.
104 *as long as she wasn't hurt:* "Aviatrix calm in Luke Field takeoff crash," HSB, March 20, 1937, page 1.

104 *to send the letter along with the car:* UASCR; exhibit "N," letter from AE to Commanding Officer, Hawaiian Air Depot, Luke Field, T.H., March 20, 1937.

104 *Bill Cogswell from the Pan Pacific Press Bureau:* "Flier, disappointed but undaunted, departs for home," HSB, March 20, 1937.

105 *Possibly the right shock absorbers:* "Earhart is amazed by events grounding her, delaying tour," OKT, March 21, 1937, pages 1 and 4.

105 *he was on his way to Los Angeles:* "Putnam goes south to await Amelia," OKT, March 21, 1937, page 4.

106 *Amelia and Fred stood:* Photograph of AE and FN standing by the rail on the SS Malolo. PCO BN./and IBA of BN, February 10, 1975. PCO EM.

Chapter 7: Preparing for the Second World Flight

107 *Following the pilot:* IBA of Theresa Minor Mantz, July 19, 1975. PCO EM.

107 *They knew the Electra:* "Earhart second takeoff May 1: Same course around world being mapped," HSB, March 27, 1937, page 1.

108 *she had talked to Manning:* IBA of Mrs. Harry Manning, circa 1978. PCO EM.

108 *Everyone was to come to her cabin:* IBA of Theresa Minor Mantz, July 19, 1975. PCO EM.

108 *A delay of another month:* "Amelia home to try again," OKT, March 25, 1937, page 1.

108 *She had several tons:* "Amelia home to try again," OKT, March 25, 1937, page 1.

108 *Manning left separately:* IBA of Theresa Minor Mantz, July 19, 1975. PCO EM.

109 *There was work to be done:* IBA of Elstrude and Fred Tomas, March 6, 1981. PCO EM.

109 *With gratitude and greetings:* Letter from AE to EE , March 25, 1937. PUL.

109 *Amelia left the study:* George Palmer Putnam. *Up in Our Country,* drawing on page 113.

109 *Altogether they were estimated:* USACR; exhibit "M," totals at bottom of unnumbered first page. NADC.

109 *When totaled, with other expenses:* USACR; Billing from Hawaiian Air Depot to AE c/o S. S. Bowman, April 5, 1937. NADC.

110 *For assembling the damaged plane:* GP's attorney's file, 1937 expense schedule "C". PCO Clyde E Holley, Esq.

110 *Saturday morning:* USACR; Board proceedings, page 6. NADC.

110 *Fred was married:* Marriage Certificate, FN and BN, Yuma, Arizona, March 27, 1937.

110 *G.P. asked Dr. Elliott:* Letter from GP to EE, March 30, 1937. PUL.

111 *Friday, April 2, the Electra was off-loaded:* GP's attorney's file, PM Air Service, Ltd. invoice No. 5007, April 30, 1937. PCO Clyde E. Holley, Esq.

111 *The investigating policeman:* "Bride of plane navigator hurt in Fresno crash," TFB, April 5, 1937.

111 *No work could be accomplished:* IBA of James M. Gerschler, August 1, 1976. PCO EM.

111 *Inspectors oversaw all shop work:* IBA of Harvey C. Christen, July 28, 1976. PCO EM.

111 *After analyzing the reports:* LAC Engineering Orders (6 pages) for repair of AE's Electra. FAA ARB.

111 *Amelia and G.P. authorized Lockheed:* GP's attorney's file, 1937 expense schedule "C". PCO Clyde E. Holley, Esq.

112 *Joe Gurr believed:* Letter from JG to FG, May 3, 1982, page 4. NZM.

112 *To back up the trailing wire:* Photo showing antenna-loading coil on top of R-1 tank, March 6, 1937. Wide World Photo, New York.

112 *They could switch to the fixed antenna:* Letter from JG to FG, May 3, 1982, page 5. NZM.

112 *Gurr believed he could improve:* Letter from JG to FG, May 3, 1982, page 7. NZM/and IBA of JG, January 20, 1976. PCO EM.

112 *Not only did this provide an escape route:* March, 1937 photos show a window; May, 1937 photos in Miami show an aluminum hatch both open and closed.

113 *He and Earhart often visited:* Amelia Earhart, *Last Flight,* pages 79 and 80.

113 *New wing tips were being installed:* LAC Engineering Order, certified by James M. Gerschler, May 19, 1937. FAA ARB.

113 *No damage had been done:* Letter from GP to G. Stanley Meikle, April 12, 1937, page 3. PUL.

113 *All four of the individual propeller blades:* Letter from GP to G. Stanley Meikle, April 12, 1937, page 3. PUL.

113 *Lockheed found the critical parts:* Letter from GP to G. Stanley Meikle, April 12, 1937, pages 3 and 4. PUL.

113 *Working after hours:* Letter from JG to FG, May 3, 1982, page 7. NZM.

113 *Gurr had the antenna mast:* Letter from JG to FG, May 3, 1982, page 7. NZM.

113 *It would not radiate as well:* Letter from JG to FG, May 3, 1982, pages 4 and 7. NZM.

113 *He tuned the transmitter's output:* Letter from JG to FG, May 3, 1982, page 7. NZM.

113 *He believed the longer antenna:* Letter from JG to FG, May 3, 1982, page 7. NZM.

113 *He was in St. Louis:* Don Dwiggins, *Hollywood Pilot,* page 105.

114 *When he was finished with everything:* Letter from JG to FG, May 3, 1982, page 5. NZM.

114 *Incidentally, he reminded Mr. Lilly:* Letter from GP to Josiah K. Lilly, May 6, 1937, page 1. PUL.

115 *This was a pleasant indication:* Letter from Gp to EE, May 8, 1937, page 1. PUL.

115 *She met Gurr at the airplane:* Letter from JG to FG, May 3, 1982, Page 5. NZM.

115 *Gurr could tell from her hesitancy:* Only once before had AE ever used the BDX radiodirection-finder. Amelia Earhart, *Last Flight,* page 64.

115 *He explained that she must set:* IBA of JG, January 20, 1976. PCO EM.

115 *A listing of the five actual loop coupler:* BDX radio direction-finder manual, (BDX buyout) Radio Research Company, Inc., manual for RDF-2-A February 1, 1937, page 12. BDX

116 *She would have to be very judicious:* IBA of JG, January 20, 1976. PCO EM.

117 *Before leaving, she posed with Gurr:* Letter from JG to FG, May 3, 1982, page 5. NZM.

117 *If not, she would quietly return:* Amelia Earhart, *Last Flight,* page 85.

117 *It would be ready for delivery:* Amelia Earhart, *Last Flight,* Page 85.

117 *"Yes sir! I am quite willing:* Letter from Josiah K. Lilly to EE, May 18, 1937, page 1. PUL.

117 *The very next morning:* "Fire delays Amelia Earhart here while she plans flight," ADS, Saturday morning, May 22, 1937, pages 1 and 5. "Thursday they flew from Burbank to Oakland and return." Amelia Earhart, *Last Flight,* page 85, "the rebuilt Electra came out of Lockheed plant on May 19. Two days later we flew it to Oakland—." Here, *Last Flight* is incorrect; flight to Oakland was made on Thursday, May 20, 1937.

CHAPTER 8: WORLD FLIGHT RESUMES— OAKLAND TO MIAMI

118 *Earhart was in Oakland:* Amelia Earhart, *Last Flight,* page 85.

118 *If Amelia was asked:* Amelia Earhart. "Miss Earhart set for flight around the world," TMH, May 29, 1937, pages 1 and 2.

118 *Exactly five years ago:* Amelia Earhart, *The Fun of It,* page 209.

118 *ten years ago Lindbergh had flown:* Chelsea Fraser, *Heroes of the Air,* Chronology, page XVI.

118 *At 3:50 P.M., Thursday:* "Amelia Earhart's plane ready for globe-girdling flight," NHT, May 22, 1937/and "Plane slightly damaged by fire shortly after arrival at Tucson Municipal Airport," ADS, May 21, 1937. "She remarked to Tucson reporters on arrival that it was five years ago today that I arrived in Ireland. The world flight left Oakland May 20, 1937.

118 *They were flying east together:* IBA of BO, October 17–18, 1975. PCO EML.

120 *He would remain in New York:* Letter from GP to Mrs. Ruth Hampton, June 23, 1937. NADC DOI.

120 *The cash and American Express Travelers Checks:* GP's attorney's file, letter to American Express Company, November 18, 1937. PCO Clyde E. Holley, Esq.

120 *A Mantz Air Service truck:* Photos taken during loading of AE's Electra at Burbank, May 21, 1937.

120 *The rest of the party:* "Fire delays Amelia Earhart here while she plans flight," ADS, May 22, 1937, pages 1 and 5.

120 *Strong surface winds:* Amelia Earhart, *Last Flight,* page 86.

121 *Again the sun was low:* "Fire delays Amelia Earhart here while she plans flight," ADS, May 22, 1937, pages 1 and 5./and "Amelia flies to Louisiana Field," ADS, May 23, 1937, page 1.

121 *"JUST TO REPORT:* Telegram from AE to BN, May 22, 1937. PCO BN.

121 *At 9:10 A.M. CST they took off:* "Noted woman flier drops in on Miami," TMH, May 24, 1937, page 2.

121 *He wanted her to hold:* "Noted woman flier drops in on Miami," TMH, May 24, 1937, page 2./and Amelia Earhart, *Last Flight,* page 87.

121 *The drift meter checked okay:* C. B. Allen. "Earhart ready to start today on globe-circling trip," NHT, June 1, 1937, pages 1 and 10.

121 *When they sighted the Florida coast:* "Noted woman flyer drops in on Miami," TMH, May 24, 1937, page 2.

122 *The creak of metal could be heard:* "Noted woman flier drops in on Miami," TMH, May 24, 1937, page 2.

122 *Could they think:* "Noted woman flier drops in on Miami," TMH, May 24, 1937, page 2.

122 *Fred had to ask Bee:* Telegram from FN to BN May 24, 1937. PCO BN.

122 *Amelia was also disturbed:* IBA of BO, October 17–18, 1975. PCO EM.

123 *They would send an instrument mechanic:* Noted woman flier drops in on Miami," TMH, May 24, 1937, page 2.

123 *so far they had not found any damage:* IBA of BO, October 17–18, 1975. PCO EM.

123 *When Bo got off the phone:* IBA of BO, Oxctober 17–18, 1975. PCO EM.

123 *The autopilot rudder had worked better:* C. B. Allen. "Delay flight start to fix instruments, TMH, May 31, 1937, pages 1 and 2.

124 *He immediately inspected:* IBA of Percy E. Pettijohn, May 15, 1975. PCO EM.

124 *Amelia was relieved:* IBA of BO, October 17–18, 1975. PCO EM.

124 *Amelia asked him about getting an accelerometer:* IBA of F. Ralph Sias, December 30, 1977. PCO EM.

124 *Once he was sure:* IBA of Percy E. Pettijohn, May 15, 1975. PCO EML.

124 *At the hotel a message was waiting:* "Noted woman flier drops in on Miami," TMH, May 24, 1937, page 2; and "Reception arranged for Merrill-Lambie," TMH, May 23, 1937, page 8A.

124 *Merrill and Lambie were presented:* "Merrill and Lambie are honored at park," TMH, May 25, 1937, page 8A.

124 *Earhart had little time to talk:* Jack L. King, *Wings of Man,* page 179.

125 *They maintained a constant:* Jack L. King, *Wings of Man,* page 182.

125 *The flight from England:* Jack L. King, *Wings of Man,* page 186.

125 *They had maintained a regular schedule:* Jack L. King, *Wings of Man,* page 186./and page 163 "WEEP radio logs,"/and photo on page 201 showing antenna details of Merrill's Electra.

125 *He showed the "G" meter:* IBA of F. Ralph Sias, December 30, 1977. PCO EM.

125 *He took several pictures:* IBA of F. Ralph Sias, December 30, 1977,./and photos taken by Sias in Miami of AE's Electra instrument panel. PCO F. Ralph Sias and EM.

125 *Because of the changes in weather:* C. B. Allen. "Miss Earhart to hop on round-world trip," TMH, May 30, 1937, page 1.

125 *She might take off for Puerto Rico:* C. B. Allen. "Miss Earhart to hop on round-world trip," TMH, May 30, 1037, page 1.

126 *The direction-finder gave good bearings:* IBA of Robert H. Thibert, November 21, 1991. PCO EM.

126 *Unfortunately Earhart wasn't able to observe:* IBA od Robert H. Thibert, November 21, 1991. PCO EM.

126 *They telephoned WQAM:* C. B. Allen. "Delay flight start to fix instruments," TMH, May 31, 1937, pages 1 and 2.

126 *He found the compasses:* C. B. Allen. "Delay flight start to fix instruments," TMH, May 31, 1937, pages 1 and 2.

127   *An hour and a half later:* C. B. Allen. "Delay flight start to fix instruments," TMH, May 31, 1937, page 1.

127   *She asked them to replace:* C. B. Allen. "Delay flight start to fix instruments," TMH, May 31, 1937, page 2.

127   *since neither she nor Fred could use the Morse code:* C. B. Allen. "Radio slip-up costly to Amelia Earhart," NHT, July 8, 1937, pages 1 and 2.

127   *It would be Tuesday morning:* C. B. Allen. "Delay flight start to fix instruments," TMH, May 31, 1937, pages 1 and 2.

127   *Without glasses, he couldn't read:* C. B. Allen. "Earhart plane ready to start today on globe-circling trip," NHT, June 1, 1937, pages 1 and 10.

127   *They agreed to have 600 gallons:* C. B. Allen. "Earhart plane ready to start today on globe-circling trip," NHT, June 1, 1937, page 1.

128   *Fred came later:* C. B. Allen. "Earhart plane ready to start today on globe-circling trip," NHT, June 1, 1937, pages 1 and 10.

128   *If not, the flight would turn:* C. B. Allen. "Earhart plane ready to start today on globe-circling trip," NHT, June 1, 1937, page 1.

128   *Somehow G.P. took this to mean:* Letter from GP to Mrs. Ruth Hampton, June 17, 1937. NADC DOI.

128   *Earhart collected a few spare parts:* C. B. Allen. "Earhart plane ready to start today on globe-circling trip," NHT, June 1, 1937, page10.

129   *her receiver would be used:* Message 8012/1320, June 12, 1937, IRTEF, page 3. NADC

129   *The hotel had been notified:* C. B. Allen. "Amelia Earhart's flight to San Juan done in quick time," TMH, June 2, 1937, pages 1 and 8A.

129   *At 4:30 they opened the hangar doors:* C. B. Allen. "Amelia Earhart's flight to San Juan done in quick time," TMH, June 2, 1937, pages 1 and 8A.

129   *Despite the early hour:* Henry Cavendish. "Suspense marks takeoff in globe-girdling flight," TMH, June 2, 1937, page 8A.

129   *In less than a half hour:* C. B. Allen. "Amelia Earhart's flight to San Juan done in quick time," TMH, June 2, 1937, pages 1 and 8A.

130   *G.P. came down from the wing:* Henry Cavendish. "Suspense marks takeoff in globe-girdling flight," TMH, June 2, 1937, page 8A.

130   *Bo followed close behind:* C. B. Allen. "Amelia Earhart's flight to San Juan done in quick time," TMH, June 2, 1937, pages 1 and 8A.

130   *She taxied across the south end:* Henry Cavendish. "Suspense marks takeoff in globe-girdling flight," TMH, June 2, 1937, page 8A.

130   *He reassured Amelia:* Henry Cavendish. "Suspense marks takeoff in globe-girdling flight," TMH, June 2, 1937, page 8A.

130   *Only 2,000 feet:* Henry Cavendish. "Suspense marks takeoff in globe-girdling flight," TMH, June 2, 1937, page 8A.

130   *They were on their way:* Amelia Earhart, *Last Flight,* page 95.

130   *She was not sure:* Amelia Earhart, *Last Flight,* page 129.

131   *G.P. stayed at the airport awhile:* C. B. Allen. "Amelia Earhart's flight to San Juan done in quick time," TMH, June 2, 1937, pages 1 and 8A.

CHAPTER 9: WORLD FLIGHT—MIAMI TO DAKAR

132   *The Electra cleared the power lines:* Henry Cavendish. "Suspense marks takeoff in globe-girdling flight," TMH, June 2, 1937, page 8A.

132 *After setting the power:* W. F. O'Reilly. "Flyer covers 1,033 miles to Puerto Rico after takeoff from Miami on second air venture," NHT, June 2, 1937, pages 1 and 22; and C. B. Allen. "Amelia Earhart's flight to San Juan done in quick time," TMH, June 2, 1937, pages 1 and 8A.

132 *"FLYING AT 3,500 FEET:* C. B. Allen. "Amelia Earhart's flight to San Juan done in quick time," TMH, June 2, 1937, pages 1 and 8A.

132 *Already the bill:* Putnam's attorney's files, expense schedule "C" 1937. PCO of Clyde E. Holley, Esq.

132 *At 7:00 A.M. the plane was passing:* AE's notes made during flight, June 1, 1937. PUL.

132 *They were bucking 25 mph headwinds:* C. B. Allen. "Amelia Earhart's flight to San Juan done in quick time," TMH, June 2, 1937, pages 1 and 8A; and "Flight to San Juan called uneventful," TMH, June 2, 1937, page 8A.

134 *The radiomen at Pan American:* C. B. Allen. "Amelia Earhart's flight to San Juan done in quick time," TMH, June 2, 1937, pages 1 and 8A.

134 *She could make out her name:* AE's notes made during flight, June 1, 1937. PUL.

134 *They followed along its north coast:* Amelia Earhart. "Miss Earhart's own account of 1st days flight," NHT, June 2, 1937, pages 1 and 22.

134 *The runway at Isla Grande:* Airport charts for Earhart flight. Isla Grande Airport, San Juan, P. R. PUL.

134 *It had taken approximately 7 hours:* "Flight to San Juan called uneventful," TMH, June 2, 1937, page 8A.

134 *She drove Amelia and Fred:* "Amelia Earhart saldr'a al amanecer hacia Brasil," *El Mundo* (San Juan, P. R.), June 2, 1937. Page 1.

134 *Early in the evening:* Amelia Earhart, *Last Flight,* pages 102 and 105.

134 *She decided they would have to stop:* Amelia Earhart. "Flier gets first glimpse of jungle in Venezuela," TMH. June 3, 1937, pages 1 and 7A.

134 *They flew across Puerto Rico:* Amelia Earhart. "Flier gets first glimpse of jungle in Venezuela," TMH. June 3, 1937, pages 1& 7A.

135 *She turned the receiver:* AE listened to WQAM while flying from Miami to San Juan, but never mentioned hearing anything after that. In Darwin Australia she admitted her receiver hadn't worked since leaving America. IBA of Wing Commander Stanley Rose, February 27, 1976. PCO EM.

135 *"Strong headwind, airspeed 160:* AE's notes made during flight, June 2, 1937. PUL.

135 *Amelia touched down:* "Miss Earhart hops from Puerto Rico to South America," TMH, June 3, 1937, page 1.

135 *They left the airport:* Letter from FN to BN, June 3, 1937. PCO BN.

136 *Fred eliminated this:* Note that FN passed to AE when approaching Dakar was in Natal time. PUL.

136 *Headwinds cut their ground speed:* AE's notes made during flight June 3, 1937. PUL.

136 *Pan American Airways employees:* Letter from FN to BN, June 3, 1937. PCO BN.

136 *Pan American Airways always flew:* Letter from FN to BN, June 5, 1937. PCO BN.

137 *Amelia decided to stay:* "Miss Earhart checks plane," LAT, June 6, 1937.

137   *Amelia mailed her flight notes:* Charts and notes AE mailed to New York from Fortaleza. PUL.

137   *After dinner they both retired early:* Letter from FN to BN, June 5, 1937. PCO BN.

137   *They departed from Fortaleza:* Amelia Earhart. "Amelia Earhart expected to fly to Africa today," NHT, June 7, 1937, page 1.

137   *With the rain coming down:* Amelia Earhart. "Amelia Earhart expected to fly to Africa today," NHT, June 7, 1937, page 1.

137   *The flight had taken:* Amelia Earhart. "Amelia Earhart expected to fly to Africa today," NHT, June 7, 1937, page 1.

138   *A photographer was there:* "Made perfect take-off," NHT, June 8, 1937, page 2.

138   *Amelia would have to use:* Amelia Earhart, *Last Flight,* page 127.

138   *It was Monday:* Chart: "Route of Miss Earhart's world flight since June 1," NHT, June 8, 1937, page 2.

139   *Amelia never knew:* "Amelia hops on sea flight," LAT, June 7, 1937.

139   *She tried listening:* Letter from FN to BN, June 8, 1937. PCO BN.

139   *Fred took his first observation:* Chart used by FN navigating to Dakar, June 7, 1937. PUL.

139   *The sun was directly in front:* In flight note from FN to AE, "By a second observation crossed with the first taken in cockpit—", June 7, 1937. PUL.

140   *A few minutes later:* In flight note from FN to AE, "By a second observation—find we are north of course—have averaged 147 m.p.h.—", June 7, 1937. PUL.

140   *It had departed Dakar:* "Has dinner with pilots," NHT, June 8, 1937, page 2.

140   *Its azimuth:* Local azimuth and elevation of the sun 1341 GMT, June 7, 1937. "Distant Suns" (computer program).

140   *Fred moved the 1240 GMT speed line:* Chart used by FN navigating to Dakar, June 7, 1937./and in flight note from FN to AE "By a second observation—have averaged 147 m.p.h.—" June 7, 1937. PUL.

141   *Fred passed a note:* In flight note: from FN to AE, "By a second observation—find we are north of course—," June 7, 1937. PUL.

141   *At 11:15 A.M. Natal time, she changed:* In flight note from FN to AE, "By a second observation—alter course to 76 degrees M." June 7, 1937. PUL.

141   *The rainwater mixed with the grease:* AE's notes made during flight, June 7, 1937. PUL.

141   *The sun's azimuth:* Local elevation and azimuth of the sun at 1630 GMT. "Distant Suns."

141   *Fred plotted the 021-201-degree line:* Chart used by FN navigating to Dakar, June 7, 1937. PUL.

141   *Because the last ten hours:* Moon was too close to sun for useful observations, June 7, 1937. "Distant Suns."

141   *Now, late in the afternoon:* Local azimuth of sun was 291 degrees at 1700 and 1800 GMT, June 7, 1937. "Distant Suns."

142   *He decided to make his approach:* Chart used by FN navigating to Dakar, June 7, 1937. PUL.

142   *The time was Natal time:* Note from FN "3:36 change to 36 degrees. Estimate 79 miles to Dakar from 3:36 pm.," June 7, 1937. PUL; and Chart used by FN

navigating to Dakar, June 7, 1937. PUL. Comparison of chart and note shows that the 3:36 p.m. was referring to Natal time.

142 *The plane picked up speed:* AE's notes made in flight, June 7, 1937. PUL

143 *The visibility in the haze:* Letter from FB to BN, June 8, 1937. PCO BN.

143 *After more than 12 hours:* Jack L. King, *Wings of Man,* page 165 and 184.

143 *He indicated for her to turn right:* Amelia Earhart, "Miss Earhart flies ocean to Africa in 13-hour hop," NHT, June 8, 1937, pages 1 and 2.

143 *"What put us north?":* "What put us north?" written by AE on bottom of "3:36 pm" note FN had passed to AE approaching Dakar, June 7, 1937. PUL.

143 *Amelia could easily have worked:* Airport charts collected for Earhart's world flight. Radio facilities at Dakar. PUL.

144 *Amelia decided it was best to turn left:* Amelia Earhart, "Miss Earhart flies ocean to Africa in 13 hour hop," NHT, June 8, 1937, pages 1 and 2.

144 *Including circling and the time to identify:* "Amelia Earhart ready to fly across Africa," NHT, June 9, 1937, page 1.

144 *Amelia Earhart was the first woman pilot:* "Has dinner with pilots," NHT, June 8, 1937, page 2.

144 *They did not believe:* "Has dinner with pilots," NHT, June 8, 1937, page 2.

144 *Amelia left the light on:* AE's notes made while at St. Louis, June 7—8, 1937. PUL.

145 *The Saint-Louis airfield:* "Amelia Earhart ready to fly across Africa," NHT, June 9, 1937, page 1.

145 *In approximately 40 minutes:* AE's notes made while flying St. Louis to Dakar, June 8, 1937. PUL.

145 *She requested that the engines:* Amelia Earhart, *Last Fight,* page 140.

145 *Amelia explained to her hosts:* AE's notes made while she was at Dakar, June 8–9,1937. PUL.

146 *He wanted to know:* Cable from GP to AE, "Tribune arranging. What are plans? Love," June 9, 1937. PUL.

146 *He complained that the radio was useless:* Letter from FN to BN, June 8, 1937. PCO BN.

146 *This time her bed was large:* AE's notes written while at Dakar, June 8–9, 1937. PUL.

CHAPTER 10: WORLD FLIGHT—DAKAR TO SINGAPORE

147 *Thursday, June 10, 1937, the Electra lifted off:* "Amelia Earhart skirts tornado; reaches Gao on world flight," NHT, June 11, 1937, pages 1 and 15.

149 *The message:* Message 6009/0931, June 9, 1937, IRTEF, page 1. NADC

149 *The local time was Greenwich mean time:* U.S. Hydrographic Office Publication No. 216, Air Navigation, page 446.

149 *Up before daylight:* AE's notes made in flight, June 11, 1937. PUL.

149 *Almost exactly on schedule:* Chart of Niamey airfield collected for AE's world flight. PUL.

150 *Amelia brought the plane down:* Chart of Ft. Lamy airfield collected for AE's world flight. PUL.

150 *It was suggested:* "Miss Earhart flies to Ft. Lamy over jungles of Africa," NHT, June 12, 1937, page 1.

150 *Both of her earlier ocean conquests:* Average dead reckoning error on flights from Harbour Grace, Newfoundland to landfall on Irish Coast in 1932, and Honolulu to landfall on the California Coast in 1935.

151 *They were airborne:* "Miss Earhart spans Sudan bad lands. Reaches El Fasher," NHT, June 13, 1937, page 1.

151 *They left El Fasher:* Amelia Earhart. "Miss Earhart reaches Red Sea, ready for long flight to India," NHT, June 14, 1937, pages 1 and 16.

151 *Of the regions of Africa:* Letter from FN to BN, June 14, 1937. PCO BN.

151 *The city of Khartoum:* Chart of Khartoum airfield collected for AE's world flight. PUL.

151 *The refueling crew:* Letter from FN to BN, June 14, 1937. PCO BN.

151 *Again, the sun:* Amelia Earhart. "Miss Earhart reaches Red Sea, ready for long flight to India," NHT, June 14, 1937, pages 1 and 16.

151 *Because Amelia preferred:* AE's notes made during flight, June 13, 1937. PUL.

152 *Amelia departed Massawa:* "Amelia hops for Arabia," LAT, June 14, 1937.

152 *She circled the area:* Chart of Assab airfield collected for AE's world flight. PUL.

152 *Sometimes, he wrote:* Letter from FN to BN, June 14–15, 1937. (Two parts to letter). PCO BN.

153 *If there was enough daylight:* Letter from FN to BN, June 14–15, 1937. (Two parts to letter). PCO BN.

153 *A greatly overloaded aircraft:* Chart of Assab airfield collected for AE's world flight. PUL.

153 *Using takeoff power:* Amelia Earhart. "Amelia Earhart in Asia; crosses 2 seas on flight," NHT, June 16, 1937, pages 1 and 23.

153 *To ensure that the engines:* SST, June 21, 1937, page 12.

154 *The right engine was gulping fuel:* Amelia Earhart. "Amelia Earhart in Asia; crosses 2 seas on flight," NHT, June 16, 1937, pages 1 and 23.

154 *In the meantime:* Amelia Earhart. "Amelia Earhart in Asia; crosses 2 seas on flight," NHT, June 16, 1937, pages 1 and 23.

154 *She followed the river:* Chart of Karachi's Drigh airfield collected for AE's world flight. PUL.

154 *They touched down:* "Dash from Assab in a day," TSO, June 16, 1937, page 1.

154 *When the propellers came to a stop:* "Dash from Assab in a day," TSO, June 16, 1937, page 1.

154 *G.P. had called from New York:* "Dash from Assab in a day," TSO, June 16, 1937, page 1.

154 *[G.P. asked]: "How do you feel:* "Miss Earhart in India phones husband here," NHT, June 16, 1937, page 23; Amelia Earhart, *Last Flight,* pages 178, 179.

155 *While they were sleeping:* ISL, June 15, 1937. NADC.

155 *It was en route:* OSL, June 16, 1937. NADC.

155 *The Imperial Airways mechanics:* Amelia Earhart. "Miss Earhart is off to Calcutta after a camel ride in Karachi," NHT, June 17, 1937, pages 1 and 25.

156 *Amelia had the 8,000 postal covers:* Portfolio of flight charts and notes mailed from Karachi to GP in New York. PUL.

156 *"GEPEPUT," in New York:* Cablegram from AE to GP, Karachi, 1405 (2:05 p.m.), June 16, 1937. PUL.

156 *"FUEL ANALYZER OUT:* Cablegram from AE to GP, Karachi, 9:55 p.m., June 16, 1937. PUL.

156 *He closed by telling:* Letter from FN to BN, June 15, 1937. PCO BN.

156 *Amelia and Fred arrived:* Amelia Earhart. "Miss Earhart is off to Calcutta after a camel ride in Karachi," NHT, June 17, 1937, pages 1 and 25.

156 *When the wheels touched down:* Amelia Earhart. "Amelia Earhart fights rain and eagles in India," NHT, June 18, 1937, pages 1 and 3.

156 *Amelia decided they would:* Amelia Earhart. "Amelia Earhart fights rain and eagles in India," NHT, June 18, 1937, pages 1 and 3.

156 *"KLM USES CAMBRIDGE CABLING:* Cablegram from GP to AE in Calcutta, "KLM uses Cambridge——," June 16, 1937. PUL.

157 *Then she pulled it off:* "Amelia Earhart wings to Siam," LAT, June 18, 1937.

157 *They were airborne:* Associated Press from Calcutta, June 18, 1937, NHT, June 18, 1937, page 1.

157 *The forecast was for thunderstorms:* India Meteorological Department Forecast, 17/1530 to 18/1530 GMT, June 17–18, 1937. PUL.

158 *They would have to wait:* Amelia Earhart. "Monsoon beats back Miss Earhart," NHT, June 19, 1937, page 1.

158 *For the second time:* Associated Press from Akyab, June 19, 1937, NHT, June 19, 1937, page 1.

158 *Then they followed the valley:* AE's notes made during flight June 19, 1937. PUL.

158 *While they waited:* Amelia Earhart, "Miss Earhart starts hop from Rangoon to Bangkok," LAT, June 20, 1937.

158 *They were airborne:* Amelia Earhart, "Miss Earhart starts hop from Rangoon to Bangkok," LAT, June 20, 1937.

159 *At approximately 10:27 A.M. in Bangkok:* SST, June 21, 1937, page 12.

159 *Because the Electra:* SST, June 21, 1937, page 12.

CHAPTER 11: WORLD FLIGHT—SINGAPORE TO LAE, NEW GUINEA

160 *Afterward, Mr. Davis drove them:* SST, June 21, 1937, page 12.

160 *They left Singapore:* SST, June 21, 1937, page 12.

160 *They were heading for Bandoeng:* K.N.I.L.M. - Koninklijke Nederlandche Indies Luchtvaarte Mattschappij.

162 *She believed that for a safe crossing:* Cable from Karachi from AE to GP, June 16, 1937. PUL.

162 *Within 30 minutes:* IBA of Francis O. Furman, March 7, 1981. PCO EM.

162 *It was approximately 10:37 A.M.:* SST, June 21, 1937, page 12.

162 *Furman recommended they stay:* IBA of Francis O. Furman, March 7, 1981. PCO EM.

163 *The Navy and Coast Guard ships:* "Amelia Earhart has Java to N.Y. chat on phone," NHT, June 22, 1937, page 1.

163 *she would send them full particulars:* Message 8025/1445, June 25, 1937, IRTEF, page 19. NADC.

163 *Furman said he would find out:* IBA of Francis O. Furman, March 7, 1981. PCO EM.

163 *The Electra would not be ready:* IBA of Francis O. Furman, March 7, 1981. PCO EM.

163 *Every day at 8:30 A.M.:* IBA of Francis O. Furman, March 7, 1981. PCO EM.

163 *Lieutenant H. F. MacComsey:* SSL, June 21, 1937. NADC.

164 *They were having difficulty:* IBA of Francis O. Furman, March 7, 1981. PCO EM.

164 *A full moon:* Phase of moon, June 24, 1937. "Distant Suns."

164 *By then it was too late:* "Miss Earhart back in Bandoeng," NHT, June 25, 1937, page 1.

164 *departed Bandoeng:* "Miss Earhart back in Bandoeng," NHT, June 25, 1937, page 1.

164 *It was 2100 hours:* ISL, June 23, 1937. NADC.

164 *She told G.P. of the delay:* "Trip to end Tuesday, Miss Earhart says," LAT, June 25, 1937.

164 *G.P.P.—Is everything:* Amelia Earhart, *Last Flight,* page 178.

165 *She hoped to make it:* "Miss Earhart back in Bandoeng," NHT, June 25, 1937, page 1.

165 *She knew that fuel management:* IBA of Francis O. Furman, March 7, 1981. PCO EM.

165 *They took off from Surabaya:* "Miss Earhart back in Bandoeng," NHT, June 25, 1937, page 1.

165 *Unfortunately, the job could not be completed:* IBA of Francis O. Furman, March 7, 1981. PCO EM.

165 *The U.S. Navy seaplane tender Swan:* SSL, June 24, 1937. NADC.

166 QUOTE ONTARIO NIDX TRANSMITTER: Message from GOAS to AE, 2230 GMT, June 23, 1937. NASB GOAS NPU.

166 *Before leaving the airfield:* Notes made by AE on back of Calcutta, India weather forecast. PUL.

167 *The mechanics had also annealed:* IBA of Francis O. Furman, March 7, 1981. PCO EM.

167 SUGGEST ONTARIO STAND BY: "BT" is a Morse code character sequence meaning "break." It is used in Morse code similar to the way a dash mark is used when writing.

167 EARHART: Message from AE via NPM to Itasca, "Suggest Ontario stand by on—," IRTEF, page 21. NADC.

168 *They landed at 2:30:* "Amelia Earhart off from Java for Australia," NHT, June 27, 1937.

168 *It was 6:30 A.M.:* "Amelia Earhart off from Java for Australia," NHT, June 27, 1937.

168 *She carefully maneuvered:* "Amelia Earhart flies Timor Sea to Port Darwin," NHT, June 28, 1937.

168 *Earhart met with the local officials:* Letter 37/477 from C. L. A. Abbott to CONSL, Sydney, Australia, August 3, 1937. NADC.

168 *He estimated the sun would set:* Local time of sunset at Darwin, June 27, 1937. "Distant Suns."

168 *They departed Koepang:* "Amelia Earhart flies Timor Sea to Port Darwin," NHT, June 28, 1937.

169 *She leveled off:* "Amelia Earhart quits Australia for New Guinea," NHT, June 29, 1937.

169 *She cross-checked the consumption:* IBA of Norman W. King, February 28, 1976. PCO EM.

169 *She circled the large airport:* SMH, June 29, 1937, page 11, column 7.

169 *He would allow them:* "Mrs. Amelia Earhart Putnam: Airwoman and navigator grounded," NOS, July 2, 1937.

169 *Dr. Curruthers would cable:* Note from Dr. Carruthers to AE at Gordon's Victoria Hotel, Darwin, Aust. PUL.

170 *Sergeant Rose pressed her:* IBA of Wing Commander Stanley Rose, February 27, 1976. PCO EM.

170 *he would have a look:* IBA of Wing Commander Stanley Rose, February 27, 1976. PCO EM.

170 *Earhart told the Quantas mechanic:* IBA of Norman W. King, February 28, 1976. PCO EM.

170 *She requested the Vacuum Oil Company:* Fuel slip signed by AE at Darwin. PUL

170 *It must not be diluted:* EHCR, page 5. (only Stanavo 87 octane gas was added at Darwin).

170 *He would supply her:* IBA of Wing Commander Stanley Rose, February 27, 1976. PCO EM.

170 *she would use voice to:* EHCR, page 1. (the 3105 frequency was apparently transposed from 96.6 to 36.6 meters).

171 *A message would be sent:* EHCR, page 1. PDI.

171 *This was to be the only time:* Letter signed by AE and FN to Ernie Crome. NASM.

171 *The cable cautioned:* Message from Itasca RB to AE at Darwin . . . , IRTEF, page 15. NADC.

171 *The second message:* Message 8025/1935, June 25, 1937, IRTEF, page 19. NADC.

171 *At the same time:* Portfolio of charts and notes AE sent from Darwin to GP in New York. PUL.

171 *They had to decline:* SMH, June 29, 1937, page 11, column 7.

171 *At the Gordon's Hotel Victoria:* Note from Dr. Carruthers to AE at Gordon's Victoria Hotel, Darwin, Aust. PUL.

172 *The cumulus cloud activity:* IBA of Walter A. Dwyer, February 12, 1976. PCO EM.

172 *They walked across the ramp:* Photo of AE's Electra inside the hangar at Darwin. PCO Norman W. King.

172 *Sergeant Rose handed Earhart:* IBA of Wing Commander Stanley Rose, February 27, 1976. PCO EM.

172 *The Electra gained speed:* SMH, June 30, 1937, page 15, column 5.

172 *Amelia turned to climb:* AE's chart prepared by CW has initial magnetic course as 069 degrees. PUL.

172 *The sun glared:* Local elevation and azimuth of sun at 7:00 a.m., June 30, 1937. "Distant Suns."

173 *Sergeant Rose transmitted:* IBA of Wing Commander Stanley Rose, February 27, 1976. PCO EM.

173 *From there, they flew:* AE's chart prepared by CW for flight between Lae, N.G. and Darwin. PUL.

173 *Rose was not surprised:* IBA of Wing Commander Stanley Rose, February 27, 1976. PSO EM./and Letter 37/477 from C. L. A. Abbott to CONSL, Sydney, Australia, August 3, 1937. NADC.

173 *She was leaning the mixture:* EHCR, page 2. PDI.

173 *Their mapmaker, Clarence Williams:* AE's chart prepared by CW for flight between Lae, N.G. and Darwin. PUL.

174 *It was 71 miles:* AE's chart prepared by CW for flight between Lae, N.G. and Darwin. PUL.

174 *At the high altitude:* EHCR, page 2. PDI.

174 *The Sperry gyro horizon instrument:* EHCR, page 2. PDI.

174 *Amelia turned to a heading:* AE's chart prepared by CW for flight between Lae, N.G. and Darwin. PUL.

174 *They spotted Lae Airport:* Lae Airport Chart No. 20/1935. PCO JC, Melbourne, Australia.

174 *They touched down:* Lae Airport Chart No. 20/1935. PCO JC, Melbourne, Australia.

174 *at approximately 3:02 P.M. Lae time:* Amelia Earhart. *Last Flight,* page 219.

CHAPTER 12: PREPARING FOR THE
LAE-TO-HOWLAND FLIGHT

176 *They would move the plane:* EHCR, page 2. PDI.

177 *"8028 FOLLOWING FOR AMELIA EARHART:* Message 8028/0910, June 28, 1937, IRTEF, page 25. NADC/and EHCR, page 3. PDI.

177 *The Salamaua radio station:* IBA of Edward F. Bishton, September 9, 1984. PCO EM.

177 *A cable to the naval radio station:* Message 0011/1045, July 11, 1937. NASB GOAS NPU.

178 *The radio operator:* IBA of Edward F. Bishton, September 9, 1984. PCO EM.

178 *The message from Darwin:* EHCR, page 2. PDI.

178 *She stayed at the hangar:* EHCR, page 2. PDI.

178 *He took the covers:* IBA of JC, February 11, 1976. PCO EM.

178 *Collopy bought Fred a scotch whiskey:* IBA of JC, February 11, 1976. PCO EM.

178 *In 1929, while he was living in New Orleans:* FN's application for pilot's license No. 22201, July 29, 1929. FAA ACB.

179 *In February 1930:* Limited commercial license No. 11833 issued to FN, February 16, 1930. FAA ACB.

179 *In mid-1930 Fred went to work:* Letter to FN at N.Y. Rio & Buenos Aires Line, Miami, July 25, 1930. FAA ACB.

179 *If you liked flying in mountains:* IBA of Bertie Heath, February 14, 1976. PCO EM.

179 *he was not apprehensive:* IBA of JC, February 11, 1976. PCO EM.

179 *With Collopy's help:* IBA of JC, February 11, 1976. PCO EM.

180 *"AMELIA EARHART LAE/CONGRATULATIONS:* Message from Oakland, Port Board to AE, 10:24 p.m., June 29, 1937. PUL.

181 *Balfour filed it at Lae:* EHCR, page 3. PDI.

181 *The message was handled routinely:* AE filed message in Lae at 2015 GCT, June 29 (6:15 a.m., June 30, at Lae). EHCR, page 3. PDI./and Itasca relayed request to Pearl Harbor at 0555 GCT, June 30. Itasca responded to AE at 0600 GCT, June 30, 1937 with message 8029/1830, July 29, 1937. IRTEF, page 28. (9 hours and 45 minutes later). NADC.

181 *"COMMANDER USS ITASCA:* EHCR, page 3. PDI.

181 *"8029 FOLLOWING FOR AMELIA EARHART:* Message 8029/1830, July 29, 1937, IRTEF, page 28. NADC.

181 *Tutuila forwarded the message:* Message 1029/1600, July 29, 1937, IRTEF, page 28. NADC.

181 *He told her the work was going well.* EHCR, page 2. PDI.

182 *Balfour said he had:* EHCR, page 8. PDI.

182 *"BLACK ITASCA VIA TUTUILA:* Message sent June 30, 1937 from AE to RB, "Black Itasca Via Tutuila. Account local conditions—stand watch for direct contact. Earhart." IRTEF, page 28. NADC.

182 *NOUGHT:* This is an archaic term for the cipher zero.

182 *So far as is known:* EHCR, page 4. PDI.

182 *"PUTNAM TRIBUNE OAKLAND:* Cablegram from AE to GP in Oakland, 5:35 p.m., June 30, 1937. PUL.

182 *"TWYCROSS RABAUL":* EHCR, page 3. PDI.

183 *He would have to come back:* EHCR, page 4. PDI.

183 *At the same time he would calibrate:* EHCR, page 4. PDI.

183 *The receiver checked okay:* EHCR, page 4. PDI.

184 *As soon as the engine cowlings:* EHCR, page 2. PDI.

184 *Howard had his assistant:* EHCR, page 5. PDI.

184 *She shut down the engines:* EHCR, page 2. PDI.

184 *This time when she ran the engines:* EHCR, page 2. PDI.

184 *Howard reminded her:* IBA of Wing Commander Roberet W. Iredale, February 11, 1976.

185 *Navy aerologist:* Message 2529/2245, June 29, 1937, IRTEF, page 29. NADC.

185 *That was almost an hour longer:* AE's chart prepared by CW for flight between Howland Island and Lae, shows total no wind time as 17 hours and 1 minute. PUL.

185 *The actual winds:* Message from Itasca to AE, 1410 GMT, June 30, 1937. PUL.

185 *"8029 REQUEST FOLLOWING BE FORWARDED:* Message 8029/1235, June 29, 1937, IRTEF, page 27. NADC.

185 *"BLACK ITASCA TUTUILA RADIO":* Message AE to RB Itasca Via Tutuila: "Ask Ontario broadcast—morning New Guinea time. Earhart." IRTEF, page 32. NADC.

186 *She also requested:* EHCR, page 4. PDI.

186 *She took off into the wind:* EHCR, page 4. PDI.

186 *As she crossed over the northwest:* Sid Marshall film of Earhart takeoff from Lae, N.G. NLA

186 *The other end of the runway:* Lae Airport Chart No. 20/1935. PCO JC, Melbourne, Australia.

186 *The Electra was in good condition:* EHCR, page 2. PDI.

187 *She thought it must be:* EHCR, page 4. PDI.

187 *He would translate Earhart's instructions:* IBA of Wing Commander Robert W. Iredale, February 11, 1976.

187 *It must not be diluted:* EHCR, page 5. PDI.

187 *The tank capacities:* 1.2 U.S. gallons equal 1 imperial gallon.

187 *At eight different times each day:* 1937 Radio Facilities Book, Listing of radio-time signals, pages 170 and 171.

187 *The stations were so far away:* EHCR, pages 4 and 5. PDI.

188 *she was unable to get a minimum:* EHCR, page 4. PDI.

188 *He advised her to pitch her voice higher:* EHCR. Page 5. PDI.

188 *She would order all the tanks:* EHCR. Page 5. PDI.

188 *They would leave at 9:30 A.M.:* EHCR. Page 5. PDI.

188 *Dick Merrill had recounted:* Jack L. King, *Wings of Man,* page 176.

188 *Earhart watched closely:* IBA of Wing Commander Robert W. Iredale, February 11, 1976. PCO EM.

189 *The first was a report:* Radiogram to AE from Nauru Island via Rabaul, "The following from Nauru—transmissions with times." July 1, 1937. PUL.

189 *the second was a coded weather report:* Message to AE from Swan via Tutuila, 2120 GMT, June 30, 1937. PUL.

189 *While they were watching Iredale:* Message from Vacuum to RB Itasca, 1955 IST, IRTEF, page 36. NADC.

189 *When Iredale was finished:* EHCR, page 5. PDI.

189 *All tanks except one:* EHCR, page 5. PDI.

189 *He would ask the Salamaua operator:* EHCR, page 5. PDI.

189 *But the ship, when contacted:* EHCR, page 6. PDI.

189 *Balfour reported that he had had no luck:* EHCR, page 8. PDI.

189 *Then Malabar reported:* EHCR, page 6. PDI.

189 *"BLACK ITASCA—TUTUILA RADIO":* Message from AE to RB Itasca, "Black Itasca - Tutuila Radio. Account local conditions—notify Ontario change BT Earhart." July 1, 1937. IRTEF, page 32. NADC.

189 *Balfour said he would keep trying:* EHCR, pages 6 and 8. PDI.

189 *Collopy inquired about the fuel:* IBA of JC, February 11, 1976. PCO EM./and Letter from JC to Civil Aviation Board, August 28, 1937. PCO JC.

190 *If they left Lae:* Local sunrise at Howland Island for July 2, 1937. "Distant Suns" (computer program).

190 *Earhart included for shipment:* Shipping list of items sent by AE and FN from Lae to U.S. PUL/and IBA of BN, February 10, 1975. PCO EM.

190 *The expansion of the gasoline:* IBA of Ela Birrell and Flora Stewart, February 16, 1976. PCO EM.

191 *"DENMARK IS A PRISON:* Telegram from AE to Press Tribune Oakland, 3:48 a.m., July 2, 1937. PUL.

191 *"WE SHALL TRY TO GET OFF:* Telegram from AE to Press Tribune Oakland, 3:59 a.m., July 2, 1937. PUL.

191 *Earhart said they would be back:* EHCR, page 6. PDI.

191   *It was from Lieutenant True:* Message 2520/1230, June 30, 1937, IRTEF, page 31. NADC.

191   *Balfour checked with Rabaul:* EHCR, page 6. PDI.

191   *Complete silence prevailed:* EHCR, page 6. PDI.

192   *Balfour was listening:* 1937 Radio Facilities Book, radio time signals, Saigon, French Indo-China, page 166.

192   *When Fred checked his chronometer:* EHCR, page 6. PDI.

192   *He was very pleased:* IBA of Mrs. Harry Balfour, February, 1976. PCO EM.

193   *He declined:* Letter from Harry Balfour to Lt. Leo G. Bellarts, October 1, 1970, page 1. Scrapbook of Lt. Leo G. Bellarts (College Park, MD), NADC.

193   *A glance at the wind sock:* Sid Marshall film of Earhart takeoff from Lae, N.G. NLA.

193   *Sid Marshall, the Guinea Airways chief pilot:* IBA of Ela Birrell and Flora Stewart, February 16, 1976. PCO EM.

193   *Fred climbed up:* Sid Marshall film of Earhart takeoff from Lae, N.G. NLA.

193   *Lowering herself down:* Sid Marshall film of Earhart takeoff from Lae, N.G. NLA.

194   *Fifty yards before it reached:* IBA of JC, February 11, 1976. PCO EM./and Letter from JC to Civil Aviation Board, August 28, 1937, page 1. PCO JC.

194   *Instead of the slightly less than 15 mph headwind:* EHCR, page 7. PDI.

194   *Local interference prevented him:* Message 2015/2335, July 15, 1937, from NPU to COMDESRON 2. (Balfour's schedule was at hour plus :20 minutes, schedule was completed at :22 minutes after the hour. Radio log entries are made at completion of message not at time scheduled for transmission). NASB GOAS NPU.

194   *"URGENT BLACK ITASCA TUTUILA RADIO:* Message from Vacuum to RB Itasca, July 2, 1937. IRTEF, page 36. NADC.

CHAPTER 13: THE *ITASCA* AND HOWLAND ISLAND

195   *The* Itasca *had traveled:* Message 6018/1210, June 18, 1937, IRTEF, page 7. NADC.

195   *USCG Lieutenant Commander Frank T. Kenner:* ISL, 0955 hours, June 16, 1937. NADC.

195   *Because Captain Thompson had never made:* ISL, 1015 hours, June 18, 1937 (reference COMHWSEC letter June 17, 1937). NADC.

197   *The Coast Guard provided a ship:* E. H. Bryan Jr. Panala'au Memoirs, pages 1–3.

197   *The communications were handled:* Message 7011/2102, June 11, 1937, IRTEF, page 3. NADC.

197   *Earlier in the year:* ISL, 1540 hours, June 16, 1937. NADC.

197   *Black was now serving:* Note "At this time—by the *Itasca.*" June 18, 1937, IRTEF, page 7. NADC.

197   *On Wednesday morning:* ISL, 0845 hours, June 16, 1937. NADC.

197   *in March, Earhart had requested:* Message 8013/1320, March 13, 1937, from COMSFDIV to USS Shoshone and COMHWSEC. NASB.

197   *When Captain Thompson learned:* Note "Mr. Richard Black—to perform its work." June 16, 1937, IRTEF, page 5. NADC.

198   *Captain Thompson requested:* Note "Due to amount of—Commander Hawai-
       ian Section." June 16, 1937, IRTEF, page 4. NADC.

198   *Instead, the dry-docked Coast Guard cutter* Taney: ISL, 1415 hours, June 16,
       1937. NADC.

198   *The communications officer:* IBA of Captain William L. Sutter, May 24, 1975,
       and July 23, 1977. PCO EM.

198   *On Thursday, June 17:* ISL, 0820 hours, June 17, 1937. NADC.

198   *Four boxes of spare parts:* ISL, 1500 hours, June 17, 1937. NADC.

198   *He concluded by informing them:* Message from Ruth Hampton, DOI, to RB
       Via Radio Washington, D. C., June 18, 1937. NASB COMDT14ND.

199   *In the midst of preparing:* IBA of Captain William L. Sutter, May 24, 1975, and
       July 23, 1977. PCO EM.

199   *Even though the ship was moored:* ISL, 0000 hours, June 16, 1937. NADC.

199   *It reported that the* Itasca's *transmitter:* Message 8018/0921, June 18, 1937,
       IRTEF, page 7. NADC.

199   *He tested the 500-watt T-16-A:* Note "This was done by Radio Electrician An-
       thony." June 18, 1937, IRTEF, page 7. NADC.

199   *It was designed exclusively:* The Coast Guard at War Communication XVI, Vol-
       ume II, page 145, para 326.

199   *(On the Bendix receiver:* BDX manual for RA-1 series receiver for aircraft,
       page 1.

199   *Anthony told them of the meeting:* IBA of AN, July 22, 1975. PCO EM.

199   *The detailed radio information:* Scrapbook of Lt. Leo G. Bellarts. (College
       Park, MD) NADC; and June 16, 1937, IRTEF, page 6. NADC.

200   *It reinforced the belief:* IBA of Captain William L. Sutter, May 24, 1975, and July
       23, 1977. PCO EM.

200   *There were airplane mechanics:* ISL, 0900 to 1600 hours, June 18, 1937.
       NADC.

200   *At 1600 HST, Friday afternoon:* ISL, 1600 hours, June 18, 1937. NADC.

200   *Richard Black had been aboard:* IBA of RB, May 11, 1976. PCO EM.

200   *Radio direction-finding:* IBO Lt. Leo G. Bellarts, April 11, 1973. PCO EM.

200   *Mr. Black wrote a message:* Message 8019/1340, June 19, 1937, IRTEF, page 10.
       NADC.

200   *Putnam's remark about "500 kilocycles:* Message 8019/1340, June 19, 1937,
       IRTEF, page 10. NADC.

201   *A message was sent:* Message 8019/1340, June 19, 1937, IRTEF, page 10.
       NADC.

201   *All messages had to be relayed:* Message NPU to Itasca, "Msg Mr. Black refer—
       American Samoa 2305." June 22, 1937, IRTEF, page 14. NADC.

201   *On Tuesday, June 22:* ISL, 1400 hours, June 22, 1937. NADC.

201   *In the case of the* Swan: Message from RB Itasca to AE at Darwin or Vandoeng
       Jarva [sic] "Following for Amelia—Itasca Stop Black." June 23, 1937, IRTEF,
       page 15. NADC.

201   *They warned that communications:* Message from RB Itasca to AE at Darwin
       or Vandoeng Jarva [sic] "Following for Amelia—Itasca Stop Black." June 23,
       1937, IRTEF, page 15. NADC.

201   *Wednesday evening, at 1930 IST:* ISL, 1930 hours, June 23, 1937. NADC.

201   *The* Itasca *moved to a position:* ISL, 2100 hours, June 23, 1937. NADC.

202 *The surface wind at Howland Island:* Message 8024/1330, June 24, 1937, IRTEF, page 17. NADC.

202 *He wanted Putnam to keep them:* Message from RB Itasca to Ruth Hampton, DOI, "Govt. Int. Hampton assistant—at stations. Black." June 24, 1937, IRTEF, page 18. NADC.

202 *Friday morning, June 25:* ISL, 0400 to 0800 hours, June 25, 1937. NADC.

202 *At 1112 IST the* Itasca *departed:* ISL, 0800 to 1200 hours, June 25, 1937. NADC.

202 *Chief Bellarts would have to calibrate:* Message 8025/1445, June 25, 1937, IRTEF, page 19. NADC.

202 *Boats were lowered:* ISL, 1200 to 1600 hours, June 25, 1937. NADC.

202 *A very long message:* Message 8026/1130, June 26, 1937, IRTEF, page 21. NADC.

202 *The information was represented:* No pertinent communications from Earhart found in files. It is possible that the information was given to USCG San Francisco by GP after his Cheyenne, Wyoming telephone conversation with AE in Surabaya.

203 *The* Itasca *was to inform her:* Message 8026/1130, June 26, 1937, IRTEF, page 21. NADC.

203 *"SHE BROADCAST ON QUARTER AFTER:* Message 8026/1130, June 26, 1937, IRTEF, page 21. NADC.

203 *The message ended:* Message 8026/1130, June 26, 1937, IRTEF, page 21. NADC.

203 *She concluded the message:* Message from AE via NPM to Itasca, "Suggest Ontario stand by—quarter to BT Earhart." June 26, 1937, IRTEF, page 21; and note, "The above message—the plane direction finder." June 26, 1937, IRTEF, page 22. NADC.

204 *The* Ontario*'s call letters:* EHCR, page 8. PDI.

204 *The transmitting power:* Message from RB Itasca to AE at Darwin or Vandoeng Jarva [sic] "Following for Amelia—Itasca Stop Black." June 23, 1937, IRTEF, page 15. NADC.

204 *San Francisco, in its earlier message:* Message 8026/1130, June 26, 1937, IRTEF, page 21. NADC.

204 *The General Electric 200-watt model:* The Coast Guard at War Communication XVI, Volume II, page 145, para 324.

205 *The only transmitter:* The Coast Guard at War Communication XVI, Volume II, page 145, para 326.

205 *They could not use both:* IBA of Lt. Leo G. Bellarts, April 11, 1973./and IBA of Chief RadiomanThomsa J.O'Hare, May 13, 1975, and December 31, 1977. PCO EM.

205 *He urgently requested:* Message 8026/1705, June 26, 1937, IRTEF, page 22. NADC.

205 *The responsibility for communications:* Message 8026/2255, June 26, 1937, IRTEF, page 23. NADC.

205 *Captain Thompson now felt secure:* message from AE via RCA Radio Manila to RB Itasca, "Black Itasca KAA suggest Ontario—possibly quarter to Earhart." June 27, 1937, IRTEF, page 23. NADC.

205 *Boats were lowered:* ISL, 0845 hours, June 27, 1937. NADC.

205 *The canvas walls of the tent:* IBA of Lt. Leo G. Bellarts, April 11, 1973./and IBA of Captain William L. Sutter, May 24, 1975, and July 23, 1977. PCO EM.

205 *A 35-ampere-hour battery:* Note following message at 0806, July 2, 1937, IRTEF. Page 43. NADC./and IBA of gunnery officer Lt. CMDR. Linford H. Hines, July 25, 1976. PCO EM.

205 *The work party cleared:* Message 8025/1935, June 25, 1937, IRTEF, page 19. NADC.

206 *"6027 SWAN ONTARIO ITASCA:* : Message 6027/1420, June 27, 1937, IRTEF, page 24. NADC.

206 *It indicated that the weather:* Scrapbook of Lt. Leo G. Bellarts (College Park, MD). NADC.

206 *Sunday had been a busy day:* ISL, 1840 hours, June 27, 1937. NADC.

206 *All hands were called:* ISL, 0633 hours, June 28, 1937. NADC.

206 *They concluded by stating:* Message 8028/0910, June 28, 1937, IRTEF, page 25. NADC.

206 *The Howland surface wind:* Message 6001/1330, July 1, 1937, IRTEF, page 33. NADC.

207 *"8012 UNITED PRESS REPORTS:* Message 8012[sic]/2130, July 1, 1937, IRTEF, page 36. NADC.

207 *In the* Itasca's *radio room:* IRL, 1557 hours, July 1, 1937. NADC.

207 *There were now two radio logs:* 1900 hours, July 1, 1937, Note [Started second watch. Two (2) logs from this point.—direction finder on Howland which kept 3rd log]. IRTEF, page 36. NADC.

207 *At 1905 IST, boats number 1 and 3:* ISL, 1905 hours, July 1, 1937. NADC.

207 *He was to take radio bearings:* "Organization of radio personnel during forthcoming flight." Scrapbook of Lt. Leo G. Bellarts (College Park, MD.) NADC

207 *"URGENT BLACK ITASCA TUTUILA RADIO:* 1955 hours, July 1, 1937, IRTEF, page 36. NADC.

207 *Earhart's estimated time of arrival:* Local sunrise at Howland Island, July 2, 1937. "Distant Suns."

208 *At 0245 IST, in a low monotone voice:* 0245–0248 hours, July 2, 1937, IRTEF, page 39. NADC.

208 *"OVERCAST—WILL LISTEN:* 0345 hours, July 2, 1937, IRTEF, page 40. NADC.

208 *At 0453 IST the* Itasca *heard:* 0453 hours, July 2, 1937, IRTEF, page 40. NADC.

208 *Her transmission came in so strong:* 0000–0004 hours, July 2, 1937, IRTEF, page 37. NADC./and IBA of Lt. Leo G. Bellarts, April 11, 1973. PCO EM.

208 *He was in charge of the mechanics:* ISL, 0610 hours, July 2, 1937. NADC.

208 *At 0614 IST, Earhart reported:* 0614 hours, July 2, 1937, IRTEF, page 41. NADC./and ISL, 0614 hours, July 2, 1937. NADC.

208 *Radioman O'Hare was working Honolulu:* IRL 0630 to 0635 hours (1800 to 1805 GCT), the *Itasca* was transmitting Morse code "A's" on 7500 kilocycles. NADC./and 0630–33 hours, July 2, 1937, IRTEF, page 41. NADC.

208 *Captain Thompson ordered the* Itasca: ISL, 0614 hours, July 2, 1937. NADC.

209 *The murky smoke:* Photo taken at 0700 hours, July 2, 1937, shows Itasca making smoke. PCO of Lt. Frank Stewart.

209 *Her signal strength was 4:* 0645 hours, July 2, 1937, IRTEF, page 41. NADC./and ISL, 0645 hours, July 2, 1937. NADC.

209 *Again, the radiomen interpreted:* 0645 hours, July 2, 1937, IRTEF, page 41.

NADC./and IBA of Chief Radioman Thomas J. O'Hare, May 13, 1975, and December 31, 1977. PCO EM.

209   *From 0700 to 0703 IST:* IRL, 0700 to 0703 hours (1830 to 1833 GCT), July 2, 1937, The Itasca was transmitting to Cipriani on Howland Island.

209   *At 0742 IST, she reported:* 0742 hours, July 2, 1937, IRTEF, page 42. NADC; and IBA of William L. Galten, September 18, 1972, and September 25, 1972. PCO EM.

209   *she had only one half hour left:* 0742 hours, July 2, 1937, IRTEF, page 42. NADC; and IBA of Chief Radioman Thomas J. O'Hare, May 13, 1975, and December 31, 1977. PCO EM.

209   *The signal strength was 5:* 0743–46 hours, July 2, 1937, IRTEF, page 42.

209   *Her signal strength was 5 plus:* 0807 hours, July 2, 1937, IRTEF page 43. NADC; and ISL, 0758 hours, July 2, 1937. NADC.

209   *In fact, Captain Thompson later noted:* 0015–0018 hours, July 2, 1937, IRTEF, page 37. NADC.

210   *When they found out:* IRL, 2224 hours, 2256 hours, and etc., July 1, 1937. NADC.

210   *NMC in San Francisco:* IRL, 2206 hours, July 1, 1937. NADC.

210   *At 0715 and 0815 IST:* IRL, 0715 and 0815 hours, July 2, 1937. NADC.

210   *Earhart's receiver:* Listed item 15, IRTEF, page 47. NADC.

210   *Chief Bellarts switched:* IRL, 0842 hours, July 2, 1937. NADC.

210   *Without warning, Earhart came on:* 0844–46 hours, July 2, 1937, IRTEF, page 45. NADC; and ISL, 0843 hours, July 2, 1937. NADC.

210   *She was loud:* 0758 hours, July 2, 1937, IRTEF, page 42; and 0807 hours, July 2, 1937, IRTEF page 43. NADC.

210   *She told them to wait:* 0844–0846 hours, July 2, 1937, IRTEF, page 45. NADC.

210   *Nothing was ever heard:* Listed item 12, IRTEF, page 47; and Listed item 12, IRTEF, page 105. NADC.

210   *Evidently, as Earhart was cranking:* Note "Itasca was purposely conservative in assuming Earhart down.", IRTEF, page 47. NADC; and Letter from WT to RW, October 18, 1937. NADC.

210   *It was indeed tragic:* EHCR, page 8. PDI.

211   *If Radioman Cipriani:* IRL, 2216 to 2240 hours, July 4, 1937, Note "Want Howland keep loop in use especially at night"—"Use Interior's batteries if necessary." NADC.

CHAPTER 14: THE SEARCH FOR EARHART

214   *She never responded:* IRL, 0800 to 2400, July 2, 1937. NADC; and Note "The Itasca steadily called the plane." July 2, 1937, IRTEF page 50; and Note item 12, IRTEF, page 105. NADC.

214   *But its battery was dead:* IRL, 0935 hours, July 2, 1937. NADC.

214   *A coded message was dispatched:* Message 6002/1015, July 2, 1937, IRTEF, page 48. NADC.

214   *Captain Thompson hurried met:* IBA of RB, May 11, 1976. PCO EM.

214   *The Itasca's executive officer:* ISL, 0-912 and 1030 hours, July 2, 1937. NADC.

216   *This reasoning was reinforced:* Message 6002/2015, July 2, 1937, IRTEF, pages 50 and 51; and Message 6016/1200, July 16, 1937, IRTEF, page 102. NADC.

216 *"6002 EARHART CONTACT 0742 REPORTED:* Message 6002/1015, July 2, 1937, IRTEF, page 48. NADC.

216 *"The visibility reported:* ISL, "Instructions for keeping the ship's log." Page (4), June, 1937. NADC.

216 *There were 1,600 gallons:* Message 6002/1018, July 2, 1937, IRTEF, page 48. NADC.

216 *At 1040 IST the* Itasca *got underway:* ISL, 1040 hours, July 2, 1937. NADC.

216 *Four men were posted:* Message from James Carey, United Press, 1550 HST, July 3, 1937, scrapbook of Lt. Leo G. Bellarts. (College Park, MD.) NADC.

216 *The watch officers themselves:* Message 6003/1220, July 3, 1937, IRTEF, page 61./and Message 6004/1515, July 4, 1937, IRTEF, page 64. NADC.

216 *The operator of the ship-to-airplane circuit:* Note "The *Itasca* steadily called the plane"; and Message 6002/2015, July 2, 1937, IRTEF, pages 50 and 51. NADC.

216 *The incessant calls of the* Itasca: Note "Since 1000 in the morning—plane was missing." July 2, 1937, IRTEF, page 52. NADC.

217 *Officials responsible for conducting the search:* Note item 13, IRTEF, page 105. NADC.

217 *"0002 USE AVAILABLE NAVAL FACILITIES:* Message 0002/1940, from SECN, July 2, 1937. NASB COMDT14ND.

217 *Gurr told him that with battery power:* IBA of JG, January 20, 1976. PCO EM.

217 *"8002 POSSIBILITY PLANE MAY ATTEMPT:* Message 8002/1910, July 2, 1937, IRTEF, page 50. NADC.

218 *The* Itasca *steadily called:* Note "This information formed—called the plane." IRTEF, page 50. NADC.

218 *The Navy dispatched:* SRNCG, page 2. NASB COMDT14ND.

218 *The Navy seaplane tender* Swan: SSL, 1635 and 1934 hours, July 2, 1937. NADC./and message from COMINBATFOR to OPNAV, 1515, July 2, 1937. NASB COMDT14ND.

218 *The* Itasca *was ordered:* Message 0002/2050, July 2, 1937, IRTEF, page 53. NADC.

218 The Colorado *would bring:* Message 0002/2115, July 2, 1937 (decoded in service cypher). NASB COMDT14ND.

218 *In the meantime, the* Itasca: ISL, 1040 to 1355 hours, July 2, 1937 (hourly passage distance in nautical miles). NADC.

218 *At 1355 IST it turned:* ISL, 1316 and 1355 hours, July 2, 1937. NADC.

218 *Covering a 15-mile swath:* Message 6012/1757, July 12, 1937, IRTEF, page 95. NADC.

218 *After dark it searched:* Message 6003/1220, July 3, 1937, IRTEF, page 61; and Message 6004/1515, July 4, 1937, IRTEF, page 64. NADC.

218 Itasca *returned to Howland:* ISL, 0710 hours, July 3, 1937. NADC.

218 *The* Achilles *heard two dashes:* Message 1002/2030, July 2, 1937, IRTEF, page 52. NADC.

219 *After many messages:* Message 6003/0940, July 3. 1937, IRTEF, page 58. NADC.

219 *Lieutenant Harvey in the PBY seaplane:* SRCO, page 3. NADC.

219 *It was imperative:* Message 6003/0800, July 3, 1937, IRTEF, page 57. NADC.

219 *"6003 NAVY PLANE REPORTS RETURNING:* USCG message 6003/0956, July 3, 1937. NASB.

219 *At 0930 IST the* Itasca *departed:* ISL, 0930 hours, July 3, 1937. NADC.

219 *They would advise the* Itasca: Message 6003/1015, July 3, 1937, IRTEF, page 58. NADC.

219 *At that time:* Message 6003/1035, July 3, 1937, IRTEF, page 58. NADC.

219 *They continued generally westward:* ISL, 1400 and 1605 hours, July 3, 1937. NADC.

219 *In the meantime the battleship* Colorado: SRCO, page 4. NADC.

219 *"8003 FOUR SEPARATE RADIOMEN:* Message 8003/2350, July 3, 1937, IRTEF, page 61. NADC.

220 *"With the information:* Note "With the information—on 4 July without result." IRTEF, page 61. NADC.

220 *From there, the* Itasca *would work:* Message 6004/1515, July 4, 1937, IRTEF, page 64. NADC.

220 *All day Sunday it cut south:* ISL, 0612 through 1828 hours, July 4, 1937. NADC.

220 *During the day:* Message 0004/1050, July 4, 1937, IRTEF, page 65. NADC.

220 *The* Ramapo *was under the direction:* SRLX, Narrative of Search, pages 2, 3, and 4. NADC

220 *The* Colorado *would refuel them at sea:* Message 1004/1305, July 4, 1937, IRTEF, page 67. NADC.

221 *It was probably of no value:* ISL, 1940 hours, July 4, 1937. NADC.

221 *At daylight:* ISL, 0000 to 0400, and 2115 hours, July 4, 1937. NADC.

221 *They expected to arrive:* Message 0004/1910, July 4, 1937, IRTEF, page 67. NADC.

221 *The captain expected results:* IRL, 2210 to 2240 hours, July 4, 1937. NADC./and hand written notes contained in scrapbook of Lt. Leo G. Bellarts. (College Park, MD.) NADC.

221 *No call sign was given:* HRL, 0035 HST, July 5, 1937 (dates of actual d/f logs are a day off). NADC./and Message 8005/0425, July 5, 1937, IRTEF, page 72. NADC.

222 *The keying was extremely poor:* Message 8005/0242, July 5, 1937, IRTEF, page 70. NADC.

222 *The* Moorby, *radio call GYSR:* Letter No. 507, from Albert M. Doyle CONSL, Sydney, Aust. to Cordell Hull, SECS, August 21, 1937. (Suitland, MD) NADC.

222 *This message received:* Note "The British steamer—281 (miles) north of Howland." IRTEF, page 70. NADC.

222 *"6005 OFFICIAL INFORMATION:* Message 6005/0255, July 5, 1937, IRTEF, page 70. NADC.

222 *"EARHART PLANE APPARENTLY DOWN:* Message from *Itasca* to Moorsby [sic]: "Earhart plane apparently—afternoon COMDR Itasca." IRTEF, page 70. NADC.

223 *All day Monday:* ISL, 0800 to 2400 hours, July 5, 1937. NADC.

223 *NO FEARS FELT FOR SAFETY:* Message 8005/1525, July 5, 1937, page 73. NADC.

223 *This message changed:* Note "This message changed—capable of transmitting on water." IRTEF, page 73. NADC.

223 *Just after dark:* ISL, 1300 and 1903 hours, July 5, 1937. NADC.

223 *At 2132 on the night of the 5th:* SRCO, page 6. NADC.

224 *A message was received from Mr. Putnam:* SRCO, page 7. NADC.

224 *He would modify it:* SRCO, page 7. NADC.

225 *At day break, Wednesday:* SRCO, page 8. NADC.

225 *Friedell had not known:* SRCO, page 2. NADC.

225 *"Upon completion the ITASCA:* SRCO, page 8. NADC.

225 *Orders to turn her around:* SRLX, Narrative of Search, pages 3 and 4. NADC.

225 *At 130 knots (150 mph):* SRLX, Estimate and Decisions, Items 10 and 11, page 1./and Item 12, page 4. (1100 gals./45.8 gph = 24 hours 1 minute) and (1100 gals./53 gph = 20 hours 45 minutes). NADC.

225 *They correctly assessed:* SRLX, Estimate and Decisions, page 7. NADC.

226 *"the most probable landing point:* SRLX, Estimate and Decisions, page 9. NADC.

226 *Though the visibility was excellent:* SRCO, page 9. NADC.

226 *At 0700 on the morning of 9 July:* SRCO, page 10. NADC.

226 *McKean Island showed unmistakable signs:* SRCO, page 10. NADC.

226 *Carondelet Reef was under water:* SRCO, page 10. NADC.

226 *At 1400 the planes were launched:* SRCO, page 11. NADC.

226 *As the planes approached Hull Island:* SRCO, page 11. NADC.

227 *"Point origin":* SRLX, Narrative of Search, page 5. NADC.

227 *Three hours and fifteen minutes later:* SRCO, page 11. NADC.

227 *"Sydney was the only Island:* SRCO, page 11. NADC.

227 *The COLORADO at 1445 in Latitude:* SRCO, page 12. NADC.

228 *The* Colorado *was detached:* SRCO, page 12. NADC.

228 *"As this is written:* SRCO, page 13. NADC.

228 *Authorization to search:* SRLX, Narrative of Search, page 6. NADC.

228 *No U.S. ship or plane:* SRLX, Appendix "C," "Earhart Search Map." NADC.

228 *Operated by the London Mission Society:* SRLX, Narrative of Search, page 8. NADC.

228 *Captain Noyes launched sixty planes:* SRLX, Narrative of Search, page 8. NADC.

229 *Five days later, at 1648:* SRLX, Narrative of search, page 13. NADC.

229 *The Itasca had been released:* Messages 0016/1706 and 6016/1722, July 16, 1937, IRTEF page 103. NADC./and Message 0016/1440, July 16, 1937, IRTEF, page 102. NADC.

229 *Captain Noyes steered the* Lexington: SRLX, Narrative of Search, page 13. NADC.

229 *The* Lexington, *after passing near:* SRLX, Narrative of Search, page 13. NADC.

229 *"No sign nor any evidence:* SRLX, Narrative of Search, page 16. NADC.

229 *From the strength of her radio signals:* Message 6002/1402, July 2, 1937, IRTEF, page 49. NADC.

CHAPTER 15: EXAMINING THE EVIDENCE

231 *"I was personally present:* Letter from WT to COMDTCG RW, October 18, 1937. NADC.

231 *"EARHART CONTACT 0742:* Message 6002/1015, July 2, 1937, IRTEF, page 48. NADC.

232 *Less than thirty minutes later:* ISL, 1040 hours, July 2, 1937. NADC.

232 *Chief Bellarts had Galten's original:* IRL, 0742 hours, July 2, 1937. NADC.

232 *O'Hare had a copy:* IRL, 0742 hours, July 2, 1937. NADC.

232 *"Gas is running low:* Notes made by Howard M. Hanzlik, United Press correspondent on Itasca July 2, 1937. PCO Howard M. Hanzlik.

232 *But now we know:* Mr. Hugh Leggatt found the Eric H. Chater letter in 1992 while going through Placer Dome, Inc. archives. The letter had been missing for 55 years.

232 *The Chater report:* EHCR, pages 5 and 8. PDI.

232 *Earhart's plane was fueled:* EHCR, page 5. PDI.

232 *But because of the 88-degree daytime temperature:* Fuel Density Vs Temperature, 87 Octane. PAA drawing No 20.006,104A, March 4, 1941. PAA.

232 *All performance figures:* LAC Report 623, March 10, 1937, page 2. LAC.

232 *Aircraft engine fuel burn rates:* U.S. Government, *Flight Engineering: U.S. Navy Training Course,* Bupers 629.19173 U525-1, 1946 edition, pages 119 and 144.

232 *Earhart reported, at 0418 GCT:* EHCR, page 8. PDI.

232 *The distance from Lae to Howland Island:* "We must be on you," 0742 hours, July 2, 1937, IRTEF, page 42. NADC.

233 *According to data:* LAC Model 10 Flight Manual, "Indicated Airspeed for Maximum Range," page 35a. LAC.

233 *Their contracts guaranteed:* LAC Report 636, Model 10, Part II, paragraph 2.7, Performance Guarantees. LAC.

233 *(Lockheed even stipulated:* LAC Report 636, Model 10, Part II, paragraph 2.7111, Performance Guarantees. LAC.

234 *Captain Thompson believed:* Message 6002/1402, July 2, 1937, IRTEF, page 49. NADC.

234 *He based this:* Item 14, IRTEF, page 47. NADC.

234 *That is bad enough:* Photograph of Eahart's cockpit instrument panel taken in Miami by PAA instrument mechanic F. Ralph Sias. IBA of F. Ralph Sias, December 30, 1977. PCO EM.

234 *This would have allowed:* LAC Model 10 Flight Manual, "Landing Speeds at Various Gross Weights," page 43. LAC.

235 *But the design of the dump valve:* LAC Drawing No. 43708, Special Equipment-Ship #1055—Drawing No. 43964, "Dump Valve Assembly"—Drawing No. 43965, "Fuselage Dump Valves"—Drawing No. 43957, "Fuel Valve and Chute Installation."

235 *"As regards the search:* Letter from WT to COMDTCG RW, October 18, 1937. NADC.

CHAPTER 16: SOLVING THE MYSTERY

238 *"partly cloudy":* 0453 hours, July 2, 1937, IRTEF, page 40. NADC.

239 *Noonan wrote that he found:* Letter from FN to PW, May 11, 1935. POPA.

241 *The next navigational event:* 0742 hours, July 2, 1937, IRTEF, page 42. NADC.

241 *Howland Island is actually:* "the position of Howland Island was found to be 5½ (nautical) miles eastward of the charted position as determined by the U.S.S. Naragansett in 1872." USCG Confidential Letter 601–64, August 12,

1936, page 1. NADC./and Position of Howland Island as shown on Earhart's chart prepared by Clarence S. Williams, February 9, 1937. NASM.

242   *The visibility at the time:* ISL, 0700 and 0800 hours weather observations, visibility 9 = greater than 20 miles, July 2, 1937. NADC.

242   *He interrupted their progress:* 0758 hours, July 2, 1937, IRTEF, page 42. NADC.

243   *Both the battleship* Colorado: "one (1) set of charts to the Commandant of the Fourteenth Naval District, Pearl Harbor," USCG Confidential Letter 601-64, August 12, 1936, page 5. NADC.

243   *A second piece of information:* ISL, 0700 and 0800 hours weather observations, wind east "Beaufort force 1 = 4 to 8 mph." NADC.

243   *When they were closest:* ISL, 0758 hours, July 2, 1937./and Note at 0758 hours, July 2, 1937, IRTEF, page 42. NADC.

244   *The* Itasca *departed Howland:* ISL, 1040 hours, July 2, 1937. NADC.

245   *The men on the* Itasca: Note 0758 hours, July 2, 1937, IRTEF, page 42./and Note 0807 hours, July 2, 1937, IRTEF, page 43./and item 14, IRTEF, page 47. NADC.

245   *"We are flying north:* 0844–46 hours, July 2, 1937, IRTEF, page 45. NADC.

Appendix

251   *In March 1937:* The telegram CJ sent to AE in Oakland at 3:54 p.m., March 11, 1937, specified that 900 gallons of fuel would be ample for the flight to Honolulu. AE actually took off from Oakland with 947 gallons.

251   *To reflect an approximate 342-pound weight reduction:* After the March crash in Honolulu the Electra had a lower antenna, the trailing wire antenna, a cabin window, and crew changed. A cabin hatch, structural stiffeners, stronger landing gear collars, oleo struts, and tires were added. The net overall change is estimated to have reduced the Electra's weight by 342 pounds.

251   *Accordingly, after the first hour:* 57 gallons weighs 342 pounds (342 / 6 = 57). The 192 gallons of extra fuel at Lae (1092−900 = 192) is reduced by 57 gallons (192−57) to 135 gallons to make the Oakland and Lae aircraft weight equivalent, from that point, for the rest of the flight.

SOURCES

THE AUTHORS AND
THEIR CONTRIBUTORS

The authors have spent more than twenty-five years searching for evidence that would solve the Earhart mystery. We interviewed over a hundred witnesses and traveled more than a hundred thousand miles doing research for this book. Early on, a probable solution was tantalizingly obvious, but decades would pass before the "smoking gun" was discovered. Only a grizzled old prospector would understand the excitement we felt when the evidence was unearthed.

Elgen began his flying career of over 40,000 hours as a radioman in Navy PBY seaplanes during World War II, and retired as senior pilot on the Boeing 747 in 1987, after forty years with the Flying Tiger Line. He was honored to receive the Fédération Aéronautique Internationale "Gold Air Medal" in 1971 as the outstanding sports pilot in the world, an Institute of Navigation "Superior Achievement Award" in 1971 as a practicing navigator, and the Air Line Pilots Association "Award for Outstanding Airmanship" in 1972. He holds more than fifteen "World Records" and "Firsts." He is the only pilot to have flown solo around the world over the North and South Poles.

The FAA has certified Captain Long as an Air Transport Pilot, Flight

Navigator, Flight Radio Operator, Powerplant Mechanic, and Accident Prevention Counselor. The FCC has issued him a Commercial 2c Radiotelegraph Operator's License and Extra Class Radio Amateur License W7FT.

Captain Long received an Associate Degree in Aeronautics from the College of San Mateo in California, and "Accident Investigation" training from the Air Safety Center at the University of Southern California and the Norton Air Force Base Crash Laboratory. He was first designated as an "Aircraft Accident Investigator" for ALPA in 1957, and is a member of the International Society of Air Safety Investigators.

Earhart was lost while attempting the first flight around the world at the equator. Captain Long, flying an unpressurized twin-engine piston plane even smaller than Earhart's, crossed her path twice as he made the first solo flight around the world over the poles. With gender roles reversed, the wife handling the publicity and the husband doing the flying, the experience of world-record-setting flying was absolutely invaluable to the Earhart research. Time and again, it provided the insight to ask the right questions and to look in the right places for obscure but vital information.

As the last active airline pilot to have taken his CAA Navigator's Rating aboard a Boeing 314, Long had navigated the flying boats as Fred Noonan had done in the salty environment of wet compass, drift meter, bubble octant, and chronometer. Consequently the techniques and procedures Noonan used when plotting his charts were as familiar as an old friend.

We tape-recorded every witness cited as a source for this book. We accumulated literally thousands of documents, photographs, and recorded interviews, which Marie catalogued, referenced, labeled, and filed. This archive of material gives our book an unprecedented richness of detail and authenticity. Many of these witnesses, as we think of them, participated in Earhart's around-the-world flight. Many of them are now dead.

Following is a partial listing of those people who offered firsthand information about Amelia Earhart and Fred Noonan. This book is their story, too, and the book is gratefully dedicated to them:

Charlotte Kamakaiwi Akina—sister of lead colonist James Kamakaiwi—**Howland Island**

Gen. Lawrence C. Aimes, US Army—Lockheed director, with Putnam at NMC—**San Francisco**

Lt. Cmdr. Henry M. Anthony, USCG—communications officer, Hawaiian Section—Honolulu

Jean L. Backus—Author; finder of Mrs. Amy Earhart's letters from Amelia—Berkeley, California

Mrs. Harry Balfour—second wife of officer in charge, radio station for Guinea Airways—Lae, New Guinea

Lt. Cmdr. Irl Vernon Beall, USCG—assistant, division communications officer—San Francisco

Lt. Leo G. Bellarts, USCG—chief radioman (code name "DC") aboard the cutter *Itasca*

Ela Gofton Birrell—at Cecil Hotel with "A.E." and Fred the morning they left—Lae

Edwin H. Bishton—radioman, Amalgamated Wireless Ltd. station—Rabaul, New Guinea

Adm. Richard B. Black, USN—Department of the Interior; was "A.E.'s" representative on the *Itasca*

Albert L. Bresnik—Amelia Earhart's personal photographer—Hollywood

Edwin H. Bryan Jr.—curator, Bishop Museum, and organizer of island colonists—Honolulu

Joseph R. Burgard—factory radio installer, radio shop, Lockheed Aircraft—Burbank, California

Adm. Harry R. Canaday, USN—Pan American pilot with Noonan on survey flights—Alameda, California

Margot de Carie—Amelia Earhart's personal assistant and driver—North Hollywood, California

Jack Cartwright—foreman, sheetmetal shop, Lockheed Aircraft, 1937—Burbank

Harvey C. Christen—manager of production, Lockheed Aircraft, 1937—Burbank

James A. Collopy—"Jim"—district superintendent, Australian Civil Aviation—Lae

Col. Daniel A. Cooper, US Army—Army Air Corps representative on USCG cutter *Itasca*

Gen. James H. Doolittle, USAF—"Jimmy"—pilot and friend of Amelia Earhart—New York

Walter A. Dwyer—meteorologist, provided "A.E." weather forecast to Lae—Darwin, Australia

Lt. Cmdr. Robert W. Findley, USCG—communications dept., headquarters—Washington, D.C.

Francis O. Furman—"Fuzz"—mechanic who worked on the Electra—Bandoeng, Java

William L. Galten—"Bill"—USCG radioman (code name "BG"), guarded Earhart radio circuit—*Itasca*

Walter A. Gaston—foreman, fuselage shop, Lockheed Aircraft, 1937—Burbank

Peter Gendron—USCG coxswain, operated boats from ship to Howland Island—*Itasca*

James M. Gerschler—"Jimmy"—assistant chief engineer, Lockheed Aircraft, 1937—Burbank

Betty H. Gillies—pilot and longtime friend of Amelia Earhart—New York

Firman C. Gray—manager, final assembly, Lockheed Aircraft, 1937—Burbank

Joseph H. Gurr—radioman UAL, changed Electra's antenna system, May 1937—Burbank

Frank C. Hannam—mechanic for Paul Mantz, worked on "A.E."'s plane—Burbank

Howard M. Hanzlik—United Press correspondent, heard "A.E." messages on radio—*Itasca*

Bertie Heath—pilot for Guinea Airways, at Cecil Hotel with "A.E." and Fred—Lae

Al Hemphill—Bendix radio engineer, worked on design of direction-finder—Baltimore

Fallon M. Herndon—Aircraft mechanic for scout planes on USS *Colorado*

Lt. Cmdr. Linford H. Hines, USCG—warrant gunnery officer on cutter *Itasca*

Clyde E. Holley, Esq.—attorney for Amelia M. Earhart and George P. Putnam—Los Angeles

Wing Cmdr. Robert W. Iredale—"Bob"—with Vacuum Oil Company; fueled the Electra—Lae

Clarence L. Johnson—"Kelly"—performance and aerodynamic engineer, Lockheed—Burbank

Capt. Roy Keeler—senior pilot with Pan American, associate of Fred Noonan—Miami

Mrs. Frank T. Kenner—"Betty"—wife of Adm. F. T. Kenner, USCG, Cmdr. Hawaiian Section—Honolulu

Adm. William W. Kenner, USCG—twin brother of Adm. Frank T. Kenner on the *Itasca*

Norman W. King—mechanic engineer, Qantas; worked on the Electra—Darwin, Australia

Col. Henry S. Lau, U.S. Army Signal Corps, visiting friends on Howland Island

William P. Lear—"Bill"—radio direction-finder designer and associate of Earhart—New York

Ah Kin Leong—colonist for Department of the Interior, living July 2, 1937, on Howland Island

Paul Yat Lum—radio operator "K6INF," colonist living July 2, 1937, on Baker Island

Yau Fai Lum—radio operator "K6GNW," colonist living July 2, 1937, on Howland Island

Vivian Bryant Maatta—secretary for "A.E.," "G.P.," and W. T. Miller—Oakland

Mrs. Harry Manning—second wife of Commodore Harry Manning; flew to Hawaii with "A.E."—New York

Mrs. Albert Paul Mantz—"Terry"—second wife of Paul Mantz; with "A.E." in Honolulu 1937—Burbank

Cmdr. Roy Minor Mantz, USN—"Terry"'s son by Roy Minor, Paul's adopted son—Burbank

Dorman J. Marshall—"Biff"—radio ship technician, Lockheed Aircraft, 1937—Burbank

Adm. Donald E. McKay—aide to Secretary of Treasury Morgenthau, on visit to Honolulu

Ruckins D. McKneely—"Bo"—was "A.E."'s personal mechanic and flew with her to Miami

Capt. Henry T. Merrill—"Dick"—flew Atlantic in Lockheed 10-E, met with "A.E." in Miami

Col. Harold A. Meyer, US Army—"Ham"—manager of logistics for Line Island colonists—Honolulu

O. Vernon Moore—Bendix radio design engineer, built d/f receiver for "A.E."—Washington, D.C.

Muriel Earhart Morrissey—"Pidge"—Amelia's younger sister—West Medford, Massachusetts

Mrs. Frederick J. Noonan—"Bee"—second wife of Fred Noonan—Oakland

John K. Northrop—"Jack"—design engineer of "A.E."'s Vega, Lockheed Aircraft—Burbank

Jacqueline Cochran Odlum—friend; flew Electra with "A.E.," N.Y. to Burbank—Indio, California

CPO Thomas J. O'Hare, USCG—radioman 3c (code name "TO"), guarded ship-to-shore radio circuit—*Itasca*

Charles Palmer—"Cap"—author and friend of George Palmer Putnam—Hollywood

Percy E. Pettijohn—"Ed"—foreman of Pan American radio shop, Dinner Key, 1937—Miami

David Binney Putnam—oldest son of G. P. Putnam; with "A.E." and "G.P." in Miami

Mrs. David B. Putnam—"Nilla" and her husband, David, were with "A.E." and "G.P." in Miami

Dorothy Binney Putnam—"Dolly"—first wife of G.P. and mother of both sons—Ft. Pierce, Florida

George Palmer Putnam III—"Junie"—youngest son of G. P. Putnam—Ft. Pierce, Florida

Jean Marie Cosigny Putnam—third wife of G. P. Putnam—Los Angeles

Margaret Haviland Putnam—"Peg"—fourth wife of G. P. Putnam—Los Angeles

Wing Cmdr. Stanley Rose—Sergeant in charge, d/f station, fixed Electra's receiver—Darwin

Lloyd Royer—precision mechanic, Lockheed Aircraft; longtime friend of "A.E."—Burbank

James L. Savage—"Doc"—Pan American mechanic, knew F. J. Noonan—Midway Island

F. Ralph Sias—Pan American instrument mechanic, 1937, worked on "A.E." 's plane in Miami

Elinor P. Smith—pilot, early associate of "A.E." and "G.P."—New York

Samuel J. Solomon—"Sam"—partner in starting Boston & Maine Airways—Washington, D.C.

Neta Snook Southern—friend of Amelia's, her first flight instructor—Los Angeles

Flora Stewart—"Ma"—owner of Cecil Hotel and host to "A.E." and Fred in Lae

Lt. Frank Stewart, USCG—chief quartermaster, *Itasca*

Capt. Roy E. Stockstill, USCG—engineering officer, *Itasca*

Clara Trenckman Studer—friend of "A.E." 's and first editor, *Ninety-Nines* magazine—New York

Lt. Cdr. Albert D. Stumpff, USCG—"Al"—chief yeoman of *Itasca* on leave in San Pedro, California

Capt. William L. Sutter, USCG—communications officer, wrote most of radio report—*Itasca*

Capt. William I. Swanston, USCG—"Bill"—navigation officer, surveyor of islands—*Itasca*

William T. Tavares—"Bill"—early and longtime colonist on Line Islands, 1937—*Itasca*

Mrs. Louise McPhetridge Thaden—original Ninety-Nine pilot and friend of "A.E."—New York

Robert H. Thibert—radioman for Pan American, calibrated Electra's radio d/f—Miami

Fred and Elstrude Tomas—cook and maid for "A.E." and "G.P.," 10042 Valley Spring Lane—North Hollywood

Evelyn Trout—"Bobbi"—original Ninety-Nine pilot and friend of "A.E."—Los Angeles

Adm. Arnold E. True, USN—aerologist, made Lae–Howland flight forecasts—Pearl Harbor

Karl E. Voelter—manager of Curtiss-Wright hangar where "A.E." parked her plane—Miami

Adm. Russell R. Waesche Jr., USCG—commandant, son of 1937 commandant—Washington, D.C.

Sgt. Horace G. Waters, US Army—Wheeler Field mechanic for "A.E.," 1935 and 1937—Honolulu

Fay Gillis Wells—original Ninety-Nine pilot and friend of "A.E." and "G.P."—New York

William P. Wentworth, Esq.—attorney for Fred and Mary B. Noonan—Oakland

Edward E. Werner—"Ed"—assistant foreman, fuselage shop, Lockheed Aircraft—Burbank

Adm. Frederick A. Zeusler, USCG—headquarters communications officer—Washington, D.C.

REFERENCES

BOOKS AND MAGAZINES

Backus, Jean L. *Letters from Amelia: An Intimate Portrait of Amelia Earhart.* Boston: Beacon Press, 1982. Includes letters from 1901 to 1937.

Blay, Roy A. "Amelia Earhart's Last Flight." *Lockheed Horizons* (Lockheed Corporation), no. 26, May 1988.

Chapman, Sally Putnam, with Stephanie Mansfield. *Whistled Like a Bird: The Untold Story of Dorothy Putnam, George Putnam, and Amelia Earhart.* New York: Warner Books, Inc., 1997.

298 • Sources

Dwiggins, Don. *Hollywood Pilot: A Biography of Paul Mantz*. Garden City, NY: Doubleday & Company, 1967.

Earhart, Amelia. "Here Is How Fannie Hurst Could Learn to Fly." *Hearst's International-Cosmopolitan,* January 1929.

Earhart, Amelia. *20 hrs. 40 mins.: Our Flight in the Friendship*. New York and London: G. P. Putnam's Sons, 1928. Original edition.

Earhart, Amelia. *Last Flight*. New York: Harcourt, Brace and Co., 1937. Arranged by George Palmer Putnam. Original edition.

Earhart, Amelia. *The Fun of It: Random Records of My Own Flying and of Women in Aviation*. New York: Brewer, Warren & Putnam, 1932; reprinted 1975 by Gale Research, New York, and in 1977 by Academy Chicago Limited. The original edition is cited.

Earhart, Amelia. "Try Flying Yourself." *Hearst's International-Cosmopolitan,* November 1928.

Fraser, Chelsea. *Heroes of the Air*. New York: Thomas Y. Crowell Company, 1926. Lindbergh's flight from New York to Paris is recorded in the chronology of the revised 14th edition, 1936.

Haggerty, James. *Aviation's Mr. Sam*. Fallbrook, CA: Aero Publishers, Inc., 1974. Sam Solomon was partner with Amelia Earhart at Boston & Maine Airways.

Jacobs, George, and Theodore J. Cohen. *The Shortwave Propagation Handbook*. Hicksville, NY: CQ Publishing, Inc., 1979; 2nd edition published 1982. The 2nd edition is cited.

King, Jack L. *Wings of Man: An Informal Biography of Captain H. T. "Dick" Merrill*. Glendale, CA: Aviation Book Co., 1981.

Lyon, Thoburn C. *Practical Air Navigation*, 10th edition. Denver, CO: Jeppesen & Co., 1970.

Morrissey, Muriel Earhart. *Courage Is the Price: The Biography of Amelia Earhart*. Wichita, KS: McCormick-Armstrong Publishing Division, 1963. Muriel Earhart Morrissey was Amelia Earhart's sister.

1998 *Information Please Almanac*, ed. Borgna Brunner. Boston: Houghton Mifflin, 1998.

Noonan, Frederick J. "A Letter from Fred Noonan to Lieut.-Comm. P. V. H. Weems." *Popular Aviation,* May 1938.

Oakes, Claudia M. "U.S. Women in Aviation: The 1930s." *Air & Space* (magazine of the Smithsonian National Air & Space Museum), Winter 1980.

Putnam, George Palmer. *Up in Our Country*. New York: Duell, Sloan and Pearce, 1950.

Putnam, George Palmer. *Wide Margins: A Publisher's Autobiography*. New York: Harcourt, Brace and Co., 1942.

Smith, Frank Kingston. *Legacy of Wings: The Harold F. Pitcairn Story*. New York: Jason Aronson, 1981; republished 1987 by T.D. Associates, Lafayette Hill, PA.

Van Cott, Harold P. *Human Engineering Guide to Equipment Design*. New York: McGraw-Hill Company, 1963; revised edition published 1972. See, in revised edition, Chapter 1, "Systems and Human Engineering Analysis" (with Jerry S. Kidd).

Weems, P. V. H. *Air Navigation*. New York and London: McGraw-Hill Book Company, Inc., 1931.

Published and Unpublished Materials—Institutional, Industrial, and U.S. Government

Bendix Radio. "RA-1 Series Receiver for Aircraft." Manual, dated 1946. Amelia Earhart had the first prototype of this receiver installed in her Electra for the world flight. The Bendix Aviation Corporation, Baltimore, MD, is presently a subsidiary of Allied Signal, Fort Lauderdale, FL.

Bowditch, Nathaniel, LL.D. *American Practical Navigator: An Epitome of Navigation and Nautical Astronomy.* Publication No. 9. Washington, DC: U.S. Hydrographic Office, 1926. Amelia Earhart bought and studied this book.

Bryan, E. H., Jr. *Panala'au Memoirs.* Honolulu: Pacific Scientific Information Center, Bernice P. Bishop Museum, 1974. A chronology of U.S. colonization of Pacific islands including Baker and Howland Islands.

Crowell, James LeRoy. "Frontier Publisher: A Romantic Review of George Palmer Putnam's Career at the *Bend Bulletin,* 1910–1914," with an extensive epilogue. Master of Science thesis, University of Oregon School of Journalism, Eugene, OR, 1966.

Dreisenstok, J. Y. *Navigation Tables for Mariners and Aviators,* 6th edition. Publication No. 208. Washington, DC: U.S. Navy Department, Hydrographic Office, 1942. The Dreisenstok Tables were used by Fred Noonan.

Hatfield, D. D. *Los Angeles Aeronautics: 1920–1929.* Hatfield History of Aeronautics, Locality Series, Alumni Library. Inglewood, CA: Northrop Institute of Technology, 1973.

Lockheed Aircraft Corporation. Lockheed reports and aircraft drawings (various dates). LAC, Burbank, CA. Now a subsidiary of Lockheed Martin Corporation, Bethesda, MD.

Maskelyne, Nevil. *The Nautical Almanac and Astronomical Ephemeris.* London: Her Majesty's Stationery Office, 1767. Now published annually as the *Nautical Almanac* by the Nautical Almanac Office of the U.S. Naval Observatory; see under U.S. Naval Observatory.

Radio Research Company, Inc. "Type RDF-2-A Direction Finder Equipment (Aircraft Use)." This manual, dated February 1, 1937, was prepared for the U.S. Navy Department, Bureau of Aeronautics contract No-52717. The Radio Research Company, Washington, DC, was acquired by Bendix Radio in early 1937.

U.S. Naval Observatory. *Nautical Almanac.* Washington and London: Nautical Almanac Office of the U.S. Naval Observatory. Issued annually and sold by the Superintendent of Documents, U.S. Government Printing Office. Back issues available at the Library of Congress.

U.S. Naval Observatory. *The Air Almanac.* Washington and London: Nautical Almanac Office of the U.S. Naval Observatory. Issued three times annually and sold by the Superintendent of Documents, U.S. Government Printing Office. Back issues available at the Library of Congress.

U.S. Government. *Air Navigation.* U.S. Navy Hydrographic Office Publication No. 216. Washington, DC: U.S. Hydrographic Office, under the authority of the Secretary of the Navy, 1955.

U.S. Government. *Flight Engineering: Navy Training Courses.* Bupers 629.19173

U525-1 edition. Washington, DC: Training Bureau of Naval Personnel, Standards and Curriculum Division, 1946.

U.S. Government. Radio facility books, including: "List of Coast Stations and Ship Stations"; "List of Stations Performing Special Services." 1937. Available at the Library of Congress.

U.S. Government. *The Coast Guard at War: Communications XVI*. Vols. 1 and 2. Washington, DC: Commandant, U.S. Coast Guard, [circa] 1947., Public Information Office, Historical Section.

Western Electric Corporation. "Radio Transmitter No. 13C and 13CB Supplement to the 13C Radio Transmitter Instruction Bulletin." Instruction Bulletin No. 782, printed in New Jersey, circa 1936. Archived at the offices of AT&T in Warren, NJ. This radio transmitter was developed by Bell Telephone Laboratories and incorporated for Western Electric.

COMPUTER-GENERATED INFORMATION

Distant Suns. Computer software program used to determine the positions of stars, sun, moon, and planets at various locations, dates, and times. Copyright 1991–1992 by Mike Smithwick, San Louis Obispo, CA.

Propman. Computer software program used to determine radio wave propagation for various frequencies at various locations, dates, and times. No. 091-0957-001, Rockwell International, Collins Avionics & Communications Division, Cedar Rapids, IA.

ARCHIVED SOURCES OF INFORMATION

I. Archives Excluding the U.S. National Archives

AEAK

Amelia Earhart Birthplace Museum, Atchison, KS.

Personal papers, letters, photographs, and memorabilia of the Earhart and Otis families at the birthplace of Amelia Earhart.

BISH

Bernice P. Bishop Museum, Honolulu, HI.

Journals, logs, maps, photographs, and histories of the colonists on the Pacific Islands, 1935–1942. Includes the files of the Pacific Scientific Information Center.

FAA

Federal Aviation Administration, FAA Airman and Aircraft Registration Branches, Mike Monroney Aeronautical Center, Oklahoma City, OK.

History and repair records of Lockheed Electra aircraft Model 10-E, serial number 1055, registration NR16020. Airman information on registered pilots Amelia M. Earhart, Harry Manning, and Frederick J. Noonan.

LAC

Aircraft Corporation, subsidiary of Lockheed Martin Corporation, Bethesda, MD (originally located in Burbank, CA).

Drawings, engineering orders, letters, reports, manuals, and photographs of

Amelia Earhart and her Model 10-E, Lockheed Electra aircraft, serial number 1055.

NASM

National Air and Space Museum Library, Smithsonian Institution, Washington, DC.

In the Amelia Earhart Collection: charts of Captain Clarence S. Williams USNR, photographs.

NHLA

Natural History Museum of Los Angeles County, Sever Center, Los Angeles, CA. Amelia Earhart Collection.

NLA

National Library of Australia, Canberra, Australia.

Original 16 mm movie film, made by Guinea Airways pilot Sid Marshall, showing Amelia Earhart's takeoff from Lae, New Guinea, on July 2, 1937; diary of Mrs. Dorothea Garsia (wife of Nauru Island's administrator, Commander Rupert C. Garsia) relating to listening and watching for Earhart's passage over Nauru Island.

NSWL

State Library of New South Wales, Sydney, Australia.

Newspapers, magazines, books, reports, photographs, maps, and the Mitchell and Dixson libraries collection specializing in information relating to Australia and the Southwest Pacific.

NZM

Chester W. Nimitz Museum, Fredericksburg, TX.

Personal collection of Frederick A. Goerner; historical records of the Pacific campaign during World War II.

PDI

Placer Dome, Inc., Vancouver, B. C., Canada.

Historical information regarding mining in New Guinea; Chater Letter, regarding the activities of Amelia Earhart and Frederick Noonan while at Lae, New Guinea. (This eight-page report, dated July 25, 1937, was written by Eric H. Chater and mailed to M. E. Griffin in San Francisco. The Chater Letter can also be retrieved from the historical section of the Placer Dome Web site at <*www.placerdome.com*>).

PUL

Purdue University Library, West Lafayette, IN.

In the Special Collections of Amelia Earhart and George Palmer Putnam and the records of the Purdue Research Foundation: notes, maps, letters, telegrams, radiograms, photographs, landing fee receipts, fuel receipts, newspaper clippings, personal albums, trip planning data, aircraft refueling diagrams, weather, airport, and en route facility charts.

SLRC

Schlesinger Library, Radcliffe College, Cambridge, MA.

Amelia Earhart Collection from Muriel Earhart Morrissey.

UOW

University of Wyoming, American Heritage Center, Laramie, WY.

Papers of Eugene L. Vidal.

WEC
Western Electric, subsidiary of Bell Telephone Laboratories, Inc., Archives Department, American Telephone and Telegraph, Archives, Warren, NJ. Letters, operating manuals, and descriptive literature.

II. The U.S. National Archives

Untold millions of documents are stored within the National Archives system. The two depositories that were used in researching this book are those in Washington, DC (NADC) and in San Bruno, CA (NASB). The outline that follows, necessarily brief, details where the source material used in the text can be located. While the system is undeniably complex, the researcher will usually find archivists on hand ready to give useful aid.

NADC
National Archives and Records Administration, Washington, DC (includes depositories at Suitland and College Park, MD). The following material has been consulted:

Record Group 26 Amelia Earhart, file 601 Earhart, reference 65-601 Itasca—Radio Transcripts Earhart Flight: A 106-page confidential report submitted July 19, 1937, by Commander Warner K. Thompson to the Commander of the USCG San Francisco Division (source for radio messages sent and received by the USCG cutter *Itasca*). Other U.S. Coast Guard records available also in Record Group 26 Amelia Earhart, file 601 Earhart: radio logs, radio messages, USCG ships' logbooks, search reports, cruise reports, letters, and general correspondence.

Record Group 45, file GU: Listing of Office of Naval Records Collection.

Record Group 24: U.S. Navy ships' logbooks.

Record Group 37, file A4-3: USS Colorado weekly publication during search for Electra.

Record Group 80, file A4-5 (5): General records of the Navy Department.

U.S. Department of State, U.S. Consulate, Sydney, Australia, Record Group 84, file 796.1: Correspondence relating to Amelia Earhart's world flight, filed by State Department as 800.79611 Putnam, Amelia Earhart/(number).

U.S. Department of Commerce, Record Group 40: miscellaneous documents.

Federal Aviation Administration (and its predecessors), Record Group 237: miscellaneous documents.

U.S. Army Overseas Operations and Commands, General Correspondence, Air officer, Hawaiian Department, Record Group 395: Complete inventory of every item in Earhart's Electra aircraft; report of U.S. Army Air Corps investigation of Earhart's crash at Luke Field, March 20, 1937.

NASB
National Archives, San Bruno, CA. The following material has been consulted:

Record Group 181, Commandant's Office, General correspondence 1925–1942 [Entry # 49], box 90, RA 2244 A: Messages sent and received by the Fourteenth Naval District. The following search reports are also available in file A4-3/Earhart: report of the Earhart search by U.S. Navy and U.S. Coast Guard July 2–18, 1937, by the Fourteenth Naval District (with enclosure of search message despatches); report of search by USCG cutter *Itasca*, June 19–29, 1937; report of Earhart

Search—Lexington Group—U.S.S. Lexington flagship, July 1937; report of Earhart search by U.S.S. *Colorado*, July 1–13, 1937.

Record Group 181, Commandant's Office, General correspondence 1926–1939 [Entry # 38], box 490, RA 3051 B: messages sent and received by the Twelfth Naval District.

Record Group 313, U.S. Naval Station American Samoa, Commandant's Office, General correspondence [Entry # 58-3440], files A4-3/Earhart (1), (2), (3), (4), and (5): Messages sent and received by Naval Radio Tutuila.

ACKNOWLEDGMENTS

As already mentioned, we had the help of hundreds of people who shared their knowledge of Amelia Earhart and her around-the-world flight. We are deeply in debt to all who contributed, and welcome this opportunity to express our gratitude in print. We must thank certain individuals and institutions for their outstanding assistance to us.

The years of research requiring worldwide travel would have been impossible without the invaluable benefit of working for the Flying Tiger Line—now merged with Federal Express Corporation—and the unfailing interest and assistance of co-workers.

Purdue University played a major role in financing Earhart's flight and in archiving Amelia and George Putnam's personal papers. Helen Schroyer, librarian at the Purdue University Library, spent countless hours helping us locate important documents. Her knowledge of the Earhart collection was an indispensable asset. Claudia Oakes, historian of women in aviation at the Smithsonian Institution, helped us through the National Air and Space Museum files in Washington. Jean L. Backus, upon completion of her book *Letters from Amelia,* entrusted us with the boxes of letters received by Amy Otis Earhart. After study, we forwarded the collection in honor of Muriel Earhart Morrissey to the Schlesinger Library, Radcliffe College, Cambridge, Massachusetts, where it is now located.

A special trip to Laramie was necessary to study the papers of Eugene Vidal at the American Heritage Library, University of Wyoming. The University of Oregon, Eugene, is a special repository for newspapers and the history of journalism in Oregon. James L. Crowell, biographer of George Palmer Putnam's publishing days in Bend, Oregon, gave us a tour of the Putnam home in Bend and a copy of his University of Oregon Master of Science thesis about Putnam, "Frontier Publisher." Louise Foudray, curator at Amelia Earhart's Birthplace Museum in Atchison, Kansas, has always answered requests for information accurately and promptly.

Over the years we became acquainted with a host of very helpful reference librarians. The stacks at the New York Public Library have our fingerprints all over them. The same could be said for the libraries of Atchison, Boston, Burbank, Cheyenne, Chicago, Cleveland, Coral Gables, Glendale, Honolulu, Juneau, Lafayette, Los Angeles, Miami, North Hollywood, Oakland, Salt Lake City, San Diego, San Francisco, San Juan, San Mateo, and Tucson. The local newspaper collections at each of these libraries were invaluable sources of contemporary information, and supplemented the major stories carried by the news wires and major newspaper syndicates. Access to the raw files of the newspaper morgues at the *Los Angeles Times, Honolulu Advertiser, Honolulu Star Bulletin, Miami Herald,* and *Oakland Tribune* yielded photographs and bits of information that had never been published.

Bilingual Japanese research assistants aided us at the library of the Japanese Diet in Tokyo, and Italian assistants helped us at libraries and archives of Rome and Foggia, Italy. Translations of Japanese documents were arranged by Ayako Lowery, Spanish by Silvia Long and Louis Romanos, and French by Alix Millen. We also did research in Australia, Hong Kong, London, Manila, and Singapore.

U.S. government agencies were wonderfully cooperative. The files of the National Archives in Suitland, Maryland, and Washington, D.C., were opened fully, with dusty old boxes and files delivered unhesitatingly for our inspection. Kathleen M. O'Connor, archivist at the National Archives in San Bruno, California, spent months of her own time gathering the pertinent Earhart files in their possession. Truman R. Strobridge, historian for the United States Coast Guard, cooperated fully and took a personal interest in helping us find our way through the bureaucratic maze at headquarters. How can we ever repay Lt. Cmdr. Robert W. Findley, who provided invaluable information about USCG radio equipment and procedures? His lifetime of Coast Guard communications experience was shared with never a thought of personal compensation or reward. Our thanks to the Coast Guard officers and radiomen who were on the *Itasca* and in Honolulu. It was the interviews, logs, messages, and photographs of Henry M. Anthony, Leo G. Bellarts, William L. Galten, Thomas J. O'Hare, and William L. Sutter that allowed us finally to piece together the communications problems faced by Earhart. O. Vernon Moore held the key to Earhart's Bendix radio receiver, and Al Hemphill led us to the solution of why the Bendix direction-finder loop failed her. Lockheed employees were crucial in verifying details of Earhart's Electra, and special thanks are owed for the personal assistance of Roy Blay, Joseph Burgard, Jack Cartwright, Harvey Christen, James Gerschler, Clarence "Kelly" Johnson, and Edward Werner. The veterans of early Pan American Airways also deserve special recognition. Adm. Harry Canaday, Capt. Roy Keeler, Percy Pettijohn, James Savage, F. Ralph Sias, and Robert Thibert all made significant contributions.

Edwin H. Bryan Jr., curator of collections at the Bernice P. Bishop Museum in Honolulu, produced records and recounted stories of the establishment of U.S. colonies on the Line Islands in the mid-1930s. Lee Mottler guided us with unerring accuracy through the voluminous collection of the Pacific Scientific Information Center. Howard M. Hanzlik, United Press correspondent aboard the *Itasca,* produced an independent contemporaneous written record of the events there. They were an invaluable cross-check of the official records and added immeasurably to our confidence in the content of the official records.

Individual members of the women's pilot organization Ninety-Nines Inc. supported our research. Special thanks to Loretta Gregg for guidance at the Oklahoma City headquarters, Thon Griffith, former president, and Gene Nora Jessen, historian and former president, for proofreading parts of the manuscript.

Earhart and Noonan departed on their final flight from New Guinea, which had been under Australian administration since 1914. Over a period of more than a decade we spent an enormous amount of time searching in various Australian repositories. The sponsorship of Lady Nancy-Bird Walton and Lady Maie Casey gained us complete access to the Australian National Archives and Australian National Library. Many records of events that took place before World War II in New Guinea and on other islands in the southwest Pacific were destroyed

ACKNOWLEDGMENTS • 307

during the hostilities. The research center and its assistants at the State
Library of New South Wales, in Sydney, were always cheerfully ready
with help as we attempted to reconstruct the lost information. The
Mitchell and Dixson Libraries contained books, periodicals, maps,
records, and photographs that effectively chronicled the entire southwest Pacific "Island Services" of Australia before the war. The newspaper and periodical collections covered the local 1937 publications of
major cities in Australia and New Zealand. Of great interest to us were
those of Darwin, Australia, and Port Moresby, Papua New Guinea. A
most important source of general information about activities on the
islands of the southwest Pacific was the *Pacific Island Monthly* magazine. Special appreciation is owed to Phillip Geeves, F.R.A.H.S.,
archivist for Amalgamated Wireless Ltd. (AWA), for his patient examination of company records for 1937. Thanks to Jack Davidson, who
helped us sift through Sid Marshall's collection at Bankstown Airport,
and Kay Brick who, during an earlier visit from the United States, had
located and copied the historic movie film Marshall made of Earhart's
takeoff from Lae.

We must acknowledge at least some of the many individuals and organizations who unfailingly supplied specialized information: Ernie A.
Crome, aviation historian; the Aviation Historical Society of Australia;
Ian Willis, Lae historian; John McGoogan and D. W. Finch, NSW secretary of the Worlds Ship Society; Alan Holmes, Melbourne central office
of the Bureau of Meteorology; Laurie Bernardos, senior airworthiness
clerk at the Department of Civil Aviation (DOT), Melbourne; P. D Wil-
son, archivist at Queensland State Archives; Ian Trevina, Air New
Guinea, Port Moresby; and Alan Arndt, secretary, Overseas Telecommu-
nications Commission Veterans Association. Through their efforts we
came away with a deep admiration for all Australians and New Zealan-
ders, and enough material for a dozen books.

In the last few years our search efforts narrowed to concentrate on
the few remaining unanswered questions. The focus was sharpened
when Hugh Leggatt of Placer Dome Inc. found the Eric Chater report.
In 1995, Roy Blay of Lockheed and Elgen Long personally examined
the papers in Vancouver, B.C., and satisfied ourselves that they were
unquestionably authentic. The information contained in the Chater report was pivotal and priceless.

The senior editor for program development at the science unit for
Nova and public broadcasting station WGBH, Stephen Lyons, offered
encouragement and advice on obtaining needed technical and institu-
tional expertise.

We owe a debt of gratitude for the contributions of G. Swenson and F. E. C. Culick, both of the California Institute of Technology, for lending their expertise in matters of aerodynamics and fuel consumption performance. Our thanks also to Lockheed for the extra effort they made to locate and furnish to Dr. Culick all of Clarence "Kelly" Johnson's reports and pertinent Model 10-E Electra reports.

David W. Jourdan, president of Nauticos, performed independent analysis using his company's proprietary Renavigation computer program. Untold hundreds of hours of research was done at the Meridian Science Division by Gary Bane, Bruce Crawford, Thomas Dettweiler, Julie Perkins, and Jeff Palshook to gather, check, and quantify all available data. It was through their offices that personnel from Rockwell Collins Division were enlisted to lend their time and unquestioned ability in the science of radio signal propagation.

The deep oceans were a complete mystery to the authors until the patient instruction of Lt. Cmdr. Malcolm Bartells, commanding officer of the bathyscaphe *Trieste II,* and R. George Rey, sonar operator on the *Titanic* search, hinted at the possibilities. Further education and guidance were provided by the Scripps Institution of Oceanography with the help of Rose Dufor, Ronald Moe, Meredith Sessions, Dr. George Shore, and archivist Stuart Smith.

An untold amount of help and counsel were offered by the finders of the gold ship *Central America,* Williamson & Associates, and its staff of geophysicists and ocean engineers. Mike Williamson, Tim McGinnis, Nicholas Lesnikowski, Richard Petters, and Captain Arthur St.Clair Wright have become more than teachers; they have become our friends. The same can be said for Ken Collins, President of Oceanworkers and an expert on Autonomous Unmanned Vehicle technology.

There could be no better friend than Capt. Fred Patterson III of World Airways, who we are convinced knows more about Lockheed Electras than anyone. His expertise and advice has been invaluable in a hundred ways.

The same must be said for our Orcas Island friend Roy A. Blay. Roy's fifty years of experience as an aeronautical engineer, aircraft accident investigator, writer, and aviation historian was lent to us unstintingly. Many know that Roy is very knowledgeable about Amelia Earhart, but few know that he played an instrumental part in solving the de Havilland Aircraft Comet disasters. His investigations led to the modern failsafe fuselage structures we enjoy in our jet airliners of today. He was generously willing to help whenever asked, and we asked often.

Researching this book has been a monumental task and has taken up much of our time over the last twenty-five years. So much so that it encroached on the time we spent with our families. We must acknowledge the patient and unfailing interest of our children and grandchildren. Mitchell, Donna, Samara, Marika, Harry, Silvia, Stephanie, and Justin, we love you for your understanding and support through the years.

After the research was finished, the book still had to be written, edited, designed, and published. Fortunately for us, into this vacuum stepped an author well known in adventuring and underwater archeology circles, Clive Cussler. Through his guidance and advice we were introduced to Bob Bender, vice president and senior editor at Simon and Schuster, and in turn editors Johanna Li, Leonard Mayhew, and Loretta Denner. No one will ever know the amount of time and effort they expended, above and beyond the call of duty, to make this book as good as it could be. The phrase "a purse out of a sow's ear" comes to mind. What can we say but thanks for your patience and diligence.

If we have accidentally left out someone, please accept our sincere apology for the unintentional omission.

INDEX

Printed in the United States
By Bookmasters